INFORMATION SECURITY AND PRIVACY

A Practical Guide for Global Executives, Lawyers and Technologists

Thomas J. Shaw Esq., Editor

Cover design by ABA Publishing.

Printed in the United States of America.

15 14 13 12 11 5 4 3 2 1

Library of Congress Cataloging-in-Publication Data

Information security and privacy: a practical guide for global executives, lawyers, and technologists / Thomas J. Shaw, editor.
p. cm.
Includes bibliographical references and index.
ISBN 978-1-61632-807-8
1. Computer security—Law and legislation—United States. 2. Data protection—Law and legislation—United States. 3. Computer security—United States. 4. Data protection—United States. I. Shaw, Thomas J.
KF390.5.C6I54 2011
342.7308'58—dc22

2011001897

Discounts are available for books ordered in bulk. Special consideration is given to state bars, CLE programs, and other bar-related organizations. Inquire at Book Publishing, ABA Publishing, American Bar Association, 321 North Clark Street, Chicago, Illinois 60654-7598.

www.ababooks.org

Contents

Foreword

Information pervades our world. With the dramatic increases in digitization of information, some of which previously existed in analog form (in books, newspapers, television, films, on records and tapes, maps, photos, in human minds) but much of which is new, digital information is everywhere we turn. So the challenge for those of us concerned with the disclosure, loss, unauthorized use, or unrequested modification of our personal or organizational data is to understand how to bring some measure of control to this chaotic whirlwind of proliferating information. To begin to accomplish this task, we have assembled a large number of legal and technology experts (more than sixty), both domestically and internationally based, to address the issues that organizations face in protecting their corporate, employee, and customer information.

We are the Information Security Committee of the American Bar Association's Science & Technology Law Section. As shown in the Contributors section, some of the leading practitioners in information security and privacy law and technology from law firms, consulting firms, corporations, universities, and government participated in this project. Our goals are to inform our audience and to provide the tools to identify and manage the business, legal, and technical risks of protecting information on a global scale. As such, beyond the general interest reader, this book speaks to two categories of readership: first, those occupying a C-suite office, be it CEO, CFO, COO, CISO, CPO, or corporate counsel, and second, the lawyers and technologists who advise them on managing these issues.

The book is laid out to assist both audiences by using a wide and deep approach. There are eight comprehensive chapters, presented sequentially to follow the methodology introduced in the first chapter. Each chapter has a high-level summary for the C-suite officers to briefly capture the issues necessary to lead their organizations ("What Global Executives Need to Know") and a series of recommendations for the legal and technology advisors, sometimes in a separate section and sometimes intertwined with the rest of the chapter. Each chapter then presents and analyzes the substantive details of each of the respective topics. The chapters cover the following areas:

- A lifecycle methodology for addressing information security and privacy
- What information security is and why it is important
- How information security relates to privacy
- U.S. federal and state laws creating information security and privacy obligations
- International laws creating information security and privacy obligations

- Other sources of information security and privacy obligations
- Legal liabilities related to information security and privacy under civil and criminal law
- How to design and use an information risk management program
- Requirements for information security controls and the frameworks to use them
- In-depth explanations of two key Internet controls: encryption and identity management
- Major control categories for information security and privacy
- Best practices in use of information security and privacy policies and controls
- How to respond effectively to a data breach
- Information security and privacy audits and certifications
- New and emerging technologies impacting information security and privacy
- The roles of lawyers and technologists as information security and privacy advisors
- A look forward and some concluding thoughts

Some of the substantive chapters may appear to be primarily targeted at lawyers, such as the chapters on statutes and legal liabilities, or at technologists, such as the chapters on information security controls and best practices. In fact, both sets of advisors need to understand all the material presented here. Lawyers need to ensure that their organization has a reasonable information security and privacy program that can withstand legal scrutiny. Such a program is built through a deep understanding of the statutory, regulatory, and contractual requirements, the legal liability exposures for information security and privacy, the appropriate policies and procedures in the areas of risk management, information security, and privacy, and the legal issues surrounding key controls such as public key infrastructures and identity management. Technologists must know of the domestic and international legal obligations and potential liabilities that inform the risk assessment and treatment processes, gain an in-depth understanding of important shared network controls such as encryption, and be ready to address the new and emerging technologies such as social networking, cloud computing and mobile computing.

Following the last chapter are several appendices. The first appendix lists the various standards and guidelines that apply to information security and privacy. The second appendix is a glossary of terms that should help the reader understand the blizzard of technical terms in this area and also tie the terms to the applicable standards in the first appendix. The third appendix summarizes some of the many U.S. state laws that apply to information security and privacy. The fourth appendix begins a collection of best practice documents, which we hope to add to rather rapidly.

While this book is now more than 400 pages long, it owes a debt of gratitude to the "first edition" of this series that was assembled in 2003 and published in 2004. That 80-page handbook, titled *Information Security: A Legal, Business, and Technical Handbook,* provided an initial view of this topic some seven years ago. So much has changed since then, and this new book reflects those changes. The 600 percent increase in content includes coverage of: international laws to provide a global perspective, a focus on executives' knowledge and responsibilities, the role of the technologists, information security and privacy audits and certifications, the significant roles of cryptography and identity management, and a chapter dedicated to new and emerging technologies, plus additional appendices. Of course the new or revised statutes, regulations, and standards related to information security and privacy are also included. And all this detail is presented as part of an overarching stable lifecycle methodology for practitioners to use and thus effectively address the information security and privacy requirements in their organizations.

Finally, I would like to thank all the volunteers who worked on this project. For no remuneration except seeing their names listed herein, scores of lawyers and technologists contributed their experience, expertise, and insight across a dizzying array of topics. From those who contributed a few hundred words to those who contributed a few thousand, those who authored and those who edited and those who did both, I owe them a debt of gratitude for creating the majority of this project's content. All contributors to this book are listed in the Contributors section, with several given notice for their additional efforts.

While this book is as complete as possible, it is merely a starting point. The necessary legal research, knowledge about risk and security frameworks, and in-depth understanding of each organization's unique business situation must work in tandem with this book. It should be facilitated by the trusted legal and technology advisors that organizations count on each day, supplemented by whatever new expertise is necessary. Expertise and experience that combine both law and technology are essential to addressing these complex requirements. It is also our intention to keep this book updated so that it never loses relevance. To do so, we will regularly provide updates to laws, technologies, and standards, using as many of the new publishing technologies as are available to us. To make this as much a living document as possible, I will list my email address here (thomas@tshawlaw.com) so that you may contact me as you have questions and I will try to refer you to the appropriate resources within the relevant ABA sections and committees and from our collective network of contacts with legal and technology expertise. We hope to be of service.

Thomas J. Shaw, Esq.
Editor and Lead Author
February 2011

About the Editor

Thomas J. Shaw, Esq., Attorney at Law, CPA, CRISC, CIPP, CISM, ERM^P, CFF, CISA, CGEIT, CCSK

Thomas J. Shaw, Esq., is an attorney based in Tokyo, Japan, who works with organizations in Asia and globally on Information law (privacy, information security, e-discovery), Internet law (cloud computing, social networking, intellectual property, e-commerce), international transactional law, compliance, information governance, and litigation and technology risk assessment/reduction. He writes extensively on Information and Internet law and technology and also on Asia-Pacific law, as he has resided in Asia for the last sixteen years. He is the editor of several American Bar Association technology law publications, including the *Information Security & Privacy News* and the *EDDE Journal* and is a coauthor of the forthcoming ABA book, *Cloud Computing—A Practical Guide for Lawyers.* A law school valedictorian, former college instructor and corporate executive, he has degrees in computer science and accounting and licenses/certifications in law, financial statement audit, information risk and controls, privacy, information security, records management, financial forensics, information systems audit, information technology governance, and cloud computing security. He can be reached via e-mail at thomas@tshawlaw.com and on the web at www.tshawlaw.com.

About the Editor

About the Contributors

Richard Abbott
Abbott Engineering Solutions, Inc., 610 King George's Way, West Vancouver, BC V7S1S3; Rabbit@shaw.ca; Oregonrabbit@hushmail.com; Attorney and IT privacy consultant.

E. Regan Adams, Esq., CIPP
Risk Tech Law/iRisk Strategic LLC, 30 Fifth Avenue, New York, NY; (908) 675-6181; E.ReganAdams@gmail.com; Information law and risk mitigation strategies: policy and strategic solutions in optimizing information utility while achieving defensible legal and regulatory data risk-related practices.

Mike Ahmadi
GraniteKey LLC, 1295 Heather Lane, Livermore, CA 94551; (925) 413-4365; mike.ahmadi@granitekey.com; www.granitekey.com; Chief Operations Officer, Security Consultant, and Integration Specialist, California Privacy and Security Advisory Board Steering Committee Member.

Michael A. Aisenberg
MITRE Corporation, 7515 Colshire Dr., McLean, VA 22102; (703) 983-1054; maisenberg@mitre.org; http://www.mitre.org/; FFRDC law/policy support to classified cyber systems of intelligence, defense, and homeland security agencies; ABA InfoSec Law Policy W-G Co-chair; former Chair, IT Sector Coordinating Council and Information Security committee.

Paul E. Ambrosio
Guidance Software, Inc., 215 North Marengo Avenue, Suite 250, Pasadena, CA 91101; (626) 229-9191; paul.ambrosio@guidancesoftware.com; www.guidancesoftware.com; Deputy General Counsel at Guidance Software—handles technology licensing and general business matters for the company.

W. Scott Blackmer
InfoLawGroup LLP, Salt Lake City, Utah; sblackmer@infolawgroup.com; www.infolawgroup.com; Founding Partner; licensed attorney in Washington, DC, Maryland, Utah, formerly Brussels and the UK; IT law practice since 1982.

Rebecca Grassl Bradley
Whyte Hirschboeck Dudek SC, 555 East Wells Street, Suite 1900, Milwaukee, WI 53202; (414) 978-5785; rbradley@whdlaw.com; http://whdlaw.com; commercial, information technology, and intellectual property litigation and transactional attorney.

***Charlene A. Brownlee, CIPP**
Davis Wright Tremaine LLP, 1201 Third Avenue, Suite 2200, Seattle, WA 98101-3045; (206) 757-8014; charlenebrownlee@dwt.com; www.daviswrighttremaine.com; Attorney who advises clients on global privacy and information management and co-authored the legal treatise "Privacy Law" (*Law Journal Press*).

Ronald L. Change, Esq., GLEG
Curtiss-Wright Corporation, 1000 Wright Way, Cheswick, PA 15024; (724) 275-5776; Ronald.change@gmail.com.

Denley Chew, CISSP
Federal Reserve Bank of New York, 33 Liberty Street, New York, NY 10045; (212) 720-8933; denley.chew@ny.frb.org; www.newyorkfed.org; FRBNY Markets Group Continuity Officer.

Kathryn R. Coburn
Partner at Health IT Law Group LLC; Pacific Palisades, CA; (310) 721-9905; kathryn@healthinfotechlaw.com; www.healthinfotechlaw.com.

Elisa Cogswell
Department of Veterans Affairs, Office of General Counsel, 810 Vermont Avenue NW, Washington, DC 22304; (202) 461-7684; elisa.cogswell@va.gov; specializes in e-discovery, HIPAA, HITECH, Privacy Act, and other VA privacy statutes.

Jon B. Comstock, JD, CIPP
Wal-Mart Stores, Inc., 702 SW 8th Street, Bentonville, AR 72712; (479) 659-1767; Jon.Comstock@walmartlegal.com; Associate General Counsel for Information Systems Security group and Privacy Office.

Rebecca H. Davis
Wal-Mart Stores, Inc., 805 Moberly Lane, Bentonville, AR 72712; (512) 917-6306; rebecca.h.davis@gmail.com; www.walmart.com; corporate law, information security.

Ben A. Eilenberg
Gresham Savage Nolan & Tilden, 3750 University Ave., Suite 250, Riverside, CA 92507; (951) 684-2171; Ben.Eilenberg@GreshamSavage.com; http://www.greshamsavage.com; lawyer specializing in litigation, intellectual property, and high tech.

Tanya L. Forsheit, Esq., CIPP
InfoLawGroup LLP, 1500 Rosecrans Ave., Suite 500, Manhattan Beach, CA 90266; (310) 706-4121; tforsheit@infolawgroup.com; www.infolawgroup.com; Founding Partner; privacy and data security compliance, outsourcing and cloud computing transactions, litigation.

Daniel B. Garrie, Esq., MA
Focused Solution Recourse Delivery Group LLC, 418 North 60th Street, Seattle, WA 98103; (215) 280-7033; dgarrie@fsrdg.com; www.fsrdg.com; Senior Managing Partner focusing on information governance, computer forensics, electronic discovery, and privacy with 70+ legal publications.

***Joanna Lyn Grama, JD, CISSP, CIPP/IT**
Purdue University, 155 S. Grant St., West Lafayette, IN 47907-2114; (765) 496-3970; jgrama@purdue.edu; www.purdue.edu; Information Security Policy and Compliance Director.

Richard A. Guida
Johnson & Johnson, 1003 US Route 202, Raritan, NJ 08869; (908) 655-4907; rguida@its.jnj.com; http://www.jnj.com; Vice President, Worldwide Information Security through January 2011; thereafter, retired, working as independent consultant; richard.guida@comcast.net; 4 Coury Road, Hillsborough, NJ 08844.

Nicholas P. Heesters, Jr., Esq.
Law Offices of Nicholas P. Heesters, Jr., LLC, P.O. Box 777, Hockessin, DE 19707; (302) 528-8404; npheesters@heesterslaw.com; www.heesterslaw.com; Attorney at Law specializing in the areas of technology law, intellectual property, and information security.

Eric A. Hibbard, CISSP, CISA, ISSAP, ISSMP, ISSEP, SCSE
Hitachi Data Systems, 750 Central Expressway, Santa Clara, CA 95050; (408) 970-7979; eric.hibbard@hds.com; www.hds.com; CTO Security and Privacy.

Marcia Hofmann
Electronic Frontier Foundation, 454 Shotwell St., San Francisco, CA 94110; (415) 436-9333; marcia@eff.org; http://www.eff.org; Senior Staff Attorney focusing on privacy and other civil liberties in the digital age.

***Robert R. Jueneman**
SPYRUS, Inc., 318 Vegas de Taos Loop, Taos, NM 87571; rjueneman@spyrus.com; www.spyrus.com; Chief Scientist, responsible for cryptographic, PKI, and information security direction; fully cleared, 50 years' experience.

Joel S. Kazin, CPA, CISA, CISSP, CISM
JeffersonWells, 99 Park Avenue, Penthouse, New York, NY 10016; (914) 564-1484; joel.kazin@jeffersonwells.com; www.jefersonwells.com; Engagement Manager.

Kevin J. Kotch
Obermayer Rebmann Maxwell & Hippel LLP, 200 Lake Drive East, Woodland Falls Corporate Park, Suite 110, Cherry Hill, NJ 08002; (856) 857-1432; kevin.kotch@obermayer.com; www.obermayer.com; Attorney specializing in commercial litigation, white collar crime, insurance recovery, and information security issues.

Gerald S. (Jerry) Levine
Focused Solution Recourse Delivery Group LLC; (908) 955-3779; jlevine@fsrdg.com; www.fsrdg.com.

Patrice A. Lyons
Law Offices of Patrice Lyons, Chartered, 910 17th St. NW, Suite 800, Washington, DC 20006; (202) 293-5990; palyons@bellatlantic.net; Corporate Counsel, Corporation for National Research Initiatives, involved in many Internet-related activities.

Edward R. McNicholas
Sidley Austin LLP, 1501 K Street NW, Washington, DC 20005; emcnicholas@sidley.com; www.Sidley.com/InfoLaw; Partner focusing on complex information technology, constitutional and privacy issues.

***David Navetta, CIPP**
Information Law Group, 1117 S. Clarkson St., Denver, CO 80210; (303) 325-3528; dnavetta@infolawgroup.com; www.infolawgroup.com; Founding Partner InfoLawGroup, Co-Chair ABA Information Security Committee.

Jon Neiditz
Nelson Mullins Riley & Scarborough LLP, 201 W. 17th St. NW, Suite 1700, Atlanta, GA 30363; (404) 322-6139; jon.neiditz@nelsonmullins.com; http://www.nelsonmullins.com/attorneys/jon-neiditz; Partner and Information Management Practice Leader; JD, Yale Law School.

Dan Oseran, JD, MBA, CISSP
PayPal, 9999 N. 90th Street, Scottsdale, AZ 85258; (480) 862-7230; doseran@paypal.com; www.paypal.com.

Paul E. Paray, Esq.
Capacity Coverage Company of NJ, Inc., One International Drive, Mahwah, NJ 07495; (201) 281-5134; paule@paray.com; risk management and litigation counsel for businesses looking to protect and grow their corporate assets.

Tallien Perry
tallienperry@verizon.net.

Michael Power
Barrister and Solicitor, 461 Roncesvalles Ave., Unit B, Toronto, Ontario, Canada M6R 2N4; (416) 723-4295; emp@michaelpower.ca; www.michaelpower.ca; Toronto-based lawyer who advises both public- and private-sector clients on privacy and information risk management issues.

Robert Radvanovsky
Infracritical, Inc., 1706 Millbrook Court, Suite 201, Geneva, IL 60134-1838; (630) 673-7740; rsradvan@infracritical.com; www.infracritical.com.

Paul Rice
Discover Financial Services, 2500 Lake Cook Road, Deerfield, IL 60015; (224) 405-2029; paulrice@discover.com; www.discover.com; operational risk management.

David G. Ries
Thorp Reed & Armstrong LLP, One Oxford Centre, 301 Grant St., 14th Fl., Pittsburgh, PA 15219; (412) 394-7787; dries@thorpreed.com; www.thorpreed.com; Partner, practices in the areas of environmental, commercial, and technology litigation, including privacy and security.

Anne M. Rogers, PMP, CISSP, CCE, EnCE
Waste Management, 1001 Fannin St., Suite 4000, Houston, TX 77002; (713) 287-2488; arogers@wm.com; www.wm.com; Director, Information Safeguards Practice: Information Security Policy and Program Management, Digital Forensics, and e-Discovery Support.

***Steven B. Roosa**
Reed Smith LLP, 136 Main Street, Suite 250, Princeton Forrestal Village, P.O. Box 7839, Princeton, NJ 08543-7839; (609) 744-5480; stevenroosa@gmail.com;_www.reedsmith.com; Partner, litigation.

Randy V. Sabett, JD, CISSP
Sonnenschein Nath & Rosenthal LLP, 1301 K Street NW, Suite 600, Washington, DC 20005; (202) 408-6830; rsabett@sonnnenschein.com; www.sonnenschein.com; co-chair of the Internet and Data Protection Practice; member of the Commission on Cybersecurity for the 44th Presidency.

Richard L. Santalesa, Esq.
InfoLaw Group LLP; 3040 North Street, Fairfield, CT 06824; (203) 292-0667; Richard@Santalesa.com; http://www.infolawgroup.com; Senior Counsel, electronic commerce and Internet issues, software and content licensing, privacy and data security, outsourcing, software and website development transactions, and other commercial arrangements.

Frederick Scholl, PhD, CISSP, CISM, CHP
Monarch Information Networks LLC, 9467 Smithson Lane, Brentwood, TN 37027; (615) 739-1039; freds@monarch-info.com; www.monarch-info.com; 25+ years business experience; information security advisor to trusted businesses.

Gary A. Schonwald
Law Offices of Gary A. Schonwald, 247 W. 87th St., Suite 3J, New York, NY 10024; (212) 495-9207; Esquiregs@gmail.com; practices in the areas of intellectual property licensing and development, mergers and acquisitions, and IP security.

Thomas J. Shaw, Esq., CPA, CRISC, CIPP, CISM, ERM^{P}, CFF, CISA, CGEIT, CCSK
See editor biography listed above.

Thomas J. Smedinghoff
Wildman Harrold, 225 West Wacker Drive, Suite 3000, Chicago, IL 60606; (312) 201-2021; smedinghoff@wildman.com; http://www.wildman.com; Partner in the Privacy, Data Security and Information Law Practice, a member of the U.S. delegation to UNCITRAL and co-chair of the ABA's Federated Identity Management Legal Task Force.

Gib Sorebo, JD, CISSP
SAIC, 1710 SAIC Drive, McLean, VA 22102; (703) 676-2605; sorebog@saic.com; http://www.saic.com; provides information security consulting and integration services to the private and public sectors.

Matt Sorensen, JD, CIPP, CISSP, CISA, GCFA, GSEC
mattsorensen@hotmail.com; http://datariskgovernance.com

Kevin D. Spease, CISSP-ISSEP, CIPP/IT
Health Net, 11971 Foundation Place, Rancho Cordova, CA 95670; (916) 935-1166; kevin.spease@healthnet.com; www.healthnet.com; Web Center of Excellence (WCOE) Senior Information Security Analyst.

Marc Techner, CISSP
SAIC, 1009 Via Sinuoso, Chula Vista, CA 91910; mtechnerlaw@aol.com; consulting on information security to the U.S. government; licensed to practice law in California and the U.S. District Court, Southern District of California.

Steven W. Teppler
Edelson McGuire LLC, 350 North LaSalle, Suite 1300, 60654; (941) 487-0050; steppler@edelson.com; www.edelson.com; leads electronic discovery, digital evidence management practice.

Lucy L. Thomson, Esq., MS, CIPP/G
915 North Quaker Lane, Alexandria, VA 22302; (703) 798-1001; lucythomson1@mindspring.com; Vice Chair, ABA Section of Science and Technology Law, Senior Principal Engineer and Privacy Advocate at a global technology company.

***Benjamin Tomhave, MS, CISSP**
Gemini Security Solutions, 4451 Brookfield Corporate Dr. #200, Chantilly, VA 20151; (703) 282-8600; btomhave@geminisecurity.com; http://geminisecurity.com/; Senior Security Analyst, Engineering Management, Specializing in Security Strategy, Architecture, Research, and Solutions.

Geoffrey P. Vickers
Baker, Donelson, Bearman, Caldwell & Berkowitz, PC, Baker Donelson Center, 211 Commerce St., Suite 800, Nashville, TN 37201; (615) 726-5649; gvickers@bakerdonelson.com; www.bakerdonelson.com; mergers and acquisitions, specializes in business technology and business process and technology outsourcing.

Nicholas Vogt
Reitler Kailas & Rosenblatt LLC, 885 Third Ave., 20th Floor, New York, NY 10022; (212) 209-3054; nvogt@reitlerlaw.com; www.reitlerlaw.com; Of Counsel, Intellectual Property.

K. Krasnow Waterman
LawTechIntersect LLC, New York, NY; (520) 591-3700; kkw@LawTechIntersect.com; Consulting—pure technology and legal technology, compliance, risk, security, privacy, access control/privilege management, data governance, e-Discovery (bars: New York and District of Columbia).

Joel Weise
Information Systems Security Association, 359 Timberhead Ln., Foster City, CA 94404; (650) 867-6836; jmweise@comcast.net; 30+ years as a security practitioner, a founder of the ISSA, chairman of *ISSA Journal* Editorial Board, Distinguished Fellow.

David Willson, CISSP, Security +
NEK Advanced Security Group, 110 S. Sierra Madre St., Colorado Springs, CO 80903; (719) 634-5523; WWW.NEKASG.Com; david.l.willson@hotmail.com; Deputy Director of Cyber Operations; licensed to practice law in New York, Connecticut, and soon Colorado, with information security and the law focus.

Benjamin T. Wilson, CISSP, MCSE, JD
DigiCert, Inc., 355 South 520 West, Canopy Building II, Suite 200, Lindon, UT 84042; (801) 701-9678; ben@digicert.com; www.digicert.com; General Counsel, Senior Vice President Industry Relations, Federated Identity, PKI Legal and Policy Infrastructures.

Amanda M. Witt
Nelson Mullins Riley & Scarborough LLP, 201 17th Street NW, Suite 1700, Atlanta, GA 30363; (404) 322-6120; amanda.witt@nelsonmullins.com; www.nelsonmullins.com; Of Counsel with practice focusing on information security and privacy, e-commerce, and intellectual property protection.

Paola Zeni, CIPP; Avvocato
Symantec, 350 Ellis Street, Mountain View, CA 94043; (650) 527-1225; paola_zeni@symantec.com; symantec.com; Senior Corporate Counsel, Privacy.

* Denotes recognition for the additional efforts of this contributor

CHAPTER 1

Introduction to Information Security

Digital information is fundamental to life today. Digital information access devices and websites are everywhere, as mobile phones, tablet PCs, notebooks, DVD viewers, personal data assistants, digital cameras, flash drives, camcorders, e-commerce sites, blogs, micro-blogs, social networking sites, and so on. Digital information permeates organizations as well, with almost all corporate data now stored electronically. The majority of organizations' asset valuations are no longer in tangible assets like plant and equipment but are embodied in intangible assets like intellectual property that may be stored digitally and therefore more easily appropriated. Consumers want their personal information kept private, while organizations have competitive and reputational interests in protecting their corporate and client data. With business and social interactions increasingly happening over the Internet, individual personal and sensitive data, corporate confidential and secret data, and government diplomatic and infrastructure data flows over open networks and is stored in locations only indirectly under the control of its owners. And as the numbers and types of websites and devices that access this information proliferate, so do the risks and challenges of staying safe and secure. What is needed among this chaotic interplay of ever-expanding data flows and changing technologies, geographies, and business needs is a stable methodology that can be used at all times to understand and manage the dynamic set of risks to personal, corporate, and customer information.

This book was written with just that need in mind—to provide corporate executives and their legal and information security advisors the techniques to create a stable set of processes to handle the challenges raised by rapidly multiplying domestic and international laws and regulations, by new technologies, by litigation and other legal claims, by increasingly complex threats and vulnerabilities from outside and inside organizations, and by changing business dynamics. These techniques are part of a methodology called the Information Security and Privacy Lifecycle.

What Global Executives Need to Know

- The phases and deliverables from the Information Security and Privacy Lifecycle
- The need for business leaders to make decisions based on a firm understanding of the information security and privacy risks and potential impacts
- The varying reasons for organizations to protect data
- The costs and other impacts of data breach and subsequent data loss and disclosure
- The relationship between information security and privacy

1.1 THE INFORMATION SECURITY AND PRIVACY LIFECYCLE

This high-level lifecycle methodology requires the design and implementation of underlying processes specific to each organization, country, and industry to address current as well as future information security and privacy risks. This Information Security and Privacy Lifecycle methodology comprises the following five phases:

1. Synthesis of all legal obligations from applicable information security and privacy laws and regulations
2. Analysis of all information security and privacy legal liability exposures
3. Creation of information security and privacy policies and assessment of information security and privacy risks
4. Selection, design, and implementation of information security and privacy controls
5. Compliance, audit and certification of the information security and privacy program

After completion of the final phase, the lifecycle starts again with the first phase in a repetitive loop, as depicted in Figure 1.1.

Before discussing this lifecycle, everyone involved in this area must fully understand an important concept: information security and privacy is not a separate discipline within each organization, like accounting or sales, but instead needs to permeate the organization and be owned and executed by every executive, employee, contractor, vendor, and customer of the organization. More than ever, top executives need to fully understand the obligations, liabilities, risks, and treatments involving information security and privacy. Leadership buy-in and follow-through are essential, as was most recently reemphasized from the top of the U.S. government:

> It is not enough for the information technology workforce to understand the importance of cybersecurity; leaders at all levels of government and industry need to be able to make business and investment decisions based on knowledge of risks and potential impacts.[1]

1. Obama Administration, *Cyberspace Policy Review—Assuring a Trusted and Resilient Information and Communications Infrastructure* (2009).

Figure 1.1
The Information Security and Privacy Lifecycle

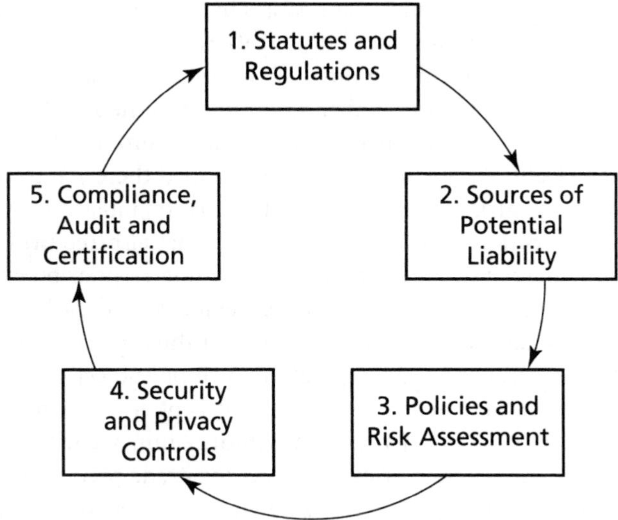

A. Phase 1: Synthesis of Statutory and Regulatory Requirements

Organizations must understand their information security and privacy obligations from statutes and regulations in each country where they do business, including any industry sector-specific rules. To craft a single set of information security and privacy rules usable worldwide, a synthesized global legal view should be created from all applicable current and prospective (where possible) laws. This can be done on a regional instead of global level but may lead to disparate and potentially conflicting policies.

The global legal view includes the laws in each region, country, and state/province in which a company operates, hosts (or outsources) data, or collects data. Once all the laws and their information security and privacy provisions have been identified, they must be synthesized in a manner that encompasses all these requirements into a single legal view. A company, for example, operating in Europe, the United States, and Japan would have to comply with the information security and privacy rules in the European Union privacy directive, the myriad U.S. state and federal laws on information security and privacy, and Japan's law on the protection of personal information, plus other regulations for the specific industries, association rules, and laws of countries where it does business electronically or stores data in the Internet cloud. Many of those domestic and international laws are covered in Chapter 2.

1. Synthesis Example

Illustrating this process of a synthesized global legal view is the very simple example of a Japanese corporation doing business only in the United States and Japan. In general Japanese law requires corporations holding customers' or employees' personal information to take the "necessary and proper measures" to exercise control over that data, including ensuring that third parties who process this corporate data implement similarly adequate levels of security protection.[2] The information security requirements are not specific but fall under the general banners of reasonableness and practicality.

In the United States, an organization may be required to adhere to sector-specific information security and privacy rules. Companies in the U.S. consumer financial sector are subject to the Gramm-Leach-Bliley Act[3] and its Safeguards Rule[4] requiring a comprehensive security program, including physical, technical, and administrative controls. Those involved with the health care industry are subject to the Health Insurance Portability and Accountability Act,[5] amended by the Health Insurance Technology for Economic and Clinical Health Act.[6] Under its Security Rule,[7] there are technical, physical, and administrative safeguards to ensure the confidentiality, integrity, and availability of electronically stored personal health information. The act also requires providing protection against reasonably anticipated threats, designating responsible individuals, providing employee training, performing risk assessments, providing breach notification, and establishing contractual compliance provisions for third-party data processors.

More generally, the company's U.S. operations will be subject to the Federal Trade Commission (FTC) Act's Section 5 for unfair or deceptive trade practices regarding information security. The lack of a reasonable information security program may be considered an unfair trade practice or even a deceptive trade practice if actual practices differ from the stated security policy. Consent decrees often require respondents to implement and maintain a comprehensive information security program to protect the security, confidentiality, and integrity of personal information, including administrative, technical, and physical safeguards considering a respondent's size, complexity, and activities and the sensitivity of the personal information. The FTC's "Red Flags Rule" for identity theft requires corporations selling and billing for goods or services to regularly assess the risk of identity theft and to develop "reasonable and appropriate" protections.[8]

At the U.S. state level, some statutes go further than current federal law in prescribing certain security requirements, so their provisions should be added to the synthesized information security and privacy legal view (the effect of potential preemption is ignored here, as a best practices synthesized statute is preferable even if not strictly required currently). For example, Nevada's encryption requirement mandates the use of encryption for any non-fax electronic transmission sent outside the sender's secure system and requires the use of the Payment Card Industry's DSS[9] standard for card payments.[10] Rhode Island's data destruction statute requires a business to take reasonable steps to destroy or make unreadable customers' personal information it no longer needs to retain.[11] California's

2. Japan, Act on the Protection of Personal Information (2005), Article 20.

3. Gramm-Leach-Bliley Act, Pub. L. No. 106-102 (1999).

4. FTC Safeguards Rule: Final Rule, 16 C.F.R. Pt. 314 (2002).

5. Health Insurance Portability and Accountability Act, Pub. L. No. 104–191 (1996).

6. Health Insurance Technology for Economic and Clinical Health Act, Pub. L. No. 111–5, Division A Title XIII, pp. 112–65, and Division B Title IV, pp. 353–98 (2009).

7. HHS Security Standards: Final Rule, 45 C.F.R. Parts 160, 162, 164 (2003).

8. FTC Identity Theft Rule, 16 C.F.R. Pt. 681 (2008).

9. Payment Card Industry, *Data Security Standard Requirements and Security Assessment Procedures* Version 2.0 (2010).

10. Nev. S.B. No. 227 (2009).

11. R.I. H 5902 (2009).

breach notification statute requires businesses that have customers' electronic personal information to notify persons whose unencrypted data is subject to unauthorized access.[12]

Massachusetts's information security law requires a comprehensive, written information security program with administrative, physical, and technical security controls as well as the following:[13]

- Developing information security policies and designating a leader for the program
- Creating an inventory of personal information and maintaining oversight of third-party service providers
- Monitoring the program and performing annual reviews
- Monitoring for unauthorized use and incident management procedures
- Establishing user authentication and access control procedures
- Encrypting transmitted records and stored data on mobile devices
- Maintaining up-to-date network and system protection software
- Providing employee security training

2. Synthesized Legal View

Consolidating the provisions from these various statutes results in a synthesized global legal view that encompasses at least the following high-level information security and privacy requirements:

Information Security/Privacy Policy	Inventory of Personal Information
Risk Assessment Process	Internal Reviews and Monitoring
Reactive and Preventive Controls	Incident Management and Monitoring
Data Destruction/De-identification	User Authentication and Access Controls
Breach Notification	Encryption (stored data)
Responsible Person	Encryption (transmission)
Competence of Personnel	Up-to-Date System/Network Software
Special Rules for Information Brokers	Employee Security Training
PCI DSS Use for Electronic Payments	Oversight of Third Parties/Provisions
Identity Theft Assessment	Special Protections for Sensitive Data
Administrative and HR Security	Physical and Environmental Security
Personal Info Collection/Use Limits	Personal Info Integrity and Correction
Third-Party Transfer Restrictions	Choice and Accountability

B. Phase 2: Analysis of Potential Exposures to Legal Liability

1. Contractual

Beyond what is mandated by law, what is unique to each organization is the particular set of contractual and other commitments to implement certain information

12. Cal. Civ. Code § 1798.82 (2002).
13. Mass. Gen. Laws ch. 93H: 201 CMR 17.03–17.04 (2008).

security and privacy controls and the possible tortious claims based on failure or absence of those controls. This phase may take significant time to complete, as it requires gathering data about the organization's relationships and its use of information security and privacy across the world. The easiest place to begin is to inventory the organization's information assets. This inventory includes the hardware, system and application software, development and testing environments, and the networks and facilities that the organization uses to transmit and host data and the owners and custodians thereof. How an organization acquired each asset will lead to a list of vendor agreements and any contractual information security and privacy requirements and restrictions. In addition, all outsourcing agreements and service level agreements (SLAs) must be obtained and examined for these provisions. A complete inventory of customer agreements is also necessary to find the information security and privacy provisions therein and to determine potential liability exposures.

2. *Torts and Other*

Possible areas of liability for tort claims should be identified proactively, so that exposures can be determined and the proper controls and legal defenses can be built in advance. Also, a complete understanding of nonregulatory information security and privacy requirements, such as industry association rules, must be obtained. A starting point is a complete understanding of the business model of the organization. Questions to ask include these: How does the company use information in delivering its products and services? Whose information is it using (i.e., its customers', its employees', or its own)? What classification levels are applied to the data? How is the data accessed and by whom? Who owns each type of data? What data and processing are outsourced, to whom, and where? What other laws and regulations is the organization subject to? What insurance coverage is in place? What countries does this organization do business in?

The contract, tort, and other sources of information security and privacy liability are covered in Chapter 3.

C. Phase 3: Information Security/Privacy Policies and Risk Assessment Frameworks

1. *Information Security/Privacy Policies*

Each organization must be guided by its own policies in information security and privacy. These policies are in response to the statutory, regulatory, and contractual commitments and business needs and risks an organization faces. The information security/privacy policy guides the corporation and its employees, customers, and vendors in the use of information security and privacy. The first step is to set the scope for the information security/privacy policy (although there can be and usually are separate information security and privacy policies, for simplicity they will be discussed as a single unit) as it can apply to all systems, organizations, technology, assets, and countries or any subset thereof. The commitment of corporate management to information security and privacy must be documented (and if not sufficient, remedied). The roles of all the stakeholders (e.g., users, custodians, managers, owners) are then documented (and assigned, if not already done). This process continues until all the legal, business, and technological directions for information security and privacy are addressed. The creation of a complete information security/privacy policy is quite involved, and whole books are devoted to the topic. Its creation and dissemination typically require many iterations, revisions, and approvals, but a typical information security and privacy policy will have at least the following high-level components:

Management's Commitment	Roles of All Stakeholders
Data Classification	Acceptable Use
Physical Security	Change Management
Malware	Media Handling
Backup/Business Continuity	E-mail/Messaging Systems
Data and Media Destruction	Encryption
Software Patching	Authentication
Monitoring and Logging	Access Control
Password Management	Network Access
Systems Development	Third-Party Compliance
Incident Management	Statutory Compliance
Use of Mobile/Wireless Devices	Human Resources
Limits on Collection, Use, and Disclosure of Personal Data	Destruction/De-identification of Unused Personal and Sensitive Data
Right of Access and Correction	Choice/Right to Object
Notice to Data Subject	Supervision of Third-Party Processors
Data Integrity	Limits on Cross-Border Transfers
Limits on Retention Periods	Limits on Direct Marketing/Opt-out
Data Subject Consent	Business Transfer Notification
Limits on Sensitive Data/Security	Data Breach Notification

2. *Risk Assessment/Management*

To realize the aspirations of the information security and privacy policy, the proper controls must be put into place to manage the various legal, business, and technical risks. To know which information security and privacy controls are needed, a risk assessment process must be undertaken. Risk assessment requires understanding the external and internal threats to an organization's information assets and the vulnerabilities of its current systems and processes. The risks are typically assessed on either a qualitative high-medium-low scale or a quantitative numerical scale, taking account of the likelihood that threats will materialize and the impact of loss based on the sensitivity and criticality of the in-scope information assets. Many risk assessment processes are available, all of which should lead to essentially the same results. Three of the most prominent risk assessment and management standards and guidelines are those from the International Organization for Standardization (ISO), the U.S. National Institute for Standards and Technology (NIST), and ISACA (formerly the Information Systems Audit and Control Association), specifically ISO 27005,[14] NIST's Risk Control Framework (RCF),[15] and ISACA's Risk IT, respectively.[16]

14. ISO/IEC 27005, *Information Technology—Security Techniques—Information Security Risk Management* (2008).

15. NIST Special Publication 800-37, Revision 1, *Guide for Applying the Risk Management Framework to Federal Information Systems* (2009).

16. ISACA, *The Risk IT Framework* (2009).

ISO 27005 describes a six-step risk management model: context establishment, risk assessment, risk treatment, risk acceptance, risk communication, and risk monitoring and review. NIST's RCF uses a six-phase model for new system implementations: categorize the system and information processed by it, select security controls for the system, implement the security controls, assess the security controls, authorize information system operation, and monitor the security controls. Risk IT has three domains with three processes in each: Risk Governance—establish and maintain a common risk view, integrate with enterprise risk management, and make risk-aware business decisions; Risk Evaluation—collect data, analyze risk, and maintain risk profile (inventory); and Risk Response—articulate risk, manage risk, and react to events (Risk IT views information security risk as just one of the risks of IT).

Before implementing the risk methodologies, an inventory and valuation of all the organization's information assets must be undertaken. Regardless which risk methodology is used, it requires a significant time and resource commitment from the organization to design, implement, and maintain. Risk assessment processes must be repeated regularly to address new threats and vulnerabilities that arise as well as changes to the business or the systems used and any new information assets that are introduced, including those that incorporate technologies new to the organization.

The information security and privacy policy and risk management frameworks are discussed in Chapters 4, 5, and 6.

D. Phase 4: Information Security and Privacy Controls

Once the risks have been assessed and the potential impacts understood, the risks must be prioritized and decisions made on how to respond. Risks can be retained, transferred/shared, or avoided, or controls can be used to mitigate the risks. For the latter, the same three organizations previously mentioned have suggested lists of controls: NIST's security control families,[17] ISO 27002,[18] and ISACA's COBIT.[19]

1. Control Groupings

The NIST controls are divided into the three classes: management, operations, and technical. In addition to project management, controls are grouped into seventeen families: Access Control, Awareness and Training, Audit and Accountability, Security Assessment and Authorization, Configuration Management, Contingency Planning, Identification and Authentication, Incident Response, Maintenance, Media Protection, Physical and Environmental Protection, Planning, Personnel Security, Risk Assessment, System and Services Acquisition, System and Communications Protection, and System and Information Integrity.

The ISO 27002 controls are divided into administrative, technical, and physical, covering organization, asset management, human resources security, physical and

17. NIST Special Publication 800-53, Revision 3, *Recommended Security Controls for Federal Information Systems and Organizations* (2009).

18. ISO/IEC 27002, *Information Technology—Security Techniques—Code of Practice for Information Security Management* (2005).

19. ISACA, *Control Objectives for Information and Related Technology 4.1* (2007).

environmental security, communications and operations management, access control, systems development and maintenance, incident management, business continuity management, and compliance. COBIT is divided into four domains: Plan and Organize, Acquire and Implement, Deliver and Support, and Monitor and Evaluate and thirty-four (34) processes (COBIT, unlike the other two methodologies, is not solely for information security). ISACA has published several mapping documents that explain in detail the differences among these control methodologies.[20]

In addition to procedural controls, contractual controls must be implemented to ensure that all external entities, including customers, vendors, and agents who interact with the organization, are processing its data with at least the same level of information security and privacy controls. Standardized provisions addressing how to protect data and later destroy data at contract termination are needed. As the controls used for information security and privacy will overlap those of other disciplines (e.g., finance, information technology, human resources, compliance), a great deal of coordination is required in selecting controls based on the information security and privacy objectives.

The information security and privacy controls are covered in Chapters 5, 6, and 7.

2. *Minimum Set of Controls*

The following is a high-level description of the minimum administrative, physical, and technical information security controls that any organization should design, implement, and continually practice and review. Detailed controls require an analysis of each organization's business.

Security Measures	Description
Administrative	
1. Separation of Duties and Environments	Critical functions of users and administrators are split among different members of the organization, and the production environment is separated.
2. Employee Training and Awareness	All employees and contractors must be trained for their controls and regularly be made aware of new security issues and procedure changes.
3. Human Resources	Security roles are defined, and training is conducted regularly.
4. Independent External Testing	Tests to ensure that networks and systems cannot be externally (or internally) penetrated and external audits of security controls are conducted.

20. ISACA, COBIT®, Mapping: Mapping of NIST SP800-53 Rev 1 with COBIT® 4.1 (2007) and COBIT® Mapping: Mapping of ISO/IEC 17799:2005 with COBIT® 4.0 (2006).

Security Measures	Description
Administrative (continued)	
5. Third-Party Access and Oversight	The service levels of third parties are contractually committed to, their access controlled, and their activities supervised.
6. Internal Audits	Tests are conducted to ensure that controls are designed properly and are working as designed and that all laws are being complied with.
7. Management Reviews	Reviews of the security policy, risk assessments, and security controls are conducted on a regular basis, including legal compliance and implementation of follow-up actions.
Physical	
8. Physical Access Controls	Controls are implemented for all entrances to secure areas and access.
9. Environmental Controls	Fires, earthquakes, floods, riots, etc., are appropriately addressed.
Technical	
10. Authentication Controls	Controls are implemented to ensure that users are who they claim to be through appropriate use of multifactor identification techniques, including password standards.
11. User Access Controls	Controls are implemented to ensure that only authorized users can access data and programs and that those who are no longer authorized (e.g., terminated employees) cannot.
12. Malware Protection	Controls are implemented to limit the impact of software viruses and other malware.
13. System Monitoring and Capacity Controls	Network and system events and operator and system administrator actions are set, monitored, and recorded into logs, which are then reviewed.
14. Encryption—Storage and Transmission	Controls are implemented for the proper use of encryption technology for data storage and transmission and the proper encryption key management controls.
15. Mobile Device and Media Controls	Controls are implemented over the use of mobile computing and storage devices and all removable media, disabling the use of such devices to the extent possible.

Security Measures	Description
Technical (continued)	
16. E-mail and e-Commerce System Controls	Controls are implemented over all applications that interact externally, including e-mail, e-Commerce, EDI, SaaS, FTP servers, websites, blogs, etc., and the use of attachments.
17. Wireless Access Points	Controls are implemented over the use of wireless access points into a corporate network.
18. Regular Backup and Business Continuity	Periodic backups are performed and sent off-site, and facilities and plans are built and tested to ensure availability during device outages or disasters.
19. Application Controls	Checks are made during data input, processing, and output.
20. Operational Procedures	Controls are implemented to ensure that ops processes are documented and available to all.
21. Change Management	Controls are implemented to ensure that application, system, and data changes are managed appropriately to minimize impact on availability, integrity, and confidentiality.
22. Incident Management	Incidents are identified, isolated, responded to, resolved, documented, and followed up.
23. Information Ownership and Classification	Controls are implemented to ensure that all information is inventoried and owned by someone who assumes responsibility for its integrity and its classification.
24. Physical and Logical Segregation of Data	Customer data is logically and physically segregated from all other customer data and from corporate data, and secret and sensitive data are separated.
25. Asset Management	Information assets are inventoried, tracked, maintained, and disposed of properly.

E. Phase 5: Compliance, Audit, and Certification

1. Compliance and Audit

After the controls are implemented, their use in the daily operations of the organization must be monitored for compliance with the information security/privacy policies and control objectives and ultimately the applicable laws and regulations. The regular monitoring and evaluation for effectiveness is from two directions—internal and external. Internal monitoring involves the response to, review, and follow-up of all security incidents that arise and periodic reviews by management of the effectiveness of the information security/privacy program. This monitoring should be part of the ongoing information security/privacy policy, risk assessment, and control review processes. External reviews include reviews by customers and by independent auditors employed by the organization itself. An example is the American Institute of CPA's (AICPA) SysTrust[21] methodology. This procedure requires an assurance audit on the five SysTrust principles (security, availability, processing integrity, confidentiality, and privacy). The security principle includes documenting, communicating, and monitoring the AICPA's security policies and procedures. Other types of external audits include those that are part of Sarbanes-Oxley[22] internal controls reviews, AICPA SAS 70/ISAE 3402[23] service provider audits, and NIST's security control assessments.[24] External vulnerability reviews for potential system and network penetration attacks should be based on an overall testing and assessment methodology such as NIST's SP 800-115 guidelines.[25]

2. Certification

To ensure they have implemented best practices, organizations may seek independent certification of their information security/privacy program. This is most typically done under the ISO 27001 certification standard.[26] This standard describes all the components that an adequate information security management system must have. In conjunction with the other ISO 27000 standards, an independent ISO-designated certifier will examine both the design and ongoing operation of the information security management program to determine if it meets the described standard, including the security policies and controls described previously. There are other audits specifically targeting privacy.

Audit and certification are covered in Chapter 6.

Before moving on to the detailed chapters, four additional concepts will help to create the foundation needed for an organization's total commitment to information security and privacy. First is an understanding of the reasons to protect data, which include both the direct costs associated with data breaches of customer, employee, or corporate information (responding to the incidents and settling claims) and the indirect costs (harm to reputation and resultant loss of business). Statutes and regulations also create general and specific requirements for information security and privacy. And corporate boards of directors and officers have a duty of care to safeguard data. Second is an explanation of just what information security is. Third is a presentation of examples of data breaches that occur when information security fails. And fourth is a discussion of the dynamic relationship between privacy and information security.

---

21. AICPA, *Trust Services Principles, Criteria and Illustrations* (2006).

22. Sarbanes-Oxley Act, Pub. L. 107-204 (2002).

23. AICPA, *Statement on Auditing Standards 70, Service Organizations* (1992), to be replaced in 2011 by both the International Standard on Assurance Engagements (ISAE) 3402 *Assurance Reports on Controls at a Third Party Service Organization* and U.S. Statement on Standards for Attestation Engagements (SSAE) 16 *Reporting on Controls at a Service Organization.*

24. NIST Special Publication 800-53A, *Guide for Assessing the Security Controls in Federal Information Systems* (2008).

25. NIST Special Publication 800-115, *Technical Guide to Information Security Testing and Assessment* (2008).

26. ISO/IEC 27001, *Information technology—Security techniques—Information security management systems—Requirements* (2005).

1.2 WHY PROTECT DATA?

A. Costs of Data Loss and Disclosure

The increase of available information on technical media contributes to fiscal motivations for the growth of "cybercrime." In the past, demonstrating technical prowess by breaking into seemingly secure sites was an adequate reason for cybercrime, but today a multi-billion-dollar industry has grown around data theft. This industry has taken hold because of the ways in which people and companies use technology resources. For example, in the United States, 8 out of 10 households now bank online.[27] The rise of online banking and the prevalence of malware on consumers' computers contribute to an annualized rate of $480 million in online banking fraud.[28] A black market exists for both industry and consumer information where stolen data is readily traded. From 2002 through 2009, the overall amount of card fraud has more than doubled, from $3 billion in losses to about $7 billion.[29] In 2010, for the first time ever, theft of information replaced theft of physical assets and stock as the leading type of fraudulent activity globally.[30]

The cost to individual businesses from information security breaches is staggering. In 2009, the average cost per incident of a data breach in the United States was over $6 million with the cost of a single breached record estimated at $204.[31] Costs are incurred in completing security repairs, performing investigations, complying with laws, and covering litigation-related expenses. If a small business has 50,000 customers in its database and has to pay $3 to mail a record to each customer in the event of a breach, it will spend $150,000 just mailing the notification to satisfy data breach laws. Loss of reputation, goodwill, and increased customer churn can often be more costly for an organization than demonstrable financial expenditures.[32]

Loss due to data breach is a global problem. A study by a protection software vendor estimates that over $1 trillion was lost by global organizations in 2009 worldwide due to loss of intellectual property and the costs of repairing data breaches.[33] The report of data breaches in countries ranges from the theft of personal information from customers of Japanese online supermarkets via SQL injection attack[34] to the loss in the United Kingdom of two password-protected CDs containing the names, birth dates, and National Insurance numbers of 25 million children, parents, guardians, and caregivers involved with the HM Revenue and Customs child benefit.[35] The costs of data breaches in several countries around the world are now being analyzed and

---

27. https://www.javelinstrategy.com/research/brochures/brochure-150.

28. http://ecommerce-journal.com/news/27287_online-banking-fraud-hovered-120-million-third-quarter-2009-fdci-reports.

29. http://storefrontbacktalk.com/securityfraud/card-fraud-soars-but-not-fraud-rate-thanks-to-visa#ixzz0t6xTNZlf, June 2010.

30 *Global Fraud Report 2010–2011*, Economic Intelligence Unit (Oct. 2010).

31. 2009 Annual Study: Cost of a Data Breach. PGP Corporation and the Ponemon Institute, LLC, January 2010, p. 4.

32. *Id.* $135 of the $204 per record cost for the United States in 2009.

33. McAfee, Inc., *Unsecured Economies: Protecting Vital Information* (2010). The amount is projected from a survey of more than 800 CIOs in Germany, Japan, China, the United Kingdom, India, Brazil, Dubai, and the United States.

34. *Supermarket Customer Data Breached by SQL Injection Hack,* JAPAN TODAY (2010).

35. *Chancellor Faces Up to UK's Worst-Ever Data Breach,* COMPUTERWORLD UK (2009).

display trends similar to those in the United States.[36] The cost of data breaches per record for Germany, Australia, France, and the United Kingdom range from $98 to $177 in the categories of detection and escalation, notification, ex-post response, and lost business.[37]

Generally, the most valuable piece of information an organization collects from its customers is the personal information of an individual. Because of its value to both the data subject and the information holder, an organization must protect personal information at all stages of the data lifecycle. An organization can protect personal information by:

- Limiting the amount and kind of personal information gathered and stored
- Notifying the person of the ways in which his or her information is used or disclosed
- Obtaining the person's consent to such uses and disclosure
- Providing means for a person to review and update his or her own personal information
- Giving the person the ability to hold someone accountable for the failure to afford these protections

Consumers have an expectation that private information will be kept secure against loss, theft, corruption, and unauthorized access, use, or disclosure. As discussed earlier, the loss or unauthorized disclosure of consumer or personal information exposes an organization to significant financial and reputational harm. Loss of personal information also creates consumer distrust of organizations that gather this information.

B. Statutory Requirements

In addition to the economic losses, failure to adequately secure personal information can expose organizations to legal or regulatory action.[38] Navigating the complexities of state and federal laws that govern the protection of consumer information is challenging for all organizations. Almost all U.S. states[39] have adopted laws that require organizations to notify individuals following a security breach involving personal information. Most of these laws are based on the original state breach notification law,[40] California's "SB 1386," enacted in 2003. Each state's law, however, has its own significant variations, which requires a fact-intensive inquiry for an organization following a loss of personal information, based on a predesigned data breach response plan.

---

36. *Five Countries: Cost of Data Breach*, PGP Corporation and the Ponemon Institute, LLC (2010).

37. *Id.* at p. 9.

38. The FTC's recent case against Dave and Buster's is an example of a regulatory body holding a company at fault for the loss of personal information. FTC File No. 0823153, *Dave & Buster's Settles FTC Charges It Failed to Protect Consumers' Information*, FTC press release dated March 25, 2010, ¶4 (2010), at http://www.ftc.gov/opa/2010/03/davebusters.shtm. Note that loss to credit card information also can lead to actions for noncompliance with the Payment Card Industry Data Security Standards.

39. As of July 2010, the four remaining states without data breach notification laws are Alabama, Kentucky, New Mexico, and South Dakota.

40. Cal. Civ. Code §§ 1798.29, 1789.82 *et seq.*

State breach notification laws generally are based on the loss of citizen consumer personal information by private entities. The definition of personal information that has been adopted by most states includes language similar to the original California SB 1386 definition, which defined personal information as "an individual's first name or first initial and last name in combination with any one or more of the following data elements, when either the name or the data elements are not encrypted: (1) Social Security number; (2) driver's license number or California Identification number; (3) account number, credit or debit card number in combination with any required security code, access code, or password that would permit access to an individual's financial account."[41] Some states require per se notification following the loss of personal information, but others only require notification if such information is likely to cause harm to the individual or result in identity theft.

In addition to the myriad state breach notification laws, organizations must also comply with a number of distinct federal security breach notification laws that are generally based on industry affiliation. Examples of these industry notification laws include the Gramm-Leach-Bliley Act for financial institutions[42] and the Health Information Technology for Economic and Clinical Health Act (HITECH Act)[43] for health care professionals. Many states also have adopted related laws that require organizations to implement security procedures to protect personal information. Security procedures may include such techniques as data encryption and/or secure destruction of media containing personal information, maintaining a comprehensive information security program applicable to any records containing personal information or the implementation of technical and physical security methods, such as encryption.[44] U.S. federal and state laws and their international information security and privacy statutory counterparts are discussed further in Chapter 2.

C. Duty of Care to Safeguard Data

The high costs associated with a breach and the sensitive information that may be disclosed create a need to safeguard data. Risks are often assumed in using the Internet or other digital means to store or send personal information, but there is an expectation that information custodians will take reasonable precautions and provide reasonable protections for valuable information. Although this concept may sound fairly simple and straightforward, in reality the legal concept of the duty of care[45] is currently being developed as it applies to digital safeguards.

The legal obligations imposed on organizations to take such reasonable precautions are becoming more defined through government regulations and private sector activity.

---

41. Cal. Civ. Code § 1798.82(e)(2005). California has since amended the definition of personal information to include "medical information" and "health insurance information."

42. *See* 15 U.S.C. §§ 6801–6809.

43. Health Information Technology for Economic and Clinical Health (HITECH) Act, Title XIII of Division A and Title IV of Division B of the American Recovery and Reinvestment Act of 2009 (ARRA), Pub. L. No. 111-5 (Feb. 17, 2009).

44. *Id.*

45. Duty of Care is defined as an "[o]bligation that a sensible person would use in the circumstances when acting towards others and the public. If the actions of a person are not made with watchfulness, attention, caution, and prudence, their actions are considered negligent. Consequently, the resulting damages may be claimed as negligence in a lawsuit" (http://www.legal-explanations.com/definitions/duty-of-care.htm).

Federal laws such as Sarbanes-Oxley and Gramm-Leach-Bliley impose certain duties on regulated entities. State laws such as data breach notification laws and/or information security requirement laws often define particular activities that holders of information must perform. Private regulations such as the Payment Card Industry's Data Security Standard also define behaviors. All of these multiple sources provide the framework for defining an organization's duty of care to secure information.[46]

The complexity of the duty of care analysis for electronic information requires evaluation of a number of factors. Different concepts must be considered, including the value and sensitivity of the information, the risk of disclosure, existing legal or contractual protection obligations, and the practical availability of technical safeguards. Modern information systems often require a multidisciplinary effort to determine the correct duty of care that includes the following groups:

- Security professionals to evaluate impacts from relevant security threats and vulnerabilities
- Information technologists to implement the appropriate solutions in a technical environment
- Attorneys to analyze legal and contractual obligations and compliance criteria

Those groups involved in the multidisciplinary approach to information security and privacy can help an organization meet the standard of due care.[47]

The measure for duty of care is whether protections provided are reasonable, and the determination of reasonableness is subject to scrutiny by others. Expectations for the standard of due care will continue to evolve as statutes, technology, and business practices evolve, effectively raising the bar on the minimum standard of due care.

Managing the business to ensure that the standard of due care is followed by an organization is the traditional fiduciary duty of the board of directors.[48] Ensuring that this fiduciary duty is followed is integral to the concept of corporate governance. Corporate governance provides the structure of setting corporate objectives, the ability to reach those objectives, and the verification of proper performance of those objectives.[49] IT governance is the subset of corporate governance that is concerned with IT supporting and enabling the corporation to achieve its objectives.[50]

IT governance often is based on guidance provided by resources such as the International Organization for Standardization (ISO) 27000 standards, Federal Information Processing Standard (FIPS) Publication 200, and Control Objectives for Information and Related Technology (COBIT) 4.1. These standards help provide organizations with

---

46. Thomas J. Smedinghoff, *Where We're Headed: New Developments and Trends in the Law of Information Security*, Privacy and Data Security L.J. (January 2007): 106.

47. Expert advice is helpful in establishing best practices. Guides such as the Federal Trade Commission's publication *Protecting Personal Information—A Guide for Business* (http://www.ftc.gov/bcp/edu/pubs/business/idtheft/bus69.pdf) also can help an organization understand reasonable security actions.

48. Clyde E. Rankin III, *United States Corporate Governance: Implications for Foreign Issuers*, in Trends and Developments in Corporate Governance 283 (Kluwer Law International, 2004).

49. Organisation for Economic Co-operation and Development (OECD), *OECD Principles of Corporate Governance* (1999), p. 11.

50. Alan Calder, IT Governance: Guidelines for Directors 20 (2005).

industry best practices for IT strategy and security. Statutes and regulations also guide behaviors for appropriate IT and security governance.

1.3 WHAT IS INFORMATION SECURITY?

A. Definition

The term "information security" is an umbrella concept. In its broadest sense, the term refers to the protection of information "assets." Information assets include not only the information itself but also computer software, hardware, networks, and the infrastructure supporting information systems.

Information may reside on disk drives, physical media, or transient memory and may constitute intellectual property or confidential information. Information systems compile, utilize, communicate, and store information. Information systems consist of hardware, such as computer servers, networks, desktop and laptop computers, personal digital assistants, pagers, and cellular phones, as well as software, such as operating systems and applications. In a broader sense, the infrastructure supporting data centers and computer systems (i.e., electricity, water, and telecommunications services, as well as heating, ventilation, and air-conditioning systems) is also an information asset.

"Information security" is an umbrella term because it encompasses a large number of disciplines. Some examples include:

- *Security Management Practices:* Actions of management to protect an organization's information assets by developing and implementing security policies and procedures, classifying and determining the value of information assets, analyzing and managing risk, auditing, and implementing business continuity and disaster recovery.
- *Physical Security:* Protecting physical facilities and infrastructure from intrusion, theft, tampering, vandalism, unauthorized access, accidents, and natural disasters.
- *Personnel Security:* Providing assurances that personnel used by an organization (employees and contractors) are competent, adequately trained, trustworthy, and managed appropriately.
- *Systems/Computer Security:* Protecting information within an information system, including securing the operating system, applications, and access to workstations.[51]
- *Network Security:* Protecting information as it is transmitted from system to system using computer networks and securing those networks from intrusion and unauthorized access.[52]
- *Telecommunications Security:* Protecting information by preventing unauthorized access to telecommunications systems other than computer networks, such as phone systems, voice-mail systems, facsimile machines, pagers, broadcasting systems, and videoconferencing systems.

51. Warwick Ford & Michael Baum, Secure Electronic Commerce 94 (2001).
52. *Id.*

- *Operations Security:* Using procedures and systems to ensure that an organization's technology operates correctly and that its operations continue without interruption. This discipline also includes designing an organization's operations to deter, detect, and recover from incidents of theft, tampering, vandalism, fraud, and unauthorized access. It includes maintaining electronic records and logs that support an organization's business, facilitate investigations of the organization's security, and provide accountability.

B. Confidentiality, Integrity, and Availability

Another aspect of information security is the protection of information by establishing "security services," or critical security goals and capabilities. The three primary measurements for these security services are confidentiality, integrity, and availability (CIA), also known as the CIA triad (see Figure 1.2). The proper balance among confidentiality, integrity, and availability is the cornerstone for every information security and privacy program.

Confidentiality is defined in the information security industry as assurance that information is not improperly disclosed to unauthorized individuals, processes, or devices.[53] Confidentiality depends on authorization restrictions for access and disclosure to protect information propriety.[54] For example, regulations may require a payment processor to treat cardholder data in a confidential manner and prevent unauthorized disclosure. To achieve confidentiality, the payment processor may employ a combination of technical, personnel, and operational controls to prevent such disclosure.

Integrity of information aims to protect content against unauthorized modification or destruction of information. In addition, integrity includes ensuring that information is authentic.[55] The Sarbanes-Oxley law requires that publicly held companies ensure their financial reporting is accurate and true. To ensure their financial information has not been improperly altered, the information technology and accounting departments will audit their "controls" to ensure that the data reported has maintained its integrity from unauthorized modifications.

Availability is defined as timely and reliable access to data and information services for authorized users.[56] Availability requires ease of access to information and is often a critical element for many industries that depend on this information to complete their tasks. For example, medical professionals often require immediate access to critical patient health history in order to properly treat a patient.

Striking the correct balance among confidentiality, integrity, and availability of information is a critical task for both information security professionals and the attorneys that counsel them. For example, a business may dictate the criticality of information availability, but if confidentiality requirements are not followed at the expense of ensuring high availability, there may be adverse consequences to the business.

---

53. Committee on National Security Systems, National Information Assurance Glossary, CNSS Instruction no. 4009 (April 26, 2010), p. 17.
54. 44 U.S.C. § 3532 (b)(1)(B).
55. 44 U.S.C. § 3532 (b)(1)(A).
56. 44 U.S.C. § 3532 (b)(1)(C).

Figure 1.2
The CIA Triad

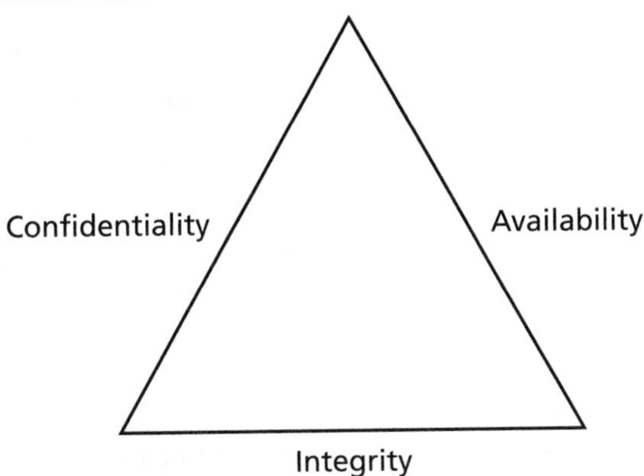

Although the CIA triad accounts for the basis of information assurance, other elements that should be understood for security services include those listed in the following table:

Service	*Definition*[56]
Authentication	Security measure designed to establish the validity of a transmission, message, or originator.
Authorization	Access privileges granted to a user, program, or process.
Accountability	Ability to trace activities to a responsible source.
Assurance	Measure of confidence that the information security and privacy features, practices, procedures, and architecture of an information system accurately mediate and enforce the information security and privacy policy.
Non-repudiation	Assurance that the sender of data is provided with proof of delivery and the recipient is provided with proof of the sender's identity, so neither can later deny having processed the data.

1.4 WHEN INFORMATION SECURITY FAILS: DATA BREACHES

Over the past several years, the information of millions of individuals has been compromised through data breaches, often resulting in identity theft and fraud. Several of the largest breaches involved sophisticated global organizations of hackers who infiltrated information systems at vulnerable points—where sensitive personal records were unsecured—even though those same records were encrypted in company

57. Committee on National Security Systems, National Information Assurance Glossary, CNSS Instruction no. 4009 (April 26, 2010).

networks. Data breaches have resulted in significant financial losses to many businesses, fraud inflicted on consumers, and even criminal indictments and civil damage actions.

Criminal cases illustrate the breadth of breach issues and the schemes that have produced many of the largest and most publicized data breaches. Indictments demonstrate methods hackers use to access computer systems remotely and steal financial and other sensitive information, including techniques such as war-driving (driving with a laptop computer and high-powered antenna to locate, and potentially exploit, vulnerable wireless computer systems),[58] installation of "sniffers" (code that allows for the capture of data in real-time as it traverses computer networks),[59] and SQL injections (Internet-based attacks that exploit vulnerabilities in database-driven websites).[60]

A. Data Breach Examples

In late 2008, an attack using hacking methods resulted in $9.5 million of loss in less than 12 hours at RBS WorldPay. According to the FBI, the breach of RBS WorldPay was one of the "most complicated and organized computer fraud attack[s] ever conducted" in which hackers exploited vulnerabilities in the RBS WorldPay computer network and attacked key aspects of the global financial infrastructure.[61] RBS WorldPay, with headquarters in Atlanta, Georgia, processes credit and debit card transactions for financial institutions around the world. As the U.S. payment processing arm of the Royal Bank of Scotland Group, it is the second-largest ATM processor in the United States. A crime group was able to crack the company's encryption algorithms, counterfeit dozens of debit cards, and change ATM withdrawal limits to facilitate the attack. Eight hackers were charged with wire and computer fraud, access device fraud, computer intrusion, aggravated identity theft, and conspiracy in a 16-count indictment.[62]

One of the largest criminal prosecutions was for information security breaches at Heartland, Hannaford, TJX, and DSW,[63] where millions of personal records were stolen. In the breach of Hannaford Brothers, an East Coast grocery store chain, hackers used a SQL injection attack to intercept data stored on the magnetic stripe of payment cards as customers used them at the checkout counter. That information was taken in transit between the point-of-sale in the grocery store and the company that pro-

---

58. *See, e.g.*, Indictment at 2, United States v. Salcedo, No. 5:03-cr-00053-LHT-1 (W.D.N.C. 2006); Indictment at 3, United States v. Gonzalez, No. 1:08-cr-10223-PBS-1 (D. Mass. 2008).

59. *See, e.g.*, Indictment at 3-4, United States v. Yastremskiy et al., No. 2:08-cr-00160-SJF-1 (E.D.N.Y. 2008); Indictment at 3, United States v. Gonzalez, No. 1:08-cr-10223-PBS-1 (D. Mass. 2008).

60. *See, e.g.*, Indictment at 5, United States v. Gonzalez, No. 1:08-cr-10223-PBS-1 (D. Mass. 2008).

61. Gordon Snow, Federal Bureau of Investigation, Statement before the House Judiciary Subcommittee on Crime, Terrorism, and Homeland Security (July 28, 2010), *available at* http://judiciary.house.gov/hearings/pdf/Snow100728.pdf.

62. Eight hackers including Victor Pleshchuk of Russia and Sergei Tsurikov of Estonia were indicted for wire fraud, computer fraud, access device fraud, computer intrusions, aggravated identity theft, and conspiracy in a 16-count indictment returned on November 10, 2009, in the Northern District of Georgia. (*See* http://atlanta.fbi.gov/dojpressrel/pressrel09/atl111009.htm.)

63. Albert Gonzalez was sentenced on March 26, 2009, to 20 years and a day, and fined $25,000 for his role in the breaches into Heartland Payment Systems, Hannaford Brothers, 7-Eleven, and other companies. The sentence will run concurrently with a 20-year sentence he received in two other cases involving hacks into TJX, Office Max, Dave & Buster's restaurants and others.

cesses credit card payments, and exposed 4.2 million credit card accounts.[64] At critical junctures, security failed because the system as a whole was not secure. Once on the networks, the hackers installed "back doors" to provide them with continued access and programmed the malware to erase evidence from the hacked networks to avoid forensic detection.

TJX, an off-price retailer selling family apparel and home fashions in over 2,500 stores worldwide, including T.J. Maxx, Marshall's, A.J. Wright, Bob's Stores, and HomeGoods stores in the United States, was the target of a data breach in 2007 when 45.6 million credit and debit card numbers were stolen by intruders over a period of more than 18 months.[65] The TJX breach exploited vulnerabilities in the TJX information system at the store level and in the software used to manage large business databases. Security "failed" at multiple points, including TJX's use of wireless technology with a weak encryption mechanism and its transmission of unencrypted authorization requests within its networks. This configuration made its information system vulnerable to attack. Intruders also had access to the TJX decryption algorithm through the use of an unsecured key or password that defeated any protection encryption might have provided on its information system. During the payment approval process, TJX transmitted payment card data (including the track 2 data on the magnetic stripe) without encryption to payment card issuers.

Heartland Payment Systems (HPS), based in Princeton, New Jersey, is the sixth-largest processor of credit and debit card transactions in the United States.[66] Using an SQL injection attack, hackers broke into the Heartland network and planted malware capable of sniffing payment card data as it moved across the company's network. Even though Heartland encrypted some of its data, its information security failed because there were opportunities for personal data to be intercepted when it was unencrypted on the company network.

In 2005, DSW discovered a data security failure that allowed hackers to gain access to sensitive credit and debit card information (name, card number, expiration date, and security code), and checking account information (bank routing number, account number, check number, and driver's license number and state) for more than 1.4 million customers.[67] Hackers gained access to the DSW computer networks through wireless access points on the networks. Intruders intercepted wireless signals and connected wirelessly to in-store networks without authorization. This information was transmitted wirelessly to a computer network located in the store and then sent to the bank or check processor.[68] Several coconspirators were indicted for this breach of the DSW computer system.[69]

64. *See* http://www.boston.com/business/articles/2008/03/18/grocer_hannaford_hit_by_computer_breach/.

65. TJX SEC Form 10-K, p. 7 (for the fiscal year ended January 27, 2007).

66. http://www.heartlandpaymentsystems.com.

67. In the Matter of DSW, Inc., No. C-4157, Complaint (March 2006), *available at* http://www.ftc.gov/os/caselist/0523096/0523096c4157DSWComplaint.pdf; Decision and Order, *available at* http://www.ftc.gov/os/caselist/0523096/0523096c4157DSWDecisionandOrder.pdf;DSW SEC Form 10-K (FY ended), *available at* http://www.sec.gov/Archives/edgar/data/1319947/000095015209003376/l35986ae10vk.htm.

68. *Id.*

69. *Id.*, ¶ 7; United States v. Gonzalez, No. 1:08-cr-10223-PBS-1 (D. Mass. 2008).

B. Statistics and Causation

In 2009, techniques such as these resulted in a record 131,032,177 business sector data records exposed.[70] Nearly 60 percent of the records breached occurred in retail companies and payment card processors. And from 2009 to 2010, the number of publicly reported data breaches doubled.[71] There are a number of causes of data breaches, particularly in the business sector. Hackers have targeted retailers and payment card processors because of the high value for identity theft of the consumer information collected and maintained by these entities. At the same time, business executives have failed to address the multitude of vulnerabilities in their networks, making them prime targets for hackers to exploit. Another aspect of lax security is the breaches that resulted from the theft or loss of laptops, computers, hard drives, backup tapes, PDAs, or other portable media containing unencrypted personal information. Many organizations collect too much sensitive data and save it much longer than is necessary to accomplish its business purposes.

For a robust approach to responding to data breaches, see Chapter 6.

1.5 RELATIONSHIP BETWEEN INFORMATION SECURITY AND PRIVACY

Several relationships exist between information security and privacy. One relationship of information security and privacy is that one enables the other. Privacy requires information security to achieve its objectives. At the same time, privacy is larger than just the information security controls designed and implemented on its behalf. There are many other aspects to privacy that are not part of what information security aims to achieve. To understand this difference, we must first define privacy before looking at its relationships with information security.

A. What Is Privacy?

More than a century ago, in their classic 1890 work *The Right to Privacy*, Samuel Warren and William Brandeis opined that privacy is the "right to be let alone."[72] Decades later, William Prosser developed this "right to privacy" into four torts,[73] still the bases for privacy tort law in many state courts and commonly referred to as (1) intrusion upon seclusion, (2) public disclosure of private facts, (3) false light, and (4) misappropriation of name or likeness. However, these articulations of the "privacy right," and privacy torts, while critical to present-day thinking and the evolution of privacy and data security statutory law in this country over the last two decades, are no longer sufficient to describe modern notions of privacy in the information/Internet age, particularly in light of the proliferation and widespread availability of electronic information.

Professor Solove, widely regarded as the father of modern privacy legal theory, has commented on the difficulties in developing a coherent theory of privacy:

> When I first began exploring privacy issues, I sought to reach a definitive conclusion about what "privacy" is, but after delving into the question, I was humbled by it. I could

70. Identity Theft Resource Center, 2009 Data Breach States (January 6, 2010) at 7 (http://www.idtheftcenter.org/artman2/uploads/1/ITRC_Breach_Stats_Report_20100106_1.pdf).

71 http://blog.imperva.com/2010/11/.

72. Samuel D. Warren & Louis D. Brandeis, *The Right to Privacy*, 4 Harv. L. Rev. 193 (1890).

73. William L. Prosser, *Privacy*, 48 Cal. L. Rev. 383, 388–89 (1960).

> not reach a satisfactory answer. This struggle ultimately made me recognize that privacy is a plurality of different things and that the quest for a singular essence of privacy leads to a dead end. There is no overarching conception of privacy—it must be mapped like terrain, by painstakingly studying the landscape.[74]

The new concept of information privacy that has emerged in modern discussion is the ability to control how personal information is collected, used, shared, and disclosed. Privacy has modernly been defined as "[t]he appropriate use of personal information under the circumstances. What is appropriate will depend on context, law, and the individual's expectations; also, the right of an individual to control the collection, use, and disclosure of personal information."[75] While oversimplified, such a definition is consistent with the notion of privacy embodied in the Fair Information Practice Principles, five core principles of privacy protection developed over the last 30 years and that have formed the basis for the vast majority of modern privacy and data security laws around the globe: (1) Notice/Awareness; (2) Choice/Consent; (3) Access/Participation; (4) Integrity/Security; and (5) Enforcement/Redress.[76]

B. How Does Privacy Relate to Information Security?

There can be no privacy without information security. The best intentions to keep confidences are useless if the information is readily hacked or leaked. NIST states: "The *security* objective of confidentiality is defined by law as preserving authorized restrictions on information access and disclosure, including means for protecting personal *privacy* and proprietary information."[77]

In information security, the focus is on protecting the confidentiality, integrity, and availability of information. Confidentiality and integrity are especially important for privacy compliance. Organizations are usually concerned with maintaining the confidentiality of their own nonpublic information, but privacy laws establish separate and additional confidentiality requirements when the organizations handle personal information. Privacy law helps determine what information must be kept confidential and sometimes how it must be kept confidential—with access controls, encryption, physical and organizational security measures, and other policies and procedures. Thus, privacy laws and policies add substantive requirements for the confidentiality aspect of information security practice. Privacy laws and policies sometimes specify aspects of data integrity (one of the Fair Information Practice Principles mentioned above), such as correcting and updating data, taking it from the

---

74. Daniel J. Solove, Understanding Privacy (Harvard University Press, 2008), at ix (Preface). *See also* Solove, *I've Got Nothing to Hide and Other Misunderstandings of Privacy*, 44 San Diego L. Rev. at 259–60 (2007), *available at* SSRN: http://ssrn.com/abstract=998565 ("there are no clear boundaries for what we should or should not refer to as 'privacy'").

75. International Association of Privacy Professionals (IAPP), Information Privacy Certification Glossary of Common Privacy Terminology, *available at* https://www.privacyassociation.org/images/uploads/CIPP%20Privacy%20Glossary_0909.pdf.

76. The Federal Trade Commission's articulation of the Fair Information Practice Principles can be found at http://www.ftc.gov/reports/privacy3/fairinfo.shtm.

77. NIST Special Publication 800-122, Guide to Protecting the Confidentiality of Personally Identifiable Information (PII), Recommendations of the National Institute of Standards and Technology, Section 3, *available at* http://csrc.nist.gov/publications/nistpubs/800-122/sp800-122.pdf (citing 44 U.S.C. § 3542) (emphasis added).

most reliable sources (often the affected individual), and maintaining information systems in such a way as to prevent and detect data corruption and restore databases to an earlier state if necessary.

This process can be conceptualized by focusing on the lifecycle of data within an enterprise and the places within that lifecycle where data might be at risk of compromise—where privacy rights, and other protected interests, might be harmed as the result of a security breach. Organizations must manage that risk, and avoid privacy and other harms, by implementing information security controls.

The Fair Information Practice Principles can serve as guideposts to information security and privacy practitioners alike:

> Privacy is much broader than just protecting the confidentiality of PII. To establish a comprehensive privacy program that addresses the range of privacy issues that organizations may face, organizations should take steps to establish policies and procedures that address all of the Fair Information Practices. For example, while providing individuals with notice of new information collections and how their personal information will be used and protected is central to providing individuals with privacy protections and transparency, it may not have a significant impact on protecting the confidentiality of their personal information. On the other hand, the Fair Information Practices related to establishing security safeguards, purpose specification, use limitation, collection limitation, and accountability are directly relevant to the protection of the confidentiality of PII.[78]

Without information security, the privacy of sensitive information at various stages of the data lifecycle is at risk. Put another way, information security controls are one mechanism for protecting the privacy of certain categories of sensitive information. This relationship has found form in U.S. state legislation that has emerged over the last several years. Massachusetts' data security regulations[79] seek to protect the *privacy* of personal information from cradle to grave by requiring companies to put in place *information security* programs including controls such as authentication measures, encryption, and other policies and procedures.[80] Similarly, the state data breach notification laws[81] aim to protect nonpublic or private personal information by requiring that companies disclose to individuals and sometimes regulators when they have expe-

78. NIST Special Publication 800-122, *supra* note 75, at § 2.3.

79. Mass. Gen. Laws c. 93H and 201 CMR §§ 17.00–17.05.

80. *See, e.g.*, Ark. Code Ann. § 4-110-104(b); Cal. Civ. Code §§ 1798.31 & 1798.81.5; Colo. Rev. Stat. Ann. § 6-1-713; Conn. HB 5658; Kan. Rev. Stat. § 365.720 to .730; Md. Com. Law Code Ann. § 14-3503; Mass. Gen. Laws ch. 93H and 201 CMR §§ 17.00-17.05; Nev. Rev. Stat. §§ 603A.210 and 603A.215 (SB 227); Or. Rev. Stat. § 646A.622; R.I. Stat. § 11-49.2-2; Tex. Bus. & Com. Code §§ 521.001 *et seq.*; Utah Code Ann. § 13-44-201; Wash. Rev. Code Ann. § 19.215.020 to .030.

81. *See* National Conference of State Legislators, State Security Breach Notification Laws as of April 12, 2010, *available at* http://www.ncsl.org/Default.aspx?TabId=13489.

rienced an information security breach that compromises "personal information."[82] Security and transparency thus promote privacy objectives.

C. Practical Guidance

The notions of privacy and privacy harms will continue to evolve, but it is unlikely that the legal framework for protecting privacy will keep up with the breakneck speed of technology. Therefore, the most important takeaway for purposes of understanding the relationship between privacy and security is that stakeholders within an organization who are tasked with one and/or the other must work together in any and all circumstances, with legal as a common thread. Privacy professionals cannot meet their objectives of protecting and managing personal information of employees and customers without the help of information technology and security experts. Conversely, information technology and security experts cannot accomplish their mission of protecting corporate information assets unless they understand the privacy values often driving compliance and risk management goals. Lawyers need to understand information security, technology, *and* privacy. Ideally, the lawyers should help to mediate and translate among these groups for purposes of promoting compliance and legal defensibility.[83] The disciplines of privacy and information security are so intertwined that their respective stakeholders can and must cooperate fully for the ultimate success of the organization's data protection programs.

---

82. Although "personal information" or "PII" as defined under these laws and U.S. federal laws discussed throughout this book has traditionally been defined as name in conjunction with Social Security number, driver's license number, financial account number (with or without passwords or other information that would grant access to the account), or in some cases medical information, regulators in this country are starting to explore the notion of protecting information beyond traditional PII, more in line with the European notion of personal information and privacy as a fundamental human right, including any data element that could be used to identify a person. *See, e.g.*, NIST Special Publication 800-122, *supra* note 75, Section 2.2 ("The following list contains examples of information that may be considered PII: name, such as full name, maiden name, mother's maiden name, or alias; personal identification number, such as social security number (SSN), passport number, driver's license number, taxpayer identification number, patient identification number, and financial account or credit card number; address information, such as street address or e-mail address; asset information, such as Internet Protocol (IP) or Media Access Control (MAC) address or other host-specific persistent static identifier that consistently links to a particular person or small, well-defined group of people; telephone numbers, including mobile, business, and personal numbers; personal characteristics, including photographic image (especially of face or other distinguishing characteristic), x-rays, fingerprints, or other biometric image or template data (e.g., retina scan, voice signature, facial geometry); information identifying personally owned property, such as vehicle registration number or title number and related information; information about an individual that is linked or linkable to one of the above (e.g., date of birth, place of birth, race, religion, weight, activities, geographical indicators, employment information, medical information, education information, financial information). *See also* "Discussion draft" of a bill "[t]o require notice to and consent of an individual prior to the collection and disclosure of certain personal information relating to that individual," introduced in May 2010 by Reps. Rick Boucher (D-Va.) and Cliff Stearns (R-Fla.), *available at* http://www.infolawgroup.com/uploads/file/Boucher%20Privacy_Draft_5-10.pdf.

83. NIST Special Publication 800-122, *supra* note 75, at ES-4 ("Organizations should encourage close coordination among their chief privacy officers, senior agency officials for privacy, chief information officers, chief information security officers, and legal counsel when addressing issues related to PII.").

CHAPTER 2

Information Security and Privacy Laws and Regulations

To create a consistent approach to information security and privacy across an entire organization, it is essential to identify all domestic and international laws that apply to the organization's global operations. Statutes and regulations concerning information security and privacy must be synthesized into a coherent body of law that can be translated into information security and privacy policies and controls (discussed in Chapters 4–6). This chapter begins with U.S. federal and state statutes and regulations that affect information security and privacy. This is followed by international privacy and information security statutes for major countries across the globe. The chapter concludes by discussing certain nonregulatory obligations, including those for business continuity and an attorney's obligation to protect client data. Due to the dynamic nature of information security and privacy statutes, regulations, and judicial review by courts in all jurisdictions, it is important to check all applicable sources for any recent revisions when undertaking the statutory synthesis process to create an organization's single global legal view.

What Global Executives Need to Know

- The statutes affecting information security and privacy in every country and locality where the organization operates
- The industry regulations and standards applicable to information security and privacy
- The types of organizational data affected by these statutes and regulations and the data's current location
- Actions required for the organization to be in compliance with these statutes and regulations
- Actions required for the organization when it is no longer in compliance (e.g., data breach)

2.1 U.S. FEDERAL LAWS

A. Gramm-Leach-Bliley Act

1. *Statutory Requirements*

The Gramm-Leach-Bliley Act (GLBA),[1] also known as the Financial Services Modernization Act of 1999, repealed the Glass-Steagall Act of 1932, which required the separation of certain types of financial companies from bank holding companies. Title V of GLBA[2] requires financial institutions,[3] among other things, to protect the nonpublic personal information of financial consumers[4] from disclosure.[5]

Personal privacy can be enhanced by giving consumers greater control over how businesses collect, use, and share their personal information. In an effort to promote a degree of financial consumer privacy, the act requires financial institutions to provide customers with (1) an initial and annual notice of the financial institution's privacy policies and practices,[6] and (2) an opportunity to prevent their information from being shared with certain third parties.[7] In November 2009, the seven financial industry regulatory agencies[8] and the FTC jointly released a model privacy notice form that, if used, meets the GLBA notice requirements.[9]

Additionally, GLBA addresses information security. Although economic and reputational factors led to the development of information security programs at financial institutions predating GLBA, the act mandates the programs and establishes an observable degree of due care across the financial sector. To accomplish this, Section 501(b) of GLBA requires financial services regulatory agencies to establish appropriate standards for financial institutions subject to their respective jurisdictions.[10] These standards are designed to promote the safeguarding of financial consumer information.[11] Safeguarding in this context is to preserve and maintain the confidentiality and integrity of this protected class of information.

---

1. The text of the bill is available at http://banking.senate.gov/conf/confrpt.htm.
2. Title V of the Gramm-Leach-Bliley Act has been codified as U.S.C. §§ 6801–6809.
3. 15 U.S.C. § 6809(3).
4. 15 U.S.C. § 6809(9). The privacy and information security requirements of GLBA apply to the information of any "individual who obtains, from a financial institution, financial products or services which are to be used primarily for personal, family, or household purposes[.]"
5. 15 U.S.C. § 6801(b).
6. *Id.* at § 6803.
7. *Id.* at § 6802. It should be noted that some information sharing in the normal course of business is unavoidable, and customers must be notified in the privacy notice that such sharing will occur, even if a customer may not opt out of the sharing without forgoing the services of the financial institution.
8. Board of Governors of the Federal Reserve System, Office of the Comptroller of the Currency (OCC), Office of Thrift Supervision (OTS), National Credit Union Administration (NCUA), Federal Deposit Insurance Corporation (FDIC), Securities and Exchange Commission (SEC), Commodity Futures Trading Commission (CFTC).
9. The Joint Release is available at http://www.ftc.gov/opa/2009/11/glb.shtm.
10. See *supra* note 3.
11. 15 U.S.C. § 6801(b). *See also* §§ 6804–6805.

Information security programs achieve the confidentiality of consumer information through administrative, technical, and physical safeguards[12] designed to:

- ensure the security and confidentiality of customer records and information
- protect against any anticipated threats[13] or hazards to the security or integrity of such records
- protect against unauthorized access[14] to or use of such records or information that could result in substantial harm or inconvenience to any customer.[15]

2. *Regulatory Requirements*

On January 17, 2001, the federal banking agencies released[16] a joint set of final guidelines[17] to implement the goals and safeguards specified in Section 501(b). Although called guidelines, they are mandatory and enforced by financial institution regulators.[18] As a general matter, these Interagency Guidelines require financial institutions to establish comprehensive, written, information security programs.

a. Information Security Programs

Information security programs are nothing less than the sum total of all the activities that a financial institution undertakes to protect information from misuse, loss, and theft. Information security programs are typically the responsibility of Chief Information Security Officers or similar executives. Coordination with compliance, risk, audit, and operational groups within the financial institution is often necessary. An information security program should include administrative, technical, and physical safeguards appropriate to the size and complexity of the financial institution.[19]

For large, complex bank holding companies, a consolidated and uniform information security program is not required so long as the subsidiaries and operating units coordinate the various elements of their programs.[20] Regardless of structure, the Guidelines require the financial institution's board of directors to: (1) approve the security policy and program, (2) exercise general oversight over the program,[21] and (3) receive man-

12. *See* Chapter 5.
13. *See* Chapter 4
14. *See* Chapter 5.
15. 15 U.S.C. §§ 6801(b) and 6801(b)(1–3).
16. Joint Press Release of the Board of Governors of the Federal Reserve System, the Federal Deposit Insurance Corporation, the Office of the Comptroller of the Currency, and the Office of Thrift Supervision, Agencies Adopt Guidelines for Customer Information Security (Jan. 17, 2001).
17. Interagency Guidelines Establishing Standards for Safeguarding Customer Information, 66 Fed. Reg. 8616 (Feb. 1, 2001); 12 C.F.R. pt. 30 (Office of the Comptroller of the Currency), 12 C.F.R. pts. 208, 211, 225, and 263 (Board of Governors of the Federal Reserve System), 12 C.F.R. pts. 308 and 364 (Federal Deposit Insurance Corporation), and 12 C.F.R. pts. 568 and 570 (Office of Thrift Supervision). The Guidelines became effective on July 1, 2001. The National Credit Union Administration and the Commodity Futures Trading Commission have also issued guidelines under the authority granted by GLBA.
18. Due to the similarity between the Interagency Guidelines, the OCC version codified at 12 C.F.R. pt. 30, app. A, will be cited throughout this section, with brief mention of the SEC and FTC versions below.
19. 12 C.F.R. pt. 30, app. B, II.A.
20. *Id.*
21. *Id.*, III.A.

agement's annual report on the effectiveness of the program.[22] Based on feedback from the board of directors, ongoing observations and decisions by management, and, most importantly, advances in technology, threats, and business changes, management must adjust the information security program accordingly.[23]

b. Risk Assessment

The most widely interpreted of the Interagency Guidelines is the requirement to assess risk. The Guidelines require management to: "identify reasonably foreseeable internal and external threats" to customer information,[24] assess the likelihood and potential damage of these threats,[25] and assess the effectiveness of a wide variety of information security controls.[26] The universe of possible threats to customer information is limited to those that are reasonably foreseeable, making the risk assessment less onerous.

In deciding how to control risks to customer information, financial institutions may consider likelihood and impact of threats, which work in tandem to set a level of due care.[27] Financial institutions should expend more resources to control those events that are highly likely and carry a high impact. When dealing with high-impact, less likely, or very infrequent threats, some mitigation is still warranted. Management may remain informed regarding current foreseeable threats by collaborating with peer institutions, participating in industry groups, and staying abreast of available technologies and information regarding the ever-changing threat landscape. Risk assessments are discussed in Chapter 4.

c. Management and Control of Risk

Under the Interagency Guidelines, the objectives of the information security program should include the protection of consumers from harms resulting from the disclosure of personal data.[28] The means of protecting the confidentiality and integrity of sensitive information include a wide array of processes, human capital, and technology. These administrative, technical, and physical safeguards are sweeping and can be broadly interpreted to include safeguards ranging from the physical security of buildings and data centers to the types of encryption used during online banking sessions. The safeguards are discussed in Chapter 5.

d. Third-Party Service Providers

The Guidelines require financial institutions to oversee third-party service providers with respect to the security of customer information that is maintained or processed on behalf of the institution.[29] Service provider organizations routinely obtain an SAS 70 report (see Chapter 6) that attests to the effectiveness of their controls. Over time,

---

22. *Id.*, III.F.
23. *Id.*, III.E.
24. 12 C.F.R. pt. 30, app. B, III.B.1.
25. *Id.*, III.B.2.
26. *Id.*, III.B.3; III.C.
27. *Id.*, III.B.
28. 12 C.F.R. pt. 30, app. B, II.B.
29. 12 C.F.R. pt. 30, app. B, III.D.

companies began to desire more assurance than that provided by the SAS 70, so companies began doing their own due diligence on service providers. In the financial services industry, GLBA mandated that financial institutions oversee service provider arrangements.[30] This has led to significant audit activity for service providers who are continually audited by their customers.

In an attempt to standardize the requirements for meeting a standard of information security due care, the BITS organization standardized the assessment of third-party service providers.[31] BITS is a nonprofit organization that developed the "BITS Framework for Managing Technology Risk for Service Provider Relationships."[32] Within the BITS Framework two tools were developed to ensure service providers had implemented controls in conformance with the ISO 27002 standard for information security controls. The first tool is called the Standardized Information Gathering (SIG) Questionnaire, which is a template based on the ISO 27002 standard and specifies the expected information security controls that should be in place at the service provider organization. The second tool is the Agreed Upon Procedures (AUP), which serve as testing procedures meant to validate the effectiveness of the controls specified in the SIG.[33] ISO 27002 and BITS AUP are further discussed in Chapter 5.

e. Data Breach Notification

The regulatory agencies issued an Interagency Guidance on Response Programs for Unauthorized Access to Customer Information and Customer Notice (Incident Response Guidance) regarding the implementation of notification programs to notify customers, regulators, and law enforcement officials of data breaches.[34] The regulations promulgated to implement the response program have been codified as Supplement A to Appendix B of 12 C.F.R. Part 30. "[E]very financial institution should . . . develop and implement a risk-based response program to address incidents of unauthorized access to customer information in customer information systems" regardless of whether the breach occurs in the financial institution's own computer systems or in those hosted by third-party service providers.[35]

3. SEC and FTC Requirements

The Securities and Exchange Commission (SEC) adopted Regulation S-P: Privacy of Consumer Financial Information to implement the privacy provisions of GLBA.[36] Regulation S-P requires organizations subject to the SEC's jurisdiction to adopt policies and procedures that address administrative, technical, and physical safeguards to protect customer information.

---

30. 12 C.F.R. pt. 30, app. B, III(D).

31. BITS was created by the Financial Services Roundtable (www.fsround.org); *see* http://www.bitsinfo.org/about.html.

32. Available at http://www.bitsinfo.org/downloads/Publications%20Page/2009Framework.pdf.

33. The SIG and the AUP can be downloaded from a BITS-sponsored website: http://www.sharedassessments.org/.

34. 70 Fed. Reg. 15736 (Mar. 29, 2005).

35. 12 C.F.R. 30, app. B, Supp. A(II).

36. 17 C.F.R. pt. 248.

The Federal Trade Commission (FTC) has also issued a final rule implementing Section 501(b) of GLBA (FTC Rule).[37] The FTC Rule is less extensive and comprehensive than the Guidelines, but it does require financial institutions subject to FTC jurisdiction to develop and implement a comprehensive security program appropriate to their size and complexity, the nature and scope of their activities, and the sensitivity of any customer information they possess.[38] It is important to note that the FTC has taken a very broad approach to defining "financial institution." Therefore, organizations that may not normally be considered a financial institution, such as a travel agency or a law firm that provides certain services, may fall under the FTC's jurisdiction.[39]

B. Health Insurance Portability and Accountability Act/Health Information Technology for Economic and Clinical Health Act

To improve the efficiency and effectiveness of the health care system, the Health Insurance Portability and Accountability Act of 1996 (HIPAA)[40] included Administrative Simplification provisions that required the Department of Health and Human Services (HHS) to adopt national standards for electronic health care transactions and code sets, unique health identifiers, and security.[41] The Office for Civil Rights (OCR) administers and enforces the Privacy Rule and Security Rule. The Enforcement Rule provides standards for the enforcement of all the Administrative Simplification Rules.

1. HIPAA Privacy Rule

To guard against technology advances eroding the privacy of health information, HIPAA mandated the adoption of federal privacy protections for individually identifiable health information. The HIPAA Privacy Rule[42] set national standards for the protection of individually identifiable health information by three types of covered entities: health plans, health care clearinghouses, and health care providers who conduct the standard health care transactions electronically. The Privacy Rule applies to protected health information (PHI) in electronic, oral, and hardcopy media. It relates to Confidentiality, Integrity, and Availability of PHI in any form and covers matters such as when patient information can be used or disclosed, how to disclose the "minimum necessary" amount of information, disclosures to Business Associates, and patient information of minors.

The Privacy Rule requires organizations subject to HIPAA to designate a Privacy Official who is responsible for developing and implementing policies and procedures to comply with the Privacy Rule and safeguard PHI created, stored, and exchanged. These policies and procedures must address a number of topics, including the provider's "Notice of Privacy Practices," patient authorization for disclosure, patient access to PHI, amending PHI, accounting for disclosures, and workforce training.

---

37. 16 C.F.R. pt. 314.

38. 16 C.F.R. pt. 314.3(a).

39. Brian J. Peretti & Dennis Dow, *Gramm-Leach-Bliley and the Bankruptcy/Collection Attorney*, Norton Bankr. L. Adviser, Feb. 2002.

40. Health Insurance Portability and Accountability Act of 1996, P.L. No.104-191 (42 U.S.C. § 1320d-2).

41. All of the HIPAA Administrative Simplification Rules are located at 45 C.F.R. pts. 160, 162, and 164.

42. Final Privacy Rule 65 Fed. Reg. 82462 (Dec. 28, 2000). The HIPAA Privacy Rule went into effect April 14, 2003.

2. HIPAA Security Rule

The second layer of HIPAA is the Security Rule,[43] which applies only to electronic protected health information (e-PHI), both when data is stored and during transmission or receipt. HIPAA mandated the adoption of security standards for health information that take into account the technical capabilities of records systems used to maintain health information, the costs of security measures, the need for training persons who have access to health information, the value of audit trails in computerized records systems, and the needs and capabilities of small health care providers and rural health care providers.[44]

An organization subject to HIPAA must maintain reasonable and appropriate administrative, technical, and physical safeguards to ensure the integrity and confidentiality of the e-PHI; protect against reasonably anticipated threats to the security or integrity of the e-PHI; prevent any unauthorized uses or disclosures of the e-PHI; and ensure compliance by its workforce.[45] An example of a Security Rule requirement is for a health care provider to develop and implement a disaster recovery plan.

Telephone calls and faxes are not considered electronic transactions subject to the Security Rule. However, "telephone voice response and 'faxback' systems (a request for information from a computer made via voice or telephone keypad input with the requested information returned as a fax) do fall under the Security Rule because they are used as input and output devices for computers, not because they have computers in them."[46]

Risk analysis is the first step in an organization's Security Rule compliance efforts. Risk analysis is an ongoing process that should provide the organization with a detailed understanding of the risks to the confidentiality, integrity, and availability of e-PHI. There are numerous methods of performing risk analysis, and no single method or "best practice" guarantees compliance with the Security Rule. Some examples of steps that might be applied in a risk analysis process are outlined in NIST SP 800-30.[47] Information risk analysis and management are further discussed in Chapter 4.

The Office for Civil Rights (OCR) is responsible for issuing annual guidance on the provisions of the HIPAA Security Rule.[48]

3. Covered Entities

HIPAA Privacy and Security Rules apply to Covered Entities, which include health care providers who transmit patient health information in electronic form in connection with a transaction covered by HIPAA. These transactions include electronic claims, eligibility requests, and claims status inquiries to health plans, other health care providers,

43. Final Security Rule 45 C.F.R. 164.302–.318. The HIPAA Security Rule went into effect April 21, 2005.

44. 42 U.S.C. § 1320d-2(d)(1).

45. 42 U.S.C. § 1320d-2(d)(2).

46. 68 Fed. Reg. 8342.

47. Risk Management Guide for Information Technology Systems, *available at* http://www.hhs.gov/ocr/privacy/hipaa/administrative/securityrule/nist800-30.pdf.

48. See the Security Series papers available on the Office for Civil Rights (OCR) website (http://www.hhs.gov/ocr/hipaa), for a detailed discussion of tools and methods available for risk analysis and risk management, as well as other Security Rule compliance requirements.

and clearinghouses. As of February 17, 2010, Business Associates of Covered Entities must comply with most provisions of the HIPAA Security Rule.

4. HITECH Act Amendments

On February 17, 2009, the Health Information Technology for Economic and Clinical Health (HITECH) Act[49] provisions were enacted as part of the American Recovery and Reinvestment Act of 2009 (ARRA)[50]—the legislation referred to as the "stimulus bill." The HITECH Act amended the HIPAA Security and Privacy Rules (see the summary of key changes in the following chart), introduced the new Breach Notification Rule, imposed higher civil fines for violations of HIPAA Standards, and required Business Associates to comply with certain provisions of the Security Rule.

The HITECH Act also established programs for Medicare and Medicaid reimbursement incentive payments to encourage the adoption of electronic health records technology. The program will make incentive payments available to certain eligible providers who can demonstrate "meaningful use" of certified electronic health records. "Meaningful use" criteria are the subject of developing regulations and are expected to evolve during the duration of the program, between 2011 and 2014.

The table on the following pages summarizes key ARRA and HITECH Act provisions that amend or reference the HIPAA Privacy Rule or Security Rule.

5. "Meaningful Use" of Certified EHR Technology

The HITECH Act established programs under Medicare and Medicaid to provide incentive payments for the "meaningful use" of certified EHR (electronic health record) technology. These programs begin in 2011 and will provide incentive payments to eligible professionals and eligible hospitals as they adopt, implement, upgrade, or demonstrate meaningful use of certified EHR technology. Patient privacy and security are important considerations in implementing the EHR incentive programs. CMS (Centers for Medicare and Medicaid Services) is working with the Office for Civil Rights and the ONC (Office of the National Coordinator for Health Information and Technology) to address the privacy and security protections under the HITECH Act.

In July 2010, HHS issued a Final Rule on the Initial Set of Standards, Implementation Specifications, and Certification Criteria for Electronic Health Record Technology in conjunction with its Final Rule on the meaningful use EHR incentive program.[51] The rule establishes the system capabilities and related standards and implementation specifications that EHR technology must include, at a minimum, to support the stage 1 meaningful objectives set for eligible professionals and hospitals. The website of the

49. Title XIII of ARRA, pp. 112–65.

50. The HITECH Act is comprised of two titles in ARRA: Title XIII (Health Information Technology) in Division A (Appropriations Provisions), pp. 226–79, and Title IV (Medicare and Medicaid Health Information Technology; Miscellaneous Medicare Provisions) in Division B, pp. 467–96. ARRA is available at http://www.thomas.gov/home/approp/app09.html#hl. The ARRA requirements were incorporated into the existing HIPAA regulations where possible. Some amendments were to other legislation, such as the Social Security Act.

51. More information is available at the CMS website http://www.cms.gov/EHRIncentivePrograms/.

ARRA Section	Summary	HIPAA Section
Business Associates		
§ 13404(a), "Application of Contract Requirements"	Requires Business Associates to comply with certain provisions of the Security Rule.	§ 164.502(e)(2) § 164.504(e)
§ 13404(b), "Application of Knowledge Elements Associated with Contracts"	Requires a Business Associate that notes any privacy noncompliance by Covered Entity to request Covered Entity to correct the situation or cease doing business with it.	§ 164.502(e) § 164.504(e)
§ 13408, "Business Associate Contracts Required for Certain Entities"	Extends Business Associate status to other entities such as health information exchanges, regional health information organizations, PHR operators, and e-prescribing gateways.	§ 164.502 § 164.308(b)
Restrictions on Disclosure		
§ 13405(a), "Requested Restrictions on Certain Disclosures of Health Information"	Extends a patient's right to request restrictions on disclosure under certain conditions (e.g., the item or service has been paid out of pocket in full).	§ 164.522(i)(A)
§ 13405(b), "Disclosures Required to Be Limited to the Limited Data Set or the Minimum Necessary"	Clarifies data holder's responsibilities in releasing requested data by providing guidance on what constitutes "minimum necessary."	§ 164.502(b)(1) § 164.514(e)(2)
§ 13405(c), "Accounting of Certain PHI Disclosures Required If Covered Entity Uses Electronic Health Record"	Revises HIPAA requirements to include treatment, payment, and operations within required disclosures; changes the accounting period to three years.	§ 164.528
§ 13405(d), "Prohibition on Sale of Electronic Health Records or PHI"	Prohibits, with some exceptions, Covered Entity or Business Associate from directly/indirectly receiving remuneration in exchange for an individual's PHI unless covered by a valid authorization.	§ 164.508
§ 13405(e), "Access to Certain Information in Electronic Format"	Requires Covered Entity to provide individuals with copies of their PHI in electronic format upon request or transmit it as directed if maintained as an electronic health record (EHR).	§ 164.524

ARRA Section	Summary	HIPAA Section
Improved Enforcement		
§ 13411, "Audits"	The Secretary of HHS must perform periodic audits to ensure Covered Entities and Business Associates, subject to HIPAA and now ARRA, are complying with all requirements.	Social Security Act
§ 13410, "Tiered Increase in Amount of Civil Monetary Penalties"	Eliminated exceptions in HIPAA where penalties did not apply and established new minimum ($50,000 per violation) and substantially higher maximum civil penalties ($1.5 million) for HIPAA violations. The minimum civil monetary penalties are tiered based on the organization's perceived culpability for the HIPAA violation.	Social Security Act
§ 13409, "Wrongful Disclosure Criminal Penalties"	Criminal penalties imposed for the wrongful disclosure of individually identifiable health information. Employees of Covered Entity and/or Business Associate may be individually prosecuted if they are involved in a violation.	Social Security Act
Breach Notification Rule[52]		
§ 13402, "Notification in the Case of Breach of Unsecured PHI"	Requires Covered Entities and Business Associates to notify patients, HHS, and potentially the media of breaches of Unsecured PHI. Enforcement began February 22, 2010. A Breach is defined as an impermissible use or disclosure under the Privacy Rule that compromises the security or privacy of the PHI such that the use or disclosure poses a significant risk of financial, reputational, or other harm to the affected individual.[53]	Adds new subpart D under § 164

52. The Interim Final Rule for Breach Notification for Unsecured Protected Health Information became effective September 2009. HHS developed a Final Rule that was submitted to the Office of Management and Budget (OMB) on May 14, 2010. HHS withdrew the Final Rule to allow for further consideration. Until such time as a new final rule is issued, the Interim Final Rule that became effective on September 23, 2009, remains in effect.

53. http://www.hhs.gov/ocr/privacy/hipaa/administrative/breachnotificationrule/index.html.

ARRA Section	Summary	HIPAA Section
Breach Notification Rule (continued)		
	There are three exceptions to the definition of "Breach."	
	The first exception applies to the unintentional acquisition, access, or use of PHI by a workforce member acting under the authority of a Covered Entity or Business Associate.	
	The second exception applies to the inadvertent disclosure of PHI from a person authorized to access PHI at a Covered Entity or Business Associate to another person authorized to access PHI at the Covered Entity or Business Associate.	
	In both cases, the information cannot be further used or disclosed in a manner not permitted by the Privacy Rule.	
	The final exception applies if the Covered Entity or Business Associate has a good faith belief that the unauthorized individual, to whom the impermissible disclosure was made, would not have been able to retain the information.	
	"Unsecured Protected Health Information" means PHI that is not rendered unusable, unreadable, or indecipherable to unauthorized individuals through the use of a technology or methodology specified by the Secretary in guidance on the HHS website, such as encryption.	
	Similar breach notification provisions enforced by the Federal Trade Commission (FTC) apply to vendors of PHRs and their third-party service providers.	

Certification Commission for Health Information Technology[54] (CCHIT) maintains a list of certified EHR technology.

6. The Patient Protection and Affordable Care Act of 2010

The Patient Protection and Affordable Care Act of 2010 (H.R. 3590) was enacted on March 23, 2010. This sweeping health reform legislation requires HHS to develop interoperable and secure standards and protocols to facilitate the enrollment of individuals in federal and state HHS programs and authorizes grants to state and local governments to promote the implementation of health information technology (HIT).

7. Industry Standards and Resources

Several standards and resources are available to assist organizations in implementing these health-care-specific and general statutes and regulations. The following are those that are not discussed elsewhere in this book. All Special Publications (SP) are from the U.S. National Institute of Standards and Technology (NIST) on their standards website.[55] NIST also has a new website dedicated to health IT standards and testing.[56]

- SP 800-66, Revision 1: An Introductory Resource Guide for Implementing the Health Insurance Portability and Accountability Act (HIPAA) Security Rule (October 2008). Part 3 links the NIST Risk Management Framework to components of the Security Rule.
- Best Practices for the Secure Destruction of Personal Health Information—Joint Publication between Ontario Privacy Commissioner and the National Association for Information Destruction (NAID) (October 2009).[57]
- Reassessing Your Security Practices in a Health IT Environment, Office of the National Coordinator for Health Information and Technology (ONC).[58]
- Application Security Questionnaire, Healthcare Information and Management Systems Society (HIMSS).[59]
- SP 800-122: Guide to Protecting the Confidentiality of Personally Identifiable Information (PII) (Draft) (January 2009).
- SP 800-111: Guide to Storage Encryption Technologies for End-User Devices, and SP 800-88 Guidelines for Media Sanitization (September 2006).
- SP 800-118: Guide to Enterprise Password Management (Draft) (April 2009).
- SP 800-52: Guidelines for the Selection and Use of Transport Layer Security (TLS) Implementations; SP 800-77: Guide to IPSec VPNs; and SP 800-113: Guide to SSL VPNs.

---

54. http://www.cchit.org/.
55. http://www.nist.gov.
56. http://healthcare.nist.gov.
57. Available at http://www.ipc.on.ca/english/Resources/Discussion-Papers/Discussion-Papers-Summary/?id=900.
58. Available at http://healthit.hhs.gov/portal/server.pt/gateway/PTARGS0107418480860018/SmallPracticeSecurityGuide-1.pdf.
59. Available at http://www.himss.org/content/files/ApplicationSecurityv2.3.pdf.

- Vital Records Programs: Identifying, Managing, and Recovering Business-Critical Records (ANSI/ARMA 5-2003).

C. Sarbanes-Oxley Act

The Sarbanes-Oxley Act of 2002 (SOX)[60] establishes corporate disclosure and governance requirements for publicly held companies. The main principles of SOX are transparency and accountability in business activities and information reporting so as to accurately portray the soundness and stability of a public company. Under SOX, a publicly held company must follow a series of governance requirements that lead to individual executive accountability. An important aspect of SOX is the potential for criminal punishment at the individual corporate executive level for failure to oversee the integrity of the business's reporting processes.

SOX regulations, comprising eleven title parts, contain numerous information integrity sections which require that a public company have a baseline of internal controls and audit functions to ensure accuracy, reliability, trustworthiness, and integrity of information systems and reporting processes. In essence, for an organization to comply with SOX, it must understand the nature of all transactions and corresponding data flows and implement appropriate controls to effectively prevent fraud, tampering, and manipulation of information. Information security and the handling of information security risk are fundamental and important parts in achieving SOX compliance.

Section 404 requires certain disclosures related to financial reporting in public companies' annual reports.[61] Annual reports must contain an internal control report that states the responsibility of management to establish and maintain adequate internal controls and procedures for financial reporting. An internal control report must also contain an assessment of the effectiveness of the company's internal control structure and procedures for financial reporting. An accounting firm that prepares or issues an audit report relating to the assessment must attest to and report on the assessment made by the company's management, consistent with standards established by the Public Company Accounting Oversight Board.[62] See Chapter 6 for further discussion on SOX audits.

Section 302 of SOX[63]—and the internal control assessment and certification regulations implementing it—requires that a public company's chief executive officer and chief financial officer certify, in each annual or quarterly report filed with the SEC, the following: that they have reviewed the report, that the report does not contain untrue statements of material facts, and that the financial information fairly presents the financial condition of the company.[64] The signing officers are responsible for establishing and maintaining internal controls to ensure that material information is made known to the officers and must report their conclusions about the effectiveness of these controls, based on an evaluation, within 90 days of making the report.[65] They must also disclose

60 Sarbanes-Oxley Act of 2002, Pub. L. No. 107-204, 116 Stat. 745 (2002).

61. 15 U.S.C. § 7262.

62. *Id.*

63. 15 U.S.C. § 7241.

64. *Id.* at § 7241(a)(1)–(3).

65. *Id.* at § 7241(a)(4).

to auditors all deficiencies in internal controls and any fraud conducted by management or employees who have a significant role in the company's internal controls.[66] The signing officers must indicate in the report whether there are significant changes in internal controls or other factors that could affect internal controls after their evaluation, including significant deficiencies and material weaknesses in the controls.[67]

If attacks on information security controls or controls that are poorly designed or operated were to result in the alteration of records or falsification of financial results, the company and its officials could be held liable for making untrue statements of material facts and inaccuracies in financial reports (especially if not disclosed in the report). Moreover, a violation could occur if members of management or employees responsible for internal controls over financial systems compromise those controls or commit fraud for the purpose of inflating the company's financial results. Finally, the failure to report compromises in internal controls or corrective actions involving computer systems holding financial records may be a violation.

It is also worth noting that SEC Rule 33-8124 (interpreting Section 302 of SOX) distinguishes "internal controls over financial reporting" from a new concept—"disclosure controls and procedures." Disclosure controls encompass information required not only on Forms 10-Q and 10-K but also on Form 8-K (material events). Thus, disclosure controls under Section 302 also include internal controls over financial disclosures required by Section 404. More information on internal controls is available from the Institute of Internal Auditors.[68] In addition to the assessment and certification of internal controls, two other important SOX requirements impact a company's information security requirements: SOX Section 802 requires the preservation of information pending a federal inquiry, investigation, or legal matter, and Section 1107 provides protection for whistle-blowers.

SOX Section 802(a)[69] is a legal hold preservation requirement similar to the Federal Rules of Civil Procedure that triggers the retention of all potentially relevant data pending an inquiry, investigation, or legal matter, and failure to do so may result in criminal fines and penalties of up to 20 years' imprisonment and $1 million. Again, the responsibility of information security personnel and legal counsel is to ensure that they have a tested and audited legal hold preservation process. This means a documented process with a clear chain of custody that evidences the integrity and authenticity of the data and refutes any and all possibility of data destruction or tampering. Section 802(a) with its criminal sanctions illustrates again the critical aspect of SOX as a criminal books-and-records law that requires a company to have a structured, data-mapped records management program. The only way a company can demonstrate the necessary controls over the data lifecycle is to know what is where and to then preserve that data accordingly. Failure to defensibly adhere to these requirements puts the corporation and its executives at risk of imprisonment and criminal sanctions.

The whistle-blowing protection requirements found in Section 1107 of SOX are also important from an information security perspective.[70] Information security is an inte-

---

66. *Id.* at § 7241(a)(5).

67. 15 U.S.C. § 7241(a)(6).

68. *See* the Institute of Internal Auditors' "Sarbanes-Oxley Section 404: A Guide for Management by Internal Controls Practitioners," 2d ed., January 2008.

69. 18 U.S.C. § 1519.

70. 18 U.S.C. § 1513(e).

gral part of a company's whistle-blowing program in several aspects. Information security personnel must have the right tools and protections in place for the collection of sensitive, confidential information from whistle-blowers. They must be able to manage ongoing security requirements for communications and quick incident response mechanisms for forensic capture of information.

SOX-regulated multinational businesses with cross-border data protection privacy requirements in foreign jurisdictions also need to be addressed. This may require customized processes and procedures that protect local privacy rights while allowing for SOX regulatory whistle-blowing protection. Information security procedures should adhere to the foreign country's data protection laws as best as possible yet also protect the regulatory needs of the U.S. multinational doing business abroad. International laws are discussed later in this chapter.

D. Federal Information Security Management Act

The Federal Information Security Management Act (FISMA)[71] replaced the Government Information Security Reform Act (GISRA), which expired in 2002, retaining GISRA's basic risk-based information security approach but with several significant changes. Congress codified information security based on principles of information integrity, confidentiality, and availability.[72] The Act broadened the Clinger-Cohen definition of information technology to also apply to IT systems used or operated by other agencies or by contractors on behalf of government agencies.[73]

Federal agencies now have responsibility to ensure the information security for the physical assets of other agencies or of contractors if they support federal operations.[74] Federal agencies must report annually to the Office of Management and Budget (OMB) and Congress regarding: (1) agency risk assessments; (2) security policies; (3) subordinate plans, (4) training; (5) annual testing and evaluation; (6) corrective actions; (7) security incident reporting; and (8) continuity of operations.[75] Agencies must conduct "testing and evaluation of information security policies, procedures and practices" no less than once a year.[76]

Section 3544(a)(1)(A) of FISMA requires federal agencies to identify and provide information security protections commensurate with the risk and magnitude of harm resulting from unauthorized access, use, disclosure, disruption, modification, or destruction of information collected or stored by the agency.[77] FISMA, however, exempts national security systems and information systems under the Department of Defense and the National Intelligence System from direct OMB authority.[78]

71. Federal Information Management Act of 2002, Pub. L No. 107-347, Title III, 116 Stat. 2899 (2002) (amending 44 U.S.C. §§ 3541–49).

72. 44 U.S.C. § 3542 (a)(1).

73. *Id.* § 3544(a)(1)(A)(ii).

74. *Id.* § 3544(b).

75. *Id.*

76. *Id.* § 3544(b)(5).

77. *Id.* § 3544(a)(1)(A).

78. *Id.* § 3543.

FISMA also modified several related sections of the U.S. Code. Sections 302[79] and 303[80] amended Title 40, directing the National Institute of Standards and Technology (NIST) of the Department of Commerce to create minimum standards and guidelines for information security. The Federal Information Processing Standards (FIPS) address unauthorized use, disclosure, disruption, modification, or destruction of information or information systems. Civilian agencies ensure compliance with the operational, management, and technical information assurance controls found in NIST Special Publication 800-53.[81] Following is a table of required processes and NIST standards that federal agencies follow in order to comply with FISMA. This is further discussed in Chapter 6. The Department of Defense applies compatible standards to its information systems using the DoD Information Assurance Certification and Accreditation Process (DIACAP).[82] FISMA also amended Section 3505 of the Paperwork Reduction Act, requiring the heads of federal agencies to make annual inventories of all major information systems under their control.[83]

FISMA Procedural Step	***Applicable NIST Standard***
Overall Process Description	NIST 800-37 Rev. 1: *Guide for Applying the Risk Management Framework to Federal Information Systems: A Security Lifecycle Approach*
Step 1: Security Categorization	FIPS 199: *Standards for Security Categorization of Federal Information and Information Systems*
	NIST 800-60: *Guide for Mapping Types of Information and Information Systems to Security Categories*
Step 2: Security Control Selection	FIPS 200: *Minimum Security Requirements for Federal Information and Federal Information Systems*
	NIST 800-53 Rev. 3: *Recommended Security Controls for Federal Information Systems*
	NIST 800-53A Rev. 1: *Guide for Assessing the Security Controls in Federal Information Systems and Organizations: Building Effective Security Assessment Plans*

79. 116 Stat. at 2956.

80. 116 Stat. at 2957.

81. *Guide for Assessing the Security Controls in Federal Information Systems,* NIST Special Publication 800-53A (Dept. of Commerce, Nat'l. Institute of Standards and Technology, July 2008).

82. *DoD Information Assurance Certification and Accreditation Process (DIACAP),* Department of Defense Instruction 8510.01, November 28, 2007.

83. 116 Stat. at 2960.

FISMA Procedural Step	*Applicable NIST Standard*
Step 3: Security Control Refinement and Risk Assessment	FIPS 200: above
	NIST 800-53 Rev. 3: above
	NIST 800-30: *Risk Management Guide for Information Technology Systems*
	OMB M04-04: *E-Authentication Guidance for Federal Agencies*
Step 4: Security Control Documentation, System Security Plan, and Contingency Plan	NIST SP 800-18 Rev. 1: *Guide for Developing Security Plans for Federal Information Systems and Organizations*
	NIST 800-34 Rev. 1: *Contingency Planning Guide for Federal Information Systems*
Step 5: Security Control Implementation	NIST 800-53: *Security Control CM-6, Configuration Settings*
	NIST 800-63: *Electronic Authentication Guidelines*
	NIST 800-70: *National Checklist Program for IT Products: Guidelines for Checklist Users and Developers*
Step 6: Security Control Assessment	NIST SP 800-53A Rev. 1: above
	NIST 800-18 Rev. 1: above
	NIST 800-37 Rev. 1: above
Step 7: Security Risk Determination and Documentation	NIST 800-37 Rev. 1: above
Step 8: System Authorization and Certification and Accreditation (C&A)	NIST SP 800-37 Rev. 1: above
Step 9: Security Control Monitoring	NIST SP 800-37 Rev. 1: above

E. Federal Trade Commission Act

Likely the most active federal regulator in the area of data security and privacy is the Federal Trade Commission (FTC). The FTC plays a central role in establishing, developing, and implementing standards and rules regarding the online and off-line collection, storage, use, disclosure, and disposal of personal information of customers and employees of most general business enterprises. It has engaged in relevant rulemaking, has conducted public forums and workshops, and has issued reports providing guidance to all stakeholders, with the ultimate goal of protecting the security, confidentiality, and integrity of personal information of consumers and employees.[84] And it has a robust Internet web presence with sites and pages that seek to educate the consumer and potential offender alike.[85]

1. *FTC's Authority*

The FTC's broad authority is set forth in Section 5 of the FTC Act,[86] which prohibits unfair or deceptive practices. The FTC typically commences an enforcement action initiated by the filing of a formal complaint alleging that an organization has failed to comply with its own publicly available privacy policy or has deviated from Fair Information Privacy Principles and that such conduct constitutes a deceptive or unfair trade practice. While the norm is for the FTC to file a complaint, it is not unusual for an interested party to seek government intervention. A typical example is the formal request of a privacy advocacy group, Electronic Privacy Information Center (EPIC), asking the FTC to open an investigation regarding Google's "Cloud Computing Services," which EPIC asserted to be both deceptive and unfair in their impact on consumers.[87]

For the most part, the FTC has focused on whether companies live up to the representations and assurances made to customers in their published, customer-facing privacy policies. For example, a company promised that it would not share customer information with a third party without the customer's consent, yet did so anyway. Or a promise was made that the customer's information would be used only for a specifically stated reason, yet its use morphed to multiple applications to satisfy the marketing department's request for more customer analytics, without regard to the earlier commitment made to the customer. The FTC usually looks at whether the conduct is primarily deceptive or primarily an unfair trade practice, but, until more recently, usually not both for the same case. But in *Gateway Learning*,[88] for instance, the FTC first alleged deceptive trade practice, because despite explicit assurances to the contrary in its privacy policy, the company rented out the information of its customers without consent, and then alleged unfairness, because the company changed its policy on this same subject without notifying its customers. Conversely, in the *CartManager*[89] case, the FTC brought primarily an unfairness case, because of inadequate disclosures about CartManager's information practices (i.e., as an online shopping cart company, CartManager did not make direct promises to the customers of its customers).

84. For example, see the FTC's brochure, "Protecting Personal Information: A Guide to Business" at http://www.ftc.gov/infosecurity/.

85. *See* http://ftc.gov/idtheft, http://www.ftc.gov/privacy/, and http://www.onguardonline.gov/.

86. 15 U.S.C. §§ 1 *et seq.*

87. http://epic.org/privacy/cloudcomputing/google/ftc031709.pdf. Remains pending. Additionally, see recent request from U.S. Representative for FTC to investigate the storage of documents on digital copy machines, http://voices.washingtonpost.com/posttech/2010/04/rep_markey_calls_for_ftc_to_in.html.

88. http://ftc.gov/os/caselist/0423047/040707cmp0423047.pdf.

89. http://www.ftc.gov/os/caselist/0423068/050426comp0423068.pdf.

While continuing its mandate to hold organizations accountable for breaches of their express privacy assurances made to customers as a deceptive trade practice, the FTC has also significantly stepped up its enforcement efforts against unfair business practices. Whereas the norm was to attempt to remediate a breach of a privacy promise, the FTC has more and more set its sights on those organizations that hold substantial amounts of personally identifiable information (PII), which has been compromised or breached in some fashion due to an organization's failure to implement a reasonable data security program. Here again, the FTC's contention is that such conduct constitutes an unfair business practice, especially where the customer has no real opportunity to have any impact on the data's security and relies exclusively on the company to adequately safeguard it.

The first significant FTC enforcement cases involving inadequate data security were brought against Guess and Tower Records. In February 2002, an SQL injection attack was used on the Guess website to obtain the unencrypted credit card numbers of customers stored in Guess's databases.[90] Similarly, in a case involving Tower Records, when Tower redesigned its website, it introduced a security vulnerability that revealed order history records, including personal information, such as the names, addresses, e-mail addresses, phone numbers, and past purchases of Tower customers.[91]

In addition to the forums and public workshops conducted by the FTC, one of the most instructive opportunities for understanding the breadth and depth of the FTC's role in protecting PII is to examine some additional FTC enforcement actions. One caution is in order. To date, most of the enforcement actions brought by the FTC have concluded with orders being entered as the result of agreed-upon settlements between the parties. Thus, there is little case law interpreting the FTC Act on unfair or deceptive trade practices in the information security context.

Nevertheless, as there are numerous enforcement actions evidencing a real-world understanding of "the way things really are," businesses should be guided by the known outcomes. There is nothing on the horizon that points to a reduced enforcement posture by the FTC. (Quite the opposite is true. If there is any clamoring going on, it is for the FTC's enforcement authority to be expanded.)

2. Example Enforcement Actions

A sampling of FTC enforcement actions follows.[92]

- *Eli Lilly:* The first action to assert the violation of an assurance in a privacy policy was in *Eli Lilly*, which involved the unintended disclosure of prescription drug users' personal information.[93] Eli Lilly is a pharmaceutical company that offered an "e-mail reminder service" designed to tell customers when it was time to refill their Prozac medication. The reminders were individualized e-mails that did not identify any other subscribers to the service. When

90. http://www.ftc.gov/os/2003/08/guesscomp.pdf.
91. http://ftc.gov/os/caselist/0323209/040421comp0323209.pdf.
92. For additional cases, see the FTC's website at http://www.ftc.gov/privacy/privacyinitiatives/promises_enf.html.
93. http://www.ftc.gov/os/2002/05/elilillycmp.htm.

announcing the termination of the service, however, Eli Lilly sent subscribers an e-mail that included all of the recipients' e-mail addresses, thereby disclosing personal information to someone other than the intended individual customer. The FTC complaint lifted verbiage from Eli Lilly's privacy policy that assured the customer that Eli Lilly had "security measures in place . . . to protect the confidentiality of any of Your Information that you volunteer."[94] A consent order was entered that concluded that Eli Lilly's failure to employ sufficient measures to meet the promise made amounted to an unfair or deceptive act under the FTCA. As part of the agreed resolution, Eli Lilly was required to establish and maintain an information security program for the protection of personally identifiable information collected from its customers.[95]

Lesson: Failing to understand how technology works or being careless in implementation can result in liability.

- *Microsoft Passport:* In 2001, a coalition of consumer groups led by the Electronic Privacy Information Center (EPIC) filed a complaint with the FTC regarding certain representations made by Microsoft in connection with its "Passport" web services. These services included Passport Single Sign-On (Passport), which allowed users to sign in at any participating website with a password and user name; Passport Wallet, which collected and stored credit card numbers and billing and shipping information for users; and Kids Passport, which allowed parents to create specialized accounts for their children. A year later, the FTC and Microsoft reached a settlement of the *Microsoft Passport* case.[96]

  It was also alleged that Microsoft engaged in deceptive practices because on the passport.com website, Microsoft made several representations regarding the privacy and security of the Passport services, including, among others, that customers were more secure using Passport and that ".NET Passport services achieves a high level of Web Security by using technologies and systems designed to prevent unauthorized access to your personal information" and that ".NET Passport is protected by powerful online security technology."[97] Microsoft was also accused of collecting more information than was stated in the Passport privacy policy. In its complaint, the FTC alleged that Microsoft's representations were false or misleading in violation of the FTCA since, in fact, Microsoft failed to document and implement procedures "that were reasonable and appropriate to: (1) prevent possible unauthorized access to the Passport system; (2) detect possible unauthorized access to the Passport system; (3) monitor the Passport system for potential vulnerabilities; and (4)

94. *Id.*
95. http://www.ftc.gov/os/2002/01/lillyagree.pdf.
96. http://www.ftc.gov/opa/2002/08/microsoft.shtm.
97. http://www.ftc.gov/os/2002/12/microsoftcomplaint.pdf.

record and retain system information sufficient to perform security audits and investigations."[98]

Lesson: Failing to implement an effective data security program that protects the customer as promised results in liability.

- *Dave & Buster's:* The FTC, in March 2010, reached its 27th settlement in a case challenging faulty data security practices by organizations that handle sensitive customer information. The FTC complaint against Dave & Buster's charged that the company left consumers' credit and debit card information vulnerable to hackers, resulting in several hundred thousand dollars in fraudulent charges. The FTC did not insist on industry best practice or "state of the art" security. The stated scope of its inquiry was whether or not the organization acted "reasonably" with regard to the effort to protect its customers' data. For Dave & Buster's the conclusion was that the effort was deficient in that the company failed to (1) take sufficient measures to detect and prevent unauthorized access to the network; (2) adequately restrict outside access to the network, including access by the company's own service providers; (3) monitor and filter outbound data traffic to identify and block the export of sensitive personal information without authorization; and (4) use readily available security measures to limit access to its computer networks through wireless access points.[99] As a result of these alleged failures, the FTC asserted that a hacker exploited certain vulnerabilities, installed unauthorized software, and accessed about 130,000 payment card accounts. The settlement required Dave & Buster's to stand up a meaningful data security program and to obtain independent audits every other year for ten years to ensure compliance with the settlement. Also, as a standard practice, record-keeping provisions to allow the FTC to monitor compliance were included as part of the agreement.[100]

  Lesson: Wireless technology has more vulnerabilities. It presents increased risk to any environment. Better do it right if you go down that path.

- *CVS Caremark:* In February 2009, the FTC settled a case with CVS Caremark wherein the allegation of the FTC was that CVS had failed to adequately protect, again through "reasonable" measures, the medical and financial privacy of its customers. *CVS* was also one of the first cases to raise privacy of employees (as opposed to just consumers) as an FTC Act compliance/enforcement issue. In a related action, CVS also agreed with the Department of Health and

---

98. *Id.*

99. http://ftc.gov/os/caselist/0823153/100325davebusterscmpt.pdf.

100. It is a general requirement in FTC consent decrees that the company and its security auditor implement a data security program. However, the company and its approved third-party security auditor are allowed to determine the appropriate technologies and audit frameworks. The requirements will vary based on the size and industry of the company and the data being held. A third-party audit is required every two years over either a 10-year or a 20-year period. Auditors are required to meet certain qualifications, and the FTC reviews the audit reports and the company's and auditors' performance.

Human Services to pay $2.25 million to settle allegations of HIPAA violations. The investigation started with media reports around the country that CVS pharmacies were throwing trash into open dumpsters that contained patient identity and health information, Social Security numbers, payment card information, and other categories of sensitive information.[101] The FTC complaint asserted a failure to implement reasonable policies and disposal procedures, inadequate training of its employees, failure to implement a method to assess compliance with existing policies, and failure to conduct a proper risk assessment. The asserted legal basis for the unfair and deceptive claim was, in part, CVS's public-facing assurances that "CVS/pharmacy wants you to know that nothing is more central to our operations than maintaining the privacy of your health information."[102] Terms of settlement include a comprehensive information security program; a third-party audit every two years for 20 years; and standard record-keeping requirements.

Lesson: Paper matters. It's not only about electronic data.[103]

- *TJX Companies, Inc.:* In 2008, the FTC, after coordinating its investigation with 39 state attorneys general, settled a case involving what to date has been one of the largest known data breaches in history in terms of number of customer records breached, amount of fraud sustained, enforcement and remediation costs, and adverse impact on the company involved. In announcing the settlement, then FTC Chairperson Deborah Platt Majoras said, "Information security is a priority for the FTC, as it should be for every business in America."[104] The complaint alleges that TJX, with over 2,500 stores worldwide, failed to use reasonable and appropriate measures to prevent unauthorized access to its networks. A hacker exploited simple vulnerabilities and obtained, among other sensitive customer information, tens of millions of credit and debit payment card numbers. The specifics of the allegations should be warning flags for businesses generally. Again, wireless access was a key culprit. TJX was alleged to have created an unnecessary risk to its customers' information by storing and transmitting it in clear text; failing to use readily available security measures to limit wireless access to its networks; allowing weak passwords by systems administrators; using firewalls inadequately; and failing to employ sufficient measures to detect and prevent unauthorized access to its networks or to conduct security investigations.[105] Settlement terms contain the now familiar 20-year requirement for third-party audits and a data security program that contains "administrative, technical and physical safeguards" appropriate to the company's size, the nature of its activi-

101. http://ftc.gov/opa/2009/02/cvs.shtm.

102. http://ftc.gov/os/caselist/0723119/090218cvscmpt.pdf.

103. A recent FTC enforcement action resulting from disposing of sensitive paper records in a dumpster was concluded in early 2010 against a stockbroker, Gregory Navone. The allegations included the assertion that Navone made misrepresentations as to his companies' data security practices (http://www.ftc.gov/os/caselist/0723067/100120navonestip.pdf).

104. http://www.ftc.gov/opa/2008/03/datasec.shtm.

105. http://www.ftc.gov/os/caselist/0723055/080327complaint.pdf.

ties, and the sensitivity of the personal information it collects. Specifically, TJX also was required to: (1) designate someone to coordinate the information security program; (2) identify internal and external risks to customer information and assess adequacy of safeguards already in place; (3) design and implement safeguards to control the risks identified in the risk assessment and monitor their effectiveness; (4) develop reasonable steps to select and oversee service providers that handle the customers' sensitive information; and (5) regularly evaluate and adjust the security program in view of changes in external threats and internal environment.[106] While the third-party audit is also required, the TJX auditor must "certify" that the company's security program meets or exceeds the requirements of the FTC's orders. That is a tall order.

Lesson: As the FTC's knowledge and expertise in this area grow, a natural outcome is that the terms of settlement become more technically refined.

- *CardSystems Solutions:* In 2006, a data breach at CardSystems was one of the largest known to date. Through the authorization process of debit and credit card transactions, CardSystems collected and stored sensitive data that came from "swiping" the card in violation of security standards that apply to payment cards, in addition to other data.[107] For a company that reportedly processed about 210 million card purchases in a single year, totaling more than $15 billion for more than 119,000 retail merchants, the full ramifications of the data breach were huge. The complaint allegations were similar to those mentioned earlier, including (1) storing information for which no legitimate business purpose was served; (2) storing it in a particularly vulnerable format; (3) failing to conduct thorough risk vulnerability assessments to known attack vectors such as "Structured Query Language" (or SQL) injection attacks and failing to implement readily available defensive postures to such risks; (4) failing to use strong passwords to prevent access by hackers; and (5) failing to employ adequate detection strategies. The FTC did not assert that any single failure was deceptive but that "taken together, [CardSystems] failed to provide reasonable and appropriate security for personal information stored on its computer network." It was alleged that "tens of millions of credit and debit cards" were compromised.[108] Settlement terms were similar to those just discussed in other cases.[109]

  Lesson: The cumulative effect of multiple factors can expose an organization's information security to attack.

- *Twitter:* The micro-blogging service Twitter settled charges with the FTC regarding its privacy and data security practices.[110] The FTC's complaint

106. http://www.ftc.gov/os/caselist/0723055/080327agreement.pdf.

107. Payment Card Industry—Data Security Standard (PCI DSS), https://www.pcisecuritystandards.org/documents/pci_dss_v2.pdf.

108. http://ftc.gov/os/caselist/0523148/0523148complaint.pdf.

109. http://ftc.gov/os/caselist/0523148/0523148consent.pdf.

110. In the Matter of Twitter, Inc., FTC File No. 0923093, Agreement Containing Consent Order.

alleged that despite Twitter's promises on its website to protect the personal information of its users, Twitter's practices failed to provide reasonable and appropriate security. Twice in 2009, intruders obtained control of Twitter administrative accounts because of deficient password security policies. Unlike many other companies that the FTC has pursued regarding their online information security practices, Twitter does not sell goods online or collect financial information from its users. The settlement bars Twitter from misleading consumers about the extent to which it protects nonpublic consumer information and it must maintain a comprehensive risk-based information security program, name a person to be in charge of the program and have periodic independent audits of this program. According the FTC, Twitter failed to prevent the unauthorized administrative control of its system by not taking "reasonable" steps, such as: requiring employees to use hard-to-guess passwords; prohibiting employees from storing administrative passwords in plain-text in their personal e-mail accounts; suspending administrative passwords after a reasonable number of unsuccessful login attempts; providing an administrative login page known only to authorized users that is separate from the ordinary user login page; enforcing periodic administrative password changes; and restricting administrative access to employees whose jobs required it.

Lesson: Oversight by the FTC in meeting the standards set in the FTC Act is not limited to those organizations who handle financial data or sell online.

- What should be apparent is that the analytical framework of the FTC's enforcement actions adheres to a well-defined template. Section 5 of the FTC Act authorizes the FTC to intervene in the face of "unfair and deceptive" trade practices that affect interstate commerce.[111] Earlier in this chapter, we introduced the Gramm-Leach-Bliley Act (GLBA). The FTC's Safeguards Rule[112] enables the FTC to enforce GLBA against "financial institutions" not regulated by the federal financial supervisory bodies. The Safeguards Rule provides the FTC with a ready checklist of the elements that should be included in a meaningful remediation plan. Any business should use the Safeguards Rule as a source for its own analysis of what a business should "reasonably" do to avoid being the subject of a complaint.

Consider that the Safeguards Rule mandates that the covered entities "develop, implement, and maintain a comprehensive information security program . . . [that] contains administrative, technical, and physical safeguards" that are appropriate for its size, its complexity, the nature of its business, and the sensitivity of the customer information collected. The stated objectives of such a program are to "(1) insure the security and confidentiality of customer information; (2) protect against any anticipated threats or hazards to the security or integrity of such information; and (3) protect against unauthorized

111. This latter requirement provides the jurisdictional basis for a federal agency to bring an enforcement action.

112. http://www.ftc.gov/os/2002/05/67fr36585.pdf.

access to or use of such information that could result in substantial harm or inconvenience to any customer."[113] When you examine the mandated "elements" of a security program, you can appreciate that the FTC considers each element as helping to satisfy or demonstrate reasonable conduct. For instance, is a particular person designated to run the security program? Has a thorough risk assessment been conducted to identify external and internal threats to the "security, confidentiality, and integrity" of customers' information?

The Safeguards Rule walks you through what is required "at a minimum" to achieve an effective risk assessment. Relevant areas of inquiry include the following: (1) employee training; (2) your information systems, including design, and information processing, storage, transmission, and disposal; (3) detection of, prevention of, and response to attacks and other failures; (4) safeguards to control risks and to monitor effectiveness over time; (5) proper vetting of service providers in the selection process, including an assessment of their security posture, not just reliance on contract terms; and (6) "[e]valuat[ion] and adjust[ment of your] information security program in light of the results of the testing and monitoring" required by this Rule, "any material changes to your operations or business arrangements, or any other circumstances that you know or have reason to know may have a material impact on your information security program."[114] For those seeking clarity as to what falls within the crevice of "unfair and deceptive" conduct, at least when it comes to data security, look closely at the FTC's Safeguards Rule.

To stay in sync with the FTC's approach to privacy and data security, there are two key points. One, whatever you tell customers you will or won't do with their data in your posted privacy policy, adhere to your promises. Second, for data security, never guarantee that personal information can be protected from unauthorized access. The FTC requires only "reasonable" (not perfect) data security.

F. Fair Credit Reporting Act/Fair and Accurate Credit Transactions Act

The Fair Credit Reporting Act of 1970 (FCRA)[115] requires consumer credit reporting agencies to implement "reasonable procedures" that are "fair and equitable to the consumer, with regard to confidentiality, accuracy, relevancy, and proper utilization" of consumer credit, personnel, insurance, and other covered information.[116]

FCRA was reauthorized and amended by the Fair and Accurate Credit Transactions Act of 2003 (FACTA or the FACT Act).[117] It includes provisions to prevent identity theft and to provide redress for victims of identity theft. Some of its key provisions in these areas include:

- provisions for fraud alerts and active duty alerts on credit reports[118]
- requirements for blocking information resulting from identity theft[119]

---

113. *Id.*
114. *Id.*
115. 15 U.S.C. §§ 1681 *et seq.*
116. 15 U.S.C. § 1681(b).
117. Pub. L. No. 108-159 (Dec. 4, 2003).
118. 15 U.S.C. § 1681c-1.
119. 15 U.S.C. § 1681c-2.

- requirements for truncation of credit and debit card numbers on receipts[120]
- requirements for consumer reporting agencies and resellers to adopt reasonable procedures to verify the identity and permissible purpose of those to whom they provide consumer reports[121]
- free disclosure to consumers of credit reports, annually and after an adverse action notice[122]
- requirements for covered financial institutions and creditors to establish identity theft prevention ("red flags") programs[123]
- prohibition of pretexting—obtaining credit information under false pretenses[124]
- requirements for secure disposal of consumer reports and information derived from them[125]

Several regulations by federal agencies implement FACTA. For example, the FTC published *Guidelines Requiring the Proper Disposal of Consumer Information* (16 C.F.R. pt. 682). The federal banking agencies included secure disposal requirements in their *Interagency Guidelines Establishing Information Security Standards.*[126] These rules require secure disposal of covered paper and electronic records.

In November 2007, the FTC and the federal banking agencies published a final interagency rule, *Identity Theft Red Flags and Address Discrepancies Under the Fair and Accurate Credit Transactions Act of 2003.*[127] The rule, referred to as the Red Flags Rule, was effective on January 1, 2008, with mandatory compliance by November 1, 2008. The FTC has extended enforcement several times (only for entities regulated by the FTC), most recently until December 31, 2010. The Rule requires "financial institutions" and "creditors" with "covered accounts" to implement a written Identity Theft Prevention Program to detect, prevent, and mitigate identity theft.

The FTC has taken a broad approach to the definition of "creditor" under the Red Flags Rule, asserting that attorneys, accountants, and doctors are covered. In December 2009, the U.S. District Court for the District of Columbia held that application to attorneys is beyond the statutory authority for the rule.[128] Accountants and doctors are also challenging its application to them.

A high-profile example of an enforcement action under FCRA is the FTC's court action against ChoicePoint, Inc. in 2006.[129] ChoicePoint is a data broker that sells information, including consumer credit information, to its subscribers. Identity thieves posed as customers of ChoicePoint and bought information that they used to commit identity theft. The FTC brought the action against ChoicePoint, alleging that ChoicePoint vio-

120. 15 U.S.C. § 1681c(g)(1).
121. 15 U.S.C. § 1681e(a).
122. 15 U.S.C. § 1681j.
123. 15 U.S.C. § 1681m(e).
124. 15 U.S.C. § 1681q.
125. 15 U.S.C. § 1681w.
126. 69 Fed. Reg. 77610-77621 (Dec. 28, 2004).
127. 72 Fed. Reg. 63718-637-75 (Nov. 9, 2007). The FTC rule is codified at 16 C.F.R. pt. 681. The banking agencies' rules are in 12 C.F.R. pts. 41, 222, 334, 364, 571, and 717.
128. American Bar Ass'n v. Federal Trade Commission, 671 F. Supp. 2d 64 (D.D.C. 2009).
129. U.S. v. ChoicePoint, Inc., No. 1 06 cv 0198, N.D. Ga., *see* http://www.ftc.gov/choicepoint.

lated FCRA and the FTC Act by failing to have reasonable procedures to screen prospective subscribers. The case settled with a consent order under which ChoicePoint agreed to pay a $10 million civil penalty, to set up a $5 million fund for redress of injured consumers, and to maintain a comprehensive information security program, with auditing by a qualified, independent professional.[130]

FCRA, as amended by FACTA, is a broad law that regulates credit reporting, including a number of provisions to protect the privacy and security of consumer credit information.

G. Computer Fraud and Abuse Act

The Computer Fraud and Abuse Act (CFAA) is the primary federal law aimed at computer fraud, intrusions, and related activity.[131] The CFAA makes it a crime to or attempt to:

- obtain national security information[132]
- intentionally access a protected computer without authorization or exceed authorized access and thereby obtain information from any protected computer[133]
- intentionally access a government computer[134]
- knowingly with intent to defraud access a protected computer without authorization or exceed authorized access and thereby further the intended fraud and obtain anything of value[135]
- knowingly cause the transmission of a program, information, code, or command and intentionally cause damage without authorization to a protected computer, intentionally access a protected computer without authorization and recklessly cause damage, or intentionally access a protected computer without authorization and cause damage or loss[136]
- knowingly and with intent to defraud traffic in passwords or other similar information used to gain access to a protected computer without authorization[137]
- engage in cyber-extortion—that is, threaten to cause damage to a protected computer without authorization or by exceeding authorization, threaten to obtain information from or compromise the confidentiality of information obtained from a protected computer, or demand money to undo damage caused to facilitate the extortion[138]

130. FTC News Release, January 29, 2006, www.ftc.gov/opa/2006/01/choicepoint.shtm.

131. 18 U.S.C. § 1030, as amended by the USA PATRIOT Act of 2001.

132. *Id.* § 1030(a)(1).

133. *Id.* § 1030(a)(2)(c). The act also prohibits accessing financial records of a financial institution, card issuer, or consumer reporting agency files on a consumer, and information from any department or agency of the U.S. government. 18 U.S.C. § 1030(a)(2).

134. *Id.* § 1030(a)(3).

135. *Id.* § 1030(a)(4). The law does not apply to a fraud committed solely to obtain the use of a computer unless the value of the use is more than $5,000 in any one-year period.

136. *Id.* § 1030(a)(5)(A).

137. *Id.* § 1030(a)(6).

138. *Id.* § 1030(a)(7).

As discussed later in this section, the CFAA also provides a civil remedy for victims of computer crime.[139]

The CFAA focuses on "protected computers," which are defined as computers used by a financial institution or the U.S. government and computers that are used in interstate or foreign commerce or communications.[140] Courts have consistently found that computers connected to the Internet are "protected computers."

Many of the provisions of the CFAA rely on the terms "unauthorized access" and "exceeding authorized access."[141] Unauthorized access means that the user has no access rights to the computer, such as a computer hacker. Exceeding authorized access means the person has some authority to use the computer but does not have access to obtain or alter the information he or she has accessed. For example, a bank employee was prosecuted for using the bank's computers to access personally identifiable information of customers whose accounts she did not manage in order to commit a fraud.[142]

The types of unauthorized or exceeding access covered by the CFAA are not always clear. For example, in civil cases, courts have reached different conclusions about whether the CFAA covers an employee who has permission to use the employer's computers but uses this access to misappropriate the employer's information.[143] In criminal cases, courts have been reluctant to criminalize what would otherwise be a simple breach of contract or a workplace policy. For example, in *United States v. Drew*, the court refused to criminalize the conscious breach of a website's terms of service, even though finding that most courts would allow a civil CFAA action for such a breach.[144]

However, one of the most important aspects of the CFAA is that it gives the victim access to the federal courts to seek damages, injunctive relief, and other equitable relief.[145] The federal courts can hear the matter if one or more persons suffered a combined loss of at least $5,000. Loss includes any reasonable costs associated with the response, damage assessments, restoring the system and data, and lost revenue.[146] The victim must file the action within two years of the date of the wrongful act or discovery of the damage.[147]

---

139. Companies should also be aware that employees' unauthorized access of third-party computers, if done while the employee is acting as an agent of the employer, may subject the organization to CFAA liability.

140. 18 U.S.C. § 1030(e)(2).

141. *Id.* § 1030(e)(6).

142. United States v. John, 597 F.3d 263, 273 (5th Cir. 2010).

143. *Compare* Shamrock Foods Co. v. Gast, 535 F. Supp. 2d 962, 968 (D. Ariz. 2008) (conduct not covered by CFAA) *with* NCMIC Fin. Corp. v. Artino, 638 F. Supp. 2d 1042, 1057–59 (S.D. Iowa 2009) (conduct covered by CFAA). These cases usually involve an employee's theft of his or her employer's information before the employee begins to work for a competitor or starts a competing business.

144. United States v. Drew, 259 F.R.D. 449, 459, 467 (C.D. Cal. 2009); *see also* State v. Riley, 988 A.2d 1252 (2009) (employee who had password access to employer's computer system did not commit a crime by violating employer's workplace policies) (interpreting a similar New Jersey state law).

145. 18 U.S.C. § 1030(g).

146. *Id.* § 1030(c)(4)(A)(i)(I). This provision includes a civil remedy for the modification or impairment of medical examination, diagnosis, or treatment; physical injury to a person; threat to public health or safety; and damage affecting a U.S. government computer involved in the administration of justice, national defense, or national security.

147. A number of states have statutes creating a state court remedy for computer-related offenses. *See* N.J.S.A. 2A:38-3 (New Jersey statute). The New Jersey statute provides that the victim can recover damages, punitive damages and reasonable attorneys' fees, and costs of investigation and litigation.

H. Digital Millennium Copyright Act

The Digital Millennium Copyright Act (DMCA), which became effective on October 28, 1998, prohibits the circumvention of technological measures implemented by copyright owners to protect their works and also prohibits tampering with copyright management information. The DMCA also added civil remedies and criminal penalties for violating such prohibitions.

As amended by the DMCA, Section 1201 of Title 17 to the U.S. Code prohibits persons from circumventing a technological measure that controls access to a work protected by the Copyright Act. Under an exception, circumvention is permitted for the purpose of identifying and disabling a technological means if such "technological measure, or the work it protects, contains the capability of collecting or disseminating personally identifying information reflecting the online activities of a natural person who seeks to gain access to the work protected."[148] Such a technological measure could include a "cookie" that could be placed on an individual's computer upon visiting a website.

Another example of a technological measure that could collect and disseminate personally identifiable information could be software installed on a consumer's electronic equipment or computer. Some Digital Rights Management (DRM) software bundled with music or movies purchased by consumers has been observed attempting to collect and disseminate personally identifiable information. However, an individual may invoke this exception only if the user is not provided with conspicuous notice or the capability to restrict or prevent such collection or dissemination, if the circumvention has no other effect on the ability of any person to gain access to any work, and the act of circumvention does not violate any other law.[149] This exception permits acts of circumvention in order to protect an individual's privacy, but fails to expressly permit the development and distribution of the means of accomplishing such circumvention.

Other notable exemptions allowing circumvention of technological measures controlling protected works permitted under the DMCA include reverse engineering,[150] encryption research,[151] and security testing.[152] The DMCA's stated goals for these exceptions are to promote research advancing the state of knowledge of cryptography and to correct security flaws and vulnerabilities; however, there are notable instances in which research in these areas has been met with industry resistance and lawsuits citing DMCA violations.

Lawsuits and threats of lawsuits may create a chilling effect on security research and publication. In one well-known instance from late 2005, a large record company distributed CDs containing software that could cause serious security vulnerabilities on consumers' computers. However, the researchers who discovered this vulnerability did not publicize their findings in a timely fashion. Instead, the researchers engaged in distracting legal discussions concerning potential DMCA liabilities with their own personal

---

148. 17 U.S.C. § 1201(i)(1) (2010).
149. *Id.*
150. 17 U.S.C. § 1201(f) (2010).
151. 17 U.S.C. § 1201(g) (2010).
152. 17 U.S.C. § 1201(j) (2010).

counsel as well as the general counsel representing their academic institution.[153] This delay left millions of consumers vulnerable while questions of DMCA liability were considered.

I. Children's Online Privacy Protection Act

The Children's Online Privacy Protection Act of 1998 (COPPA)[154] prohibits websites from collecting, using, or disclosing personal information from a child under the age of 13 without obtaining verifiable consent from the child's parent.[155] Parental consent may be obtained by using postal mail, telephone, facsimile, e-mail with copy of digitized signature, a digital certificate, or a PIN or password through an allowed verification method. No parental consent is needed if the collection of name and online contact information for the parent or child is solely to obtain parental consent, to provide notice to the parent, to respond to a one-time request, for the safety of the child, for public safety, or for the security or integrity of the website. To date, the Federal Trade Commission (FTC) has brought approximately fourteen enforcement actions under COPPA against websites that collected personal information from children under the age of thirteen without obtaining prior parental consent.[156]

Section 1301(b)(1)(D) of COPPA directs the FTC to promulgate regulations requiring website operators to "establish and maintain reasonable procedures to protect the confidentiality, security, and integrity of personal information collected from children."[157] The FTC's COPPA regulations can be found at 16 C.F.R., part 312. However, it basically repeats the COPPA security provision just quoted (*see* 16 C.F.R., §§ 312.3(e) and 312.8).

The FTC usually relies on its power to regulate deceptive or unfair trade practices under the FTC Act rather than on COPPA for information security matters.[158] However, in 2010, as part of its five-year rule review process and because of the change in the online environment and children's increased use of mobile technology, the FTC requested comments as to whether 16 C.F.R. § 312.8 was sufficiently clear to protect the confidentiality, security, and integrity of personal information collected from children.[159]

---

153. Deirde K. Mulligan & Aaron Perzonowski, *The Magnificence of the Disaster: Reconstructing the Sony BMG Rootkit Incident*, 22 Berkeley Tech. L.J. 1198 (2007).

154. 15 U.S.C. §§ 6501–6506.

155. 16 C.F.R. § 312.2 defines "obtaining verifiable consent" as "making any reasonable effort (taking into consideration available technology) to ensure that before personal information is collected from a child, a parent of the child: (a) Receives notice of the operator's personal information collection, use, and disclosure practices; and (b) Authorizes any collection, use, and/or disclosure of the personal information."

156. Statement of FTC to U.S. Senate, April 29, 2010, http://www.ftc.gov/os/testimony/100429coppastatement.pdf.

157. 15 U.S.C. § 6502(b)(1)(D).

158. For more information on the FTC's COPPA enforcement, *see*: http://www.ftc.gov/privacy/privacyinitiatives/childrens.html and http://www.ftc.gov/privacy/coppafaqs.shtm.

159. *See* 75 Fed. Reg. 17,089 and comments at http://www.ftc.gov/os/comments/copparulerev2010/index.shtm.

J. Veterans Affairs Information Security Act

The Veterans Affairs Information Security Act[160] requires the Department of Veterans Affairs (VA) to establish and maintain VA-wide information security protocols to protect VA security systems and information.[161] In doing so, the VA must comply with the Federal Information Security Management Act of 2002, and the VA's security measures must meet the requirements issued by NIST and OMB. Under the act, the VA's security program must include risk assessment procedures; information security controls and plans for providing security for networks and facilities; annual security awareness training for all VA employees, contractors, and all other users of VA sensitive information; periodic testing of security controls; a process for planning, developing, implementing, and evaluating remedial actions to address security deficiencies; procedures for detecting and immediately reporting security breaches; and plans and procedures to ensure the continuity of operations for VA systems.[162]

In the event of a data breach[163] of sensitive personal information (SPI),[164] either a non-VA entity or the VA's Office of Inspector General will conduct a risk analysis of the breach.[165] If the risk analysis shows the potential for misuse of the data, the VA has to provide credit protection services.[166] Incidents with potentially significant consequences have occurred.[167]

The law also requires that VA contracts include breach-related language where the VA discloses SPI.[168] Specifically, Section 5725(a)(1) requires that as a condition of the contract, the contractor cannot disclose the VA's SPI unless expressly authorized by the contract. Contractors also have to report all data breaches to the VA.[169] In addition, contracts must include liquidated damages the contractor or subcontractor will pay in the event it causes a data breach.[170] Money paid to the VA under Section 5725's liquidated damages clause will be used exclusively for credit protection services.

---

160. Title IX of the Veterans Benefits, Health Care, and Information Technology Act of 2006, P.L. 109-461.

161. 38 U.S.C. § 5722(a).

162. *Id.*

163. Data breach means the loss of, theft of, or other unauthorized access, other than that incidental to the scope of employment, to data containing sensitive personal information, in electronic or printed form, that results in the potential compromise of the confidentiality or integrity of the data. 38 U.S.C. § 5727(4).

164. Sensitive personal information is defined as any information about the individual maintained by the VA, including the following: (A) education, financial transactions, medical history, and criminal or employment history; (B) information that can be used to distinguish or trace the individual's identity, including name, Social Security number, date and place of birth, mother's maiden name, or biometric records. 38 U.S.C. § 5727(19).

165. 38 U.S.C. § 5724(a)(1).

166. *Id.* at (a)(2).

167. On May 3, 2006, burglars stole a VA laptop from a VA data analyst's home. The laptop contained the names, Social Security numbers, and birth dates of about 26.5 million veterans and their families as well as about 1.1 million active military personnel, 430,000 National Guard members, and 645,000 reserve personnel. The laptop was recovered and an FBI forensic examination showed that the data had not been compromised or even accessed. CRS Report RL33612, *Department of Veterans Affairs: Information Security and Information Technology Management Reorganization,* by Sidath Viranga Panangala (Aug. 14, 2006).

168. 38 U.S.C. § 5725.

169. *Id.* at (a)(2).

170. *Id.* at (b).

K. Federal Privacy Act

The purpose of the Privacy Act of 1974 is to regulate the collection, use, maintenance, and security of information that executive branch agencies collect about individuals. Under the act, records collected and actually accessed or retrieved by a personal identifier must be maintained in a system of records. Government agencies can collect only information that is relevant, accurate, timely, and necessary to accomplish their purpose. An agency's failure to maintain a system of records, however, will not insulate the agency from liability if it is in fact retrieving information about an individual using a personal identifier. Individuals about whom the information pertains have a right to access and amend their information. However, neither deceased individuals, next-of-kin, nor executors have any Privacy Act rights. An unauthorized disclosure occurs when an agency discloses information contained in a system of records either without consent by the individual to whom the information pertains or without an exception.[171]

Among other requirements, the government must "establish appropriate administrative, technical and physical safeguards to insure the security and confidentiality of records and to protect against any anticipated threats or hazards to their security or integrity which could result in substantial harm, embarrassment, inconvenience, or unfairness to any individual on whom the information is maintained."[172]

The Privacy Act provides for civil remedies and criminal penalties for unauthorized disclosures of information. Two of the four distinct civil causes of actions under the act provide for injunctive relief and two provide compensatory relief.[173] The criminal penalties make an agency employee who knowingly and willfully discloses individually identifiable information subject to a $5,000 fine and misdemeanor conviction.[174]

L. Federal Rules of Civil Procedure

In 2006, the Federal Rules of Civil Procedure were amended to clarify the process of retrieving, saving, and producing electronically stored information (ESI)[175] in anticipation of and during litigation. In part these Rules were necessary to clarify inconsistent developing case law and disparate local rules. The Rules now require that ESI be treated like any other document with regard to litigation. Therefore, once a party reasonably anticipates litigation, the duty to preserve potentially relevant ESI arises.

---

171. The Privacy Act lists 12 exceptions for the disclosure of information. 5 U.S.C. § 552a(b).

172. 5 U.S.C. § 552a(e)(10).

173. *Id.* at (g)(1)(A)–(D).

174. *Id.* at (i)(1)–(2).

175. Neither the Advisory Committee on Civil Rules' Notes to 2006 package of amendments to the Federal Rules of Civil Procedure nor the amendments themselves define "electronically stored information." However, it is generally understood to mean "information created, manipulated, communicated, stored, and best utilized in digital form, requiring the use of computer hardware and software. Electronically stored information is distinguished from information derived from 'conventional' media, such as writing or images on paper, photographic images, analog recordings, and microfilm." K. Withers, *Electronically Stored Information: The December 2006 Amendments to the Federal Rules of Civil Procedure,* 4 Nw. J. Tech. & Intell. Prop. 171, ¶ 9, *available at* http://www.law.northwestern.edu/journals/njtip/v4/n2/3.

The Rules do make accommodations for the differences between ESI and regular documents. Specifically:

- Unless requested in a specific format, *Rule 34(b)* allows the responding party to produce ESI in any reasonable format. This can include printouts or PDFs or native format if there are concerns about producing metadata.
- Under *Rule 26(b)(2)*, a responding party does not need to produce ESI that is not reasonably accessible unless the requesting party shows "good cause." The court also has discretion to split the cost between the parties or even require the requesting party to pay for everything.
- Due to the massive amounts of information when producing ESI, *Rule 26(b)(5)* allows a party who inadvertently produces privileged or protected information to "claw back" the material after producing it. However, courts interpreting this provision have still required that parties be diligent in both their original production and in finding their inadvertent disclosures, otherwise the privilege may be waived.
- *Rule 37(f)*, also known as the "Safe Harbor Provision," provides that, absent exceptional circumstances, a court may not impose sanctions on a party for failing to provide ESI lost as a result of the routine, good-faith operation of an electronic information system. (Please see the following section on data retention and destruction policies.)

Ultimately, the Federal Rules of Civil Procedure seek to treat ESI like any other document, while acknowledging the nature of those documents and the security implications of releasing them.

1. Data Retention and Destruction Policies

To avoid sanctions for lost information, a party must show that the ESI was lost due to the "routine operation of an electronic information system." In other words, the party must have destroyed the information in good faith. The Rules highlight the need to have a data retention policy that covers both paper and electronic data. The policy should address how often backup tapes are routinely purged and contain guidance on when such automatic processes should be put on hold with respect to data when litigation can be reasonably anticipated.

Courts have become more stringent on what constitutes good faith. However, there are three consistent factors that the courts have looked at to determine if a party has acted in good faith:

- Was the information destroyed under a data retention and destruction policy?
- Did the party consistently follow the policy?
- Was the policy reasonable?

Data retention and destruction policies have become increasingly important. In determining whether a policy is reasonable (and therefore protects the party), the courts have looked at a number of factors:

- The policy cannot have been instituted to thwart production during litigation.

- The policy must include a litigation hold (i.e., once a party is aware that litigation may begin, the party is required to take whatever steps are necessary to prevent the further deletion of any data that might be required).
- The policy must set forth clear guidelines on what is to be destroyed and at what intervals.

As is covered in more detail elsewhere in this handbook, ESI is found throughout any computerized system. All that information is potentially discoverable under the Federal Rules of Civil Procedure. To adequately protect a party, a data retention policy should cover all forms of ESI, including but not limited to: servers, e-mails, digital copy machines, backup tapes, temporary files, desktops, automatic archives, flash drives, laptops, proprietary systems, CDs/DVDs, telecommuters' home computers, tablets, and voicemail systems.

If a party creates a reasonable data retention and destruction policy and follows it, a court is far less likely to sanction it for any lost information.

2. *Federal Rule of Civil Procedure 5.2*

In December 2007, the Federal Rules of Civil Procedure (Fed. R. Civ. P. 5.2), Criminal Procedure (Fed. R. Crim. P. 49.1), Bankruptcy (Fed. R. B. P. 9037), and Appellate Procedure (Fed. R. App. P. 25(a)(5)) were amended to protect privacy of individuals identified in court documents by requiring redaction of Social Security numbers, taxpayer identification numbers, birth dates, the names of minors, and financial account numbers.

M. Family Educational Rights and Privacy Act

"Computer systems at colleges and universities have become favored targets because they hold many of the same records as banks but are much easier to access."[176]

The Family Educational Rights and Privacy Act (FERPA) of 1974, as amended,[177] applies to educational agencies and institutions (elementary, secondary, or postsecondary institutions, and school districts) that receive funds from the U.S. Department of Education (US ED). FERPA Regulations can be found in Section 99 of Title 34 of the Code of Federal Regulations. Generally, FERPA prohibits educational agencies and institutions from disclosing "students' education records"[178] without written parental consent, unless such disclosure falls within one of the enumerated conditions provided in 34 C.F.R. § 99.31. Once a student reaches 18 years of age or is attending a postsecondary institution, he or she is considered an "eligible student," and the rights accorded to parents under FERPA transfer to the student.

---

176. 73 Fed. Reg. 74,806, 74,843 (Dec. 9, 2008).

177. Pub. L. 93-380, codified at 20 U.S.C. § 1232g.

178. The term "education records" is defined in 34 C.F.R. § 99.3 as "those records that are: (1) Directly related to a student; and (2) Maintained by an educational agency or institution or by a party acting for the agency or institution." This includes financial information submitted to the school by the student's parents, but excludes alumni records collected and maintained by alumni associations because they are not directly related to the individual as a student.

Under a 2002 decision of the U.S. Supreme Court, FERPA provides no private right of action.[179] However, the Secretary of Education may issue an administrative complaint to compel compliance through a cease and desist order under 20 U.S.C. §§ 1234c and 1234e. Another potential sanction for a FERPA violation includes the cut-off of federal funds to the postsecondary institution, school, or school district, subject to the following conditions:

- That sanction may be applied only for a "policy or practice" of making unauthorized disclosures of education records.
- The law requires US ED to seek voluntary compliance before seeking any funding remedy.
- A state educational agency that violates FERPA's nondisclosure provisions is not subject to a cut-off of federal funds, but could be barred from receiving education records for a period of not less than five years.[180]

In the Federal Register notice cited earlier, US ED provided additional guidance and amended the regulations to better address information security concerns. For instance, 34 C.F.R. § 99.31(a)(1)(i)(B) addresses "direct control" over third-party service providers, and 34 C.F.R. § 99.31(a)(1)(ii) requires the implementation of adequate access controls over education records.

N. Communications Act and FCC Regulations

Every telecommunications carrier has a duty to protect the customer proprietary network information (CPNI) of, and relating to, other telecommunications carriers, equipment manufacturers, and customers, including telecommunications carriers reselling telecommunications services provided by a telecommunications carrier.[181] CPNI includes information about a customer's telephone services and information contained in the customer's bill.[182] CPNI is comprised of three categories: (1) Call Detail Information (i.e., time, date, number called, and duration of call); (2) Subscription Information (i.e., what services a customer subscribes to); and (3) General Account Information, including name, address, phone number, personal information (i.e., maiden name, Social Security number) and bill amount. CPNI does not include "subscriber list information" (i.e., directory information).[183]

Carriers must take "reasonable measures" to: (1) identify the locations of CPNI across their infrastructure; and (2) protect both the data and access to it from unauthorized disclosure. The FCC does not mandate specific technologies to protect CPNI. Carriers

---

179. Gonzaga Univ. v. Doe, 536 U.S. 273 (2002).

180. Under 34 C.F.R. § 99.33(e), if US ED finds that a third party involved in an unauthorized disclosure or breach has not complied with the regulations, the educational agency or institution may not share education records with it for at least five years.

181. Section 222(a) of the Communications Act of 1934, as amended, 47 U.S.C. § 222, and FCC Regulations 47 C.F.R. § 64.2010.

182. *Id.* § 222(h)(1).

183. *Id.* § 222(h)(3). "Subscriber list information" is typically name, address, and telephone number.

must also train their personnel as to when they are and are not authorized to use CPNI, and have an express disciplinary process in place.[184]

Carriers must properly authenticate a customer prior to disclosing CPNI based on customer-initiated telephone contact, online account access, or an in-store visit.[185]

- *Telephone access to CPNI.* Carriers may disclose call detail information over the telephone, based on customer-initiated telephone contact, only if the customer first provides the carrier with a password (see requirements below). If the customer does not provide a password, the carrier may only disclose call detail information by sending it to the customer's address of record or by calling the customer at the telephone number of record. If the customer is able to provide call detail information to the carrier during a customer-initiated call without the carrier's assistance, then the carrier is permitted to discuss the call detail information provided by the customer.
- *Online access to CPNI.* A carrier must authenticate a customer without the use of readily available biographical information or account information prior to allowing the customer online access to CPNI related to a telecommunications service account. Once authenticated, the customer may obtain online access to CPNI related to a telecommunications service account only through a password, as described below, which is not prompted by the carrier asking for readily available biographical information or account information.
- *In-store access to CPNI.* A carrier may disclose CPNI to a customer who, at a carrier's retail location, first presents to the carrier or its agent a valid photo ID matching the customer's account information.
- *Establishment of a Password and Backup Authentication Methods for Lost or Forgotten Passwords.* To establish a password, a carrier must authenticate the customer without the use of readily available biographical information or account information. Carriers may create a backup customer authentication method in the event of a lost or forgotten password, but such backup customer authentication method may not prompt the customer for readily available biographical information or account information. If a customer cannot provide the correct password or the correct response for the backup customer authentication method, the customer must establish a new password.[186]

The rules further require carriers to obtain opt-in consent from customers before using their CPNI to market services not currently received from the provider, whereas the older rules only required opt-in consent for disclosure of call detail information to third parties.[187] Carriers must maintain a record of all instances where CPNI was disclosed or provided to third parties, or where third parties were allowed access to CPNI.[188]

---

184. 47 C.F.R. § 64.2009(b).
185. 47 C.F.R. § 64.2010(a)–(d).
186. 47 C.F.R. § 64.2010(e).
187. 47 C.F.R. § 64.2005(b).
188. 47 C.F.R. § 64.2009(c).

The FCC rules establish breach notification and reporting requirements.[189] Carriers must document and retain for a minimum of two years a record of any breaches discovered and notifications made to law enforcement and to customers.[190] The record must include, if available, dates of discovery and notification, a detailed description of the CPNI that was the subject of the breach, and the circumstances of the breach. A "breach" has occurred when a person, without authorization or exceeding authorization, has intentionally gained access to, used, or disclosed CPNI.

O. Dodd-Frank Wall Street Reform and Consumer Protection Act

A part of this new statute[191] regulating the financial industry is the "Consumer Financial Protection Act of 2010."[192] This act creates a new Bureau of Consumer Financial Protection, whose purpose is to implement and enforce federal "consumer financial law consistently for consumer financial products and services and [ensures] that markets for consumer financial products and services are fair, transparent, and competitive." It has the authority to create and enforce regulations for financial institutions and those organizations that provide financial products or services. The Bureau will create rules to prevent "unfair, deceptive, or abusive acts or practices" or discrimination. The "unfair and deceptive" standard is used frequently by the FTC, as explained above. Combined with the new standard for "abusive acts or practices," the Bureau should have a broad authority to focus on information security and privacy practices related to the provision of financial products and services.

2.2 U.S. STATE LAWS

U.S. states have passed numerous laws aimed at the protection of the consumer's privacy.[193] This section covers those concerning data breach, protection of Social Security numbers, spyware programs, secure data disposal, information security requirements and state and individual enforcement of federal information security and privacy laws and regulations. A list of many of these state laws is presented in Appendix C.

---

189. 47 C.F.R. § 64.2011(d).

190. 47 C.F.R. § 64.2011(b) ("As soon as practicable, and in no event later than seven (7) business days, after reasonable determination of the breach, the telecommunications carrier shall electronically notify [the U.S. Secret Service and FBI] through a central reporting facility. . . . (1) Notwithstanding any state law to the contrary, the carrier shall not notify customers or disclose the breach to the public until 7 full business days have passed after notification to the USSS and the FBI except as provided in paragraphs (b)(2) and (b)(3) of this section.").

191. Dodd-Frank Wall Street Reform and Consumer Protection Act. Public Law 111-203, July 21, 2010.

192. *Id.* at Title X.

193. By one estimate in mid 2010, states have in recent years passed more than 100 privacy and information security related laws. This tally includes data breach laws in 46 states plus the District of Columbia, Puerto Rico, and the U.S. Virgin Islands, 10 state information security laws, 19 state secure data disposal laws, 13 state radio frequency ID privacy laws, 22 state phishing laws, 15 state spyware laws, 37 state spam laws, 24 state online sexual predator laws, two state recent credit history privacy laws, and three state online privacy laws. *In the Matter of the Request for Comments on Information Privacy and Innovation in the Information in the Internet Economy,* Docket No. 100402174-0175-01, Before the Department of Commerce Internet Policy Task Force, Comments of the State Privacy & Security Coalition (June 2010). Other types of such laws are in legislation, such as the New Jersey Assembly Bill No. 2975, which would require the destruction of "records stored on a digital copy machine."

A. State Data Breach Notification Laws

Almost all states and the District of Columbia, Puerto Rico, and the U.S. Virgin Islands have enacted data breach notification laws[194] requiring disclosure when data that includes defined types of personal information is exposed or accessed by an unauthorized person.[195] The laws are generally applicable to any person, business, or state agency that does business in the state and owns or licenses computerized data that contains personal information.[196] A nonowner maintaining data concerning state residents on behalf of an owner is generally subject to the law and must immediately, subject to certain limitations, notify the data owner upon discovering or reasonably suspecting a data breach, regardless of whether the entity conducts business in that state. In the majority of states, an entity is not subject to the state data breach law if the breached data is encrypted.[197]

The first data breach notice law was the California Security Breach Information Act (Senate Bill 1386), which was effective in 2003. This law has been credited with initiating the flood of high-profile data breach disclosures that started in early 2005. Most of the other laws are modeled on this California law, but there are many variations.

1. Definition of Data Breach

States differ slightly in their definitions of what constitutes a "breach" of covered data. Most state statutes define a data breach as the unauthorized acquisition of and access to unencrypted or unredacted computerized data that results in the compromise of the security, confidentiality, or integrity of personal information maintained by the person or business experiencing the breach. Nine states require that the compromise to the individual's security, confidentiality, or integrity be "material."[198]

---

194. For a list of current laws, see National Conference of State Legislatures State Security Breach Notification Laws, *available at* http://www.ncsl.org/default.aspx?tabid=13489. For a detailed discussion of laws in effect as of the date of its publication, see JOHN P. HUTCHINS ET AL., U.S. DATA BREACH LAWS: STATE BY STATE (American Bar Ass'n 2007).

195. The District of Columbia, Puerto Rico, and the Virgin Islands also have data breach laws. Alabama, Kentucky, New Mexico, and South Dakota do not have a data breach law.

196. Wisconsin and Massachusetts both reach beyond entities doing business in the state to those who own or use personal information pertaining to state residents. Certain states exempt their own state agencies or entities that are already regulated under federal privacy laws such as HIPAA and GLBA. The following states' data breach laws apply both to computerized and hard copy data: Alaska, ALASKA STAT. § 45.48.010; Hawaii, HAW. REV. STAT. § 487N-2; Indiana, IND. CODE ANN. § 24-4.9-3-1; North Carolina, N.C. GEN. STAT. § 75-65. Wisconsin, WIS. STAT. § 134.98, and Massachusetts, ALM GL ch. 93H, by neglecting to specify whether data must be computerized or hard copy, apply to both computerized and noncomputerized data.

197. In twelve states, however, a breach of information that is either "not encrypted or redacted, or is encrypted and the encryption key has been accessed or acquired" is subject to the state data breach law: Alaska, ALASKA STAT. § 45.48.010; Hawaii, HAW. REV. STAT. § 487N-2; Indiana, IND. CODE ANN. § 24-4.9-3-1; Kentucky, proposed, 2010 Bill Text KY H.B. 581; Massachusetts, ALM GL ch. 93H, § 3; 201 MASS. CODE REGS. 17.03; Michigan, MICH. COMP. LAWS SERV. § 445.72; Minnesota, MINN. STAT. § 325E.61; New York, N.Y. GEN. BUS. LAW § 899-aa; North Carolina, N.C. GEN. STAT. § 75-65; Oregon, OR. REV. STAT. § 646A.604; Texas, TEX. BUS. & COM. CODE § 521.053; Virginia, VA. CODE ANN. § 18.2-186.6.

198. Arizona, ARIZ. REV. STAT. § 44-7501; Florida, FLA. STAT. § 817.5681; Idaho, IDAHO CODE ANN. § 28-51-105; Montana, MONT. CODE ANN., § 30-14-1704; Nevada, NEV. REV. STAT. ANN. § 603A.220; Oregon, OR. REV. STAT. § 646A.604; Pennsylvania , 73 PA. STAT. § 2303; Tennessee, TENN. CODE ANN. § 47-18-2107; Wyoming, WYO. STAT. § 40-12-502.

Generally, no harm or actual loss to an individual whose data has been breached is required in order to trigger applicability of the law. In certain states, however, a threshold of harm must be reached, such that there is a "material" or "significant" or "substantial" risk of harm before any notification or disclosure requirements are required. Harm can include economic loss,[199] identity theft[200] or fraud,[201] or general loss or harm.[202] Other states require some degree of identity theft or fraud,[203] harm,[204] loss, or injury[205] to have occurred or be reasonably likely to occur, but do not specify any definitive threshold.

Almost every state provides a good-faith exception to the standard breach definition, which provides that a breach is deemed not to have occurred when there is an unauthorized disclosure to an agent or employee of the entity, the information disclosed is used for the entity's legitimate purposes, and the information thereafter is not subject to further unauthorized disclosure or misuse. Similarly, information that is publicly available is not subject to data breach laws.

2. *Definition of Personal Information/Information Subject to a Breach*

Most commonly, states for purposes of data breach statutes define "personal information" as an individual's first name or first initial and last name in combination with any one or more of the following data elements: Social Security number; driver's license number; and/or account number or credit or debit card number, in combination with any required security code, access code, or password that would permit access to an individual's financial account. Other elements that may be included in the definition are: unique electronic identifier or routing code in combination with access information;[206] medical information;[207] health insurance information;[208] unique biometric data;[209] employer ID number;[210] parent's legal surname prior to marriage or mother's maiden

199. Arizona, ARIZ. REV. STAT. § 44-7501.

200. Michigan, MICH. COMP. LAWS SERV. § 445.72; Ohio, OHIO REV. CODE ANN. § 1349.19; Rhode Island, R.I. GEN. LAWS § 11-49.2-3; Wisconsin, WIS. STAT. § 134.98.

201. Massachusetts, 201 MASS. CODE REGS. 17.03; Michigan, MICH. COMP. LAWS SERV. § 445.72; Ohio, OHIO REV. CODE ANN. § 1349.19; Wisconsin, WIS. STAT. § 134.98.

202. Michigan, MICH. COMP. LAWS SERV. § 445.72; North Carolina; N.C. GEN. STAT. § 75-65; South Carolina, S.C. CODE ANN. § 39-1-90.

203. Indiana, IND. CODE ANN. § 24-4.9-3-1; Utah, UTAH CODE ANN. § 13-44-202.

204. Connecticut, CONN. GEN. STAT. § 36a-701b; Hawaii, HAW. REV. STAT. § 487N-2.

205. Montana, MONT. CODE ANN., § 30-14-1704; Pennsylvania, 73 PA. STAT. § 2303; Wyoming, WYO. STAT. § 40-12-502.

206. Iowa, IOWA CODE § 715C.2; Missouri, MO. REV. STAT. § 407.1500; Nebraska, NEB. REV. STAT. § 87-803; North Carolina, N.C. GEN. STAT. § 75-65.

207. Arkansas, ARK. CODE ANN. § 4-110-105; California, CAL. CIV. CODE § 1798.29; Kentucky (proposed), 2010 Bill Text KY H.B. 581; Michigan, MICH. COMP. LAWS SERV. § 445.72; Missouri, MO. REV. STAT. § 07.1500; Texas, TEX. BUS. & COM. CODE § 521.053; Virginia, 2010 Bill Text VA H.B. 1039; Virginia (enrolled), VA. CODE § 32.1-127.1:05 (effective Jan. 1, 2011).

208. California, CAL. CIV. CODE § 1798.29; Michigan, MICH. COMP. LAWS SERV. § 445.72; Missouri, MO. REV. STAT. § 07.1500; Texas, TEX. BUS. & COM. CODE § 521.053.

209. Iowa, IOWA CODE § 715C.2; Nebraska, NEB. REV. STAT. § 87-803; North Carolina, N.C. GEN. STAT. § 75-65; Wisconsin, WIS. STAT. § 134.98.

210. North Dakota, N.D. CENT. CODE § 51-30-02.

name;[211] date of birth;[212] digital signature;[213] and Internet account numbers or Internet identification names.[214] In Indiana, if an individual's Social Security number alone is compromised, the individual must be notified.[215]

3. Notice Requirement

Typically, state statutes require disclosure to individuals after a "breach of the security of the system," in the most expedient manner possible and without unreasonable delay. In a notable instance, the Connecticut Attorney General asserted that the defendant's inability to produce a "log file" of the lost disk's contents further increased the risk of disclosure by unreasonably delaying disclosure to affected individuals and therefore prevented otherwise timely mitigation of the data breach.[216] A few states establish a deadline of 45 days.[217] Delaying notification for purposes of aiding law enforcement is permitted across the board.

Each state provides its own requirement for what information shall be included in the notification. In certain states, no notification is required if the entity conducts a reasonable investigation and discovers there is no risk of harm.[218]

The content of a security breach notice is mandated in various states. Notification of data breach may be given in the following ways: written notice, telephonic notice, or electronic notice in certain circumstances.[219] Almost every state allows for substitute notice procedures if providing notice will cost more than the amount listed in the statute or the affected class exceeds a certain number of individuals dictated in the statute. The content of a security breach notice is mandated in various states. Substitute notice typically involves

---

211. North Carolina, N.C. Gen. Stat. § 75-65; North Dakota, N.D. Cent. Code § 51-30-02. In North Carolina, this information is considered personal information only if it would permit access to a person's financial account or resources.

212. North Dakota, N.D. Cent. Code § 51-30-02.

213. North Carolina, N.C. Gen. Stat. § 75-65; North Dakota, N.D. Cent. Code § 51-30-02.

214. North Carolina, N.C. Gen. Stat. § 75-65. In North Carolina, this information is considered personal information only if it would permit access to a person's financial account or resources.

215. Ind. Code Ann. § 28-1-2-30.5.

216. See the Complaint to an action against Health Net of the N.E. Inc. and affiliate entities, Civ. No. 3:10CV57(PDC), which resulted in a July 6, 2010 Stipulated Judgment, in connection with violations of HIPAA's data protection requirements and Connecticut's data breach statute.

217. Florida, Fla. Stat. § 817.5681; Ohio, Ohio Rev. Code Ann. § 1349.19; and Wisconsin, Wis. Stat. § 134.98. In Florida, an entity that maintains computerized data that includes personal information on behalf of another business entity has ten days to disclose a breach to the entity.

218. Investigation for the purpose of confirming breach has occurred: Arizona, Ariz. Rev. Stat. § 44-7501. Investigation to confirm information has been or is likely to be misused: Colorado, Colo. Rev. Stat. § 6-1-716; Delaware, 6 Del. Code § 12B-102; Idaho, Idaho Code Ann. § 28-51-105; Kansas, Kan. Stat. Ann. § 50-7a02; Maryland, Md. Code Ann., Com. Law § 14-3504; Nebraska, Neb. Rev. Stat. § 87-803; New Hampshire, N.H. Rev. Stat. Ann. § 359-C:20; Utah, Utah Code Ann. § 13-44-202. Investigation to confirm there is no reasonable likelihood of harm to customers: Louisiana, La. Rev. Stat. § 51:3074; Mississippi, 2010 Bill Text MS H.B. 583; Oregon, Or. Rev. Stat. § 646A.604 (Oregon requires the results of an investigation to be kept on file for five years.). Investigation to confirm there is no significant risk of identity theft to affected individuals: Rhode Island, R.I. Gen. Laws § 11-49.2-3.

219. Electronic notice is permitted if the entity's primary method of communication with the individual is by electronic means or is consistent with the provisions regarding electronic records and signatures set forth in the Electronic Signatures in Global and National Commerce Act.

contacting the affected individual electronically if possible, conspicuously posting the notice on the website of the breached entity, and notifying applicable local and statewide media.[220]

Some states, such as Indiana, Maryland, Massachusetts, New Hampshire, and New York, include provisions for notice to the state attorney general for some breaches, in addition to affected individuals.[221] New Jersey requires reporting to law enforcement for investigation and handling.[222] New York also requires notification to the New York Consumer Protection Board and the New York State Office of Cyber Security and Critical Infrastructure and Coordination as to the timing, content, and distribution of the notices and approximate number of affected persons.[223] Several states also require notification to respective consumer reporting agencies if the number of affected individuals reaches a certain threshold.[224]

Various states also maintain databases of reported incidents, which provide examples of the notices sent to individuals for each incident.[225]

For comprehensive guidance concerning protection against and prevention of data breaches and preparing for and issuing notifications, see the California Office of Privacy Protection's publication, "Recommended Practices on Notice of Security Breach Involving Personal Information."[226]

4. *Penalties*

Penalties for failure to provide notification of a data breach range greatly from state to state. A handful of states have no specific penalties in place. A number of states provide that the state attorney general, or, in some cases, the district attorney of a county, have the authority to seek injunctive relief and damages if the data breach violation is willful and knowing. The attorney general may also enjoin an entity to enforce future compliance, and many states provide for civil monetary penalties, where generally a specific fine is defined for each violation of the statute with a certain maximum fine provided. At least one state, Michigan, provides criminal penalties for providing notice of a security breach that has not occurred where such notice is given with the intent to defraud.

B. Social Security, Spyware, and Data Disposal Laws

1. *Social Security Laws*

Recognizing the risk inherent in the possession of Social Security numbers (SSNs), 34 states have passed laws restricting use of SSNs. Many of these laws apply specifically to educational institutions and public agencies.

---

220. *See e.g.*, MONT. CODE ANN. § 30-14-1704.

221. IND. CODE ANN. § 24-4.9-3-1; MD. CODE ANN., COM. LAW § 14-3504(h); MASS. ANN. LAWS ch. 93H, § 3; N.H. REV. STAT. ANN. § 359-C:20; N.Y. GEN. BUS. LAW § 899-aa.

222. N.J. STAT. § 56:8-163.

223. N.Y. GEN. BUS. LAW § 899-aa.

224. IOWA CODE § 715C.2; 54 D.C. REG. 393; MASS. ANN. LAWS ch. 93H, § 3 (no threshold required.). Proposed legislation in Colorado requires this as well: 2010 Bill Text Colo. H.B. 1422.

225. Examples of the notices sent to individuals for each incident can be found in the databases of reported incidents that Maryland and New Hampshire maintain. *See* Maryland Information Security Breach Notices, http://www.oag.state.md.us/idtheft/breacheNotices.htm; New Hampshire, Notice of Security Breaches, http://doj.nh.gov/consumer/breaches.html.

226. *See* Recommended Practices on Notice of Security Breach Involving Personal Information, *available at* http://www.dhcs.ca.gov/formsandpubs/laws/priv/Documents/PrivacyProtection.pdf.

Generally, such SSN laws prohibit entities from: (1) intentionally communicating or otherwise making available to the general public an individual's SSN; (2) intentionally printing or imbedding an individual's SSN on any card required for the individual to access products or services provided by the person or entity; (3) requiring an individual to transmit his or her SSN over the Internet unless the connection is secure or the SSN is encrypted; (4) requiring an individual to use his or her SSN to access an Internet website, unless a password or unique personal identification number or other authentication device is additionally required to access the Internet website; (5) printing an individual's SSN on any materials that are mailed to the individual, unless state or federal law requires the SSN to be on the document to be mailed; or (6) selling, leasing, lending, trading, renting, or otherwise intentionally disclosing an individual's SSN to a third party without written consent to the disclosure from the individual, when the party making the disclosure knows or in the exercise of reasonable diligence would have reason to believe that the third party lacks a legitimate purpose for obtaining the individual's SSN.

Many states likewise prohibit educational institutions from using a student's SSN as his or her identification number on student identification cards provided by the institution. It is important to review the state laws applicable to a party's intended use of an SSN prior to requesting or using such SSN.[227]

2. *Spyware Laws*

At least fifteen states directly regulate or prohibit spyware.[228] There is no uniformly accepted definition of spyware. "Spyware" is a loosely defined type of software installed on a computer without the user's direct knowledge or informed consent. As the name suggests, spyware gathers information without the user's knowledge. As a result it creates a series of problems, ranging from the mere nuisance—slowing down a computer—to a serious threat that can totally compromise security. Spyware can surreptitiously capture information on a computer and store it for later access by another or transmit it to another location, all without the knowledge of the user. A particularly pernicious category of spyware is the "key logger," which captures every keystroke entered, even if it is changed or not saved. Spyware can be used to steal personal or confidential information, like passwords, account numbers, or trade secrets. Like viruses, spyware is often designed to be difficult to remove or to reinstall itself if it is uninstalled. It should be noted, however, that some spyware can have legitimate purposes, like monitoring children or employees, and may be legal when used in accordance with applicable laws. If used to deliver pop-ups or other forms of advertising, it is called "adware."[229]

---

227. A list of enacted SSN laws is available at http://www.ftc.gov/bcp/edu/microsites/idtheft/law-enforcement/state-laws-social-security.html.

228. Alaska, Arizona, Arkansas, California, Georgia, Illinois, Indiana, Iowa, Louisiana, Nevada, New Hampshire, Rhode Island, Texas, Utah, and Washington. For a list of these laws, see National Conference of State Legislators, "State Spyware Laws," *available at* www.ncsl.org/default.aspx?tabid=13452.

229. For general information on spyware, see Patricia Figliola, *Spyware: Background and Policy Issues for Congress* (Congressional Research Service, Dec. 9, 2009); Federal Trade Commission, Spyware Microsite, http://www.ftc.gov/bcp/edu/microsites/spyware/index.htm; and the Anti-Spyware Coalition, http://www.antispywarecoalition.org.

In addition to potentially violating specific state spyware laws, spyware may violate general laws like the Computer Fraud and Abuse Act,[230] the Electronic Communications Privacy Act,[231] the Federal Trade Commission Act,[232] and their state equivalents.

3. Data Disposal Laws

Effective January 2005, a California statute required most businesses that own or license personal information about California residents to implement and maintain reasonable security procedures to protect personal information from unauthorized access, destruction, use, modification, or disclosure, and to contractually bind third parties who obtained such information to maintain reasonable security procedures.[233] In addition to California, twenty-three other states have laws that require the secure destruction of personal information and/or the implementation of security measures to protect such information. Although most of these laws apply to businesses, some specifically require compliance by state or governmental agencies as well.[234] Secure destruction methods that satisfy such requirements generally include shredding or slurrying for paper documents. For electronic documents acceptable techniques include degaussing of hardware and overwriting of software a number of times deemed sufficient to prevent data recovery.

C. Security Program Laws

Data security laws require reasonable measures to protect defined categories of personal information. At least ten states[235] have data security laws that generally require "reasonable security," or its equivalent for covered information, with some variances in the scope of their coverage and the specificity of their requirements.

Just as California led the country with its breach notice law, it likewise enacted the first data security law in 2004, requiring businesses to "implement and maintain reasonable security procedures and practices" to protect covered information about California residents.[236]

To date, the most comprehensive data breach law is that of Massachusetts (MASS. GEN. LAWS ch. 93H), which became effective on March 1, 2010 (via implementing regulation 201 MASS. CODE REGS. 17.00).[237] Some observers believe that this law will become a model for comprehensive protection of personal information and will be adopted either at the federal level or extensively at the state level. The impact of statewide or federal adoption would be dramatic because the Massachusetts law reaches beyond individuals and entities doing

---

230. 18 U.S.C. § 1030 *et seq.*

231. 18 U.S.C. § 2510 *et seq.*

232. 15 U.S.C. §§ 41–58.

233. CAL. CIV. CODE § 1798.81.5.

234. *E.g.*, Alaska, California, Hawaii, Kansas, Massachusetts [with respect to secure disposal], Michigan, Nevada, New Jersey, and Oregon.

235. Arkansas, California, Connecticut, Maryland, Massachusetts, Nevada, Oregon, Rhode Island, Texas, and Utah.

236. CAL. CIV. CODE, § 1798.5(b).

237. *See* http:// www.mass.gov/Eoca/docs/idtheft/201CMR1700reg.pdf; *see also* Massachusetts Office of Consumer Affairs and Business Regulation, Identity Theft FAQ Regarding 201 MASS. CODE REGS. 17.00, *available at* http://www.mass.gov/Eoca/docs/idtheft/201CMR17faqs.pdf.

business within the state to all "persons who own, license, store or maintain personal information about a resident of the Commonwealth of Massachusetts." With its broad coverage of "persons," this law may well be applied to persons nationwide as long as they possess or deal in covered information and have sufficient contacts with Massachusetts to satisfy personal jurisdiction requirements. The law's definition of covered "personal information" is similar to that of most other state laws, including Social Security numbers, driver's license numbers, state-issued identification card numbers, financial account numbers, and credit card numbers.

In addition to dramatically expanding to whom its law applies, Massachusetts' law institutes fairly new requirements on all covered persons. Specifically, the law requires covered persons to "develop, implement, and maintain a comprehensive information security program that is written in one or more readily accessible parts and contains administrative, technical, and physical safeguards." The written information security program must include a risk assessment as well as implement a host of other detailed requirements. The regulation also establishes detailed requirements for the security of a covered person's computer system, including (1) encryption of all covered information that either travels across public networks, is transmitted wirelessly, or is stored on laptops or other portable devices; (2) secure user authentication and access control; (3) reasonable monitoring to detect unauthorized access; (4) reasonably up-to-date firewall protection and security software, including current patches and virus definitions; and (5) employee education and training.

D. State Attorneys General and Private Rights of Action

The Health Insurance Portability and Accountability Act of 1996 (HIPAA)[238] contains what's known as the "Privacy Rule," or Standards for Privacy of Individually Identifiable Health Information, which provides federal protections for "personal health information" (PHI) held by "covered entities," both defined terms within the HIPAA context, and also permitting the disclosure of PHI as needed for patient care and other limited purposes. HIPAA also includes the "Security Rule," known more formally as the Security Standards for the Protection of Electronic Protected Health Information, which specifies a series of administrative, physical, and technical safeguards for covered entities to use to ensure the confidentiality, integrity, and availability of electronic protected health information.

Although one of the many purposes of HIPAA was to protect individually identifiable health information, it was commonly believed that HIPAA's protection of health information was not strong enough in light of changing technology, practices, and exponential growth in data storage. In response, the Health Information Technology for Economic and Clinical Health (HITECH) Act, enacted as part of the American Recovery and Reinvestment Act of 2009 and signed into law on February 17, 2009, was intended to enhance enforcement of the HIPAA privacy and security protections.[239] Among its many provisions, the HITECH Act strengthened the civil and criminal enforcement provisions of HIPAA. Key provisions of the HITECH Act are discussed earlier in this chapter.

---

238. Pub. L. No. 104-191 (1996) (Health Insurance Portability and Accountability Act of 1996).
239. Pub. L. No. 111-5 (2009) (American Recovery and Reinvestment Act of 2009).

1. Enforcement of HIPAA by State Attorneys General

One of the most important new enforcement provisions provided by the HITECH Act is the introduction of an amendment to Section 1176 of the Social Security Act (42 U.S.C. § 1320d-5) that allows enforcement of HIPAA by state attorneys general who believe that residents of their state have been affected by violations of HIPAA.[240]

Under § 1320d-5, a state attorney general can bring a civil action in federal court to enjoin further violations and/or seek statutory damages of up to $100 per violation, limited to $25,000 in a calendar year for violations of the identical requirement or prohibition. In addition, if the action is successful, the attorney general may recover reasonable attorneys' fees and costs to the state.

A state attorney general wishing to pursue such action in federal court must first provide notice to the Secretary, giving the Secretary the opportunity to intervene in the action. If the Secretary has brought an action under this section, the state attorney general is prohibited from bringing its own action during the pendency of the Secretary's action.

It is important to note that, by filing an action under § 1320d-5, a state attorney general is not prohibited from pursuing similar actions under state laws.

2. Practical Application of State Attorneys General's Authority

Many states have health information privacy and security laws that can be enforced by the state's attorney general. In addition, many states have enacted privacy and security laws applicable to a broad range of personal or financial information (not necessarily limited or related to health care). These state general personal information privacy and security laws sometimes contain express provisions related to the privacy and security of health information. These various state information privacy and security laws can contain provisions for injunctive relief, civil and criminal penalties, or both. The following are a few examples.

Under Rhode Island law, any person who discloses a patient's confidential health care information without proper consent in violation of the statute may be liable for actual and punitive damages, and a court may award attorneys' fees. If the violation is intentional, the person can be fined not more than $5,000 for each violation, or imprisoned not more than six months for each violation, or both.[241]

Maryland's Confidentiality of Medical Records Act provides for restrictions on the disclosure of patient medical records and for the handling of electronic claims.[242] A health care provider or other person who knowingly violates the act is liable for actual damages.[243] In addition, a health care provider or any other person, including an officer or employee of a governmental unit, who knowingly and willfully violates any provision

240. Pub. L. No. 111-5 (2009) (American Recovery and Reinvestment Act of 2009) at § 13410(e) and 42 U.S.C. § 1320d-5(d).

241. R.I. Gen. Laws, Title 5, Chap. 5-37.3, Confidentiality of Health Care Communications and Information Act, § 5-37.3-4.

242. Md. Code Ann., Title 4, Subtitle 3, Maryland's Confidentiality of Medical Records Act (MCMRA) §§ 4-301 *et seq.*

243. Maryland's Confidentiality of Medical Records Act (MCMRA), § 4-309(f).

of the Maryland Act is guilty of a misdemeanor and on conviction is subject to a fine not exceeding $1,000 for the first offense and not exceeding $5,000 for each subsequent conviction for a violation.[244]

HIPAA recognizes the existence of state laws that contain protections similar to those in HIPAA, and therefore provides that HIPAA will supersede such state laws where they are contrary to HIPAA.[245] However, HIPAA will not preempt state laws, where the Secretary of HHS determines that the state law is necessary: to prevent fraud and abuse, to insure appropriate regulation of insurance and health plans, for state reporting of health care delivery or costs, or for other purposes.[246]

As a result, in cases where a state's laws provide remedies similar to those of HIPAA, the question will arise as to whether the state attorney general can or should pursue remedies under state law, HIPAA, or both. Due to the complexity inherent with state/federal preemption matters, such questions will need to be answered on a case-by-case basis.

State attorneys general are aware of the challenges. In analyzing the impact of the HITECH Act changes on enforcement of state health information privacy and security laws by state attorneys general, an article in a newsletter published by the National Association of Attorneys General stated:

> The federal law pre-empts state law on the subject of individually identifiable health information to the extent that the state law is less stringent than the federal regime. The stimulus bill extends the pre-emption and its limitation to its new provisions of HIPAA. (Section 13421, applying 42 USC 1320d-7 to the new provisions). State Attorneys General will recognize that this provision follows the familiar formula characterizing the federal law as the "floor," and state law as a higher standard. Existing HIPAA case law does not provide much guidance as to how state enforcement may develop, because almost all federal enforcement has been conducted in an administrative and collaborative setting, rather than as adversarial litigation. While it seems that HIPAA enforcement could reasonably be combined with supplemental jurisdiction state law privacy claims, it is unclear how frequently such claims will arise. It remains to be seen how state Attorneys General will make use of this new-found authority.[247]

3. The First Action by a State Attorney General

On January 13, 2010, the first action was filed by a state attorney general against a health care entity for violation of HIPAA. The Attorney General of Connecticut filed a lawsuit in U.S. District Court against Health Net of the North East, Inc. and its affiliates (collectively "Health Net") for failing to secure the patient medical records of over 500,000 Connecticut citizens. Health Net had either lost or had stolen a portable computer hard drive containing unencrypted protected medical information along with individuals' personal and financial information.

---

244. Maryland's Confidentiality of Medical Records Act (MCMRA), § 4-309(d).
245. Pub. L. No. 104-191 (1996) (Health Insurance Portability and Accountability Act of 1996), at § 1178(a)(1).
246. Pub. L. No. 104-191 (1996) (Health Insurance Portability and Accountability Act of 1996), at § 1178(a)(1).
247. *NAAGazette*, Vol. 3, No. 2, March 25, 2009.

In addition to the HIPAA violation, the Attorney General pursued state law claims under the Connecticut State Unfair Trade Practices Act.

The matter was settled six months later with Health Net paying $250,000 to the State, with an additional contingent payment to the State of $500,000, should it be established, within a defined time, that the lost hard drive was subsequently accessed and personal information used illegally, thereby impacting health plan members. In addition, Health Net agreed to provide credit monitoring, cover costs for security freezes and identity theft insurance, and implement a detailed "Corrective Action Plan."

4. Private Rights of Action

HIPAA does not provide for a private right of action for individuals harmed by violation of the statute. As modified via the HITECH Act, although there is still no private cause of action for HIPAA violations, HHS is now directed to adopt a methodology for allowing affected individuals to share in those civil monetary penalties imposed under HIPAA. Such a methodology must be in place within three years of HITECH's enactment, by 2012. Once implemented, this provision will substantially increase the incentive for individuals to file privacy and security complaints with HHS.

However, private rights of action are available to individuals under certain state health information privacy and security statutes. For example:

- *Texas law* allows patients the right to injunctive relief and damages for unauthorized release of health care information by hospitals.[248]
- Under *Montana law*, any person aggrieved by the unauthorized disclosure of health care information by a health care provider *not* subject to HIPAA may recover damages for pecuniary loss. If the violation results from willful or grossly negligent conduct, the aggrieved person may recover up to $5,000, exclusive of any demonstrated economic loss.[249]
- Under *California law*, any patient whose medical information is disclosed and who sustains an economic loss or personal injury as a result is entitled to recover compensatory damages, punitive damages (not to exceed $3,000), attorneys' fees (not to exceed $1,000), and the costs of litigation.[250]

As one of its broad and numerous functions, HIPAA is aimed at protecting the privacy and security of patient individually identifiable health information. However, HIPAA is not the exclusive method of achieving this goal, as other avenues exist under state laws, many of which, unlike HIPAA, do allow individuals a private right of action. Given the dramatic state of flux in the health care markets and health care legislation, it remains unclear how all of these numerous federal and state statutes, regulations, rules, protections, and remedies will interact over the next few years.

248. Tex. Health & Safety Code Ann. § 241.156.
249. Mont. Code Ann. §§ 50-16-553, 50-15-505.
250. Cal. Civ. Code § 56.35.

2.3 INTERNATIONAL LAWS

The legal approach to privacy in the United States is often characterized as a patchwork quilt of sectoral laws at federal and state levels, with an overlay of judicial and regulatory contract, tort, and fair trading doctrines. These laws address confidentiality and data security in specific contexts and industry sectors where there is an identified harm, such as fraud, identity theft, child predation, discrimination, or adverse decisions based on inaccurate information in governmental or commercial databases. There is little harmonization of terminology, standards, procedures, or remedies across the range of U.S. privacy-related laws.

By contrast, the majority of other industrialized nations have enacted more comprehensive privacy legislation applicable in many cases to both the public and private sectors. The privacy legislation then drives the information security requirements as provisions in these statutes. These international privacy laws are generally based on one of two models:

- The European data protection scheme established by the 1995 Data Protection Directive[251]
- The OECD Guidelines[252] and the Privacy Framework of the Asia-Pacific Economic Cooperation (APEC)[253]

International privacy and information security laws often recognize a constitutional right to privacy in personal and family life and generally establish fair information practices. Fair information practices include the principles of purpose limitation, data quality, notice, consent, individual rights of access and objection, security, and accountability. The security principle typically requires maintaining "reasonable and appropriate" safeguards to protect personal information. Regulations and official guidance in some countries establish specific requirements such as written security policies and the implementation of security measures such as encryption. Data breach notification is increasingly recommended or required under global privacy laws.

In addition, comprehensive privacy schemes often establish a governmental agency to enforce the law and assist individuals impacted by a privacy violation. In Europe, supervisory authorities are often referred to generically as "data protection authorities." The European data protection model is commonly viewed as the most restrictive, requiring companies processing personal information to register with data protection authorities or (in some countries) establish an in-house data protection officer with statutory responsibilities, as well as prohibiting data transfers to countries, including the United States, that lack similar comprehensive data privacy laws unless certain conditions are met.

---

251. *EU Data Protection Directive, Directive 95/46/EC of the European Parliament and of the Council of 24 October 1995 on the protection of individuals with regard to the processing of personal data and on the free movement of such data,* http://eur-lex.europa.eu/LexUriServ/LexUriServ.do?uri=CELEX:31995L0046:EN:HTML.

252. *OECD Guidelines on the Protection of Privacy and Transborder Flows of Personal Data* (1980), http://www.oecd.org/document/18/0,2340,en_2649_34255_1815186_119820_1_1_1,00.html.

253. *APEC Privacy Framework* (2004), http://www.apec.org/apec/news_media/2004_media_releases/201104_apecminsendorseprivacyfrmwk.html.

This chapter looks at the four countries/regions of the world outside the United States with the most developed information security and privacy law: Canada, Europe, Asia-Pacific, and Latin America. As it is essential to develop a fundamental understanding of the privacy statutes in each country where an organization operates, numerous external references are provided.

A. Canada

Canada is a federal state with a number of data protection laws governing the processing of personal information. Comprehensive legislation, for private-sector organizations, exists in the form of the federal Personal Information Protection and Electronic Documents Act[254] (PIPEDA), as well as provincial statutes in British Columbia,[255] Alberta,[256] and Quebec.[257] Determining which laws apply requires an analysis of a number of factors, but PIPEDA contains a mechanism to avoid duplicate coverage by exempting organizations already subject to "substantially similar" provincial legislation."[258]

The federal law incorporates the Canadian Standards Association's *Model Code for the Protection of Personal Information*[259] (the CSA Code) as a Schedule to PIPEDA, and the text of the statute either adds to or varies the obligations found in the CSA Code. Provincial laws enacted to date take a different form by incorporating the substance of the Code directly into legislative provisions. Both federal and provincial approaches to privacy/data protection are similar, and there is a considerable degree of cooperation between Canadian federal and provincial privacy commissioners to minimize multiple enforcement proceedings. Several provinces[260] have also enacted sector-specific legislation that governs personal health information and the protection of such data.

Canadian data protection legislation is less prescriptive than U.S. statutes and regulations on required security measures. Canadian requirements are general in nature and focus on "reasonableness" linked directly to the "sensitivity" of the information: the greater the sensitivity of the information (e.g., health information, financial information), the greater the expected degree of protection to be afforded.

254. S.C. 2000, ch. 5.

255. Personal Information Protection Act, S.B.C. 203, ch. 63.

256. Personal Information Protection Act, S.A. 2003, ch. P-6.5.

257. An Act Respecting the Protection of Personal Information in the Private Sector, R.S.Q., ch. P-39.1.

258. *See* s. 26(2)(b) of PIPEDA, which provides the federal Governor-in-Council with the power to issue orders exempting an organization, activity, or class from the application of the statute.

259. CAN/CSA-Q830-96.

260. As of October 2010, the following statutes were in force: Alberta, Health Information Act, R.S.A. ch. H-4.8; Saskatchewan, Health Information Protection Act, S.S., ch. 0.021; Manitoba, Personal Health Information Act, C.C.S.M. ch. P33.5; Ontario, Personal Health Information Protection Act, 2004, S.O. 2004, ch. 3, Sch. A; New Brunswick, Personal Health Information Privacy and Access Act, S.N.B. 2009, ch. P-7.05. Other provinces have introduced or enacted such legislation but not all are yet in force: Newfoundland, Personal Health Information Act, S.N.L. 2008, ch. P-7.01; Nova Scotia, Personal Health Information Act (introduced Nov. 4, 2009).

Principle 7 of the CSA Code, found in PIPEDA's Schedule 1, is representative and states the security requirement simply: "Personal information shall be protected by security safeguards appropriate to the sensitivity of the information."[261]

The comprehensive statutes in British Columbia and Alberta[262] call for "reasonable security arrangements to prevent unauthorized access, collection, use, disclosure, copying, modification or disposal or similar risks."

Quebec's statute[263] requires the following: "A person carrying on an enterprise must take the security measures necessary to ensure the protection of the personal information collected, used, communicated, kept or destroyed and that are reasonable given the sensitivity of the information, the purposes for which it is to be used, the quantity and distribution of the information and the medium on which it is stored."

The Personal Information Protection Act (PIPA), drafted in concert but enacted separately in each of the provinces of Alberta and British Columbia, specifies a standard for "reasonable" as "what a reasonable person would consider appropriate in the circumstances."[264] Security that meets the "reasonable" standard is generally accepted to encompass physical, technical, and procedural security measures that reflect good personal information handling practices (i.e., policies, procedures, retention schedules). Such practices are to be diligently and consistently executed, which depends, in turn, on ongoing privacy training of staff and management. Organizations are encouraged to conduct risk assessments and implement appropriate preventive measures.[265] Such assessments should consider key factors such as the reasonable foreseeability of risk, the likelihood of risk, and the seriousness of potential harm.[266]

Accountability is another concept found in Canadian privacy laws that is relevant to the security aspects of Canadian privacy statutes where third parties provide services in various "outsourcing" scenarios. Generally, data protection statutes consider personal information handled by third-party service providers to be the responsibility of the party

---

261. *See* PIPEDA, Schedule 1. The balance of the text associated with Principle 7 is short and reproduced here:

4.7.1: The security safeguards shall protect personal information against loss or theft, as well as unauthorized access, disclosure, copying, use, or modification. Organizations shall protect personal information regardless of the format in which it is held.

4.7.2: The nature of the safeguards will vary depending on the sensitivity of the information that has been collected, the amount, distribution, and format of the information, and the method of storage. More sensitive information should be safeguarded by a higher level of protection. The concept of sensitivity is discussed in Clause 4.3.4.

4.7.3: The methods of protection should include (*a*) physical measures, for example, locked filing cabinets and restricted access to offices; (*b*) organizational measures, for example, security clearances and limiting access on a "need-to-know" basis; and (*c*) technological measures, for example, the use of passwords and encryption.

4.7.4: Organizations shall make their employees aware of the importance of maintaining the confidentiality of personal information.

4.7.5: Care shall be used in the disposal or destruction of personal information, to prevent unauthorized parties from gaining access to the information (see Clause 4.5.3).

262. *See* § 34 of each of the Alberta and British Columbia Personal Information Protection Acts.

263. Section 10.

264. *See* § 2 of the Alberta and British Columbia statutes.

265. *See*, as examples, federal Privacy Commissioner reports in PIPEDA Case Summaries #2007-377 and #2008-395.

266. *See* Alberta PIPA Advisory #8, *Implementing Reasonable Security*, for a useful guide to appropriate physical, technical, and procedural security measures in a variety of situations.

contracting out the service—usually but not always the initial "collector" of the personal information.[267] Accordingly, organizations that contract out must ensure that such third parties have a comparable level of protection in place for the personal information they process.[268] This protection is usually accomplished through the use of specific security and incident notification provisions in, or appended to, the service agreement.

Data breach notification requirements are currently in force in two provincial statutes: Ontario's Personal Health Information Protection Act[269] (PHIPA) and Alberta's PIPA.[270] Several personal health information statutes, in the process of being fully enacted in Atlantic Canada, also contain data breach notification provisions. Ontario's PHIPA breach notification provisions, enacted in 2004, are the oldest in Canada and provide a requirement to "notify the individual at the first reasonable opportunity if the information is stolen, lost, or accessed by unauthorized persons."[271]

Alberta has recently amended its PIPA to require organizations to notify Alberta's Privacy Commissioner of incidents involving loss of, unauthorized access to, or other disclosure of personal information where a reasonable person would consider that there exists a real risk of significant harm to an individual. In the event of a breach the Privacy Commissioner may require the organization to notify those individuals to whom there is a real risk of substantial harm. This power attaches regardless of whether breach has been properly reported.

The federal government has taken a "two-stage" approach similar to that found in Alberta by amending PIPEDA[272] to address security breaches and impose a notification requirement. Upon enactment and coming into force, these amendments would require any "material" breach of security safeguards involving personal information to be reported to the Privacy Commissioner of Canada. Whether a breach is "material" would depend on the sensitivity of the information, the number of individuals affected, and whether there is a systemic problem.

If it is reasonable to believe that the breach in question creates a "real risk" of significant harm to individuals, then such individuals are to be notified as soon as feasible. Whether a "real risk" exists depends on the sensitivity of the information and the probability that the personal information has been, is being, or will be misused. Such notifications are to contain sufficient information to allow the individuals affected to understand the significance of the breach and permit them to take steps to reduce or mitigate the risk of any resulting harm.

---

267. The "initial collector" and associated responsibilities may be considered somewhat analogous to the European concept of a "data controller."

268. *See, e.g.*, PIPEDA Case Summary #2007-377.

269. *See* § 12 of Ontario's Personal Health Information Protection Act.

270. *See* § 37.1 of Alberta's Personal Information Protection Amendment Act, 2009.

271. *See* § 12(2) of PHIPA.

272. Bill C-29 introduced into Parliament on May 25, 2010.

B. Europe

1. EU Law

The European Commission and Parliament promulgate directives, which must be approved by a weighted majority vote of the EU Member State governments, designed to harmonize national laws in the EU. A directive[273] is not legislation; rather, it serves as a framework or model law establishing minimum requirements each Member State must "transpose" into national legislation by the implementation date.[274] The European Commission is responsible for ensuring that "EU law," including harmonization directives, is applied throughout the EU.[275]

The 1995 EU Data Protection Directive (DPD)[276] is an example of such a measure. Thus, a multinational company with entities located in several European countries must comply with the national laws of each jurisdiction in which it collects, stores, or otherwise processes personal data. Those laws will be similar, but they will also reflect some local differences in substance and procedure.

Those differences may be significant for global organizations, as the following examples illustrate:

- **Breach Notice.** While harmonized security breach notice rules are still under consideration at EU level, several countries have moved forward with their own approaches to requiring notification of security breaches involving personal data. Germany and Austria have now legislated security breach notice obligations, while other countries, prominently France, are considering similar legislation. Section 42a of the German BDSG (federal data protection act), as amended in 2009, requires notice to both affected individuals and the relevant data protection authority in the event of a significant breach involving sensitive personal data, including bank account or payment card details. These provisions apply to data collected in Germany, even if the breach occurs elsewhere.[277] The 2010 amendments to the Austrian data protection act (DSG) added paragraph 2a to Section 24, requiring notification of systematic and serious security breaches that may entail harm to the data subjects.[278]
- **Labor Law.** The interaction of German data protection law and labor law results in a requirement that companies obtain a favorable written opinion from both an internal data protection officer and from a works council of elected employee representatives before allowing German employee data to be

273. http://ec.europa.eu/community_law/directives/directives_en.htm.

274. A timetable for implementing EU directives nationally is available at http://ec.europa.eu/community_law/directives/directives_echeancier_en.htm.

275. http://ec.europa.eu/community_law/index_en.htm. The EU institutions also promulgate regulations and decisions, but in the field of data protection the relevant instruments have been harmonization directives.

276. *See* footnote 251.

277. An English translation of the amended BDSG is available at http://www.bfdi.bund.de/cae/servlet/contentblob/1086936/publicationFile/87568/BDSG_idFv01092009.pdf.

278. The amended DSG is available (in German) at http://www.ris.bka.gv.at/GeltendeFassung.wxe?Abfrage=Bundesnormen&Gesetzesnummer=10001597.

processed by an outsourcing vendor in India or accessed by a global headquarters in the United States.[279]

- **Encryption.** Spanish data protection regulations generally require encryption of sensitive personal information.[280]
- **Prior Authorization.** The French data protection authority CNIL advises employers that they must seek prior authorization to transfer sensitive employee data (including social security numbers, bank account details, and family information) to a global HR system.[281] The EU DPD applies by treaty not only to the 27 EU Member States[282] but also to the three additional members of the European Economic Area—Iceland, Liechtenstein, and Norway.[283] In addition, several countries outside the EU/EEA, such as Switzerland and Russia, have adopted data protection legislation modeled on the EU Data Protection Directive.

2. *European Data Protection Authorities*

European data protection supervisory authorities (DPAs) have investigative powers and can typically issue administrative orders, impose fines, and refer suspected violations to public prosecutors. In addition, they publish guidance documents and, in many countries, operate a central registry of data-processing activities involving personal information. The DPAs are national in most countries, but in Germany's federal system each state has a data protection authority responsible for supervising data controllers in the private sector.

The Article 29 Working Party on the Protection of Individuals with regard to the Processing of Personal Data is an independent advisory body established by Article 29 of the EU DPD. It is composed of representatives from the national data protection authorities of the EU Member States, the European Data Protection Supervisor, and the European Commission. The Article 29 Working Party is competent to examine any question covering the application of a data protection directive to ensure the uniform implementation of the directives. It carries out this task by issuing recommendations, opinions, and working documents.[284]

---

279. *See, e.g.*, H.-J. Reinhard, *Information Technology and Workers' Privacy: The German Law*, 23 Comp. Law & Policy J. 398 (2005), available online at http://www.law.uiuc.edu/publications/cll&pj/archive/vol_23/issue_2/ReinhardCountryArticle23-2.pdf.

280. *See* Royal Decree 994/1999 (adopting Regulation on Mandatory Security Measures), Art. 23 (unofficial English translation available from the Spanish data protection authority at https://www.agpd.es/portalwebAGPD/english_resources/regulations/common/pdfs/reglamento_ingles_pdf.pdf).

281. *See Guide pour les employeurs et les salariés*, p. 17 (CNIL, 2010) available online, in French, at http://www.cnil.fr/fileadmin/documents/Guides_pratiques/CNIL_GuideTravail.pdf).

282. The EU Member States currently are: Austria, Belgium, Bulgaria, Cyprus, Czech Republic, Denmark, Estonia, Finland, France, Germany, Greece, Hungary, Ireland, Italy, Latvia, Lithuania, Luxembourg, Malta, Netherlands, Poland, Portugal, Romania, Slovakia, Slovenia, Spain, Sweden, and the United Kingdom.

283. http://ec.europa.eu/external_relations/eea/.

284. http://ec.europa.eu/justice_home/fsj/privacy/workinggroup/index_en.htm.

3. 1995 Data Protection Directive

The primary source of data privacy requirements in the EU is the DPD.[285] The DPD applies to any commercial use of "personal data," defined as data relating to a natural person—a "data subject"—who is identified or identifiable from the data.

Any use of personal data is referred to as "processing," defined broadly as: "Any operation or set of operations which is performed upon personal data, whether or not by automatic means, such as collection, recording, organization, storage, adaptation or alteration, retrieval, consultation, use, disclosure by transmission, dissemination or otherwise making available, alignment or combination, blocking, erasure or destruction" (Art. 2(b)).

National laws implementing the DPD regulate data "controllers"—entities that, alone or jointly with others, "determine the purposes and means of the processing of personal data" (Art. 2(d)). Data "processors," who process data on behalf of a data controller, are required to use the data only as directed by the controller and to secure the data by appropriate "technical and operational measures."

The national law that applies is the law of any country in which an act of "processing" takes place, excluding the transmission or transit of data across a Member State (Art. 4). A data controller established in a Member State is responsible for ensuring compliance with the laws of that country, as well as the laws where the controller's offices or affiliates are located. Where a data controller is not "established" in the EEA but "makes use of equipment" situated in a Member State, the controller must designate a legal representative in such Member State.

Each Member State must establish an independent supervisory authority (a DPA) with authority to investigate complaints and impose administrative sanctions such as "stop-processing" orders (Art. 28).

Procedures for notification and publication of data processing vary among Member States. The United Kingdom, for example, has an online registration form for all data controllers to complete. Others, such as Spain, require detailed notification in most cases.

The DPD requires Member States to include in their national laws judicial remedies for injured persons, including compensation and suitable sanctions (Art. 22–24).

The DPD embodies principles of fair information practices. Personal data must be collected for "specified, explicit and legitimate purposes" and processed "fairly and lawfully." The data must be "adequate, relevant, and not excessive" in relation to the purpose for which it was collected and retained no longer than necessary to fulfill the purpose of collection.

The DPD generally requires prior notice to collection. Consent is not always required. A data controller may process personal data without consent if, for example, it can establish a legal obligation or a legitimate interest that outweighs the privacy interests. Data subjects have the right to access, modify, and request deletion of their personal data.

The DPD defines certain types of data as "sensitive" requiring "explicit prior consent" from the data subject to process the data unless one of the exceptions applies (Art. 8).

285. *See* footnote 251.

"Sensitive" data includes information relating to racial or ethnic origin; political opinions; religious or philosophical beliefs; trade-union membership; health or sex life; and criminal history. Some Member States have expanded the definition of sensitive data in their national laws. France, for example, considers Social Security numbers to be sensitive data, requiring consent or official authorization to share such data.

4. Data Transfers

Under Article 25 of the DPD, the transfer of personal data to "third countries" (i.e., outside the EEA) is prohibited unless the country receiving the data provides an "adequate level of protection." The European Commission determines whether the laws of another country are adequate. Article 26 offers some exceptions, such as transfers made with the fully informed and unambiguous consent of the data subject, transfers necessary for the performance of a contract, and transfers subject to contractual safeguards ("Model Contracts")[286] or "Binding Corporate Rules" approved by the European Commission.

These alternatives are important, as the United States (along with most of the other countries outside Europe) has not been found to afford an "adequate level of protection." A company in the United States may avail itself of another option—self-certification of compliance with the "Safe Harbor Privacy Principles" negotiated between the European Commission and the U.S. Department of Commerce in 2000.[287] The Safe Harbor Privacy Principles include a general security obligation.

The European Commission found the Swiss Federal Act on Data Protection to provide adequate protection for the transfer of personal data from the EU to Switzerland. In late 2008, U.S. and Swiss officials created the U.S.-Swiss Safe Harbor Framework.[288] The Safe Harbor Principles of the EU-U.S. Safe Harbor are the same as those for the U.S.-Swiss Safe Harbor. An organization can join either or both Safe Harbors.

In October 2009, the United States and the EU recognized a set of core privacy principles intended to ensure the protection of personal data transferred in connection with law enforcement and security.[289] Referred to as the High Level Contact Group (HLCG) Principles, they identify common principles of an effective regime for privacy. While the Principles are not binding, they are a further step toward a binding international agreement. The HLCG was formed in late 2006 to enable the EU and the United States to work more efficiently together in the cross-border exchange of law enforcement data while ensuring adequate data protection safeguards.

5. Information Security

The provisions of the DPD are supplemented by Directive 58/2002, the e-Privacy Directive,[290] which requires providers of public electronic communication services (including ISPs) to take appropriate technical and organizational measures to secure their services. Both Directives require security measures to be appropriate to the risk

286. *See* http://ec.europa.eu/justice_home/fsj/privacy/modelcontracts/index_en.htm.
287. *See* www.export.gov/safeharbor.
288. http://www.export.gov/safeharbor/swiss/index.asp.
289. http://useu.usmission.gov.
290. Available at http://eur-lex.europa.eu/LexUriServ/LexUriServ.do?uri=CELEX:32002L0058:EN:HTML.

presented by the data processing with regard to available technology and the cost of implementation. "Technical" safeguards may include encryption, firewalls, and antivirus software, while "organizational" measures typically include management of access privileges, policies, employee training, and vendor management.

The DPD requires data controllers to implement appropriate technical and organizational measures to protect personal data against loss, unauthorized destruction, alteration, disclosure or access, and unlawful processing (Art. 17). Some Member States, such as Italy and Spain, have included detailed security requirements in their national laws. Where a data controller outsources the processing of personal data, it must exercise due diligence in selecting the processor. It must further require under a contract that the third party use the data only as instructed by the data controller and implement data security measures.

6. *Data Breach Notification*

EU law does not include a general requirement to provide notice of a security breach. Member State DPAs have, however, opined that such an obligation may be inferred from the general obligation to provide notice to individuals, DPAs, or internal data protection officers. The e-Privacy Directive, amended by Directive 136/2009, requires telecommunications service providers and ISPs to report data security breaches to the applicable national authority.[291] Where there is a likelihood of adverse impact on the personal data or privacy of a subscriber, the service provider must also notify the affected subscriber. Member States must implement this requirement into national law by May 2011. The e-Privacy Directive also requires Member States to address the appropriate form of user notice and consent for Internet cookies and related tracking technologies.[292]

C. Asia-Pacific

In Asia each country has its own approach to data privacy, requiring an analysis of the laws of each jurisdiction. While many countries have adopted a regional framework and have incorporated the framework's principles into their national laws, the framework and other regional agreements are not mandatory. As a result, variations exist among the countries. This section, after introducing the regional framework, discusses each of the major countries in the region. Asia-Pacific is a very large geographic area containing many nations, ranging from Russia in the north to New Zealand in the south, from India in the west to Japan in the east. While the parties to this regional framework agreement are from both sides of the Pacific Ocean, those on the eastern side are discussed in the U.S., Canada, or Latin America sections of this chapter while those on the western side of the ocean are discussed in this section.

291. Directive 2009/136/EC Of the European Parliament and of The Council of 25 November 2009 amending Directive 2002/22/EC on universal service and users' rights relating to electronic communications networks and services, Directive 2002/58/EC concerning the processing of personal data and the protection of privacy in the electronic communications sector, and Regulation (EC) No 2006/2004 on cooperation between national authorities responsible for the enforcement of consumer protection laws.

292. *Id.* at recital 66.

1. The APEC Privacy Framework

Most Asia-Pacific countries are members of the Asia-Pacific Economic Cooperation (APEC)[293] and have incorporated the principles of the APEC Privacy Framework into their respective national laws or have made a commitment to APEC to do so.

The APEC Privacy Framework[294] consists of the following nine principles:

1. *Preventing Harm:* To individuals from the wrongful collection and misuse of personal information.
2. *Notice:* Individuals should be provided either before or at the time of collection of personal information clear and easily accessible statements about the data collector's practices and policies.
3. *Collection Limitation:* Personal information should be lawfully collected and limited to adequate information.
4. *Uses of Personal Information:* Personal information should be used only for the purposes it was collected unless an exception applies.
5. *Choice:* Individuals should have choice regarding the collection, use, and disclosure of their personal information.
6. *Integrity of Personal Information:* Personal information should be accurate, complete, and current.
7. *Security Safeguards:* Personal information should be protected against loss, unauthorized access, unauthorized destruction, use, modification, or disclosure.
8. *Access and Correction:* Individuals should be able to access, correct, and delete their personal information.
9. *Accountability:* The information controller is accountable for compliance and should obtain consent prior to any data transfers. Reasonable steps should be taken to ensure that the recipient will protect the information consistently with these Principles.

The principles of the APEC Privacy Framework closely track the OECD Guidelines but with greater attention on notice and choice and a new principle—prevention of harm—added.

2. Cross-Border Privacy Rules

To further the implementation of the APEC Privacy Framework, a Cross-Border Privacy Rules (CBPRs) system was developed in 2007. CBPRs are intended to facilitate cross-border information flows while providing oversight and enforcement. "Accountability agents" as well as regulators would ensure businesses comply with their privacy promises.[295] Accountability agents include privacy commissioners, government agencies, and privacy trustmarks, which are well established in a number of countries in Asia. In

293. APEC member countries are Australia, Brunei Darussalam, Canada, Chile, People's Republic of China, Hong Kong, Indonesia, Japan, Republic of Korea, Malaysia, Mexico, New Zealand, Papua New Guinea, Peru, the Philippines, Russia, Singapore, Chinese Taipei (Taiwan), Thailand, the United States, and Vietnam.

294. http://www.apec.org/apec/apec_groups/committee_on_trade/electronic_commerce.html.

295. For a detailed summary and action plan for Cross-Border Privacy Rules, please see http://aimp.apec.org/Documents/2008/ECSG/ECSG1/08_ecsg1_024.doc.

July 2010, the APEC Cross-Border Privacy Enforcement Arrangement (CPEA)[296] was established as a framework for the voluntary sharing of information and provision of assistance among Privacy Enforcement Authorities in APEC member economies.[297]

3. *Australia*

The primary federal statute applying to the public sector is the Federal Privacy Act of 1988.[298] The Act established the Office of the Privacy Commissioner. This law was amended by the Privacy Amendment Act of 2000 that applies to the private sector and contains ten National Privacy Principles (NPPs) that an organization must follow unless it drafts a privacy code that is approved by the Privacy Commissioner. These principles cover limits on collection, use and disclosure, data quality, data security, openness, access and correction, identifiers, anonymity, and sensitive information.

This law applies to all health service providers and only those organizations (including nonprofits) with annual revenues exceeding AUD 3 million. It also applies to organizations that sell or rent personal information but does not apply to the journalism activities of media organizations or to an action by an employer in the context of the employment relationship. The transfer of personal information to a foreign country is permitted only if the recipient follows similar privacy principles, if consent is obtained, or for performance of a contract to which the individual is a party or that is in his or her interest.

Personal information controllers should protect personal information that they hold with appropriate safeguards against risks, such as loss or unauthorized access or unauthorized destruction, use, modification, or disclosure. Such safeguards should be proportional to the likelihood and severity of the harm threatened, the sensitivity of the information, and the context in which it is held and should be subject to periodic review and reassessment. Personal information must be destroyed or de-identified if it is no longer needed.

This law may be enforced directly by an individual, or the Office of the Privacy Commissioner may initiate an investigation. Before the Commissioner may take action on behalf of an individual, the individual must first attempt to resolve the matter directly with the organization. Most complaints are resolved in this manner. If the complaint is not resolved, the Commissioner will attempt to mediate the dispute. If mediation fails, the Commissioner can make a formal determination of violation, which is enforceable by a federal court.

While Australia has not yet enacted data breach legislation, the Privacy Commissioner published a voluntary Guide to Handling Personal Information Security Breaches in 1998.[299] The steps and actions outlined in the guide are not specifically required under the Privacy Act of 1988. In mid-2010, Australia released its roadmap for updating of the

---

296. The full text of the Cross-Border Privacy Enforcement Arrangement is available at http://aimp.apec.org/Documents/2010/ECSG/DPS1/10_ecsg_dps1_013.pdf.

297. The CPEA Factsheet is available at http://www.apec.org/apec/news_media/fact_sheets/ 201006cpea.html.

298. The Privacy Act of 1988 is available at http://www.privacy.gov.au/law/act.

299. Available at http://www.privacy.gov.au/materials/types/guidelines/view/6478.

Privacy Act with the Australian Privacy Principles, including new focus on transborder data disclosures instead of data flows and on direct marketing, with additional releases forthcoming on health information and credit reporting.[300]

4. China

China has no single, comprehensive statute for data privacy. China's Constitution (Article 38) provides for a limited right of privacy.[301] Criminal privacy sanctions, civil statutes covering privacy of personality and reputation, provincial consumer protection regulations, and sectoral regulations (covering banking, outsourcing, employees, managing computer information networks, etc.) provide additional safeguards.

The Administrative Regulations for Employment Services and Employment, effective January 2008, require employers to keep employees' data confidential and obtain prior written consent before publicizing the data. For information security, regulations enacted in 2009 require companies in China providing outsourcing services to implement security measures to protect confidential information received in the course of providing those services.

The Tortious Liability Law of 2009 amended China's Criminal Law, imposing penalties for the illegal sale of personal data collected by certain organizations. The law recognizes privacy as a legally protected interest. The law requires medical personnel to keep patient records confidential and provides for fines where a violation causes harm. It provides for criminal penalties, including fines and imprisonment, for the illegal sale or disclosure of personal information collected by a government or financial entity, a telecom, a transportation provider, or an educational or medical institution.

Article 7 of the Computer Information Network and Internet Security, Protection and Management Regulations provides that the freedom and privacy of network users is protected by law and that no one may use the Internet to violate the privacy of others. The law also specifies that individual users must be registered and that all those engaged in the Internet business are subject to security supervision, inspection, and guidance.[302]

Measures for the Administration of Internet E-mail Services, implemented in 2006, protect the privacy of correspondence in using Internet e-mail services.[303] Exceptions allow a public security organization to inspect the contents of correspondence when required by national security or investigation of crimes.

Electronic banking regulations require financial institutions to take proper protective measures and guarantee the safety of their electronic banking facilities, equipment, and data.[304] Specific information security requirements include:

---

300. Australia, *Australian Privacy Principles,* Exposure Draft (2010).

301. Constitution of the People's Republic of China.

302. *See* http://www.fas.org/irp/world/china/netreg.htm.

303. Article 3, Measures for the Administration of Internet E-mail Services, *available at* http://www.chinaitlaw.org/?p1=print&p2=060604172055.

304. The "Measures Governing Electronic Banking." adopted by China's Banking Regulatory Commission and effective March 1, 2006, *available at* http://fdi.gov.cn/pub/FDI_EN/Laws/Banking/t20060620_52045.jsp.

- **Article 37.** Use of firewalls, antivirus software, and other safe products and technologies to guarantee that electronic banking has enough anti-attack capacity, antivirus capacity, and intrusion prevention capacity;
- **Article 38.** Use of proper encryption technologies and measures to guarantee the safety and confidentiality of transmission of electronic transaction data, as well as the entirety, authenticity, and undeniability of the transmitted transaction data; and
- **Article 40.** Adoption of proper measures and technologies to identify and verify the authentic identities of customers of electronic banking services.

5. Hong Kong

The Personal Data (Privacy) Ordinance of 1995 (PDPO) establishes the following six Data Protection Principles and limits automated reporting, direct marketing, and external data transfers.

- *Purpose and Manner of Collection of Personal Data (P1):* Data should be collected in a lawful purpose and manner, directly related to the purpose of collection, with notice given to the individual.
- *Accuracy and Duration of Retention of Personal Data (P2):* Data must be accurate and not kept any longer than necessary.
- *Use of Personal Data (P3):* Data must be used for purposes directly related to collection, unless consent is obtained from the individual.
- *Security of Personal Data (P4):* Security measures must prevent unauthorized access, use, or loss of data.
- *Information to Be Generally Available (P5):* Data user has to make available information about his or her policies and procedures, the information held, and the main purposes thereof.
- *Access to Personal Data (P6):* Individuals have the right to access and correct their data.

In 2010, the Hong Kong Data Commissioner published data breach guidelines. Businesses should notify data subjects of a breach when a "real risk of harm is reasonably foreseeable." Organizations should also notify law enforcement, the Office of the Privacy Commissioner, and relevant regulatory agencies. The Commissioner has published a template form[305] for organizations to use when providing notice to the Commissioner.

The Privacy Commissioner is empowered under the PDPO to serve an enforcement notice to a data user who contravenes a requirement under the PDPO (Section 50). A data user who contravenes the PDPO requirements (other than contravention of data protection principles) commits an offense and is liable on conviction to fine and imprisonment (Section 64). Section 66 of the PDPO provides that an individual who suffers damage due to a contravention of a requirement of the PDPO by a data user shall be entitled to compensation from the data user for that damage.

305. http://www.pcpd.org.hk/english/publications/files/Notification_Form_e.pdf.

6. India

India does not currently have a comprehensive information security and privacy law. Protection is possible under other laws dealing with contracts, criminal acts, intellectual property, and information technology. The right to privacy has been recognized by the Supreme Court of India as an integral part of the fundamental right to life and personal liberty, guaranteed to every individual under the Constitution of India. Fundamental rights, however, can only be enforced against the state. The Indian courts have also addressed privacy rights and data protection. The courts in India have interpreted the provisions of the Constitution of India, the Indian Contract Act,[306] the Indian Penal Code (IPC),[307] the Specific Relief Act (Relief Act),[308] the Indian Copyright Act of 1957 (Copyright Act),[309] and other existing legislation to protect the privacy rights of individuals in India.

The existing Information Technology Act of 2000 (IT Act)[310] prohibits unauthorized access to and theft of data from computers and networks but does not have provisions explicitly dealing with data privacy. The IT Act addresses computer crime, hacking, damage of source code, breach of confidentiality, and viewing of pornographic material. In addition, the Central Bureau of Investigation has set up the Cyber Crime Investigation Cell (CCIC), with a mandate to investigate offenses under the IT Act and other crimes involving use of technology.[311]

Software companies and business organizations within India, including the National Association of Software and Service Companies (NASSCOM), have created compliance guidelines to be followed by companies.[312] In the absence of a specific law, parties have to rely on contractual provisions to protect data privacy. These provisions include terms to make contracts compliant with the GLBA, HIPAA, FACTA, the U.K. Data Protection Act of 1998,[313] and other related laws and information security standards such as ISO 27001 (see Chapter 5). Generally, these contracts specify the manner in which information may be disclosed and provide for implementation of safeguards that appropriately protect the confidentiality and integrity of the data provided to the outsourcing companies.[314]

However, the use of contractual safeguards and self-regulatory measures does not completely satisfy all the foreign companies. For this reason, the Data Security Council of India (DSCI) was created to establish, popularize, monitor, and enforce privacy and data protection standards for India's outsourcing industry.[315] DSCI seeks to adopt the best global practices, drawing on U.S. laws, the EU Directive, and other guidelines in designing a model Code of Conduct for the outsourcing industry. In furtherance of its

306. Act No. 9 of 1872, 1* (April 25, 1872).
307. IPC, Act No. 45 of 1860.
308. Act No. 47 of 1963.
309. *See* http://www.education.nic.in/cpract.pdf.
310. The Information Technology Act of 2000 (ITA-2000) is an Act of the Indian Parliament (No. 21 of 2000).
311. *See* http://cbi.nic.in/aboutus/manuals/Chapter_18.pdf.
312. *See* http://infotech.indiatimes.com/articleshow/730193.cms.
313. *See* www.ico.gov.uk.
314. *See* http://www.nasscom.in/Nasscom/templates/NormalPage.aspx?id=28502.
315. *See* http://www.nasscom.in/Nasscom/templates/NormalPage.aspx?id=51973.

objectives, DSCI intends to put in place security standards by introducing certification marks for the outsourcing industry.[316]

7. Indonesia

Indonesia does not have a comprehensive privacy law. However, the Electronic Information and Electronic Transactions Law[317] establishes a general right of privacy. While this right is not specifically described, the law allows the government to develop implementing regulations to align Indonesia's laws with the APEC Privacy Framework. The law requires consent for use of an individual's private or personal information through electronic media, with certain exceptions. This requirement does apply to employee data held by employers.

In addition, the other laws address data protection. Article 14 of Act No. 39 of 1999 concerning human rights provides that all people have the right to communicate and obtain the information they need to develop themselves as individuals and to develop their social environment and to seek, obtain, own, store, process, and impart information using all available facilities. Article 2 of Act No. 6 of 1963 requires that all medical workers keep medical records confidential, except upon permission of the court for the purposes of criminal investigation. Act No. 8 of 1981 prohibits publication of the content of police investigation reports.[318]

Indonesia's legal framework does not include information security requirements. Indonesia's Criminal Code (Article 322.1) imposes penalties for the intentional disclosure of confidential information.

8. Japan

Japan's 1946 Constitution proclaims that "[f]reedom of assembly and association as well as speech, press and all other forms of expression are guaranteed." The 1988 Act for the Protection of Computer Processed Personal Data Held by Administrative Organisations and the 1990 Protection of Computer Processed Personal Data Act (based on the OECD Guidelines) provides partial regulation of some national government agencies.

The Personal Information Protection Act of 2003 applies to "Personal Information," which is defined as "[any] information that may make a living individual distinguishable from others." This would include a person's name, address, birth date, birthplace, phone number, financial history, employment history, academic history, occupation, medical history, sex, race, religion, sexual orientation, and so on.

The law applies only to information concerning individuals and does not cover information concerning corporations. The law does not specifically address international data transfers.

316. http://www.dsci.in/images/certification_mark_for_outsourcing_industry_soon.pdfandhttp://economictimes.indiatimes.com/infotech/ites/DSCI-to-implement-data-security-practices-in-IT/BPO-firms-soon/articleshow/5694649.cms.

317. Law No. 11 of 2008.

318. www.pcpd.org.hk/english/infocentre/files/indo_2.doc.

Privacy requirements include:[319]

- *Proper Acquisition* (Articles 17 and 19): The business must obtain personal information by lawful and nondeceptive means and maintain the accuracy of the data.
- *Notice of the Purpose of Utilization at the Time of Acquisition* (Article 18): The business must notify the individual when the information is acquired or its purpose changed, except in certain circumstances described in the act.
- *Supervision* (Article 21): The business must exercise appropriate supervision over its employees and third-party delegates who handle personal data.
- *Restriction of Provision to a Third Party* (Article 23): Personal data cannot be provided to third parties, except if the individual consents or if an exception applies. Outsourcing the processing of personal data to achieve the purpose (e.g., payroll outsourcing) is not defined as a "transfer to a third party."

Information security measures are set forth in Article 20 and require organizations to implement appropriate security controls to prevent loss, leakage, or destruction of personal data. There is no express provision in the law creating an obligation to notify data subjects and/or data authorities in the event of a data security breach. However, there are a number of guidelines issued by government ministries. Some guidelines (e.g., the Guidelines issued by the Financial Service Agency applicable to banking) create an obligation to notify data subjects and/or governmental authorities that issued the guidelines in the event of a data security breach.

The individual may request changes to his or her personal data to correct it, and the business must make such changes. Relevant authorities may issue administrative orders in the case of noncompliance with the law, and criminal penalties may be imposed for failure to observe such administrative orders.

9. Malaysia

Malaysia's Federal Constitution does not specifically recognize a right to privacy. The Personal Data Protection Act of 2010 is Malaysia's first comprehensive privacy legislation.[320] Requirements include notice and consent for the use of personal data, registration of data users, and special requirements for the handling of sensitive personal data such as health information, political and religious beliefs, and criminal allegations.

With certain exceptions, the transfer of personal data outside of Malaysia is prohibited unless the government designates the country receiving the data as providing data protections equivalent to those required by the act. Exceptions include consent and cases in which the data controller has taken all reasonable precautions and exercised all due diligence to ensure the data will not be processed offshore in violation of the act.

---

319. Thomas Shaw, *Asia-Pacific Data Privacy Laws: Model Corporate Privacy Principles*, The Privacy Advisor (March 1, 2010), *available at* https://www.privacyassociation.org/publications/2010_03_01_asia-pacific_data_privacy_law_model_corporate_privacy_principles/.

320. The Personal Data Protection Act is *available at* http://www.parlimen.gov.my/billindexbi/pdf/DR352009E.pdf.

The Act includes data security and data integrity principles, requiring organizations to take reasonable steps to protect personal data and ensure that it is accurate, complete, and not misleading. The Act also establishes the Office of the Data Protection Commissioner, empowered to regulate direct marketing and exports of personal data.

The Act does not create a private right of action, but allows individuals to petition the Commissioner for enforcement. If reasonable grounds are established that a violation of the law has occurred, the Commissioner can commence a formal investigation.

10. New Zealand

New Zealand was the first country in the Asia-Pacific region to have a full privacy statute, the Privacy Act of 1993. With few exceptions, the act applies and regulates access to law enforcement information by various public-sector agencies across the public and private sectors. The Act contains 12 Information Privacy Principles (IPPs) that cover the collection, security, quality, use, and disclosure of personal information. The Principles also provide individuals with rights to access and correct personal information.

There had been no cross-border privacy protection in respect of international transfers of personal information, until the passing of a new law that empowers the Privacy Commissioner to stop outbound transfers of personal information.[321] This prevents New Zealand from becoming an intermediary for data transferred from countries relying on New Zealand's safeguards that is subsequently transferred on to third countries with inadequate safeguards. The Act does not have anything explicit about cross-border enforcement cooperation arrangements. This law provides that personal information must be protected by security safeguards that are reasonable in the circumstances. It specifically requires government agencies handling personal information to ensure that the data is protected against loss, unauthorized access, use, or modification by implementing reasonable security safeguards.

The Privacy Commissioner has the power to issue legally enforceable codes of practice under the act, including codes governing the health, telecommunications, and credit reporting sectors. The Commissioner investigates complaints by individuals and promotes settlements and issues nonbinding opinions but can issue legally binding opinions only if the complaint involves charges imposed by private-sector agencies for granting access or correcting personal information. The Commissioner has the power to investigate, on its own initiative, an action that may be a violation of the act.

If a complaint has not been settled, the Commissioner may refer it to the Director of Human Rights Proceedings, who may institute proceedings in the Human Rights Review Tribunal. The aggrieved individual may also bring such proceedings. Remedies include declaratory relief, orders in the nature of an injunction, damages, and an order that the defendant take action to remedy the breach. There is a right of appeal from the Tribunal to the High Court, Court of Appeal, and Supreme Court.

321. New Zealand, *Privacy (Cross-border Information) Amendment Act 2010,* Public Act 2010 No 113.

11. The Philippines

The Philippines does not have a specific data privacy law or a data privacy authority. However, as an APEC member economy, the Philippines has committed to enacting legislation aligned with the APEC Privacy Framework. Data privacy protection is limited to the voluntary guidelines issued by the Department of Trade and Industry (DTI) in 2006.[322] The guidelines are intended to encourage organizations to adopt privacy policies for the protection of personal data in information and communications systems in the private sector.

The Civil Code of the Philippines[323] provides that "[e]very person shall respect the dignity, personality, privacy, and peace of mind of his neighbors and other persons." The Electronic Commerce Act of 2000 governs the privacy and security of electronic data in the public sector.[324]

12. Russia

The Constitution of the Russian Federation establishes certain privacy rights. Article 23, for example, grants, in the absence of a court order, the right of privacy to "correspondence, telephone communications, mail, cables and other communications." Article 24 forbids the gathering, storing, use, and dissemination of information on the private life of any person without his or her consent.[325]

Federal Law No. 152-FZ "On Personal Data," enacted in July 2006,[326] required data operators to encrypt their databases to protect personal information.[327] This requirement was removed by December 2009 amendments.[328] The amendments also extended the registration date for databases containing personal data from January 1, 2010, to January 1, 2011. Personal information in databases must be encrypted by January 1, 2011.

Russia's data protection regulator is the Russian Federal Service for Oversight of Communications, Information Technology and Mass Media (the Roscomnadzor). While violations of law may be enforced by the Roscomnadzor (and include civil, criminal, administrative, and other measures), there have been no court cases in Russia to date.[329] With the extended database compliance deadline, any legal actions arising from personal data violations are not likely until after 2011.[330]

---

322. *Prescribing Guidelines for the Protection of Personal Data in Information and Communications Systems in the Private Sector*, Administrative Order (DAO) No. 08, Series of 2006 (issued July 21, 2006), *available at* http://www.dti.gov.ph/dti/index.php?p=598.

323. Rep. Act No. 386 (June 18, 1949), Article 26, *available at* http://www.dti.gov.ph/dti/index.php?p=598.

324. Available at http://www.dti.gov.ph/dti/index.php?p=598.

325. The Constitution of the Russian Federation is available at http://www.constitution.org/cons/natlcons.htm

326. Russia's Federal Law No. 152-FZ is available, in Russian, at http://www.rg.ru/2006/07/29/personaljnye dannye-dok.html.

327. *Id.*, Article 19.1.

328. Federal Law No. 363-FZ, available (in Russian) at http://www.garant.ru/hotlaw/federal/218169/.

329. *Id.*, Article 24.

330. For more on Russian privacy laws, see I.U.Bogdanovskaya and L.K.Tereshchenko, *The Legal Protection of Personal Data—The Russian Model*, INFO. SEC. & PRIVACY NEWS (newsl. ABA Sec. Sci. &Tech. L.), Volume 1, Issue 4 (Autumn 2010).

13. Singapore

Singapore has not yet enacted comprehensive data privacy legislation. The Model Data Protection Code for the Private Sector[331] (the Model Code), summarized next, is intended to be adopted by the entire private sector, but it does not have the force of law. In 2002, the National Trust Council (NTC) adopted the Model Data Protection Code under its TrustSg program for online businesses.[332] The Model Code has no legal force; compliance is voluntary. The Model Code establishes data protection guidelines that apply only to electronic data.

The Model Code is based on the ten principles set forth in the Canadian Standards Association's Model Code for the Protection of Personal Information.[333] The same CSA principles were incorporated as a schedule to Canada's federal legislation, PIPEDA.[334]

Singapore's Electronic Transactions Act (ETA) enacted in 1998 was repealed and reenacted effective July 1, 2010, to address issues arising from the use of electronic contracts and digital signatures.[335]

The Model Code (Principle 7: Safeguards) requires organizations to implement appropriate controls to protect personal data from unauthorized access, modification, disclosure, or loss, including during destruction. As the Model Code is voluntary, there are no enforcement mechanisms.

14. South Korea

The Constitution of the Republic of Korea protects an individual's right to privacy and control of his or her personal information. The Act on the Protection of Personal Information Maintained by Public Agency provides protection for personal information processed by public agencies.

The Law on the Promotion of Utilization of Information and Communication Networks and the Protection of Data[336] applies to "providers of information and communications services" and certain offline services, namely travel services. The law establishes requirements for the collection, use, and disclosure of personal information. The term "personal information" is defined as information concerning anyone living that contains the code, letter, voice, sound, and/or image that allows for the possibility of that individual being identified by name and resident registration number (including information which, if not by itself, allows for the possibility of identification when combined with other information). In most cases, opt-out consent from the data subject is required, with prior consent required for certain sensi-

331. Summarized at http://www.ida.gov.sg/Sector%20Development/20090319164535.aspx.

332. The privacy policy of TrustSg which is based on the Model Code is available at http://www.trustsg.org.sg/privacy.html.

333. The Canadian Standards Association's Model Code for the Protection of Personal Information (CAN/CSA-Q830-96) (the CSA Privacy Code) is available at http://www.csa.ca/cm/ca/en/privacy-code.

334. *Id.*

335. The full text of the ETA can be found at the Singapore Statutes website at http://statutes.agc.gov.sg/non_version/cgi-bin/cgi_legdisp.pl?actno=2010-ACT-16-N&doctitle=ELECTRONIC%20TRANSACTIONS%20ACT%202010%0a&date=latest&method=part&sl=1.

336. http://likms.assembly.go.kr/bill/jsp/BillDetail.jsp?bill_id=ARC_Y0D7A1X2G2U8T1W52D8I5Q3T7D7Z3.

tive information. Enforcement is complaint-driven and occurs via the judicial system and the Personal Information Mediation Committee.

The Act Relating to Use and Protection of Credit Information of 1995 regulates the collection and use of personal information by operators of credit information businesses.

The Protection of Personal Information Maintained by Public Agency Act requires public agencies to implement information security measures to secure the safety of personal data against loss, theft, leakage, or forgery. An individual whose rights and benefits have been infringed upon by act or omission of the head of a public agency may request an administrative appeal.

15. Taiwan

Privacy of correspondence is a constitutionally protected right in Taiwan.[337]

The Computer-Processed Personal Data Protection Law of R.O.C.[338] enacted in 1995 regulates the processing of personal information by government agencies and private-sector organizations. The law requires personal information data controllers to comply with "the collection limitation principle "and "the use of personal information principle."

Article 3 defines "personal data" as "the name, date of birth, I.D. Card number, characteristic, fingerprints, marital, family, educational, occupational, and health status, medical history, financial conditions, social activities of a natural person and other data which can serve to identify said specific person." The law was revised in 2010 (effective 2011) by the Personal Data Protection Act of 2010 to cover the entire private sector and add provisions for compensatory damages.

Prior to the 2010 amendments, the act was limited to "computer-processed" data. It now applies to all types of personal data, including national identification numbers, passport numbers, and fingerprints. A category of "sensitive data," including health data, criminal records, and genetic information, was also created.

Data controllers are required to disclose the purposes for which data is being collected and obtain the prior written consent of the data subject, unless specific exemptions apply. The media is not required to obtain prior consent of data subjects before publishing information on them, provided that the disclosure is in the public interest.

Personal data is also afforded some protection from the common law and sector-specific laws such as the Banking Act, Statistics Act, the Official Secrets Act, and the Statutory Bodies and Government Companies (Protection of Secrecy) Act.[339]

Data controllers must protect personal information with appropriate safeguards against risks, such as loss or unauthorized access to personal information, or unauthorized destruction, use, modification, or disclosure of information or other misuses. Safeguards should be proportional to the likelihood and severity of the harm threatened, the sensitivity of the information, and the context in which it is held.

---

337. The full text of the Constitution and its Additional Articles is available at http://www.gio.gov.tw/info/news/constitution.htm.

338. Available at http://eng.selaw.com.tw/FLAWDAT01.asp?lsid=FL010627.

339. http://www.ida.gov.sg/Policies%20and%20Regulation/20060627155443.aspx.

A data subject may report violations to regulators, who will intervene, requiring the data controller to take appropriate measures. Violations of the law that result in harm to the data subject are punishable by fines, criminal penalties, and imprisonment.

16. Thailand

Thailand's 1997 Constitution seeks to protect a "person's family rights, dignity, reputation or the right of privacy," indicating that "the assertion or circulation of a statement or picture in any manner whatsoever to the public, which violates or affects a person's family rights, dignity, reputation or the right of privacy, shall not be made except for the case which is beneficial to the public" and that "persons have the freedom to communication with one another by lawful means."

Legislation and administrative directions under the Constitution have primarily concerned data handled by government agencies, rather than the private sector. See, for example, the 1997 Official Information Act discussed next.

Administrative agencies, Parliament, courts, and local governments are subject to the Official Information Act (Private Sector).[340] Information related to ongoing trials is an exception to the rule and may be withheld.[341]

The objectives of the act include the following:

- To ensure people's right to know state agency information;
- To define clearly what kind of official information may not be subject to disclosure; and
- To protect the personal information held by a state agency.

The Official Information Act (Section 23) requires state agencies to implement appropriate safeguards to protect personal information stored in agency systems.

The Official Information Commission (OIC) is comprised of government ministers, ministerial advisors, and experts appointed by the cabinet. The Commission issues advice on the operation of the law. Where an appeal is made against the nondisclosure of information, an Information Disclosure Tribunal hears the appeal and issues a decision that is binding on the government. An unfavorable decision can be appealed by filing suit in court.

Thailand is in the final stages of consultation on its draft Data Protection Law, which was approved by the Council of State and is being processed to the congress.

Also, as an ASEAN member country, Thailand shares a commitment to harmonize its data protection laws by 2015.

17. Vietnam

Vietnam does not have a comprehensive data privacy law. Vietnam's Civil Code does provide that information and materials on the private life of an individual may not be collected or published without consent (Article 2) and that letters, telephone calls, tele-

---

340. Official Information Act (OIA), B.E. 2540 (1997) Legislation is available at the website of Thailand's Official Information Commission (OIC), http://www.oic.go.th/content_eng/default_eng.asp.

341. Conference on Freedom of Information and Civil Society in Asia, May 21, 2010, *available at* http://www.jclu.org/katsudou/universal_principle/articles/330asiaconf.html.

grams, or other forms of electronic information of individuals shall be safely and confidentially guaranteed (Article 3).

The Law on E-Transactions[342] provides that agencies, organizations, and individuals must not use, provide, or disclose information on private and personal affairs, or information of other agencies, organizations, and/or individuals that is accessible by them or under their control in e-transactions, without the individuals' consent. The Law on Information Technology, as supplemented by Decree No. 63/2007/ND-CP, establishes information security requirements and provides for enforcement through fines.

Vietnam's data protection scheme does not specify information security requirements. Vietnam does not have a designated data privacy authority. The Criminal Code provides for penalties in case of repeated violations.

D. Latin America

Data privacy laws in Latin America vary among the region's 28 states. Some Latin American countries, including Argentina and Mexico, have detailed privacy laws, while others, such as Peru,[343] are general and subject to discretion.

The Ibero American Data Protection Network (IDPN) is an organization shaping the future of data privacy in Latin America. The IDPN conducts outreach efforts to promote data protection laws similar to the EU Directive. Chambers of Commerce and other business associations have also actively promoted data privacy throughout the region. In Mexico, for example, the Mexican Internet Association (AMIPCI), along with the Ministry of the Economy and the Office of the Federal Attorney for Consumer Protection, introduced the AMIPCO trusted site seal, designed to identify sites that comply with data privacy regulations.

1. Habeas Data

A fundamental concept in Latin American data privacy law is habeas data. Habeas data, literally translated as "you should have the data," is a constitutional right in many countries, including Argentina and Brazil. Although its details vary by country, habeas data generally creates the right of an individual to petition a court to help it protect his or her privacy, including his or her image, privacy, honor, and freedom of information. The action can be brought against anyone holding information, and it empowers the complaining party to request a correction or even destruction of personal data held by a third party.

Brazil became the first country to officially enact a habeas data law in 1988, when it passed a new constitution. Thereafter, Colombia adopted the habeas data right in its new constitution in 1991, Paraguay in 1992, Peru in 1993, Argentina[344] in 1994, Ecuador in 1996, and Bolivia in 2004.

---

342. http://civillawnetwork.wordpress.com/2010/01/24/law-on-e-transactions/.

343. Peru does not have a specific data privacy law or a data privacy authority. Comprehensive legislation is in draft form—the Law of Protection of Personal Data. Privacy is a constitutionally protected right in Peru. A sectoral data protection law (Law No. 27.489 of 2001) regulates credit bureaus, limiting the sources of information they can use without consent.

344. Constitución de la Nación Argentina (1994), http://www.constitution.org/cons/argentin.htm (in Spanish).

2. *Data Protection Laws*

Several Latin American states have adopted comprehensive data protection laws that are summarized next. Argentina is regarded as having the most advanced legislation and is the only country that is considered adequate for data protection purposes under the EU Data Protection Directive.[345] The Argentinean Data Protection Agency, responsible for enforcement of its law, is thought to have the potential to take precedent-setting actions with potentially region-wide repercussions.

Chile, which never enacted habeas data, was the first Latin American country to enact a data protection statute.[346] That law covers the intake and use of personal data in both personal and private sectors, as well as the rights of individuals to access, correct, and control that data. The law covers the use of financial, commercial, and banking data and addresses governmental use of private data.

3. *Argentina*

Argentina's constitutional guarantee of habeas data rights was supplemented with a comprehensive data protection law, the Law for the Protection of Personal Data (the LPPD),[347] in November 2000. The LPPD is based on the EU Data Protection Directive and the Spanish Data Protection Act of 1992 and includes within its scope the protection of personal data recorded in public data files, registers, or databanks, as well as data in private files if they are used to provide reports. Collection of "sensitive data" is given extra protection and is prohibited without consent of the data subject.[348]

Consistent with the EU Data Protection Directive, transfer of personal data to countries that do not ensure adequate protection of the data is prohibited under the LPPD. The National Directorate for the Protection of Personal Data (the Directorate)[349] has the authority to investigate and enforce the LPPD and may impose administrative and criminal penalties.

The Directorate has implemented the National Registry of Databases,[350] requiring all non-personal-use databases, electronic and hard copy, containing personal data of private citizens, corporate officials, or an organization's members, intended to be shared with third parties, to be registered. Transferring databases to third parties without written consent of the data subjects is prohibited. The data transfer restrictions apply to intra-group and intracompany transfers, such as the transfer of a database between two

---

345. Argentina is one of nine countries and territories outside the EEA considered by the European Commission to provide adequate protection for personal data. Australia, Canada, Switzerland, Faeroe Islands, Guernsey, Jersey, the Isle of Man, and the United States (under safe harbor or for airline passengers) are the remaining jurisdictions. The list of approved countries is *available at* http://ec.europa.eu/justice/policies/privacy/thirdcountries/index_en.htm.

346. The Law for the Protection of Private Life, passed Oct. 28, 1999.

347. Law No. 25.326, available at http://www.protecciondedatos.com.ar/law25326.htm.

348. *Id.*

349. The website of the National Directorate of Data Protection of the Republic of Argentina is https://www.agpd.es.

350. Haskel, *Argentina Implements Mandatory Registration Requirement for Databases,* 4 PRIVACY & SEC. L. REP. (BNA) No. 9, at 241 (Feb. 28, 2005). For more information about the data registration requirements, see http://www2.jus.gov.ar/dnpdp (Spanish only).

companies with the same parent corporation or between two business units within one organization (if one legal entity or division is located outside the EU).[351]

For information security, Section 9 of the LPPD requires persons holding personal data to take "such technical and organizational measures as are necessary to guarantee the security and confidentiality of personal data, in order to avoid their alteration, loss, unauthorized consultation or treatment, and which allow for the detection of any intentional or unintentional distortion of such information." Personal data cannot be recorded unless it meets these standards of "technical integrity and security."

4. Brazil

The Constitution[352] for the Federative Republic of Brazil was the first to incorporate habeas data in 1988.[353] Notably, the Brazilian habeas data right provides the data subject with the right of correction (not update or deletion) but if there is a dispute, the ability to add a corrective annotation to the data stored on a registry.[354]

The Habeas Data Act of 1997 regulates the right of access and provides the relevant procedural and venue guidelines for habeas data.[355] Depending on the party against whom a habeas data action is brought, the venue is different. For example, actions against the president or congress are to be brought in the Superior Federal Tribunal, whereas actions against the federal authorities are to be brought in front of regional federal judges.[356]

In July 1997, Brazil enacted the General Telecommunications Law, which provides that users of telecommunications services are entitled to have their privacy respected in the use of their personal data.[357] The Brazilian Civil Code of 2003 provides further data protection, requiring the judiciary, at the request of an individual, to adopt measures to protect against actions to the contrary.[358]

Further data protection is achieved by several supplementary statutory protections. The 1990 Consumer Protection Law provides that consumers have access to personal data, consumer files, and other information about themselves and the sources of these data.[359] The law further requires that consumer files and data be objective and accurate and not contain derogatory information for more than five years.[360] The Financial Institutions Secrecy Law provides that "financial institutions will preserve secrecy in their active and passive operations and services."[361] Information exchanged among financial institutions,

351. Haskel, *supra* note 349.

352. An English version of the Constitution is available at http://www.v-brazil.com/government/laws/preamble.html.

353. Guadamuz, *Habeas Data vs. the European Data Protection Directive*, Refereed Art. 3 J. INFO., L. AND TECH. (2001), http://papers.ssrn.com/sol3/papers.cfm?abstract_id=569106.

354. *Id.*

355. Law No. 9,507 (Nov. 12, 1997).

356. Guadamuz, *supra* note 352.

357. Law No. 9,472 (July 16, 1997) Book 1, Art. 3, IX, *available at* http://www.commsmanagement.org/tvl/docs/leigeral_english_anatel.pdf.

358. Law No. 10,406 (Jan. 12, 1997).

359. Law No. 8,078, Art. 43 (Sept. 11, 1990).

360. *Id.*

361. *Id.*

the reporting of information requested by the Federal Revenue and Customs Secretariat, and the reporting of illegal activity are all exempt from the law's applicability.[362]

5. Chile

Chile enacted its Law for the Protection of Private Life in 1999, the first in Latin America. While the law was effective in 2000, it lacked effective enforcement mechanisms until amendments in 2009. The Chilean law is based in part on Spain's Data Privacy law and covers processing and use of personal data in both the public and private sectors. It does not, however, create a data protection authority or restrict transfers of data out of Chile.

Under the law, individuals have rights of data access, correction, and judicial control. The law specifically regulates the use of financial, commercial, and banking data and creates rules addressing the use of information by government agencies.

6. Mexico

Mexico's data privacy law, the Federal Law Protecting Personal Data in Private Possession, was enacted in July 2010.[363] Like the EU Data Protection Directive and the Canadian federal PIPEDA legislation, Mexico's statute requires a lawful basis and prior consent for the collection and use of personally identifiable information.

The law regulates private parties that "process" personally identified or identifiable data, with exceptions for credit reporting agencies (which are covered by separate legislation) and individuals recording data exclusively for personal use. Definitions are similar to those of the EU Data Protection Directive, including a broad definition of "processing" and the concepts of "data controller" and "data processor."

There is no requirement to report processing activities to a government body, as in many European countries, but companies handling personal data must provide notice to the affected persons. Individuals have rights of access, correction, and objection (on "legitimate grounds") to processing or disclosure.

A federal agency, the Institute for Access to Information and Data Protection (IFAI), enforces Mexico's law. The IFAI investigates complaints as well as initiates its own investigations. Violations of the law result in administrative sanction and criminal prosecution. The IFAI, and existing sector authorities, must issue regulations by July 2011 before enforcement of the law begins in January 2012.

Data controllers and data processors must establish and maintain physical, technical, and administrative security measures to protect personal data from loss, alteration, and unauthorized disclosure or use. Potential harm, the likelihood of security breaches, the sensitivity of the data, and technological developments are taken into account in determining appropriate security measures.

Data transfers to a third party (other than for processing on behalf of the data controller) generally require an agreement requiring the transferee to assume the same

---

362. *Id.*

363. Federal Law on the Protection of Personal Data Held by Private Parties (Ley federal de protección de datos personales en posesión de los particulares), http://www.dof.gob.mx/nota_detalle.php?codigo=5150631&fecha=05/07/2010. An unofficial English translation is available at http://dgroups.org/ViewDiscussion.aspx?c=caf8f8bf-0ff2-410e-b0d5-7adacbe19c5a&i=bbb047a8-8768-432e-bf13-ae883f9c43f6.

obligations as found in the privacy notice provided by the transferor. A data transfer requires the consent of the individual unless one of the enumerated exceptions applies.

The law does not establish a formal procedure for approval of foreign data transfers. Data controllers should be able to move data within a corporate group without individual consent, inside and outside Mexico, so long as the parent or affiliate does not handle the data in a manner contrary to the privacy notice furnished by the affiliate in Mexico.

A security breach affecting personal information of a Mexican resident held by a U.S. parent, affiliate, or vendor could trigger the breach notice requirements of the Mexican law. Security breaches occurring at any stage of processing that materially affect the property or moral rights of data owners will be reported immediately by the data controller to the data owner, so that the latter can take appropriate action to defend its rights.[364]

2.4 NONREGULATORY OBLIGATIONS

A. Business Continuity

Although certain emergencies and disruptions cannot be prevented, various processes and protective measures can be implemented that will reduce risk and increase the speed of recovery. This is the objective of sound business continuity management practices.[365] Increasingly, for many businesses, a disaster recovery or business continuity plan is also becoming a de facto legal requirement. Although states have largely forgone regulating businesses in this area, there is nevertheless an emerging standard of care from industry initiatives, the common law, and a patchwork of federal regulations and guidelines which broadly suggest that a duty exists on the part of businesses to take reasonable steps to ensure business continuity.

Recent case law suggests that a business may be potentially liable to any number of plaintiffs for failing to take steps to prevent, cope with, or recover from disasters and emergencies—even acts of terrorism—that are reasonably foreseeable.[366] Furthermore, an expanding number of organizations and businesses have also begun to address disaster planning and recovery issues explicitly with their customers and vendors through customized service-level agreements that eliminate "act of God" provisions and incorporate foreseeable disaster scenarios directly into agreed-upon service levels.

In the federal arena, various agencies have issued specific guidance that either requires or strongly urges businesses to provide for emergency planning and business continuity. For instance, the Occupational Safety and Health Administration (OSHA) requires that facilities with more than ten employees have various written emergency action plans.[367] In the case of Sarbanes-Oxley, federal regulations require every broker and dealer to undertake substantial efforts to preserve a wide variety of financial records.

---

364. *Id.*, Article 20.

365. *See, e.g.*, XO Communications LLC, "Business Continuity & Today's 'Always On' Business Environment" 4 (2009), *available at* http://www.xo.com/.

366. *See* Nash v. Port Authority of New York and New Jersey, 51 A.D.3d 337 (N.Y. App. Div. 1st Dept. 2008) (holding, relative to the 1993 World Trade Center bombing, that a business that has reason to believe it is at high risk for terrorist attack has a duty to take reasonable steps to prevent or mitigate such an attack).

367. 29 C.F.R. § 1910.38(b).

Specifically, every broker and dealer must "[p]reserve the records exclusively in a non-rewritable, non-erasable format."[368] Still other bodies of federal law and federal agencies either implicitly or explicitly require certain businesses to have disaster recovery/business continuity plans, including HIPAA/HITECH,[369] FERC,[370] and FISMA.[371]

Among the federal financial regulators, the Board of Governors of the Federal Reserve System, the Office of the Comptroller of the Currency, and the Securities and Exchange Commission collectively issued a white paper entitled: "Interagency Paper on Sound Practices to Strengthen the Resilience of the U.S. Financial System."[372] This paper identified three new business continuity objectives that had special importance in the post-9/11 risk environment for all financial firms. It also identified four sound practices to ensure the resilience of the U.S. financial system by minimizing the immediate systemic effects of a wide-scale disruption of critical financial markets. In addition, the Federal Financial Institutions Examination Council (FFIEC) issued a revised Examination Handbook in March 2008 specifically on the topic of Business Continuity Planning.[373] This FFIEC Handbook, though designed for federally supervised financial institutions, contains a good deal of general business continuity best practices applicable to virtually any business interested in sound business continuity planning and implementation.

The nature and scope of any particular business continuity plan will depend on the specific industry in which a company operates and the characteristics of the various stakeholders, customers, and affected parties. Based on current trends, these requirements will likely grow in number and sophistication in the future.

B. Payment Card Industry Data Security Standard

The payment card industry has instituted a strict set of mandatory data security requirements known as the Payment Card Industry Data Security Standard (PCI-DSS).[374] PCI-DSS, true to its name, is intended to provide a uniform, private security standard for

---

368. 17 C.F.R. § 240.17a-4(f)(2)(ii).

369. 45 C.F.R. § 164.308(a)(7) (requiring a "contingency plan" in the event of "fire, vandalism, system failure, and natural disaster," as well as a "data backup plan," "disaster recovery plan," and "emergency mode operation plan").

370. *See, e.g.*, U.S. Federal Energy Regulatory Commission, Supplement to Commission Procedures During Periods of Emergency Operations Requiring Activation of Continuity of Operations Plan, Docket No. RM 10-28-000, Order No. 738 (Aug. 5, 2010) (de facto continuity plan governing electric utilities' mandatory purchase obligations in the event of an emergency disruption in communications with the Commission's headquarters), *available at* http://www.ferc.gov/coop/order 738.pdf.

371. As part of a U.S. federal agency's Certification & Accreditation (C&A), FISMA requires supporting documentation that includes a multilayered security plan, several risk assessments, and business continuity/disaster recovery plans. National Institute of Standards and Technology, U.S. Department of Commerce, Contingency Planning Guide for Federal Information Systems, Special Publication 800-34 Rev. 1 (May 2010), *available at* http://csrc.nist.gov/publications/nistpubs/800-34-rev1/sp800-34-rev1.pdf.

372. Board of Governors of the Federal Reserve System, Office of the Comptroller of the Currency, Securities and Exchange Commission, Interagency Paper on Sound Practices to Strengthen the Resilience of the U.S. Financial System (2003), *available at* http://www.newyorkfed.org/banking/circulars_archive/11522.pdf.

373. FFIEC, Information Technology Examination Handbook (2008), *available at* http://www.ffiec.gov/ffiecinfobase/html_pages/it_01.html#bcp.

374. PCI Security Standards Council, *About the PCI Data Security Standard* (2010), https://www.pcisecuritystandards.org/security_standards/pci_dss.shtml.

the administration and handling of payment card data. PCI-DSS has been adopted by all of the major card brands (e.g., VISA, MasterCard, AMEX, Discover, and JCB) and applies to stakeholders in the payment card industry that store, process, or transmit payment card information, including merchants, payment gateways, payment processors, and service providers.

The owners of the major payment card brands created an entity, the PCI Security Standards Council, to draft, develop, and manage PCI-DSS and the various processes and documentation related to it.[375] While PCI-DSS is a common security standard, the card brands still retain their own operating policies and rules that dictate procedures aimed at achieving PCI-DSS compliance.[376] These policies and rules include fines and penalties for noncompliance, as well as recovery mechanisms allowing issuing banks to recover costs arising out of a payment card security breach.[377]

When considering compliance with payment card security requirements, merchants must address PCI-DSS as well as the security-related operating regulations for each relevant payment card company. If a merchant works with all five major payment card brands, the merchant must comply with PCI-DSS and each company's security program. That means six different sets of "rules" of which to be aware.

The duty to comply with PCI-DSS is created contractually through a chain of contracts and, depending on the state in question, may also be encompassed within statutory requirements. For example, the state of Nevada makes compliance with PCI-DSS mandatory for companies that accept payment cards in the course of their business.[378]

With respect to contractually created duties, the payment card brands sit on top of the chain of contracts. The brands work through merchant banks. The "membership agreement" between merchant banks and payment card brands is therefore the first link in the PCI chain. The merchant banks (or payment processors working with the merchant banks) process the payment card transactions for the payment card brands with which they contract. If a merchant wishes to accept payment cards to transact business, it must be vetted by a merchant bank and enter into a contractual relationship with that merchant bank (and/or the merchant bank's payment processor) to set up a merchant account. The contract that exists between a merchant and merchant bank (or processor) is often known as a "merchant agreement" and represents the next link in the PCI chain. Finally, merchants that use the payment card network sometimes enter into relationships with service providers for the processing, storage, or transmittal of payment card data. These contractual agreements that exist between merchants and service providers constitute the final link in the PCI chain.

In each link of the PCI chain, obligations to comply with PCI-DSS are passed to the downstream party. The individual contracts dictate the scope of the PCI-DSS responsibilities. Typically, there is no direct contractual relationship between merchants and

375. *Id.*

376. *See, e.g.*, VISA, *VISA International Operating Regulations* (2010), http://usa.visa.com/merchants/operations/op_regulations.html.

377. *See, e.g.*, VISA, *Account Data Compromise Recovery* (2010), http://usa.visa.com/merchants/operations/adcr.html.

378. Nev. Rev. Stat. § 603A.215.

card brands or issuing banks (banks that issue credit cards to individuals). Rather, if a merchant fails to comply with PCI-DSS or suffers a security breach, fines and penalties are passed down from the card brands to the merchant banks (using the membership agreement), who in turn pass them on to the merchant (using the merchant agreement).

In order to fully comply with PCI-DSS, it is necessary to adhere to numerous technology and process requirements. The core of the PCI-DSS is a group of principles and accompanying requirements, around which the specific elements of the DSS are organized:[379]

- **Build and Maintain a Secure Network**
  Requirement 1: Install and maintain a firewall configuration to protect cardholder data
  Requirement 2: Do not use vendor-supplied defaults for system passwords and other security parameters
- **Protect Cardholder Data**
  Requirement 3: Protect stored cardholder data
  Requirement 4: Encrypt transmission of cardholder data across open, public networks
- **Maintain a Vulnerability Management Program**
  Requirement 5: Use and regularly update antivirus software
  Requirement 6: Develop and maintain secure systems and applications
- **Implement Strong Access Control Measures**
  Requirement 7: Restrict access to cardholder data by business need-to-know
  Requirement 8: Assign a unique ID to each person with computer access
  Requirement 9: Restrict physical access to cardholder data
- **Regularly Monitor and Test Networks**
  Requirement 10: Track and monitor all access to network resources and cardholder data
  Requirement 11: Regularly test security systems and processes
- **Maintain an Information Security Policy**
  Requirement 12: Maintain a policy that addresses information security

Validation of compliance may include quarterly network security scans and annual PCI security assessments.[380] The assessments are performed either by qualified security assessors or in-house personnel using a self-assessment questionnaire. The type of assessment that must be performed depends on the applicable merchant level or service provider level as defined by the card brands.[381]

PCI-DSS is another example of private industry standards being critical to determining norms of conduct, reciprocal obligations of commercial parties, and, ultimately, the legal liability of entities that are subject to those standards.

---

379. *See* https://www.pcisecuritystandards.org/documents/pci_dss_v2.pdf.

380. *See, e.g.*, MasterCard, *Merchant Levels Defined* (2010), http://www.mastercard.com/us/sdp/merchants/merchant_levels.html.

381. *See, e.g.*, VISA, *Cardholder Information Security Program* (2010), http://usa.visa.com/merchants/risk_management/cisp_merchants.html#anchor_2.

C. System-Wide Operating Rules

Security requirements can also arise from consortium rules. These rules can be binding through contracts or a network of contracts. Members may be required to sign such contracts as a condition of participating in a particular industry group, network, or consortium.

For instance, the Electronic Payments Association (NACHA, owing to its former name, the National Automated Clearing House Association) oversees the development, operating rules, and governance of the Automated Clearing House (ACH) network for electronic payments used in e-commerce, automated bill payment, and various financial transactions.[382] NACHA develops and maintains the NACHA Operating Rules, which are enforced through contracts among financial institutions and other parties that are participants in ACH transactions.[383] The NACHA Operating Rules delineate the rights, responsibilities, security requirements, and the business foundation for ACH transactions.[384]

The process by which NACHA develops its rules and policies is open and deliberative in nature, allows for comment by affected parties, and is largely modeled on the federal Administrative Procedure Act.[385] The stated goal of this approach is to instantiate private-sector rulemaking that will "provide the flexibility to promptly identify and respond to participant requirements and new technologies" as well as foster innovation and efficiency.[386]

D. Safeguarding Client Data: Lawyers' Ethical and Legal Obligations

Confidential data in computers and information systems, including those used by lawyers and law firms, faces greater security threats today than ever before. Lawyers have ethical, common law, and statutory obligations to protect information relating to clients. In addition, protection of confidential information is sound business and professional practice. It is critical for attorneys to understand and address these obligations and to exercise constant vigilance to protect client data.

The threats to attorneys and law firms are substantial and real. Attacks have taken a variety of forms, such as phishing scams and social engineering attacks—for example, using e-mail to trick attorneys into becoming involved in fraudulent collection schemes for foreign "clients"—as well as sophisticated technical exploits that result in intrusions into a law firm's network to steal information related to pending litigation.[387] In one instance, attackers were in the firm's network for a year when law enforcement notified the firm that it had been hacked. By then, the attackers had gained access to thousands of e-mails and attachments from mail servers and had obtained illegal access to every server, desktop, and laptop on the firm's network.[388]

---

382. NACHA, The Electronic Payments Association, *Introduction to NACHA*, http://www.nacha.org/c/aboutus.cfm.

383. NACHA, The Electronic Payments Association, *ACH Rules*, http://www.nacha.org/c/achrules.cfm.

384. *Id.*

385. *Id.*

386. *Id.*

387. Alejandro Martínez-Cabrera, *Law Firms Are Lucrative Targets of Cyberscams*, S.F. Chron., March 20, 2010.

388. Kim Zetter, *Report Details Hacks Targeting Google, Others*, Wired Magazine, Feb. 3, 2010, *available at* http://www.wired.com/threatlevel/2010/02/apt-hacks/.

1. Rules of Professional Conduct

Compliance with ethical obligations can be difficult because the standards governing the professional conduct of attorneys are generally a matter of state law and vary across jurisdictions. Nevertheless, the ABA Model Rules of Professional Conduct ("Model Rules") have been adopted in numerous jurisdictions and serve as a baseline for analyzing ethical issues.

Because competent representation and confidentiality are at the foundation of the attorney-client relationship, it is little surprise that the rules relating to these fundamental notions provide the starting point for analyzing the attorney's duty to safeguard client data. Model Rule 1.1 covers the general duty of competent representation:

> A lawyer shall provide competent representation to a client. Competent representation requires the legal knowledge, skill, thoroughness and preparation reasonably necessary for the representation.[389]

Model Rule 1.1 is broad enough in scope to reasonably include competence and skill in managing the technology associated with the delivery of legal services.

Model Rule 1.6 sets forth the duty of confidentiality generally. The Model Rule prohibits attorneys from revealing information relating to the representation of a client:

> (a) A lawyer shall not reveal information relating to the representation of a client unless the client gives informed consent, the disclosure is impliedly authorized in order to carry out the representation or the disclosure is permitted by paragraph (b).[390]

Significantly, Model Rule 1.6 broadly extends to "information relating to the representation of a client." Comment 16 to the Model Rule requires reasonable precautions to safeguard and preserve all such information:

> Acting Competently to Preserve Confidentiality
>
> [16] A lawyer must act competently to safeguard information relating to the representation of a client against inadvertent or unauthorized disclosure by the lawyer or other persons who are participating in the representation of the client or who are subject to the lawyer's supervision. See Rules 1.1, 5.1 and 5.3.[391]

The State Bar of Arizona has issued two ethics opinions, one in 2005 and one in 2009, that apply these rules to information security requirements. The 2005 opinion responds to an inquiry about the steps a law firm must take to safeguard client data from hackers and viruses. It states that attorneys are duty bound to understand the threats to electronic files and to take the necessary technological steps to prevent the disclosure and destruction of data:

> [Ethics Rules] 1.6 and 1.1 require that an attorney act competently to safeguard client information and confidences. . . . [T]o comply with these ethical rules as they relate to the client's electronic files or communications, an attorney or law firm is obligated to take competent and reasonable steps to assure that the client's confidences are not disclosed to third parties through theft or inadvertence. In addition, an attorney or law

389. Model Rules of Prof'l Conduct R. 1.1 (2007).

390. Model Rules of Prof'l Conduct R. 1.6 (2007).

391. *Id.* at cmt. 16.

> firm is obligated to take reasonable and competent steps to assure that the client's electronic information is not lost or destroyed. In order to do that, an attorney must either have the competence to evaluate the nature of the potential threat to the client's electronic files and to evaluate and deploy appropriate computer hardware and software to accomplish that end, or if the attorney lacks or cannot reasonably obtain that competence, to retain an expert consultant who does have such competence.[392]

The 2009 opinion from the State Bar of Arizona deals with an online file storage and retrieval system for client access to documents. It restates the ethical requirement of competent and reasonable measures to protect client confidences. It cautions that lawyers should recognize their own competence limitations regarding computer security measures and take the necessary time and energy to become competent or, alternatively, consult available experts in the field.[393]

The 2009 opinion discusses specific safeguards for lawyers to consider, such as cryptographic protocols like SSL (Secure Sockets Layer/Transport Layer Security), firewalls, password protection schemes, other encryption, and antivirus measures. It also states that lawyers should "periodically review security measures in place to ensure that they still reasonably protect the security and confidentiality of the clients' documents and information."[394]

Several other states' ethics opinions also address requirements for safeguarding client electronic data—for example, New Jersey Committee on Professional Ethics Opinion 701 (April 24, 2006), Nevada Standing Committee on Ethics and Professional Responsibility Formal Opinion 33 (February 9, 2006), and Virginia Standing Committee on Legal Ethics Opinion 1818 (September 3, 2005). While they vary in their degree of specificity, at their core they all require lawyers to take reasonable measures to protect the confidentiality of client information.

In addition to protecting computers and information systems, the duty of confidentiality requires attorneys to take reasonable precautions to safeguard confidential information transmitted in electronic form. Electronic modes of communication, including e-mail, have become routine for attorneys and other professionals. They are fast, convenient, and inexpensive but also present risks, particularly in the area of confidentiality. Respected security professionals have compared e-mail to postcards written in pencil.[395]

Several ethics opinions have concluded, with some qualifications, that encryption is not generally required for attorney e-mail.[396] The ABA accepted the approach taken by

392. State Bar of Arizona, Opinion No. 05-04 (July 2005) (Formal Opinion of the Committee on the Rules of Professional Conduct) (emphasis in original).

393. State Bar of Arizona, Opinion No. 09-04 (Dec. 2009) (Formal Opinion of the Committee on the Rules of Professional Conduct).

394. *Id.*

395. Bruce Schneier, E-Mail Security: How to Keep Your Electronic Messages Private, at 3 (1995); Bruce Schneier, Secrets & Lies: Digital Security in a Networked World, at 200 (2000) ("The common metaphor for Internet e-mail is postcards: Anyone—lettercarriers, mail sorters, nosy delivery truck drivers—who can touch the postcard can read what's on the back."); Larry Rogers, *Email—A Postcard Written in Pencil*, Special Report (Software Engineering Institute, Carnegie Mellon University, 2001).

396. *See, e.g.*, ABA Formal Opinion No. 99-413, *Protecting the Confidentiality of Unencrypted E-Mail* (March 10, 1999). However, an opinion of the New Jersey Advisory Committee on Professional Ethics, *Electronic Storage and Access of Client Files*, Opinion 701 (April 2006), states in a footnote that confidential documents sent over the Internet should be password protected "since it is not possible to secure the Internet itself."

these opinions in amendments to Model Rule 1.6 that were part of the Ethics 2000 revisions. Comment 17, which requires reasonable precautions to safeguard information in electronic communications, was added to the rule:

> [17] When transmitting a communication that includes information relating to the representation of a client, the lawyer must take reasonable precautions to prevent the information from coming into the hands of unintended recipients. This duty, however, does not require that the lawyer use special security measures if the method of communication affords a reasonable expectation of privacy. Special circumstances, however, may warrant special precautions. Factors to be considered in determining the reasonableness of the lawyer's expectation of confidentiality include the sensitivity of the information and the extent to which the privacy of the communication is protected by law or by a confidentiality agreement. A client may require the lawyer to implement special security measures not required by this Rule or may give informed consent to the use of a means of communication that would otherwise be prohibited by this Rule.[397]

What constitutes "special circumstances" is not entirely clear from the Comment, and the test is likely to be one of reasonableness, which will often be judged from hindsight. Encryption is being increasingly required in areas like banking and health care and by new laws such as the ones in Nevada and Massachusetts that require certain personal information to be encrypted when it is electronically transmitted.[398] These laws apply to attorneys. Accordingly, the best practice is to discuss with clients in advance the use of e-mail and other forms of electronic communication for confidential communications, the circumstances under which they will or will not be used, and the protection which will be given to them, including potential use of encryption or protection through a virtual private network. It is also important to determine which state's rules of professional conduct or statutory law apply to the client relationship as well as the communications and data storage incident to that relationship. Last, most attorneys should have encryption available for storage and transmission of information for use in appropriate circumstances.

2. *Common Law Duties*

In addition to the duties arising from rules of professional conduct, there are also parallel common law duties. These duties are defined by case law in the various states. The *Restatement (3rd) of the Law Governing Lawyers* (2000) summarizes this area of the law.[399] Breach of these common law duties may result in malpractice liability.

Attorneys may also have contractual duties to protect client data. This is particularly the case for clients in regulated industries like financial services and health care that have regulatory requirements to protect privacy and security.

3. *Statutes and Regulations*

In addition to ethical and common law duties to protect client information, there are federal and state statutes and regulations that require protection of defined categories of personal

---

397. Model Rules of Prof'l Conduct R. 1.6, cmt. 17.

398. NEV. REV. STAT. § 603A.215; MASS. GEN. LAWS ch. 93H.

399. *See* Restatement (3rd) of the Law Governing Lawyers § 16.d. (2000).

information. Many of these requirements apply to attorneys, although many attorneys are not aware of them. If an attorney possesses information that is subject to protection under these laws, either about the attorney's employees, clients, clients' employees or customers, opposing parties, their employees, or even witnesses, then the requirements set forth in these laws may apply. These laws are described in detail in the previous sections.

For example, several state laws now require safeguards for defined types of personal information. They generally cover Social Security numbers, driver's license numbers, and financial account numbers. Some also cover health information. They include laws requiring reasonable security, breach notice laws, and secure disposal laws. Forty-six states (all but Kentucky, Mississippi, New Mexico, and South Dakota), the District of Columbia, and the Virgin Islands now have laws that require notification concerning data breaches. While there are differences in their scope and requirements, they generally require that those entities that own, license, or possess defined categories of personally identifiable information notify affected individuals if there is a data breach. In the event of an improper disclosure, some of these laws require notice to a state agency in addition to notice to affected individuals.

At least 24 states now have laws that require specified protection for Social Security numbers. At least 19 states now have laws that require secure disposal of paper and electronic records that contain defined personal information. The FTC's Disposal Rule, 16 C.F.R. Part 682, has similar requirements for consumer credit reports and information derived from them. At least ten states now have general security laws that require reasonable measures to protect defined categories of personal information. These laws vary in the scope of their coverage and the specificity of their requirements.

To date, the most comprehensive law of this type is in Massachusetts.[400] The implementing regulations require encryption of covered personal information that is transmitted over public and wireless networks or stored on laptops and portable media.[401] With its broad coverage of all "persons who own, license, store or maintain" covered information, it may be applicable to persons outside the state, so long as they have sufficient contacts with Massachusetts to satisfy personal jurisdiction requirements.

An attorney who receives protected, individually identifiable health information (PHI) from a covered entity under the Health Insurance Portability and Accountability Act (HIPAA) will generally be a "business associate" and be required to comply with the HIPAA security requirements. The 2009 HITECH Act enhanced HIPAA security requirements, extended them directly to business associates, and added a new breach notification requirement.

4. Standards for Competent and Reasonable Measures

Legal standards that apply in other areas, like financial services, can be helpful in providing a framework for security, even though they do not legally apply to the practice of law. The FTC's Safeguards Rule under the Gramm-Leach-Bliley Act provides a helpful framework that lawyers can use to assist in complying with their obligations to safeguard client data.[402] For larger firms, standards like ISO 27001 (see Chapter 5) provide a good framework.

400. Mass. Gen. Laws ch. 93H.
401. 201 Mass. Code Regs. 17.00.
402. *Standards for Safeguarding Customer Information,* 16 C.F.R., Pt. 314.

Confidential data in attorneys' computers and information systems today faces substantial and real security risks. It is critical for attorneys to understand and address these risks in order to comply with their ethical, common law, and regulatory obligations to safeguard client data.

CHAPTER 3

Information Security and Privacy Liability

Organizations must be able to understand and plan for legal liability exposures that may arise from a number of sources. These include claims based on the information security and privacy laws and regulations discussed in Chapter 2 and from criminal statutes. Claims also arise based on conduct involving contracts between parties, tortious conduct, and consumer protection regulatory actions. This chapter analyzes all these potential sources of claims, grouped around the following areas of civil law: business contracts, such as contracts with service and software providers; intentional and negligence tort law; federal and state regulatory actions; and other types of claims, such as in lawsuits initiated by shareholders or from class action lawsuits. In addition, criminal liability for cybercrimes can arise under a number of statutes, from both U.S. and international law.

What Global Executives Need to Know

- The organization's contractual obligations and relationships impacting information security and privacy
- The potential sources of tort claims regarding information security and privacy
- The sources of potential regulatory actions involving information security and privacy
- The sources of potential information security and privacy claims from nonregulatory sources
- The potential for criminal liability arising out of cybercrimes

3.1 CONTRACT-BASED CLAIMS

This section discusses some of the causes of action and theories that may be asserted against a party that fails to maintain reasonable security controls or that suffers a data security breach.[1]

A. Contracting with Service Providers

Information technology and the processing, storage, and transmission of information are ubiquitous. At the same time (and likely as a result of this ubiquity), the regulatory and legal liability environments pose increased risks and potential for enormous liability. Additionally, whether with cloud computing providers or via more traditional avenues for outsourcing information technology functions (e.g., ASP, hosting, and storage), companies are increasingly outsourcing their information technology functions to third-party service providers to stay competitive and efficient. It is likely that adoption of these practices will continue to increase.

This reality poses significant information security, privacy, and legal challenges. Internal security and privacy professionals find themselves ceding control over significant decisions concerning the implementation, maintenance, enhancement, and enforcement of information security and privacy measures to third parties (service providers). Unfortunately, an organization's legal risks and compliance obligations do not simply disappear just because a service provider is used. In most cases they remain with the organization that chooses to outsource. Of course, from the service provider's perspective, the main goals in offering outsourcing services include: (1) ensuring secure revenue; (2) keeping expenses down with standardized offerings; and (3) avoiding liability. These motivations, however, are often counter to the goals of the company seeking to outsource (the customer).

These tensions between the customer and the service provider play themselves out during the contract negotiations. It is at this juncture that the role of the customer's information security and privacy attorney, working closely with the customer's internal security and privacy professionals, becomes increasingly important. At the same time, the service provider's lawyer must understand and manage the risks presented by the customer. To navigate these waters an understanding of data security and privacy law, contract drafting, litigation risk, and negotiation tactics is crucial. However, equally important is a solid understanding of technology and substantive security and privacy issues and how they relate to and interplay with the law. The net result is often intense negotiations around the contract's data security and privacy terms, which may be in the form of an information security and privacy schedule or exhibit ("InfoSec-Privacy Schedule," or "Schedule"). In addition, the parties may take outsourced computing risks

1. Although a civil action could be commenced against an attacker initiating a security breach, there are at least two reasons why such an approach might not be practical. First, even with present advances in tracking and forensic technology, the attacker is usually difficult, if not impossible, to identify or locate. Second, the attacker (to the extent he or she can be found) will likely be subject to criminal penalties, the enforcement of which may outweigh the benefit gained through a civil lawsuit.

into account in negotiating liability, indemnity and damages clauses, warranties relating to confidentiality and availability, and any service-level agreement.

This section explores the function, purpose, and liability impact of InfoSec-Privacy Schedules and discusses how they might be employed.

1. *The Multiple Functions of an InfoSec-Privacy Schedule*

InfoSec-Privacy Schedules serve multiple functions, some of which extend beyond the contractual relationship. Schedules function in traditional ways by establishing the relative duties of the parties and allocating risk of loss. Schedules may also proactively mandate third-party implementation of certain measures in an attempt to prevent security breaches and ensure compliance with certain laws. In addition, InfoSec-Privacy Schedules may serve an internal compliance function that could mitigate liability in the event of a regulatory action or lawsuit. Finally, these schedules effectively serve as the basis for incident response between the outsourcing service provider and customer.

2. *Proactive Nature of an InfoSec-Privacy Schedule*

InfoSec-Privacy Schedules generally require service providers to implement measures designed to prevent an incident that could result in a security breach or exposure, as well as prevent resulting legal liability. Contrast Schedules with a traditional nondisclosure agreement (NDA). NDAs often do not dictate how a service provider must protect confidential information, much less indicate the specific security controls that must be implemented, but rather simply mandate that service providers refrain from disclosing or exposing such information and secure the customer's data as they would their own confidential information. If such exposure occurs, the customer's typical remedy is to seek equitable relief, most often in the form of an injunction, and sue the service provider for damages.

In contrast, one of the overarching goals of the Schedule is to contractually ensure that the service provider actively implements specific measures and policies to prevent a confidentiality breach in the first instance. Most customers would prefer that their service provider never suffer a security breach, rather than having to initiate a lawsuit to recover for the service provider's violation of the NDA after a security breach. This is especially true where the customer's recovery is capped by limitation of liability clauses, consequential damages disclaimers, and the like.

Moreover, to the extent that the service provider essentially becomes an extension of the customer's internal operations, consistency between the customer's internal security environment and the security environments of its service providers is operationally desirable. A detailed Schedule is more likely to achieve this aim than relying on a general obligation to keep customer information confidential.

3. *The InfoSec-Privacy Schedule as a Compliance Document*

Another crucial purpose of an InfoSec-Privacy Schedule is its compliance function. Chapter 2 outlines many of the laws and regulations that effectively impose security obligations on organizations. Lawyers should consider how the Schedule addresses specific requirements imposed by applicable information security and privacy laws and how the Schedule reflects efforts to maintain "reasonable security." Many laws (especially in the financial services and health care sectors) require customers to contractually obligate service providers to employ specific security and privacy measures, and the Schedule should reflect those obligations as well. Ultimately, lawyers negotiating a Schedule should ask themselves the following question:

> If put before a privacy regulator in a regulatory action, or a judge or jury in a lawsuit, will the security and privacy terms in this document reflect a compliant status and offer "reasonable security"?

To address this point, lawyers should consider several items in developing a Schedule:

- **Security assessment process.** Although the Schedule can serve as a useful document to support a customer's compliance needs, it should typically be coupled with a security assessment or investigation. Conducting a security assessment of a service provider's security measures allows the customer to determine whether appropriate controls are in place to mitigate risk. It also allows the customer to assess whether specific compliance obligations can be met by the service provider's systems and processing functionalities. This process should be documented so that the customer can establish (for a regulator or in a litigation context) that it properly vetted its service provider prior to allowing it to process, store, or transmit sensitive or protected information. Without a due diligence process, the effectiveness of the Schedule in establishing compliance will be diminished. A Schedule filled with hollow promises may be an inadequate compliance tool. Moreover (as discussed next), the security assessment process informs the customer of the specific requirements that should appear in the Schedule. The best policy in this situation (as in many others) is to "trust, but verify" the service provider's security and privacy measures.
- **Applicable information security and privacy laws.** The Schedule should specifically reference laws with which the service provider must comply, such as the Health Insurance Portability and Accountability Act of 1996 (HIPAA), the Gramm-Leach-Bliley Act (GLBA), Canada's Personal Information Protection and Electronic Documents Act (PIPEDA), or national laws based on the EU Data Protection Directive. This can be done by incorporating a definition for "Privacy Laws" or "Security Laws" that specifies all applicable laws. Using this approach, customers put service providers on notice concerning their obligations and also demonstrate that applicable law was addressed.
- **Customer's internal control structure.** When outsourcing, a customer should view its service provider as an extension of the customer. Many customers have gone through an extensive process of measuring their internal information security and privacy risks and implementing security and privacy measures to mitigate those risks to a reasonable level. When sensitive information or systems are outsourced to a service provider, those internal measures may no longer fully apply. Even if the customer has a measure of control in configuring security settings and monitoring the processing by the service provider, many security measures remain largely under the control of the service provider. Problems may arise when the service provider's measures provide less protection than the customer's own internal controls, a situation that may be

difficult to defend in litigation or a regulatory action. Moreover, the customer may be placed in the position of defending the service provider's decisions and practices and demonstrating how they comport with specific regulatory requirements, industry standards, or customary industry practices. Therefore, the Schedule should reflect an allocation of risks and controls between the customer and service provider, and the service provider's security and privacy measures should meet or exceed those of the customer.

- **Specific controls.** Depending on the circumstances, including the nature of the services being outsourced, it may be necessary to set forth specific security and privacy measures and policies that a service provider must have in place. For example, the Schedule might specify 256-bit encryption of data at rest, or require antivirus protection. Some of these specific requirements may be dictated by specific legal obligations[2] or by the customer's internal infrastructure. Another approach is to tie the service provider's existing security measures (assessed during the customer's security assessment process) to the Schedule, with requirements to update those measures periodically, especially for long-term contracts.
- **Reasonable security.** In addition to specific security and privacy measures, the Schedule should impose a broad duty on the service provider to maintain "reasonable security." The Schedule may also impose obligations to comply with industry standards, preferably naming any published information security standards (such as ISO 27001/2, PCI-DSS, or NIST guidelines) that govern the services and serve as a test of reasonableness in the context of the service agreement. While a court may reference such standards—as well as industry custom and practice—in defining reasonableness, it is also possible that industry standards and customary practices will not be found to meet the level of reasonableness required as a matter of law,[3] especially where a court determines that service providers should have been aware of new threats and corresponding protective measures. As such, the service provider's reasonable security obligation should include, but not be limited to, industry standards.
- **Return/destruction of data.** The parties should also stipulate their expectations for data return or destruction upon termination or expiration of their agreement. As with expectations-setting for data exchange and data processing, the party-to-party expectations for data return or destruction will typically be molded by a party's desire to keep compliant with the particular data handling laws or regulations to which such party is subject.[4] Because this likely means that the recipient of data will also be asked to comply with such laws

2. *See* Mass. Code Regs. tit. 201 § 17.00 et al. (2009); *see also* Nev. Rev. Stat. § 597.970 (2005).
3. *See In re* Eastern Transportation Co. (The T.J. Hooper), 60 F.2d 737 (2nd Cir. 1932).
4. For example, a health care entity will be focused on complying with 45 C.F.R. § 164.310(d)(2)(i) and (ii) (covered entities implement policies and procedures to address the final disposition of electronic PHI and/or the hardware or electronic media on which it is stored, as well as to implement procedures for removal of electronic PHI from electronic media before the media are made available for re-use). On the other hand, an entity that falls within GLBA will focus its compliance efforts on 16 C.F.R. § 314.2(c) (*i.e.*, "the administrative, technical, or physical safeguards you use to . . . dispose of . . . customer information").

or regulations, it is in a recipient party's best interest to be sensitive to the specific data destruction requirements imposed on the disclosing party, so that the recipient can (a) confirm that its data destruction policies would comply with the disclosing party's particular requirements, (b) be in a position to develop a data destruction policy to meet the disclosing party's requirements, or, knowing that it cannot or will not comply, (c) attempt to negotiate this requirement out of the agreement.[5] When the return or destruction obligation is triggered, if the parties decide to waive this requirement, agreements often state that the recipient of the data remains obligated to preserve the confidentiality of the data.

- **Assessment and enforcement rights.** Circumstances in the information security and privacy world change rapidly—new vulnerabilities arise; safer security measures are developed—and service providers can become lax or fall behind. This is especially true in the context of long-term contracts. Schedules should provide a customer with rights to conduct periodic security assessments to confirm compliance with the Schedule and regulations and impose on the service provider the obligation to adopt reasonable additional security measures in light of the existing risk environment. The Schedule can also require the service provider to give the customer access to its own internal assessments or provide notice if it is in noncompliance with applicable standards. The Schedule may also refer to periodic benchmarking against the practices of peer companies. If noncompliance is found there should be contractual consequences, including potentially the right to terminate the contract for cause (often providing for a period in which the service provider may cure the default). These provisions serve two functions. First, the customer's right to conduct an assessment can act as a deterrent; service providers are more likely to stay in compliance if they fear an assessment and contractual remedies. Second, an assessment allows the customer to understand the security and privacy risks it faces and to know whether the service provider is addressing these risks and maintaining compliance with applicable laws. This second function is especially important for long-term contracts where the risk environment is likely to change over time.

The need to address the preceding issues may vary depending on the nature of the transaction. Moreover, the relative bargaining power of the parties and the positions taken by the service provider may impact a customer's ability to successfully negotiate certain terms. Regardless, when drafting information security and privacy terms, parties should consider how those terms might be viewed from a compliance standpoint or in a litigation context.

5. There may be a temptation to assume that meeting the data destruction requirements of one statutory/regulatory framework will be sufficient to meet other frameworks. This is not always the case. A comment by the U.S. Federal Trade Commission in its final rules pursuant to 16 C.F.R. § 314 (commonly known as the "Safeguard Rules") raises this point, if indirectly, in addressing the idea that complying with the Fair Credit Reporting Act, HIPAA, or the Fair Debt Collection Practices Act should automatically mean compliance with the Safeguard Rules: "[T]he Commission does not intend to impose undue burdens on entities that are already subject to comparable safeguards requirements . . . [; h]owever, because such other rules and laws do not necessarily provide comparable protections in terms of the safeguards mandated, data covered, and range of circumstances to which protections apply, compliance with such standards will not automatically ensure compliance with the [Safeguard] Rule."

4. Security Incident Response Planning

Customers should view a service provider as an extension of the customer not only with respect to the controls the service provider maintains but also in regard to the service provider's response to a security incident. Toward that end, the Schedule should afford the customer the most control possible in responding to, and mitigating the impact of, a security incident.

The customer should investigate the service provider's security incident response procedures for the following components: controls and policies to detect an incident; upon detection, a chain of communication that escalates the incident to appropriate personnel; procedures for ascertaining the risk and potential impact posed by a security incident; and processes to allow for rapid remediation of a security breach. Moreover, because a forensic analysis or security assessment will often be necessary post-breach, the customer should investigate what information is retained by the service provider and for how long. The Schedule should obligate the service provider to retain certain information that may be relevant to a breach (e.g., access logs, records of system errors and corrective actions taken, information concerning the starting and finishing time of operations, change records, etc.).

Further, the customer should consider how the service provider and customer will interact in the event the service provider suffers a security breach impacting the customer's information, systems, or ability to conduct business. The Schedule should require the service provider to identify an incident response coordinator to serve as the communication point for the customer. Communication obligations can include a point of contact within the customer's organization, including in some instances a security breach emergency phone number. The Schedule should impose "deadlines" for providing notice of security breaches to the customer (e.g., "immediately," "within 24 hours" of discovery, etc.). The Schedule should include a general cooperation clause and, in some cases, specific incident response procedures allocated between the service provider and customer.

In addition, the Schedule should require the service provider to provide reports and information concerning the security incident, including performing a root cause analysis identifying what information or systems were impacted and specifying the remediation taken and planned by the service provider. The Schedule should also provide the customer with the ability to conduct its own independent forensic analysis and security assessment after a breach. Because litigation or regulatory action is possible following a breach, the Schedule should include mechanisms for seeking injunctive relief, initiating a litigation hold, and preserving information that may be relevant in a litigation context, as well as procedures for responding to information requests by regulators or litigants.

5. Risk of Loss

While most of the items just discussed are rather unique to the information security and privacy realm, risk of loss provisions are common in most contracts. These provisions include warranty disclaimers, consequential damages disclaimers, limitation of liability clauses, and indemnification clauses. Risk of loss terms should also be included with respect to information security and privacy. In this context there are some additional considerations worth noting.

First, it is not unusual for a security incident to yield consequential damages in addition to direct damages, including loss of profits, lost customers, attorney fees, breach notice costs, and other similar expenses plus the typically largest expense of reconstituting the data. If the contract contains a consequential damages disclaimer, the customer should endeavor to negotiate an exception for reasonably foreseeable consequential damages arising out of a security incident and/or breach of the Schedule.

Second, the customer's damages arising out of a security incident can be enormous. They can include loss of profits, litigation (often multiple lawsuits for large breaches) and regulatory action defense costs, awarded or settled damages, imposed fines and penalties, costs to provide notice to individuals whose personal information was breached, credit monitoring expenses, call center expenses, and third-party forensic analysis expenses. If a limitation of liability clause is in the contract, a customer should consider whether the liability cap would be sufficient to make it whole in the event of a security breach. If not, the customer should attempt to negotiate an exception to the limitation of liability (or perhaps a different limit for liability arising out of security incidents or breaches of the Schedule).

Additionally, enhanced indemnification language should be considered. Anticipating that a breach or a security incident may lead to litigation or a regulatory action, the Schedule should include an indemnification clause imposing the obligation to pay for the defense of any actions and indemnifying the customer for all damages, fines, penalties, and other costs arising out of or connected to such actions.

Likewise, the Schedule should also impose a duty on the service provider to indemnify the customer for certain breach notice–related expenses. Almost all states[6] have passed breach notice laws that require companies to provide notice to individuals whose personal information *may have* been compromised. Many expenses arise out of the legal requirement to provide notice, including forensic expenses, attorney fees, and mailing costs (discussed next). In addition, some customers may also want to provide affected individuals with a dedicated website, call center, and preventive measures such as card replacement or credit monitoring. Many of these expenses have a "multiplier" component that can result in compounded damages. For example, one year of credit monitoring could cost anywhere from $10 to $360 per year per individual. If credit monitoring is provided to one million affected individuals, a low-end estimate of the cost would be about $10 million. Therefore, the customer may attempt to negotiate indemnification for these costs that is not subject to the liability cap.

Organizations should consider insurance as another method for transferring risk of loss. Cyber insurance coverage (discussed in Chapter 4) is available for many types of loss that arise out of a security or privacy breach and goes beyond what protections may exist in a commercial general liability policy. This coverage includes loss of income, remediation expenses, data restoration, attorney fees, damages, fines and penalties, forensic expenses, breach notice expenses, and credit monitoring and call center expenses. The Schedule should require the service provider to carry both errors and omissions and cyber risk coverage with appropriate limits of liability. The customer

6. *See* http://www.ncsl.org/default.aspx?tabid=13489.

should attempt to mandate that it be named as an additional insured under the service provider's policy, although some insurers are unwilling to provide "additional insured" coverage. In addition, customers should consider purchasing their own cyber policy to provide direct coverage. These types of insurance coverage provide resources to allow a service provider to pay certain liability obligations regardless of the service provider's financial condition.

An information security and privacy Schedule that sets forth service provider security and privacy obligations and corresponding customer rights is an increasingly important and necessary part of an information technology, outsourcing, or cloud computing transaction. Lawyers charged with developing such Schedules should be aware that the Schedules serve several simultaneous purposes that are specific to the compliance and liability risk associated with data security and privacy. The Schedule is a classic example of where "hybrid" knowledge of the law and security is required. A large part of the Schedule involves translating legal compliance and risk issues in a manner that can be understood by security and privacy professionals. Accordingly, lawyers should work closely with their clients' respective information security and privacy teams in developing security assessment processes and in drafting and negotiating the terms of Schedules with service providers.

B. Breach of Contract

1. *Material Breaches*

Failure to meet information security obligations contained in a contract typically triggers the material breach clauses. These material breach provisions typically give the nonbreaching party the right to terminate the agreement (often immediately), compel specific performance, and/or collect damages.[7] The material breach section of a contract may address specific data safeguards such as password protection of files, encryption of data in databases, or securing the transmissions of data.

However, information security and privacy obligations can be complex, increasing an organization's risk of an inadvertent data or system breach.[8] Whether simple or complex, the cost of remediating a breach or paying damages or fines as a result of a breach can far exceed the total monetary value of the agreement between the parties. Thus, the significant financial risk associated with poor data security and privacy and related regulatory problems makes it imperative that the information maintained for the customer

---

7. "A party is not automatically excused from the future performance of contract obligations every time the other party commits a breach; if a breach is relatively minor and not of the essence, the plaintiff is still bound by the contract and may not abandon performance . . . . A party is discharged from further performance . . . only when there is a material breach . . . ." 23 WILLISTON ON CONTRACTS (4th ed.), § 63:3.

8. Many U.S. financial institutions contractually require their technology vendors to comply with the Interagency Guidelines Establishing Information Security Standards. *See* 12 C.F.R. pt. 30 et al. (Final Rule). Many business concerns also choose to leverage information security standards developed by certain standards-setting entities, for example, ISO/IEC 27001/27002 (formerly 17799) (Information security management systems and code of practice), which are international standards issued by the American National Standards Institute (ANSI) as the U.S. representative to the International Organization for Standards (ISO), and also via the U.S. National Committee to the International Electrotechnical Commission (IEC).

be secured and not disclosed without authorization or otherwise in contravention of the terms of the agreement protecting the information.

2. *Breach of Warranty*

Information security contracts generally provide generic warranties (e.g., warranties that the vendor is incorporated and in good standing), as well as additional warranties specific to data security and privacy, such as warranties of compliance with all applicable laws and regulations, warranties against security vulnerabilities (e.g., using commercially reasonable virus detection), and warranties that the vendor will refrain from intentionally including computer viruses in the licensed software.[9] Information security agreements may also disclaim all warranties beyond those explicitly set forth, and the remedy for breach of warranty may be subject to a limitation of liability clause unless specifically excluded. Contractual liability may result from a breach of whatever warranty standard (such as "commercially reasonable") or express warranty is agreed between the parties.

3. *Breach of Privacy Policy*

Many if not most companies that store, collect, or process personal identifiable information or other sensitive data have privacy policies. An organization's privacy policy may state that the organization will not disclose certain information without the consent of the information's owner or will maintain "reasonable and appropriate" security measures to protect the information. If the owner of the information construes the privacy policy to be an agreement on which he reasonably relies to his detriment,[10] the organization's failure to use reasonable and appropriate security measures, resulting in data being lost, stolen, or otherwise damaged, or intentionally or inadvertently disclosed without consent, could subject the organization to contractual or quasi-contractual liability if the owner suffers measurable harm.[11] Additionally, the organization may face potential liability for unfair and deceptive practices.[12] This is further discussed from a noncontractual regulatory perspective next.

C. Confidentiality/Nondisclosure Agreements

Confidentiality/Nondisclosure agreements (NDAs) govern how and when nonpublic information may be shared between parties and how and when such information may be disclosed to third parties, if at all. Properly drafted NDAs focus on information that is valuable or protected and that is not already publicly available. The information may have commercial value (such as nonobvious technical information, confidential com-

---

9. While a vendor warranty against intentionally including computer viruses in its own software may sound unusual, the United States Department of Justice has for years had a criminal practice group dedicated to combating virus writers, hackers, and disgruntled engineers. The Computer Crime and Intellectual Property Section (CCIPS, available at http://www.cybercrime.gov/) has had numerous prosecutions for intentional backdoors, Trojan horses, computer viruses, and worms.

10. *See* Meyer v. Christie, 2007 WL 3120695, at *5 (D.Kan., Oct. 24, 2007).

11. *See, generally,* Cargill Global Trading v. Applied Development Co., 2010 WL 1568457, at *14, *18 (D.N.J. Apr. 21, 2010). *See also In re* Jetblue, 379 F. Supp. 2d at 327 (holding that even if plaintiffs demonstrated a contract based on privacy policy, plaintiffs' breach claim failed because they could not allege loss).

12. *See* 15 U.S.C. §§ 41–58.

mercial information, or information that would be considered a trade secret) or may be information (such as employee or customer personal information) whose unauthorized disclosure to third parties could subject the data owner to legal liability.[13]

NDAs may refer to applicable security standards or guidelines. Several industries are required to protect specific, statutorily defined confidential or nonpublic data, particularly the health care[14] and financial services industries.[15] The U.S. government often incorporates NIST guidelines in government contracting.[16] Parties handling credit or debit card details may refer to the Payment Card Industry Data Security Standard, while others may consult guidance published by nonprofits such as Counsel[17] and EPIC.[18] Even if a specific security standard is not mentioned, it is not unusual for an NDA to require the recipient of confidential information to protect that information with the same care that the recipient uses to protect its own confidential information.

NDAs create a contractual relationship between the parties obligating them to protect confidential, nonpublic, and/or proprietary information from the other party or certain third parties. Thus, an organization may be contractually obligated to protect a customer's, employee's, or business partner's personal or confidential information. Provisions addressing confidentiality often include a requirement to provide "commercially reasonable" protection of confidential information that is at least what the organization

---

13. The information protected by an NDA may include the company's own confidential data as well as a third-party's confidential data. Examples of such information might include nonpublic customer information, such as credit card or bank account information, the disclosure of which could subject an organization to financial loss and legal penalties. *See* 16 C.F.R. § 313.3(o)(2). This might include potential liability for unauthorized disclosure of protected personal information, privileged communications (such as lawyer-client or doctor-patient communications), national secrets, or the trade secrets of the company or its business partner.

14. The Health Insurance Portability and Accountability Act of 1996 (HIPAA) utilizes the concept of Protected Health Information (PHI), which is health information collected from an individual, created or received by a health care provider, health plan, employer, or health care clearinghouse, and which relates to (i) the past, present, or future physical or mental health or condition of an individual; (ii) the provision of health care to an individual; or (iii) the past, present, or future payment for the provision of health care to an individual, and such information either identifies the individual or with respect to which there is a reasonable basis to believe the information can be used to identify the individual. *See* 15 C.F.R. § 160.103.

15. The term "nonpublic personal information" means personally identifiable financial information (i) provided by a consumer to a financial institution; (ii) resulting from any transaction with the consumer or any service performed for the consumer; or (iii) otherwise obtained by the financial institution. *See* 15 U.S.C § 6809(4).

16. In addition to the definitions discussed above in GLBA and HIPAA, U.S. law and regulations contain confidentiality and nondisclosure rules addressing different contexts. The Freedom of Information Act, 5 U.S.C. § 552(b) lists certain information not subject to disclosure, including trade secrets and privileged or confidential commercial or financial information obtained from a person. *See* 5 U.S.C. § 552(b)(4). The U.S. Federal Acquisition Regulations contain rules that require confidential treatment of certain contractor or other offeror information. *See, e.g.*, 48 C.F.R. § 9903.202-4 (If the offeror or contractor notifies the contracting officer that the Disclosure Statement contains trade secrets and commercial or financial information, which is privileged and confidential, the Disclosure Statement shall be protected and shall not be released outside the Government.)

17. https://www.pcisecuritystandards.org/index.shtml.

18. http://epic.org/.

uses to protect its own confidential data.[19] Where such a term is a part of the contract, a party whose information is compromised may assert a claim against the party agreeing to provide security for the information.[20] Significantly, a particular contract may also have a data security or privacy exhibit or schedule. Practitioners should endeavor to reconcile the security provisions in an NDA with those that might exist in such an exhibit or schedule.

After establishing the definitions and applicable regulations, the agreement should establish the expectations for data exchange, processing, and disposal. Depending on the sensitivity of the data, encryption in transit or storage may be appropriate.

The parties to an NDA often place restrictions on the processing of data once received, including the individuals or functions that will have access and whether the data may be reused for other activities such as testing or aggregation with other sources. In some cases, business partners establish a "least privileges" model where only those with a need to know have access to perform only the agreed-upon activities.

D. Remedies

As with any contract, information security agreements have typical contractual remedies: termination, specific performance, and/or monetary damages. While the parties to the contract clearly have these remedies (subject to any contractual limitation of damages), a customer or third-party beneficiary of the contract may not have standing to assert a breach of contract claim, and even if so, may find it very difficult to prove damages in an information security contract matter.[21] Unless there is a showing of loss or damages incurred by the third party, there can be no recovery for the breach.[22]

---

19. Many confidentiality agreements contain provisions similar to the following: Recipient agrees to take reasonable measures to ensure that all employees, agents, or individuals to whom recipient disclosed the confidential information shall keep confidential the discloser's confidential information. At a minimum, recipient shall apply the same internal security procedures that it applies to its own confidential information to the discloser's confidential information.

20. For example, a HIPAA-covered entity may disclose PHI to a "business associate" performing tasks on its behalf only if the HIPAA-covered entity obtains satisfactory assurance that the business associate will safeguard the information. *See* 45 C.F.R. §§ 164.308(b)(1) and 164.502(e)(1)(i). The business associate thus becomes bound to security obligations by contract as well as being subject to additional restrictions under the Health Information Technology for Economic and Clinical Health Act of 2009 (HITECH), which extends HIPAA penalties to business associates.

21. *See, e.g.*, Ruiz v. Gap, Inc., 622 F. Supp. 2d 908 (N.D. Cal. 2009) (court determined that plaintiff could not show he was actually damaged by pointing to his fear of future identity theft); Pisciotta v. Old Nat. Bancorp, 499 F.3d 629 (affirming district court's decision that "there could be no action for breach of contract under Indiana law in the absence of . . . cognizable damages"); Forbes v. Wells Fargo Bank, N.A., 420 F. Supp. 2d 1018 (D. Minn. 2006) (granting summary judgment in favor of defendant on lost-data plaintiff's breach of contract claim under Minnesota law); Hendricks v. DSW Shoe Warehouse, Inc., 444 F. Supp. 2d 775 (W.D. Mich. 2006) (dismissing contract claim of plaintiff who claimed as damages "the costs of protecting herself against a risk that the stolen data will, in the future, be used to her detriment" because plaintiff had "failed to allege damages of a type cognizable under Michigan common law applicable to contract actions").

22. *See, e.g.*, Sovereign Bank v. BJ's Wholesale Club, Inc., 533 F.3d 162, 172–73 (3d Cir. 2008) (holding that an intended third-party beneficiary of a credit card agreement may enforce information security provisions of that agreement if the third party suffered cognizable harm, such as the cost of replacing thousands of credit cards).

1. *Allocation of Costs Associated with a Breach*

Information security breaches may not only damage a company's business reputation, they are also expensive. A 2009 study examined the costs various companies incurred because of data security breaches and found that, on average, a single data breach cost the affected company $6.75 million in terms of data restoration, lost business, legal fees, customer notifications, and fines/penalties.[23]

Responsibility for the costs associated with a breach may be allocated by the agreement itself, by a court, or by a regulatory agency. Indemnification clauses negotiated into the agreement (discussed earlier) may allow a contracting party to recover some of these costs from the service provider. Customers may also sue under general contract theories if they can establish a loss. This being said, laws and/or regulations that focus on data deemed sensitive (financial and health care, among others) may hold a company ultimately accountable for a security breach related to its data, regardless of where the data is stored and regardless of who was "guarding" the data.

3.2 TORT CLAIMS

A. Intentional Torts

1. *Fraud/Misrepresentation*

While fraud is an element of federal and state criminal statutes too numerous to list here in full,[24] in the civil tort context "fraud" is generally known as the intentional tort of misrepresentation.[25] The well-recognized elements of intentional misrepresentation are: (1) the making of a representation of fact, opinion, intention, or law, which (a) the maker knows or believes is not as represented, (b) for which the maker lacks confidence in the accuracy of the representation as stated, or (c) the maker knows he does not have a basis for making; (2) for the purpose of inducing another to act or to refrain from action in reliance on the representation; (3) with the maker's intent that the recipient rely on the representation; (4) whereby the recipient justifiably relies on the maker's representation; and (5) the recipient suffers pecuniary loss resulting from the action or inaction in reliance upon the representation (but only if the loss would reasonably be expected to result from the reliance).[26]

In the context of information security, misrepresentation is a commonly pled cause of action, not merely as to perceived violations of online agreements (in particular website terms of use agreements) or misrepresentations about security actually or claimed to be provided, whether through a privacy policy or otherwise, but also in actions arising

---

23. Ponemon Institute, *Fourth Annual U.S. Cost of Data Breach Study* (Jan. 2009), *available at* http://www.ponemon.org/local/upload/fckjail/generalcontent/18/file/2008-2009%20US%20Cost%20of%20Data%20Breach%20Report%20Final.pdf.

24. *See, e.g.*, Computer Fraud and Abuse Act, 18 U.S.C. § 1030, the Federal Trade Commission Act, and others covered in Chapter 2.

25. Keeton, Prosser and Keeton on The Law of Torts, § 105 at 725–28 (5th ed. & Supp. 1988).

26. Restatement (Second) of Torts, §§ 525–49; *see also* Kent D. Stuckey, Internet and Online Law, § 3.02[2] at 3–15 (1996 & Release 14 2003).

from "cyberthefts," from results gained through "phishing" or financial transactions,[27] as well as in actions alleging intentional misrepresentation by an online user to other users (e.g., online auction sales). In addition, misrepresentation is a common element in state consumer fraud and deceptive trade practice acts that have figured prominently in recent data breaches[28] and has likewise been a basis for various Federal Trade Commission actions, as deceptive practices, against companies who have suffered data breaches.[29] In such cases the issues of whether "reasonable" and legal defensible security was provided, in light of industry best practices, applicable regulatory mandates, and the companies' own representations, can all factor into whether a claim of misrepresentation is successful.[30]

2. *Invasion of Privacy*

Invasion of privacy is an intentional tort based on the intrusion upon seclusion of another or publicity given to private life. A party is liable where he intentionally intrudes on the seclusion of another or her or his private affairs and the intrusion is highly offensive to a reasonable person.[31] A party is also liable if he gives publicity to the private life of another if the matter publicized would be highly offensive to a reasonable person.[32]

The invasion of privacy tort faces significant hurdles in the typical data breach or lost laptop case. In *Randolph v. ING Life Insurance and Annuity Co.*, the court dismissed invasion of privacy claims where a burglar stole a laptop containing personal information of plan participants.[33] The court found that the failure to establish appropriate safeguards to protect the data on the laptop (even when characterized as a willful and intentional failure) was not an intentional tort but was more like a negligence claim.[34] Moreover, there were no allegations that the information on the laptop had been viewed or publicized.[35] The court did note that allowing the unauthorized viewing of personally identifiable information, including Social Security numbers, can be an intrusion highly offensive to a reasonable person.[36]

---

27. *In re* Crowson, 2010 WL 2402928 (Bankr. D. Wyo. 2010) (NO. BKR. 09-20032, ADV. 09-2009).

28. *See, e.g.*, the widely covered 2007 TJX Companies, Inc. data breach, *In re* TJX Companies Retail Sec. Breach Litigation, 564 F.3d 489 (1st Cir. 2009), where millions of credit and debit cards' data were stolen leading to claims, among other things, of breach of Massachusetts' unfair trade and deceptive practice acts, chapter 93A, codified at MASS. GEN. LAWS ch. 93A; *see also* the Hannaford Bros. 2008 data breach, *In re* Hannaford Bros. Co. Customer Data Security Breach Litigation, 613 F. Supp. 2d 109 (D. Maine 2008), in which over 4 million credit and debit card accounts were stolen, and the Maine Unfair Trade Practices Act implicated, *available at* http://www.mainelegislature.org/legis/statutes/5/title5ch10.pdf.

29. *See generally*, *A New Frontier: Litigation Over Data Breaches*, 20 PRAC. LITIGATOR, 47 (July 2009); Michael D. Scott, *FTC, the Unfairness Doctrine, and Data Security Breach Litigation: Has the Commission Gone Too Far?* 60 ADMIN L. REV. 127 (2008). *See also* § 3.1.e, FTC Act, and § 4.1.3a, FTC Regulatory Actions.

30. *See* David J. Navetta, *The Legal Defensibility Era Is Upon Us*, ISSA JOURNAL, May 2010, at 12–17.

31. Restatement (Second) of Torts § 652B.

32. Restatement (Second) of Torts § 652D.

33. 973 A.2d 702, 710 (D.C. Ct. App. 2009).

34. *Id.* at 711.

35. *Id.* at 711–12.

36. *Id.* at 710. A small number of courts have recognized a negligent invasion of privacy tort. *See* Bailer v. Erie Ins. Exchange, 687 A.2d 1375, 1389 (Md. 1997) (Chasanow, J., dissenting) (collecting cases).

To avoid potential liability from a claim of misrepresentation, organizations should actively and regularly review all their information security and privacy policies and procedures (both those circulated internally and those used externally in, for example, a website security policy) to ensure they accurately and fully reflect the current state of the organization's information security and privacy programs while comporting with all updates to applicable regulations and laws. Organizations should not make any guarantees, absolute statements, or broad unqualified representations as to the level of information security and privacy that an outside party should expect (and thereby rely upon), which could expose them to such liability.

B. Negligence

1. *Duty, Breach, Causation, Damages*

Negligence is defined as the "failure to use such care as a reasonably prudent and careful person would use under similar circumstances."[37] A plaintiff must establish four elements to prove a negligence claim: (1) the defendant owed a duty of care to the plaintiff; (2) the defendant breached that duty; (3) damages; and (4) that the breach was the proximate cause of the damages.

For example, where a hacker gains access to an organization's database and obtains names, addresses, and Social Security numbers that the hacker then uses to commit identity theft, the individuals whose private information was misappropriated may be able to assert negligence claims against the organization, contending that in failing to use industry standard security measures such as firewalls or an intrusion detection system, the organization failed to protect the victims' personal information and thereby proximately caused their damages. A more detailed discussion of the elements and potential defenses follows.

a. Duty and Breach of the Duty

In order to establish negligence, the defendant must owe a legal duty of care toward the plaintiff. While the issue has not yet been extensively litigated, some courts appear to recognize that some businesses that collect certain personal information from their customers owe a duty to their customers to protect that data.[38] The potential existence of this obligation may be reinforced through written privacy policies assuring customers that the company will take reasonable precautions to protect the customer data. It is less clear whether a duty exists in the case of information security breaches when the parties do not have a preexisting relationship, whether contractual or otherwise. Where a company shares its customer data with a third-party vendor, the vendor may be liable if it has an obligation to the company's customers[39] (see also the discussion about business associates' obligations

---

37. Black's Law Dictionary 1032 (6th ed.).

38. *See* Shames-Yeakel v. Citizens Fin. Bank, 677 F. Supp. 2d 994 (N.D. Ill. 2009) (bank owed a duty to its customers to use state-of-the-art technology to protect their information); Jones v. Commerce Bancorp, No. 06 Civ. 835 (HB), 2006 U.S. Dist. LEXIS 32067 (S.D.N.Y. May 23, 2006) (bank had a duty to protect customer information); Daly v. Metro. Life Ins. Co., 4 Misc. 3d 887, 782 N.Y.S.2d 530 (N.Y. Sup. Ct. 2004) (life insurance company had a duty to secure information provided by applicants).

39. *See* Bovan v. Am. Family Life Ins. Co., 897 N.E.2d 288, 295 (Ill. App. Ct. 2008) (an agent is liable in tort to a third party harmed by the agent's conduct when the agent breaches a duty that she owes to the third party) (quoting Restatement (Third) of Agency § 7.02, at 138 (2006)).

under HIPAA in Chapter 2). Given the increasing focus globally on the individual's privacy interest in her or his PII, companies who come into possession of an individual's PII as part of their businesses may find that they owe some duty to protect that information.[40]

The more difficult question is the extent of the duty of care owed to the plaintiff. There is no "one-size-fits-all" duty of care. The law requires that the party take "reasonable" care under the circumstances; it does not require that a party take every conceivable precaution.[41] In evaluating the duty owed, a number of relevant factors are considered, including: (1) the likelihood of something happening; (2) the risk and severity of the resulting harm; (3) the cost for the defendant to prevent or minimize the risk or harm; (4) the victim's inability to protect himself; (5) the relationship between the parties; (6) whether the victim bestowed any economic benefit on the defendant; and (7) the societal interest in protecting against this harm.[42] There is considerable uncertainty over what constitutes "reasonable care" with respect to computer security due to the fact that: (a) security needs of organizations vary widely and (b) security technologies and industry standards are constantly evolving.

The courts may look to industry standards and state and federal statutes governing the conduct to determine if a party was negligent. Violation of a statute may be considered negligence per se if the breach leads to the type of injury the statute seeks to prevent.[43] Violation of an industry standard can be offered as evidence of negligence (by not meeting the standard of care). However, industry standards and statutes are often viewed as the minimum degree of care required, and compliance with them does not necessarily mean that a party has met the standard of care required under the specific circumstances of the case.[44]

b. Damages

A plaintiff must prove actual damages caused by a security breach, such as fraud losses or lost business income suffered by a victim of identity theft.[45] The inability to prove compensable damages is the biggest factor limiting lawsuits arising out of a security

---

40. *See* Remsburg v. Docusearch, Inc., 149 N.H. 148, 816 A.2d 1001 (2002) (holding a private investigatory firm liable where they had sold information, including the Social Security number and work address of plaintiff's daughter, to a man who had been stalking and then killed plaintiff's daughter, reasoning that a private investigator owed a duty to exercise reasonable care to not subject a third party to an increased risk of criminal misconduct, including stalking and identity theft).

41. Atoka Coal & Mining Co. v. Miller, 170 F. 584, 586 (8th Cir. 1909).

42. Bell v. Michigan Council 25 of the Am. Fed'n. of State, County and Mun. Employees, AFL-CIO, Local 1023, No. 246684, 2005 Mich. App. LEXIS 353 (Mich. Ct. App. Feb. 15, 2005).

43. For example, if a driver runs a red light and hits a car in the intersection, the driver is negligent per se. The law against running red lights is designed to prevent such a collision. Similarly, laws to prevent the loss or theft of PII or to minimize the resulting harm may give rise to a finding of negligence per se if not followed.

44. The T.J. Hooper v. Northern Barge Corp., 60 F.2d 737 (2d Cir. 1932). For example, although the speed limit on a highway may be 65 miles per hour, this is probably not a reasonable speed in an ice storm. Meeting the minimum industry or statutory standard for protecting PII may not be sufficient if the party fails to address a known risk unique to its system or if it holds unusually sensitive information. *But see* Guin v. Brazos Higher Educ. Serv. Corp., Civ. A. No. 05-668 (RHK/JSM), 2006 U.S. Dist. LEXIS 4846 (D. Minn. Feb. 7, 2006) (in a stolen laptop case, court granted summary judgment where there was no evidence to show defendant failed to comply with the Gramm-Leach-Bliley Act).

45. Jones v. Commerce Bancorp, Inc., No. 06 Civ. 835 (HB), 2006 U.S. Dist. LEXIS 32067, at *6-7 (S.D.N.Y. May 23, 2006).

breach.[46] Most courts have indicated that the mere exposure to an increased risk of harm, standing alone, does not constitute cognizable harm under the law,[47] even though it may be sufficient for federal rules on standing.[48] Thus, courts have held that a party cannot recover credit monitoring and other costs associated with the increased risk.[49] A party cannot recover for the aggravation associated with the loss; a party cannot recover for emotional injury absent some physical injury.[50] The ability to recover certain damages (e.g., loss of income) may also be limited by the "economic loss" doctrine (discussed later in this chapter).

c. Proximate Cause

The breach of the duty must be closely enough related to the plaintiff's injury to be considered the cause of, or at least a substantial factor in causing, the harm and must occur in an unbroken sequence from the injury.[51] In the security breach context, it may be difficult to prove that an individual case of identity theft was caused by a given data breach. For example, in *Stollenwerk v. Tri-West Healthcare Alliance*, someone attempted to open credit accounts in the plaintiff's name on six occasions. The court found that because the plaintiff's address, including his Social Security number, was disclosed to others on multiple occasions, the use of such information in acts of identity fraud does not permit the inference that unidentified identity thieves obtained it from the defendant.[52] However, causation may be established where numerous members of an affected class suffered identity theft or where there is specific evidence that the perpetrator of identity theft used the plaintiffs' personal information to purchase goods in the plaintiffs' names.[53] While unforeseen criminal acts are usually intervening causes breaking the chain of causation, in the context of data thefts, the risk of criminal breaches is becoming a foreseeable risk and the failure to protect against them can be said to be the cause of the loss.[54]

---

46. Randolph v. ING Life Ins. & Annuity Co., 973 A.2d 702, 710 (D.C. Ct. App. 2009); *In re* Hannaford Bros. Co. Customer Data Sec. Breach Litig., 2010 ME 93, 2010 Me. LEXIS 97 (Me. Sept. 21, 2010); Randolph v. ING Life Ins. & Annuity Co., 486 F. Supp. 2d 1, 6–8 (D.D.C. 2007); Bell v. Acxiom Corp., No. 4:06CV00485-WRW, 2006 U.S. Dist. LEXIS 72477 (E.D. Ark. Oct. 3, 2006); Key v. DSW, Inc., 454 F. Supp. 2d 684 (S.D. Ohio 2006); Giordano v. Wachovia Sec., Civ. A. No. 06477 (JBS), 2006 U.S. Dist. LEXIS 52266 (D.N.J. July 31, 2006).

47. Ruiz v. Gap, Inc., No. 09-15971, 2010 WL 2170993 (9th Cir. May 2010), Hammond v. The Bank of New York Mellon Corp., Case No. 1:08-CV-06060 (S.D.N.Y. June 2010), Randolph v. ING Life Ins. & Annuity Co., 973 A.2d 702, 710 (D.C. Ct. App. 2009); *In re* Hannaford Bros.Co. Customer Data Sec. Breach Litig., 2010 ME 93, 2010 Me. LEXIS 97 (Me. Sept. 2010).

48. Krottner v. Starbucks Corp., No. 09-35823 (9th Cir. Dec. 2010).

49. *Compare* Pisciotta v. Old National Bancorp, 499 F.3d 629, 639–40 (7th Cir. 2007) (Indiana law does not recognize recovery of credit monitoring costs where there was only an increased risk of identity theft) *with* Ruiz v. Gap, Inc., No. 09-15971, 2010 U.S. App. LEXIS 10984, at *4 (9th Cir. May 28, 2010) (California courts have not decided whether time and money spent on credit monitoring are damages sufficient to support a negligence claim).

50. Melancon v. Louisiana Office of Student Fin. Assistance, 567 F. Supp. 2d 873, 874 (E.D. La. 2008).

51. Black's Law Dictionary 1225 (6th ed.).

52. No. Civ. 03-0185-PHX-SRB, 2005 U.S. Dist. LEXIS 41054, at *17-21 (D. Ariz. Sept. 8, 2005).

53. Bell v. Michigan Council 25 of the Am. Fed'n. of State, County and Mun. Employees, AFL-CIO, Local 1023, No. 246684, 2005 Mich. App. LEXIS 353 (Mich. Ct. App. Feb. 15, 2005).

54. *See* Sovereign Bank v. BJ's Wholesale Club, Inc., 395 F. Supp. 2d 183, 195–96 (M.D. Pa. 2005) (plaintiff's claim can proceed alleging that "BJ's should have realized that its negligence in retaining customer information created a situation where third parties might avail themselves of the opportunity to steal cardholder information") (citing Restatement (Second) of Torts § 448).

d. Other Defenses

There are several defenses to a negligence action based on either the availability of a contract action or damages being limited to unrecoverable economic losses.

e. Economic Loss Doctrine

The economic loss doctrine bars recovery of economic damages in tort actions where there has been no personal injury or property damage. The doctrine originated in product liability cases, where courts dismissed tort actions when the product only injured itself; that is, it failed with no resulting personal injury or damage to other property.[55] In these cases, economic loss included the decreased value of the product (that is, the product is worth less because it is inferior or does not work), the costs to repair or replace the defective product, and consequential loss of profits and use.[56] These types of damages should be remedied in actions for breach of contract or warranty and not tort actions. Courts have applied the economic loss doctrine in areas other than product liability with varying results.

Courts have reached different results in data breach cases concerning the economic loss doctrine. For example, in *In re Hannaford Brothers Co. Customer Data Security Breach Litigation*, the court held that the economic loss doctrine did not bar a negligence claim where a third party stole a grocery store's customers' credit and debit card information.[57] The court concluded that the groceries sold to the customer were not the defective product and, even assuming that the store's payment system could be construed as the defective product, the state's economic loss doctrine would not apply because this was not a case about "insufficient product value."[58] In *Sovereign Bank v. BJ's Wholesale Club, Inc.*, however, the court, interpreting a different state's law, found that the economic loss doctrine would bar a negligence claim by a credit card issuing bank against a merchant seeking the costs to replace credit cards and the amounts it reimbursed customers for fraudulent purchases.[59]

f. "Gist of the Action" Doctrine

A tort claim is barred by the gist of the action doctrine if: (1) it arises solely from a contract between the parties; (2) the duties allegedly breached were created and grounded in the contract; (3) the liability stems from a contract; and (4) the tort claim essentially duplicates a breach of contract claim or the success of the tort claim is wholly dependent on the terms

---

55. Banknorth, N.A. v. BJ's Wholesale Club, Inc., 442 F. Supp. 2d 206, 211–12 (D. Me. 2006) (discussing Oceanside at Pine Point Condo. Owners Ass'n v. Peachtree Doors, Inc., 659 A.2d 267 (Me. 1995)).

56. Moorman Mfg. Co. v. Nat'l. Tank Co., 435 N.E.2d 443 (Ill. 1982); Indemnity Ins. Co. of North Am. v. Am. Aviation, Inc., 891 So. 2d 532 (Fla. 2004). For example, where a tire fails and results in only a flat tire, the owner cannot sue the manufacturer in tort to replace the tire and for business lost when the owner missed a meeting. However, when the tire fails and an accident with injuries results, the injured parties can sue the tire manufacturer in tort for personal injuries, lost income, and damage to the cars.

57. 613 F. Supp. 2d 108, 127–28 (D. Me. 2009) (interpreting Maine law).

58. *Id.*

59. Sovereign Bank v. BJ's Wholesale Club, Inc., 533 F.3d 162, 175–78 (3rd Cir. 2008) (interpreting Pennsylvania law); *see also In re* TJX Companies Retail Sec. Breach Litig., 524 F. Supp. 2d 83, 90–91 (D. Mass. 2007) (economic loss doctrine barred negligence claim by credit and debit card issuing banks to cover the costs flowing from compromised cards and lost card verification codes).

of the contract.[60] Where the parties' relationship is defined solely by a contract, the gist of the action doctrine provides that the proper remedy is contractual; the parties do not have a separate tort claim. However, the doctrine would not bar a negligence claim where there is a duty in the absence of contract. For example, a bank has a duty to protect customer data even if there is no contract (see above); it does not matter that the bank may also have a contractual obligation to protect customer data (e.g., a written privacy policy).

2. *Gross Negligence*

Gross negligence is a "conscious, voluntary act or omission in reckless disregard of a legal duty and of the consequences to another party."[61] Gross negligence has also been called "reckless negligence," "wanton negligence," "willful negligence," and "willful and wanton negligence."[62] In some jurisdictions, gross negligence is a separate cause of action.[63] In other jurisdictions, gross negligence is simply a more culpable state of mind needed to obtain punitive damages or, depending on the parties' contract, to avoid application of an exculpatory clause.[64] Although the phrases used to describe it and the exact standards differ from state to state, gross negligence is something more than ordinary or simple negligence and usually involves a showing that the defendant was aware of a substantial risk of serious harm and chose to disregard it.[65]

"Gross negligence" becomes important in cases where simple negligence may not support a cause of action. The parties may have limited their liability through a contractual exculpatory clause, limitation on liability, or disclaimer.[66] The contract may seek to limit liability for anything from simple negligence to all liability for any injury. Some courts have held that exculpatory provisions will only bar claims for simple or ordinary negligence.[67] In those jurisdictions, such provisions will not bar claims for gross negligence, recklessness, or intentional misconduct.

---

60. Grimm v. Washington Mut. Bank, Civ. 02:08cv0828, 2008 U.S. Dist. LEXIS 55628, at *7 (W.D. Pa. July 22, 2008); *see* Sovereign Bank v. BJ's Wholesale Club, Inc., 395 F. Supp. 2d 183, 196–97 (M.D. Pa. 2005) (gist of the action applies only when there is a contractual relationship between the parties).

61. Gage v. HSM Elec. Prot. Services, Inc., Civ. A. No. 09-2141 ADM/JJG, 2010 U.S. Dist. LEXIS 58407, at *9 (D. Minn. June 14, 2010) (quoting Black's Law Dictionary 1062 (8th ed. 2004)).

62. *Id.*

63. *Compare* Liu v. Arrow Fin. Services, LLC, Civ. A. No. H-08-3116, 2010 U.S. Dist. LEXIS 48241, at *26 (S.D. Tex. May 17, 2010) (setting forth the Texas cause of action for gross negligence) and Resolution Trust Corp. v. Fortunato, Civ. A. No. 94 C 2090, 1994 U.S. Dist. LEXIS 12326, at *8 (N.D. Ill. 1994) (Illinois does not recognize a separate claim for "gross negligence" but does recognize an equivalent cause of action for "willful or wanton misconduct") *with* Ward v. County of Cuyahoga, Case No. 1:09-cv-415, 2010 U.S. Dist. LEXIS 64328, at (N.D. Ohio June 29, 2010) (Ohio does not recognize a separate cause of action for willful, wanton, and reckless misconduct).

64. *See* Cincinnati Ins. Co. v. Oanacea, No. L-04-1050, 2004 WL 1810347 (Ohio Ct. App. Aug. 13, 2004) ("Willful, wanton and reckless misconduct is technically not a separate cause of action, but a level of intent which negates certain defenses which might be available in an ordinary negligence action.").

65. *Liu*, 2010 U.S. Dist. LEXIS 48241, at *26.

66. For example, the current MySpace terms of service contains the following disclaimer: "MySpace assumes no responsibility for any error, omission, interruption, deletion, defect, delay in operation or transmission, communications line failure, theft or destruction or unauthorized access to, or alteration of, any User or Member communication." http://www.myspace.com/index.cfm?fuseaction=misc.terms.

67. *See* Stelluti v. Casapenn Enterprises, 975 A.2d 494 (N.J. Super. Ct. 2009) (ruling that exculpatory clause in fitness club contract covering "all injuries which may occur" only barred claims based on ordinary negligence), *cert. granted*, 983 A.2d 1110 (N.J. 2009).

"Gross negligence" may also support a claim for punitive damages.[68] Punitive damages are not to compensate a plaintiff for its injury but to punish the defendant and to deter that defendant and others from committing similar acts in the future. The amount of punitive damages awarded will depend on, among other things, the wealth of the defendant, the degree of the bad state of mind, and the resulting harm. There must also be a rational relationship between the damages awarded to compensate for the injury and the award of punitive damages.[69]

3.3 REGULATORY ACTIONS

The Federal Trade Commission and other federal agencies have been active in protecting the privacy and security of consumer information. At the state level, various attorneys general have brought enforcement actions in this area.

A. Federal Trade Commission

The Federal Trade Commission (FTC or the Commission) is the federal agency tasked with ensuring the efficient operation of the marketplace by protecting consumers from unfair and deceptive trade practices and promoting competition among businesses.[70] While the FTC enforces various antitrust and consumer protection laws,[71] this section discusses the Commission's enforcement of the Federal Trade Commission Act (FTCA) and other statutes designed to protect the privacy of consumer information.[72] Data security is one of the top priorities under the FTC's privacy agenda.[73] The FTC is also responsible for coordinating the federal response to identity theft and assistance for victims of identity theft.[74]

1. Authority

The FTC's enforcement authority is derived from the FTCA, as discussed in Chapter 2.[75] The FTC's primary means for taking action based on privacy violations is 15 U.S.C. § 45, more commonly known as Section 5 of the FTCA, which declares "unfair or deceptive

68. *Liu*, 2010 U.S. Dist. LEXIS 48241, at *26. These damages are also referred to as exemplary damages. *Id.*

69. State Farm Mutual Auto Ins. Co. v. Campbell, 538 U.S. 408 (2003).

70. *Emerging Financial Privacy Issues: Hearing Before the H. Comm. on Banking and Financial Services Subcomm. on Financial Institutions and Consumer Credit,* 105th Cong. (1999) (statement of Chairman Robert Pitofsky, FTC).

71. *See generally* FTC, Office of the General Counsel, *A Brief Overview of the Federal Trade Commission's Investigative and Law Enforcement Authority* (Sept. 2002), http://www.ftc.gov/ogc/brfovrvw.htm (*Brief Overview*).

72. Many enforcement actions initiated by the FTC arguably involve consumer privacy issues. The enforcement actions selected for inclusion in this chapter, however, were specifically identified as privacy-related by the FTC. *See, i.e.*, FTC, *Unfairness & Deception: Enforcement*, http://www.ftc.gov/privacy/privacyinitiatives/promises_enf.html; FTC, *Children's Privacy: Enforcement*, http://www.ftc.gov/privacy/privacyinitiatives/childrens_enf.html; FTC, *Pretexting: Enforcement*, http://www.ftc.gov/privacy/privacyinitiatives/pretexting_enf.html; FTC *Credit Reporting: Enforcement*, http://www.ftc.gov/privacy/privacyinitiatives/credit_enf.html.

73. Keynote address by FTC Chairman Jon Leibowitz at February 27, 2009, workshop, "Securing Personal Data in the Global Economy."

74. Identity Theft and Assumption Deterrence Act, 18 U.S.C. §1028 note.

75. 15 U.S.C. §§ 41–58, as amended; 15 U.S.C. § 45(a).

acts or in or affecting commerce . . . unlawful."[76] Other laws also give the Commission specific power to enforce privacy through authority conferred by the FTCA, including the Children's Online Privacy Protection Act, the Gramm-Leach-Bliley Act, the Telemarketing and Consumer Fraud Abuse and Prevention Act, and the Fair Credit Reporting Act.[77]

The Children's Online Privacy Protection Act (COPPA) generally requires commercial websites and online services aimed at children to obtain parental consent before collecting or using personal information from a child under the age of 13.[78] The requirements of COPPA have been implemented by an FTC rulemaking known as the COPPA Rule.[79] A violation of the COPPA Rule is treated as an unfair or deceptive trade practice pursuant to Section 5 of the FTCA for purposes of FTC enforcement.[80]

The Gramm-Leach-Bliley Act (GLBA), also known as the Financial Services Modernization Act and discussed in Chapter 2, was passed in 1999 to remove legal barriers between and among banks, security firms, insurance companies, and other financial services companies.[81] While facilitating the broad exchange of consumer information among financial institutions, GLBA provides some safeguards for personal financial information collected and maintained by such entities.[82] The FTC shares responsibility for enforcing the privacy requirements of GLBA with several other federal agencies and state insurance authorities.[83] The FTC published the Financial Privacy Rule to implement these provisions of GLBA.[84] GLBA also requires financial institutions to establish safeguards to protect the privacy of consumers' nonpublic financial information.[85] The FTC promulgated the Safeguards Rule to implement this provision of the law.[86] The rule requires financial institutions to develop and execute security plans to protect the confidentiality and integrity of consumers' personal information by developing a

---

76. 15 U.S.C. § 45(a)(1).

77. There are additional laws that confer consumer protection authority upon the FTC. The Commission has consumer protection enforcement responsibilities under nearly 40 separate statutes. *See* FTC *Legal Resources—Statutes Relating to Consumer Protection Mission*, http://www.ftc.gov/ogc/stat3.htm. The laws and rules discussed in this section, however, have specifically been implicated in the Commission's privacy-related enforcement actions.

78. 15 U.S.C. § 6502; 13 C.F.R. § 312.9. For purposes of COPPA, a "child" is defined as "an individual under the age of 13." 15 U.S.C. § 6501(a)(1); 13 C.F.R. § 312.2.

79. 15 U.S.C. § 6502(b); 16 C.F.R. pt. 312.

80. 15 U.S.C. § 6502(c).

81. Edward J. Janger & Paul M. Schwarz, *Modern Studies in Privacy Law: Notice, Autonomy, and Enforcement of Data Privacy*, 86 Minn. L. Rev. 1219, 1224 (Summer 2002).

82. *Id.*

83. 15 U.S.C. § 6904. Other agencies responsible for enforcing GLBA against specific financial institutions are the Office of the Comptroller of the Currency, the Board of Governors of the Federal Reserve System, the Board of Directors of the Federal Deposit Insurance Corporation, the Office of Thrift Supervision, the Board of the National Credit Union Administration, the Securities and Exchange Commission, and state insurance authorities. 15 U.S.C. § 6905(a)(1)–(7).

84. 16 C.F.R. pt. 313; *see also* FTC, *The Gramm-Leach-Bliley Act: The Financial Privacy Rule*, http://www.ftc.gov/privacy/privacyinitiatives/financial_rule.html.

85. 15 U.S.C. § 6801.

86. 16 C.F.R. pt. 314; *see also* FTC, *The Gramm-Leach-Bliley Act: The Safeguards Rule*, http://www.ftc.gov/privacy/privacyinitiatives/safeguards.html.

comprehensive information security program with reasonable administrative, technical, and physical safeguards.[87]

The Telemarketing and Consumer Fraud Abuse and Prevention Act (Telemarketing Act) was passed by Congress to protect consumers against fraudulent and abusive telemarketing practices.[88] The Commission promulgated the Telemarketing Sales Rule in response to the Telemarketing Act's requirement that the FTC engage in rulemaking to prohibit deceptive telemarketing acts and practices.[89]

The Fair Credit Reporting Act (FCRA), as discussed in Chapter 2, regulates the collection and disclosure of information about consumers' creditworthiness by consumer reporting agencies.[90] The law protects the privacy of sensitive financial information by restricting the circumstances in which it may be disclosed by a reporting agency. Violations of the FCRA constitute unfair or deceptive acts or practices under Section 5.[91]

2. *Enforcement*

The FTC has pursued numerous administrative actions and some judicial actions over the past several years to protect the privacy and security of consumers' personal information. Enforcement actions in privacy and security cases were originally based on two legal theories: (1) false promises or representations concerning privacy and security, constituting "deceptive trade practices" under the FTCA, and (2) breaches of express requirements for privacy and information safeguards under laws like COPPA and GLBA. In 2005, the FTC added a third enforcement approach: inadequate security for consumer information, by itself, was deemed an "unfair trade practice," in violation of the FTCA, even where there is no false security promise or representation and no legal safeguard requirement.

The FTC has explained its enforcement approach in this area as follows:

> Although the Commission has brought its cases under different laws, all of the cases stand for the principle that companies must maintain reasonable and appropriate measures to protect sensitive consumer information. What is "reasonable" will depend on the size and complexity of the business, the nature and scope of its activities, and the sensitivity of the information at issue. The principle recognizes that there cannot be "perfect" security, and that data breaches can occur even when a company maintains reasonable precautions to prevent them. At the same time, companies that put consumer data at risk can be liable even in the absence of a known breach.[92]

As a result of its enforcement activities, the FTC has entered into numerous consent decrees with organizations to settle regulatory actions.[93] The various FTC consent decrees concerning a company's privacy and security practices generally bar future mis-

---

87. 16 C.F.R. § 314.3.

88. 15 U.S.C. § 6101 *et seq.*

89. 15 U.S.C. § 6102(a); 16 C.F.R. pt. 310.

90. 15 U.S.C. § 1681 *et seq.*

91. *Id.*

92. Prepared Statement of the FTC, "Identity Theft: Victims Bill of Rights," Before the Subcommittee on Information Policy, Census, and National Archives, Committee on Oversight and Government Reform, U.S. House of Representatives, June 17, 2009.

93. *See* http://www.ftc.gov/privacy/privacyinitiatives/promises_enf.html.

representations about the companies' practices (where misrepresentations are involved), require the establishment of a comprehensive security program regularly audited by an independent professional, and impose reporting and record-keeping requirements to allow the FTC to monitor compliance with the terms of final orders.[94]

Early FTC actions were brought under the "deceptive practices" prong of Section 5 against companies that made security representations and promises in their privacy policies, but where the measures in place allegedly did not match those representations and promises and resulted in a failure to protect consumers' privacy. For example, the FTC brought an action against Guess? Inc., a company that manufactures and sells clothes and accessories in stores and through the website www.guess.com.[95] Guess?'s online privacy policy and "frequently asked questions" web page assured consumers that personal data, including name, address, and credit or debit card number and expiration date, were encrypted and protected by security measures.[96] The FTC alleged, however, that www.guess.com was vulnerable to commonly known attacks by hackers and that consumer information was not always stored in an encrypted format.[97] The Commission argued that Guess?'s privacy policy was thus false and misleading, and the company's practices were unfair or deceptive within the meaning of Section 5.[98]

Using enforcement authority under GLBA as well as Section 5 of the FTC Act, the Commission filed an administrative complaint against student loan company Goal Financial, LLC, based on its failure to provide reasonable and appropriate security for sensitive consumer information in loan applications.[99] In the course of its business, Goal collected extensive personal information from consumer loan applications and other sources, such as name, address, telephone number, driver's license number, Social Security number, date of birth, income, debt, and employment information.[100] Goal assured consumers that it secured nonpublic personal information with appropriate physical, electronic, and procedural safeguards.[101] According to the FTC's complaint, however, Goal engaged in practices that collectively failed to appropriately protect consumers' personal information.[102] Specifically, Goal failed to adequately assess risks to information it collected and stored in paper and electronic files; did not adequately restrict access to personal information to authorized employees; failed to implement a comprehensive

94. *See, e.g.*, Press Release, FTC, BJ's Wholesale Club Settles FTC Charges (June 16, 2005), http://www.ftc.gov/opa/2005/06/bjswholesale.htm and Agreement Containing Consent Order, *TJX*, FTC File No. 072 3055 (2008), http://www.ftc.gov/os/caselist/0723055/080327consent.pdf.

95. Press Release, FTC, Guess Settles FTC Security Charges; Third FTC Case Targets False Claims About Information Security (June 18, 2003), http://www.ftc.gov/opa/2003/06/guess.htm.

96. Complaint ¶¶ 4, 6–7, *Guess?, Inc.*, FTC File No. 022 3260 (2003), http://www.ftc.gov/os/2003/06/guesscmp.htm.

97. *Id.* ¶¶ 8–13.

98. *Id.* ¶¶ 13, 15–16.

99. Press Release, Fed. Trade Comm'n, Student Lender Settles FTC Charges That It Failed to Safeguard Sensitive Consumer Information and Misrepresented Its Security Practices (March 4, 2008), http://www.ftc.gov/opa/2008/03/studlend.shtm.

100. Complaint ¶ 4, Goal Financial, LLC, FTC File No. 072 3013 (2008), http://www.ftc.gov/os/caselist/0723013/080415complaint.pdf.

101. *Id.* at 10.

102. *Id.* at 5.

security program, including policies and procedures to regulate the collection, handling, and disposal of personal information; did not properly train employees to handle and protect personal information and respond to security incidents; and failed repeatedly to require third-party service providers to adequately protect personal information.[103]

As a result of these security weaknesses, Goal employees transferred more than 7,000 consumer files to third parties without authorization, and one employee sold to members of the public hard drives containing sensitive personal information about approximately 34,000 consumers in easily accessible clear text.[104] The Commission alleged that Goal's representations to the public about its security practices were false and misleading, and therefore deceptive under Section 5.[105] The complaint also alleged that Goal did not comply with GLBA's Privacy Rule because it was a financial institution that did not provide consumers a clear and conspicuous notice that accurately represented its privacy policies and practices.[106] In addition, the FTC argued, Goal failed to implement reasonable security policies and procedures in violation of GLBA's Safeguards Rule.[107] Goal settled the FTC's charges, agreeing to common settlement terms discussed earlier and agreeing to refrain from violating the Privacy and Safeguards Rules in the future.[108]

More recently the FTC has increasingly used the "unfairness prong" to enforce Section 5 against companies that allegedly do not sufficiently safeguard personal information, even when they have not explicitly promised consumers that their personal information is adequately protected.

In the first case of this kind, the Commission filed an administrative complaint alleging that BJ's Wholesale Club, Inc., a membership club that sells food and various merchandise, failed to take appropriate measures to protect the security of sensitive information about thousands of customers.[109] According to the complaint, BJ's Wholesale collected sensitive information from customers when they purchased goods, including names and credit or debit card numbers and expiration dates.[110] The FTC claimed that BJ's Wholesale did not take reasonable and appropriate measures (here to encrypt the data during wireless transmission) to protect this information in its computer systems, and consequently it was accessed and used by unauthorized individuals to make about $13 million in fraudulent purchases.[111] The FTC alleged that the failure of BJ's Wholesale to adequately protect consumer information was an

---

103. *Id.*

104. *Id.* ¶ 6.

105. *Id.* ¶¶ 10–12.

106. *Id.* ¶¶ 13–14.

107. *Id.* ¶¶ 13–14.

108. Decision and Order, *Goal Financial*, FTC File No. 072 3013 (2008), http://www.ftc.gov/os/caselist/0723013/080415decision.pdf.

109. Press Release, FTC, BJ's Wholesale Club Settles FTC Charges (June 16, 2005), http://www.ftc.gov/opa/2005/06/bjswholesale.htm.

110. Complaint ¶ 4, *BJ's Wholesale Club, Inc.*, FTC File No. 042 3160 (2005), http://www.ftc.gov/os/caselist/0423160/092305comp0423160.pdf.

111. *Id.* ¶¶ 7–8.

unfair act or practice in violation of Section 5.[112] BJ's settlement agreement with the FTC included common settlement terms discussed earlier.[113]

The FTC also pursued an administrative action against discount clothing retailer TJX Companies, Inc., alleging that TJX engaged in various practices that, as a whole, failed to reasonably and appropriately secure sensitive consumer information stored on its computer networks.[114] Specifically, the Commission alleged that TJX stored and transmitted personal information in clear text on its in-store and corporate networks; failed to use readily available security measures to limit wireless access to its networks; failed to require network administrators and others to use strong passwords or different passwords to access TJX's computers, networks, and programs; did not use readily available security measures (such as firewalls) to restrict access among TJX computers and the Internet; and did not take sufficient steps to detect and prevent unauthorized access to computer networks or to perform security investigations.[115]

The FTC alleged that these practices, taken together, enabled a hacker to gain unauthorized access to TJX's computer networks and download tens of millions of debit and credit card numbers, as well as personal information about approximately 455,000 consumers who had returned merchandise.[116] The breach also compromised tens of millions of payment cards and resulted in tens of millions of dollars in fraudulent charges.[117] The FTC claimed that TJX's failure to adequately protect consumer information was an unfair practice under Section 5.[118] The company's settlement with the FTC included common settlement terms discussed earlier.[119]

In addition, the Commission has initiated several Section 5 enforcement actions against purveyors of "spyware," which is software downloaded and installed on a consumer's computer that monitors or hijacks the computer's functions without the consumer's knowledge or permission. For example, the FTC filed a lawsuit against CyberSpy, LLC, and its owner in a case involving Remote Spy, a spyware program that could be remotely installed.[120] The spyware was advertised as a "100% undetectable" way to "Spy on Anyone. From Anywhere." The FTC alleged that the spyware and marketing practices violated Section 5. The settlement reached among the parties bars the defendants from providing a means to disguise the software as an innocent file or e-mail

---

112. *Id.* ¶¶ 9–10.

113. Decision and Order, *BJ's Wholesale*, FTC File No. 042 3160 (2005), http://www.ftc.gov/os/caselist/0423160/092305do0423160.pdf.

114. Press Release, FTC, Agency Announces Settlement of Separate Actions Against Retailer TJX, and Data Brokers Reed Elsevier and Seisint for Failing to Provide Adequate Security for Consumers' Data (March 27, 2008), http://www.ftc.gov/opa/2008/03/datasec.shtm.

115. Complaint ¶ 8, *The TJX Companies, Inc.*, FTC File No. 072 3055 (2008), http://www.ftc.gov/os/caselist/0723055/0803027complaint.pdf.

116. *Id.* ¶ 9.

117. *Id.* ¶ 11.

118. *Id.* ¶ 13.

119. Agreement Containing Consent Order, *TJX*, FTC File No. 072 3055 (2008), http://www.ftc.gov/os/caselist/0723055/080327consent.pdf.

120. Press Release, FTC, Spyware Seller Settles FTC Charges; Order Bars Marketing of Keylogger Software for Illegal Uses (June 2, 2010), http://www.ftc.gov/opa/2010/06/cyberspy.shtm.

attachment, requires a warning that it may violate federal or state law, requires measures to reduce risk of misuse, and requires removal of improperly installed legacy versions.[121]

In a high-profile case involving both Section 5 and the FCRA, the FTC filed a complaint in federal court against ChoicePoint, Inc., a data broker that collects, maintains, and sells consumer credit reports and other extensive personal information about thousands of consumers.[122] In Spring 2005, ChoicePoint informed about 163,000 consumers that it might have disclosed their personal information to individuals who did not have a lawful reason to access it.[123] The individuals had applied and were approved to become subscribers to ChoicePoint's services, even though their applications contained false information that ChoicePoint failed to investigate.[124] ChoicePoint also ignored unauthorized subscriber activity, even after receiving subpoenas from law enforcement authorities indicating that certain accounts were likely fraudulent.[125] At least 800 cases of identity theft occurred as a result of ChoicePoint's disclosures to subscribers involved in criminal activity.[126]

The FTC alleged that these practices violated the FCRA's requirement that consumer reporting agencies provide credit reports only for permissible purposes.[127] The complaint also claimed that ChoicePoint violated the FCRA by failing to make reasonable efforts to confirm the identities of prospective subscribers and their intended uses of the credit reports, particularly because ChoicePoint had reason to believe the information would not be used for a permissible purpose.[128] The FTC also alleged that ChoicePoint's failure to use reasonable and appropriate security measures to protect consumer information was unfair within the meaning of Section 5 and that the representations it had made on its website about its measures for protecting consumer information were deceptive under the law.[129]

The settlement agreement reached by ChoicePoint and the FTC ordered the company to pay a $10 million civil penalty, as well as $5 million for consumer redress.[130] The order also prohibited ChoicePoint from disclosing credit reports to anyone who does not have a permissible purpose for the information and required the company to implement detailed procedures to ensure that only legitimate subscribers would be furnished credit reports.[131] ChoicePoint was also ordered to implement a comprehensive information security program to safeguard the security and confidentiality of consumer infor-

121. Stipulated Order, FTC v. Cyberspy Software, LLC, No. 6:08-cv-1872-ORL-31GJK (M.D. Fla., Apr. 22, 2010) (FTC File No. 082 3160).

122. Press Release, FTC, ChoicePoint Settles Data Security Breach Charges; to Pay $10 Million in Civil Penalties, $5 Million for Consumer Redress (Jan. 26, 2006), http://www.ftc.gov/opa/2006/01/choicepoint.htm.

123. Complaint ¶ 12, United States v. ChoicePoint, Inc., No. 06-CV-0198 (N.D. Ga. 2006) (FTC File No. 052 3069), http://www.ftc.gov/os/caselist/choicepoint/0523069complaint.pdf.

124. *Id.* ¶ 13.

125. *Id.* ¶ 14.

126. *Id.* ¶ 12.

127. *Id.* ¶¶ 15–17.

128. *Id.* ¶¶ 18–24.

129. *Id.* ¶¶ 25–32.

130. Stipulated Final Judgment and Order Sections I & V, *ChoicePoint*, No. 06-CV-0198 (N.D. Ga. 2006) (FTC File No. 052 3069), http://www.ftc.gov/os/caselist/choicepoint/0523069stip.pdf.

131. *Id.* § I.

mation, which was to be regularly assessed and certified by an independent third-party professional.[132] The agreement also included extensive reporting and record-keeping requirements to allow the FTC to monitor compliance with the settlement terms.[133]

In a recent case involving off-line data, the FTC pursued an administrative enforcement action in partnership with the Department of Health and Human Services against a large pharmacy franchise that failed to adequately protect health information about consumers, which allegedly violated the Health Insurance Portability and Accountability Act (HIPAA).[134] According to the Commission, CVS Caremark Corporation routinely collected extensive personal information about its customers, including financial and health data, in the course of its business.[135] The pharmacy represented to its customers through privacy policies and other statements that it took steps to maintain the privacy of "protected health information," but the Commission claimed that CVS failed to provide reasonable and appropriate security for that data.[136]

Specifically, the FTC alleged that CVS failed to: implement policies and procedures for securely disposing of personal information; properly train employees to securely dispose of information; ensure compliance with policies and procedures for securely disposing of information; or take steps to identify or mitigate risks to customers' personal information.[137] As a result of these failures, CVS threw away materials with customers' personal information printed in clear text in unsecured dumpsters.[138] The FTC claimed that these actions were unfair and deceptive in violation of Section 5.[139] CVS settled the FTC's charges, agreeing to common settlement terms discussed earlier.[140] The company also paid the Department of Health and Human Services a $2.25 million civil penalty.[141]

B. Other Federal Agencies

While the FTC has been the most active federal agency in protecting the privacy and security of confidential consumer information, other federal agencies have brought enforcement actions in this area. Examples include the Department of Health and Human Services, the Securities and Exchange Commission, and the Commodities Futures Trading Commission.

The Department of Health and Human Services (HHS) has been active in protecting the privacy and security of patient information under HIPAA. Its first formal enforcement action was against Providence Health and Services. HHS alleged that on several occasions between September 2005 and March 2006, backup tapes, optical disks,

132. *Id.* §§ III & IV.

133. *Id.* §§ VI, VII, & VIII.

134. Press Release, FTC, CVS Caremark Settles FTC Charges (Feb. 18, 2009), http://www.ftc.gov/opa/2009/02/cvs.shtm.

135. Complaint ¶ 4, CVS Caremark Corp., FTC File No. 072 3119 (2009), http://www.ftc.gov/os/caselist/0723119/090623cvscmpt.pdf.

136. *Id.* ¶¶ 6–7.

137. *Id.* ¶ 7.

138. *Id.* ¶ 8.

139. *Id.* ¶¶ 9–11.

140. Decision and Order, *CVS*, FTC. No. 072 3119 (2009), http://www.ftc.gov/os/caselist/0723119/090623cvsdo.pdf.

141. CVS Press Release, *supra* note 133.

and laptops, all containing unencrypted electronic protected health information, were removed from the Providence premises and left unattended. The media and laptops were subsequently lost or stolen, compromising the protected health information of over 386,000 patients. In a Resolution Agreement, Providence agreed to pay $100,000 and implement a detailed Corrective Action Plan to ensure that it would appropriately safeguard identifiable electronic patient information against theft or loss. In its news release on this settlement, HHS reported that it had successfully resolved over 6,700 Privacy and Security Rule cases by requiring the entities to make systemic changes to their health information privacy and security practices.[142]

More recently, HHS brought the coordinated enforcement action with the FTC against CVS, discussed earlier, involving disposal of confidential customer information in dumpsters. The settlement included a $2.25 million civil penalty, as well as a requirement for corrective action. A subsequent enforcement action against Rite Aid Corporation, also involving disposal of prescription information, resulted in a settlement including a $1 million civil penalty and corrective action.[143]

The Securities and Exchange Commission brought an enforcement action under the GLBA Safeguards Rule against LPL Financial Corporation for failing to adopt policies and procedures to safeguard its customers' personal information, leaving at least 10,000 customers vulnerable to identity theft following a series of hacking incidents involving LPL's online trading platform. The FTC found that LPL conducted an internal audit in mid-2006 that identified inadequate security controls to safeguard customer information at its branch offices, including a risk from hacking. The SEC's order found that LPL failed to take timely corrective action because, by the time hacking incidents began in July 2007, the firm had not implemented increased security measures in response to the identified weaknesses.[144] In a settlement, LPL agreed to cease and desist from committing future violations of the Safeguards Rule, to pay a $275,000 penalty, and to undertake certain remedial actions, including retaining an independent consultant to review LPL's policies and procedures required by the Safeguards Rule.[145]

The Commodities Futures Trading Commission brought an action under the GLBA against Interbank FX, LLC, for failing to protect the confidential personal information of its consumers. One of its employees placed files containing the confidential personal consumer information of approximately 13,000 customers and prospective customers on a personal website that was accessible on the Internet for at least a year. In a settlement, Interbank agreed to pay a $200,000 penalty and to establish, implement, and maintain a documented comprehensive security program for the protection of consumer information. It further agreed to obtain an assessment of that program from a

142. HHS News Release, Providence Health & Services Agree on Corrective Action Plan to Protect Health Information (July 17, 2008).

143. HHS News Release, Rite Aid Agrees to Pay $1 Million to Settle HIPAA Privacy Case (July 27, 2010).

144. SEC Press Release, SEC Charges LPL Financial for Failing to Protect Customer Privacy (Sept. 11, 2008).

145. *Id.*

certified security professional within 180 days of the entry of the order and annually for the next five years.[146]

It is likely that other federal agencies will become more active in protecting consumer information.

C. State Attorneys General

At the state level, attorneys general have been active in protecting the privacy and security of consumer information. In one example, 41 state attorneys general entered into a joint settlement with the TJX Companies, Inc. in actions arising from the same data breach that led to the FTC action, where TJX agreed to pay $9.75 million to the states and to implement and maintain a comprehensive information security program designed to safeguard consumer data and address any weaknesses in TJX's systems in place at the time of the breach.[147]

The Florida Attorney General brought an enforcement action under state consumer protection laws against Certegy Check Services, Inc., a financial services company that experienced a data breach that exposed personal identification information from approximately 5.9 million consumer files. The data was reportedly stolen by a former employee.[148] Under a settlement, Certegy agreed to maintain a comprehensive information security program that assesses internal and external risks to consumers' personal information, implements safeguards to protect that consumer information, and regularly monitors and tests the effectiveness of those safeguards. Certegy and its related entities also agreed to adhere to payment card industry data security standards, to contribute $125,000 to the Attorney General's Seniors versus Crime Program, and to pay $850,000 for the state's investigative costs and attorney's fees.[149] Certegy also settled a number of class action claims to include credit and bank account monitoring and reimbursement of out-of-pocket costs for identity theft, check printing, and monitoring.[150]

The Connecticut Attorney General brought the first enforcement action under the HIPAA enforcement powers given to state attorneys general under the HITECH Act discussed in Chapter 2. The action was against Health Net, a health insurer that allegedly lost a computer disk drive containing protected health and other private information of 1.5 million consumers nationwide including 500,000 Connecticut residents. The missing disk drive, which was likely stolen, contained names, addresses, Social Security numbers, protected health information, and financial information. The action was

146. Commodities Futures Trading Commission Press Release, CFTC Sanctions Foreign Currency Broker Who Allowed Confidential Personal Information of Its Customers to Appear on the Internet (June 29, 2009).

147. Press Release, Massachusetts Attorney General, Attorney General Martha Coakley Announces Multi-State Settlement with the TJX Companies, Inc., over Massive Data Breach (June 23, 2009), http://www.mass.gov/?pageID=cagopressrelease&L=1&L0=Home&sid=Cago&b=pressrelease&f=2009_06_23_tjx_settlement2& csid=Cago.

148. Press Release, Florida Attorney General, Attorney General Reaches Settlement with Centergy Check Services over Data Breach (April 16, 2010), http://www.myfloridalegal.com/newsrel.nsf/newsreleases/889FA9C2A2A31 AA88525770700578C1B.

149. *Id.*

150. In the Matter of Centergy Check Services, Inc., Florida Case No. L-07-3-1109 (2010), *available at* http://myfloridalegal.com/webfiles.nsf/WF/MRAY-84KKQN/$file/CertegyAVC.pdf.

brought under HIPAA and state privacy protection laws, alleging a failure to safeguard the data and a delay in notifying consumers and the state.[151]

In a settlement of the action, Health Net and affiliates agreed to a Corrective Action Plan under which Health Net was required to implement measures to protect health information and other private data in compliance with HIPAA. The plan included continued identity theft protection, improved systems controls, improved management and oversight, improved training and awareness for its employees, and improved incentives, monitoring, and reports. It also included a $250,000 payment of statutory damages to the state and an additional contingent payment to the state of $500,000, should it be established that the lost disk drive was accessed and personal information used illegally. For consumers, the settlement included two years of credit monitoring, $1 million of identity theft insurance, and reimbursement for the costs of credit freezes.[152]

Enforcement actions by state attorneys general are likely to be a growing part of the protection of consumer privacy and data security, especially because federal laws like HIPAA provide state attorneys general the right to enforce such statutes.

3.4 OTHER TYPES OF CIVIL CLAIMS

A. Shareholder Derivative Suits

Corporate directors and officers have a fiduciary duty of care, which includes the protection of corporate assets. Because most information today is digitally created, oversight of information security and privacy falls within the duty owed by officers and directors in conducting the operations of a corporation.[153]

Corporations incorporated in the United States generally follow the Delaware (where the majority of U.S. corporations are incorporated) "business judgment" rule. This rule provides for a standard of care for the organization's directors and officers that a rea-

151. Press Release, Connecticut Attorney General, Attorney General Announces Health Net Settlement Involving Massive Security Breach Compromising Private Medical and Financial Info (July 6, 2010), http://www.ct.gov/ag/cwp/view.asp?A=2341&Q=462754.

152. *Id.*

153. Gantz et al., *The Diverse and Exploding Digital Universe*, March 2008, *available at* http://www.emc.com/collateral/analyst-reports/diverse-exploding-digital-universe.pdf; *see, e.g.*, Hadjilloucas and Haller, *Building and Enforcing Intellectual Property Value 2009*, *available at* http://goo.gl/WUYa. Prior studies reported that while in 1978 only 20% of corporate assets were intangible assets, and 80% of corporate assets were tangible assets, by 1997 the relative value of tangible and intangible assets had practically reversed, with 73% of corporate assets being intangible assets. Following the introduction of the International Financial Reporting Standard for Business Combinations (IFRS3) and similar standards in the United States (Financial Accounting Standard 141), valuing intangibles is becoming less an option and more a responsibility. Kenneth E. Krosin, *Management of IP Assets*, AIPLA BULLETIN 176 (2000 Mid-Winter Meeting Issue) (stating that 80% of corporate assets as of that date were digital); *Cybercrime*, BUSINESS WEEK, Feb. 21, 2000.

sonably prudent director or officer of a similar corporation would have used.[154] There are high-risk situations where higher standards apply to directors and officers, such as acquisitions, takeovers, responses to shareholder suits, and distribution of assets to shareholders in preference over creditors.[155] In these circumstances, directors and officers are required to obtain professional assistance or perform adequate analyses to mitigate the risks that ordinarily accompany these activities.[156] Some enterprise risk and information assurance experts assert that a "higher degree of care will also be required of Directors and Officers regarding the complex nature of issues involved in information assurance."[157] It is likely that in order for directors and officers to be deemed to have acted reasonably, they must take meaningful precautions to protect information systems and the information within. If corporate directors and officers, in the exercise of their business judgment, have made a good-faith effort to ensure that the corporation has implemented a risk management system with appropriate information security and privacy controls (as described in Chapters 4 and 5), and if they utilize a reporting system designed to ensure that information about the corporation's ordinary operations comes to their attention so that they may take action if required, they may be found to have carried out their fiduciary duties of loyalty and oversight.[158]

---

154. Delaware law, in cases of director and officer liability, is generally instructive. *See, e.g., In re* Walt Disney Derivative Litigation, Case No. 411, 2005 (Del. June 8, 2006) (restating the business judgment rule); Malone v. Brincat, 722 A.2d 5, 10 (Del. 1998) ("The directors of Delaware corporations stand in a fiduciary relationship not only to the stockholders but also to the corporations upon whose boards they serve. The director's fiduciary duty to both the corporation and its shareholders has been characterized by this Court as a triad: due care, good faith, and loyalty. That tripartite fiduciary duty does not operate intermittently but is the constant compass by which all director actions for the corporation and interactions with its shareholders must be guided."); Aronson v. Lewis, 473 A.2d 805, 812–13 (Del. 1984); Smith v. Van Gorkom, 488 A.2d 858, 872–73 (Del. 1985) ("[A] director's duty to exercise an informed business judgment is in the nature of a duty of care."); Nagy v. Bistricer, 770 A.2d 43, 49 n.2 (Del. Ch. 2000) (To fulfill the duty of good faith, a director must not intentionally disregard his duties to the company and its stockholders.); Cede & Co. v. Technicolor, 634 A.2d 345, 361 (Del. 1993) (a director must act so that "the best interest of the corporation and its shareholders takes precedence over any interest" of his own); Emerald Partners v. Berlin, 2001 Del. Ch. LEXIS 20, *87–88 (Del. Ch. Feb. 7, 2001) (Delaware courts have noted that the duty of good faith is part and parcel of the duty of loyalty).

155. Zichichi and Ragaini, eds., *International Seminar on Nuclear War and Planetary Emergencies 30th Session*, p. 414, *available at* http://goo.gl/JaXe (discussing Dr. John H. Nugent, CPA, *Corporate Officer and Director Information Assurance (IA) Liability Issues: A Layman's Perspective*, Dec. 15, 2002).

156. *Id.*

157. *Id.*

158. *See, e.g.*, Lawlor, Kichline, & Newman, *Federalizing Fiduciary Duties through Shareholder Lawsuits: Three Reasons for Court Scrutiny* (Washington Legal Found. Working Papers Ser., No. 173, July 2010). "The boards of every major pharmaceutical company, including Pfizer, have long had in place extensive reporting systems designed to keep the boards informed of day-to-day operations. Such systems will never be able to prevent all violations of federal regulatory requirements, but simply because violations occur is not a reason to conclude that an outside director has been disloyal to the corporation. Thus, for example, a federal district court recently threw out a stockholder derivative suit filed against the directors of Cephalon, Inc. The suit alleged breach of the duty of oversight following Cephalon's $425 million settlement of federal claims that it improperly promoted three of its pharmaceutical products. The court held that the suit was unmeritorious in the absence of detailed allegations demonstrating that the Cephalon board consciously chose to do nothing about illegal activity it knew (or should have known) to exist. *See King v. Baldino*, 648 F. Supp. 2d 609 (D. Del. 2009)."

The primary basis for a shareholder suit for failure to protect data is the 1996 decision in *In re Caremark International Inc. Derivative Litigation.*[159] The Delaware Court of Chancery noted that officer/director liability arises in two contexts: (1) from losses arising out of ill-advised or negligent board decisions (which are broadly protected by the business judgment rule as long as the decision resulted from a process that was rational or employed in a good-faith effort), and (2) from situations in which the board failed to act in circumstances where "due attention" would have prevented the loss.[160] In the latter situation, the *Caremark* court noted that:

> [I]t would . . . be a mistake to conclude that . . . corporate boards may satisfy their obligation to be reasonably informed concerning the corporation, without assuring themselves that information and reporting systems exist in the organization that are reasonably designed to provide to senior management and to the board itself timely, accurate information sufficient to allow management and the board, each within its scope, to reach informed judgments concerning both the corporation's compliance with law and its business performance . . .
>
> Obviously the level of detail that is appropriate for such an information system is a question of business judgment . . . . But it is important that the board exercise a good faith judgment that the corporation's information and reporting system is in concept and design adequate to assure the board that appropriate information will come to its attention in a timely manner as a matter of ordinary operations, so that it may satisfy its responsibility.

The *Caremark* case involved a settlement that the board approved of approximately $250 million regarding criminal and civil charges against the corporation for payments related to kickbacks paid to physicians treating Medicare and Medicaid patients. The derivative suit was filed to address future actions by the corporation, including initiating a committee to monitor such future conduct, and was subsequently settled.[161] This case provides a basis for a shareholder suit against officers and directors for failure to implement an information and reporting system with respect to the security of corporate networks and data. Liability could arise if they fail (1) to determine that the company is adequately meeting statutory, regulatory, or contractual obligations to protect certain data from theft, disclosure, or inappropriate use and (2) to be assured that the data critical to normal business operations, share price, and market share are protected.[162] Indeed, *Caremark* has also provided a basis for what are called "federal *Caremark* claims"—U.S. state court claims against a company's directors and officers for the corporation's violations of federal law.[163] These cases may be pursued because the state of incorporation has the

159. 698 A.2d 959 (Del. Ch. 1996).

160. *Id.*

161. *Id.*

162. *See, e.g., id.*

163. *See, e.g.,* Midwestern Teamsters Pension Trust Fund v. Deaton, Civ. A. No. H-08-1809, 2009 U.S. Dist. LEXIS 50521, *23 (S.D. Tex. May 7, 2009) (derivative lawsuit based on Federal Corrupt Practices Act violations); King v. Baldino, 648 F. Supp. 2d 609 (D. Del. 2009) (misdemeanor violation of Food, Drug, and Cosmetic Act led to shareholder lawsuit).

authority to regulate a corporation's internal structure and stock prices (for example), which may be affected by breaches of federal law.[164]

Because of the potential for "federal *Caremark* claims," laws such as the Sarbanes-Oxley Act (SOX) discussed in Chapter 2 show that directors and top managers must become actively involved with intellectual property asset management and information security in order to avoid both civil and criminal liability under SOX and shareholder derivative suits for breach of the fiduciary duty to adequately protect intellectual property assets.[165] SOX and other laws and regulations require public corporations to make adequate disclosures, in public filings and public communications, of relevant risks to the corporation and its assets. In addition, if a company has already been found in violation, the Federal Sentencing Guidelines allow, as a condition of probation, "regular or unannounced" examinations of a corporation's "books or records."[166]

Studies in the early 21st century showed that if a company is a victim of an attack on its information systems, whether from an insider or an outside attacker, the attack could result in a lack of confidence in the company and even a drop in the company's stock price.[167] This result was proven in the 2008 Heartland Payment Systems data breach, the biggest data breach of its kind as of that time.[168] By January 25, 2009, Heartland's stock had lost more than fifty (50) percent of its value from the prior twelve months with Visa and MasterCard showing losses as well.[169] Consequently, shareholders may also decide to initiate a derivative suit for loss to stock price or market share caused by inadequate attention by officers and directors to information security. In the Heartland data breach, numerous derivative suits were also filed on behalf of Heartland against the directors, who "failed to establish and maintain adequate network security, concealed news about security breaches and our network security from our shareholders, and then

164. *See, e.g.*, VantagePoint Venture Partners 1996 v. Examen, Inc., 871 A.2d 1108, 1112 (Del. 2005) ("The internal affairs doctrine is a long-standing choice of law principle which recognizes that only one state should have the authority to regulate a corporation's internal affairs—the state of incorporation.").

165. R. Mark Halligan, *Duty to Identify, Protect Trade Secrets Has Arisen*, NAT'L. L.J. (Aug. 29, 2005). Sarbanes-Oxley imposed new duties of disclosure and corporate governance. "Section 302 of the act requires the chief executive officer and chief financial officer of public companies to certify that their annual and quarterly reports contain no untrue or misleading statements of material fact or material omissions, and to certify that the financial information in the report fairly presents the financial condition of the company. Section 404 requires companies to document and certify the scope, adequacy and effectiveness of the internal control structure and procedures for financial reporting and controls. Section 906 imposes civil and criminal penalties for violations of the Sarbanes-Oxley Act."

166. Federal Sentencing Guidelines § 8D1.4. The Gibson Dunn law firm states, as of April 13, 2010, that the Justice Department is seeking to expand this to a "reasonable number of regular or unannounced examinations of facilities subject to probation supervision" in the 2011 amendment cycle. *See* http://goo.gl/Gloj.

167. *See, e.g.*, The Internet Security Alliance, and the American National Standards Institute, *The Financial Management of Cyber Risk*, *available at* http://webstore.ansi.org/cybersecurity.aspx; The Internet Security Alliance, and the American National Standards Institute, *The Financial Impact of Cyber Risk: Fifty Questions Every CFO Should Ask*, *available at* http://webstore.ansi.org/cybersecurity.aspx; A. Marshall Acuff, Jr., *Information Security Impacting Securities Valuations: Information Technology and the Internet Changing the Face of Business*, Salomon Smith Barney 3-4 (2000), *available at* http://www.ciao.gov/industry/SummitLibrary/InformationSecurityImpactingSecuritiesValuations.pdf.

168. *Heartland Breach as Bad as Tylenol Poisonings?*, *available at* http://goo.gl/lCyR.

169. *Id.*

failed to correct network security problems and/or prevent their recurrence."[170] While the derivatives suits were eventually dismissed voluntarily, a related securities suit was filed regarding the steep losses for certain shareholders of Heartland stock but the court dismissed it, as the plaintiffs could not prove that there were material misrepresentations made about the general state of security or that they were intentionally made.[171]

These legal precedents indicate that directors and officers need to undertake a certain level of involvement and oversight in ensuring that the organization is properly secured against an information security breach and other manners of personal, confidential, and secret data loss or disclosure, in order to protect against shareholder derivative suits. Chapters 4 and 5 discuss how organizations can start to address the management of the risk of data loss and disclosure.

B. Banking Customer Claims and Negligent Misrepresentation Claims

In addition to the legal theories and claims previously outlined, plaintiffs have asserted other theories of liability in attempts to recover for security breaches in various contexts.

In relation to the Uniform Commercial Code and online banking transactions, a series of lawsuits[172] have been filed by banking customers in the wake of online banking security breaches. These lawsuits allege violations of U.C.C. Section 4A-202[173] or state variations of the same. These matters involve the compromise of a banking customer's user login credentials, which allows thieves to wire transfer money out of the customer's account. The sued banks have refused to reimburse their customers for the lost funds. U.C.C. Section 4A-202 allocates responsibility between the bank and the customer in these situations, and that allocation is tied to "commercially reasonable security":

> (b) If a bank and its customer have agreed that the authenticity of payment orders issued to the bank in the name of the customer as sender will be verified pursuant to a security procedure, a payment order received by the receiving bank is effective as the order of the customer, whether or not authorized, if (i) the security procedure is a commercially reasonable method of providing security against unauthorized payment orders, and (ii) the bank proves that it accepted the payment order in good faith and in compliance with the security procedure and any written agreement or instruction of the customer restricting acceptance of payment orders issued in the name of the customer. The bank is not required to follow an instruction that violates a written agreement with the customer or notice of which is not received at a time and in a manner affording the bank a reasonable opportunity to act on it before the payment order is accepted.

In short, under U.C.C. Section 4A-202(b), as long as the bank and its customer have agreed that the customer will be verified pursuant to a "security procedure," a payment order received from the customer will be considered an effective order by the customer, whether or not it was actually authorized by the customer, but only if the security proce-

170. Heartland Payment Systems Inc. 10-Q – 20100507—Legal Proceedings.

171. *In re* Heartland Payment Systems Inc. Securities Litigation, N.J. Civ. No. 09-1043 (2009).

172. *See* http://www.infolawgroup.com/2010/01/articles/reasonable-security/online-banking-and-reasonable-security-under-the-law-breaking-new-ground/.

173. *See* http://www.law.cornell.edu/ucc/4A/4A-202.html.

dure was "commercially reasonable" and followed by the bank, and only if the bank can establish that it acted in "good faith."

One decision has considered the issue of commercially reasonable security in the online banking context, and while not specifically focused on the U.C.C. (it involved a negligence claim), it may be instructive in terms of how courts may consider the issue of reasonable security. In *Shames-Yeakel v. Citizen Financial Bank*,[174] the plaintiff survived a motion for summary judgment on the issue of whether the bank employed reasonable security. In that case the bank was not using two-factor authentication to validate the identity of online banking users despite a guidance document published by the Federal Financial Institutions Examination Council (FFIEC) entitled *Authentication in an Internet Banking Environment*, which suggested that single-factor authentication by itself may not be adequate security. As such, the court held that a reasonable finder of fact could find that the bank breached its duty, and denied the bank's motion for summary judgment. In another case, *EMI v. Comerica Bank*,[175] a federal court denied the bank's motion for summary judgment despite the fact it was using token-based two-factor authentication. In that case, interpreting Michigan's version of U.C.C. Section 4A-202,[176] the court ruled that the bank had utilized commercially reasonable security, but decided that a question of fact existed as to whether the bank acted in good faith in accepting a series of fraudulent wire transfers.

Another theory of liability that has been used in a data security breach context is negligent misrepresentation. This theory was advanced in one of the lawsuits that arose out of the TJX breach.[177] In that case, the plaintiffs were issuing banks seeking to recover from the merchant (TJX) that suffered a breach and TJX's acquiring bank. As recognized by the court, the plaintiffs were essentially alleging that by accepting credit cards and processing payment authorizations, the defendants impliedly represented that they would comply with MasterCard and Visa regulations that prohibit the storage of sensitive authentication data related to payment cards.

The court examined Massachusetts law, which follows Section 552 of the Restatement of Torts for purposes of negligent misrepresentation:

> One who, in the course of his business, profession or employment, or in any other transaction in which he has a pecuniary interest, supplies false information for the guidance of others in their business transactions, is subject to liability for pecuniary loss caused to them by their justifiable reliance upon the information, if he fails to exercise reasonable care or competence in obtaining or communicating the information.[178]

While the First Circuit Court of Appeals denied the dismissal of the plaintiffs' theory of negligent misrepresentation on a motion to dismiss, it indicated that dismissal of the claim might be appropriate on a motion for summary judgment. The court indicated

174. 677 F. Supp. 2d 994 (2009).

175. 2010 WL 2720914 (E.D. Mich. 2010). *See also* http://www.infolawgroup.com/2010/08/articles/reasonable-security/emi-v-comerica-court-finds-banks-security-is-commercially-reasonable-bank-loses-motion-for-summary-judgment/.

176. Mich. Comp. Laws Ann. §§ 440.4702 and 440.4703.

177. *In re* TJX Companies Retail Sec. Breach Litigation, 564 F.3d 489 C.A.1 (Mass. 2009).

178. *See* Nycal Corp. v. KPMG Peat Marwick LLP, 426 Mass. 491, 495–96, 688 N.E.2d 1368 (1998) (quoting the *Restatement*).

that typically conduct alone could not amount to a misrepresentation unless there was a tight link between the conduct and an actual alleged misrepresentation. The court also referenced a case suggesting that words in addition to conduct might establish the tight link it described. Notably, the First Circuit cited a similar case that employed the same theory of liability, and that case was ultimately dismissed.[179]

C. Class Actions

Class action litigation is a growing field for information security litigation, although the success by plaintiffs has been limited. In 2009, over 170 million personal records were released in two incidents.[180] A 2008 study found that financial fraud affected 7.5 percent of Americans in 2008, and data breaches spawned 19 percent of that fraud.[181] Data breaches in 2008 increased by 47 percent over the previous year.[182] In 2009, the Identity Theft Resource Center reported 400 breaches affecting 220 million records (nearly equal to the previous four years combined).[183] Affected parties then initiate litigation. For example, within a few months of the announcement of the Heartland data breach, seventeen consumer class action suits and ten financial institution class action suits had been filed.[184]

Class action certification, under U.S. federal guidelines, requires numerosity, a common question of law or fact, that the class representative's claim is typical of others in the class and that the class representative provides adequate representation (i.e., there are no conflicts of interest and there will be a vigorous prosecution of the action).[185] Difficulties have arisen in being certified in data breach cases. For example, in the TJX data breach where information on over 100 million credit cards and customers was stolen, a class action suit by several banks was denied class certification because of the difficulty of proving the required actual reliance of each class member and that such reliance was reasonable and justifiable.[186]

Plaintiffs in these class action lawsuits generally allege that a business collected their personal information for the business's purposes and then allowed a third party to improperly access that personal information[187] or, in the case of banks who issue credit cards in the credit card breach cases previously described, their and their customers' information, and caused them financial losses. The methods used by third parties to gain access to information have ranged from taking the information with no indication they were targeting the information to targeting the information itself.[188] Although the

179. CUMIS Ins. Soc., Inc. v. BJ's Wholesale Club, Inc., 23 Mass. L. Rep. 550 (Mass. Super. 2005).

180. In January 2009, as many as 100 million credit card records were exposed when it was discovered that hackers broke into the network of credit card processor Heartland Payment Systems. In October 2009, the personal information of more than 70 million U.S. military veterans was compromised when an improperly erased hard drive was sent out for repair by the Department of Veterans Affairs.

181. Gartner, Inc., *2008 Data Breaches and Financial Crimes Scare Consumers Away*, *available at* http://goo.gl/YsT8.

182. The Identity Theft Resource Center, *2008 Data Breach Total Soars*, *available at* http://goo.gl/hnE3.

183. *Id.*

184. Heartland Payment Systems Inc. 10-Q – 20100806—Legal Proceedings.

185. Fed. R. Civ. P. 23(a).

186. *In re* TJX Companies Retail Security Breach Litigation C.A. No. 07-10162-WGY (D. Mass. 2007).

187. Derek A. Bishop, *No Harm No Foul: Limits on Damages Awards for Individuals Subject to a Data Breach*, [4] Shidler J. L. Com. & Tech. [12] (May 23, 2008), *available at* http://goo.gl/GaWK.

188. *Id.*

circumstances establishing these allegations vary greatly, these elements are at the core of each of the negligence class actions brought.[189]

The recommendation for organizations for data breach class actions is to not focus only on the result of the litigation. For example, courts have held that, when there is no evidence that the information acquired in a breach was misused (i.e., there is no actual damage to the plaintiff), the damage to the plaintiff is too speculative to serve as the basis for recovery.[190] And fear of identity theft has not been enough to sustain claims for damages.[191] Rather, organizations should understand that any class action litigation may be expensive to defend. Even when the class action certification has been denied, settlements with the affected parties (e.g., credit card issuers and issuing banks) have been substantial. For example, TJX agreed to pay $40.9 million to Visa and Visa card-issuing banks for their non-lawyer costs, with the total costs to TJX well over $100 million in regard to this breach.[192] Any organization collecting personal data must at least initiate and maintain an information risk management program as described in Chapters 4 and 5. While to date no court has found that a class was damaged by the mere release of customer information, courts may eventually find such damages if the information was fraudulently used as a result of the breach and the plaintiffs suffered actual losses that could not have been avoided through reasonable information security and privacy programs.

3.5 CYBERCRIMES

A. Computer Fraud and Abuse Act

The Computer Fraud and Abuse Act (CFAA) makes it a crime to, among other things, gain unauthorized access to a protected computer and obtain information such as financial records or any information from a computer involved in interstate commerce.[193] "Obtaining" includes merely viewing the information without downloading or copying

---

189. *Id.*

190. *See* Key v. DSW, Inc., 454 F. Supp. 2d 684 (S.D. Ohio 2006); Stollenwerk v. Tri-West Healthcare Alliance, 2005 WL 2465906 (D. Ariz. Sept. 6, 2005) *aff'd in part, rev'd in part*, 254 Fed. App'x 664 (9th Cir. 2007); Guin v. Brazos Higher Education Service Corp. Inc., 2006 WL 288483 (D. Minn. Feb. 7, 2006); Forbes v. Wells Fargo, 420 F. Supp. 2d 1018 (D. Minn. 2006); Giordano v. Wachovia Securities, L.L.C., 2006 WL 2177036 (D.N.J. July 31, 2006); Bell v. Acxiom Corp., 2006 WL 2850042 (E.D. Ark. Oct. 3, 2006); Walters v. DHL Express, 2006 WL 1314132 (C.D. Ill. May 12, 2006); Randolph v. ING Life Insurance & Annuity Co., 486 F. Supp. 2d 1 (D.D.C. Feb. 20, 2007). *See also* Pisciotta v. Old Nat'l. Bancorp, 499 F.3d 629, 639–640 (7th Cir. 2007) ("Although some of these cases involve different types of information losses, all of the cases rely on the same basic premise: Without more than allegations of increased risk of future identity theft, the plaintiffs have not suffered a harm that the law is prepared to remedy. Plaintiffs have not come forward with a single case or statute, from any jurisdiction, authorizing the kind of action they now ask this federal court, sitting in diversity, to recognize as a valid theory of recovery under Indiana law.").

191. *See, e.g.*, Ruiz v. GAP, Inc., ___ F.3d ___, Case No. 07-5739 (S.C.), N.D. Cal. 2009 (April 6, 2009) (discussing Stollenwerk v. Tri-West Healthcare Alliance, 2005 WL 2465906 (D. Ariz. Sept. 6, 2005), *aff'd in part, rev'd in part*, 254 Fed. App'x 664 (2007)) (holding that lost-data plaintiffs who presented no evidence of identity theft would not be able to meet Arizona's standard for recovery of monitoring costs.).

192. *Id.* It may be that the risk of liability arising from losses to customers caused by a data breach may not be as large as the risk of liability arising from banks that compensated customers or reissued credit and bank cards as a result of customers' losses.

193. 18 U.S.C. § 1030.

it.[194] Under the CFAA it is also a crime to distribute malicious code that damages a protected computer; traffic in passwords to gain unauthorized access to a protected computer and commit cyber-extortion (that is, threaten to damage a computer); threaten to obtain information from, or compromise the security of, a protected computer; or to demand money to undo damage caused.[195] It is also a crime to do so with the intent to defraud and to obtain anything of value, including its use, in excess of a stated amount.[196] The CFAA also makes it a crime to enter into a conspiracy to commit any of these acts.[197] The contours of the CFAA are discussed more fully in Chapter 2.

The maximum penalty for violating different parts of the CFAA ranges from one to twenty years in prison for each separate offense. The sentence imposed by the court is largely driven by the amount of harm and loss caused.[198] Loss may include any reasonable costs incurred by a victim, such as response costs, costs to do a damage assessment, costs to restore data or the system, and any lost revenue caused by an interruption of service. In setting an appropriate sentence, courts will also consider other factors, such as the number of victims, the substantial inconvenience of repairing a victim's reputation or damaged credit record, a defendant's intent to obtain or publicly disclose personal information, and whether the offense involved sophisticated means. Only the most extreme cases will warrant the maximum sentence.[199]

The court will also strip the criminal defendant of the fruits of the crime. The defendant must pay restitution based on the loss resulting from the crime.[200] The restitution ultimately paid will depend in large part on the defendant's ability to pay. The court will also order that the defendant forfeit any equipment used to commit the crime as well as the proceeds of the crime.[201] In one case, a company seeking to provide online load-matching services for the trucking industry used fraudulent login credentials to gain access to, and then hack, its main competitor's website. The case went to verdict and the jury awarded the plaintiff $150,000 in damages for the defendants' violation of the CFAA, which, together with other claims—including necessary remedial measures as a result of the hack, including hardening the system to future exploits—made for a total

---

194. *See* America Online, Inc. v. National Health Care Discount, Inc., 121 F. Supp. 2d 1255 (N.D. Iowa 2000).

195. 18 U.S.C. § 1030.

196. 18 U.S.C. § 1030(a)(4).

197. The acts prohibited by the CFAA may also be covered by state criminal laws. *See, e.g.,* 18 Pa. C.S.A. §§ 7611, 7616 (Pennsylvania state law prohibiting unauthorized access of a computer and the distribution of malicious code). While federal prosecutors usually have greater resources available to them and an easier time reaching outside the state and country to prosecute computer crimes, federal prosecutors may decline to prosecute a case because of limited resources or other factors that do not touch upon whether a crime has in fact occurred. The victim of a computer crime can approach the state or local prosecutor and request that he or she prosecute the crimes under state law.

198. U.S. Sentencing Guidelines Manual § 2B1.1 & Application Notes (2009).

199. For example, Albert Gonzalez, the accused mastermind of the TJX and Heartland security breaches, received two 20-year sentences, to be served concurrently.

200. 18 U.S.C. §§ 1030(g), 3663A, 3664.

201. 18 U.S.C. § 1030(i). Restitution is paid to victims before the government will take the proceeds by forfeiture. 18 U.S.C. § 3612(c). The government will often seek a forfeiture order in the event victims cannot be located to return the proceeds of the crime.

damages award against the defendants of approximately one million dollars, which was affirmed on appeal.[202]

In another case, a court entered an injunction against a company for having obtained proprietary information from its competitor's former employee in order to create "scraper" software or a "bot" to collect all the competitor's pricing information from the competitor's website.[203] Other courts have held scrapers and bots to violate the CFAA even in the absence of proprietary information, so long as the subject conduct violated the website's terms of use.[204] It should also be noted that although some courts have used website terms of use to define the scope of authorized access under the CFAA,[205] other courts have rejected this approach when the website is publicly available and does not require any login, password, or other individualized grant of access.[206]

B. Electronic Communications Privacy Act

The Electronic Communications Privacy Act of 1986 (ECPA) consists of three statutes: the Wiretap Act, the Pen Register statute, and the Stored Communications Act.[207] The ECPA prohibits access to, and disclosure of, certain categories of electronic communications, including stored communications, under certain circumstances. It also sets forth specific procedures regarding how law enforcement may access or intercept wire or electronic communications. The ECPA defines "electronic communication" as "any transfer of signs, signals, writing, images, sounds, data, or intelligence of any nature transmitted in whole or in part by a wire, radio, electromagnetic, photoelectronic, or photo-optical system that affects interstate or foreign commerce."[208]

---

202. Creative Computing v. Getloaded.Com LLC, 386 F.3d 930, 933–935 (9th Cir. 2004).

203. EF Cultural Travel BV v. Explorica, Inc., 274 F.3d 577 (1st Cir. 2001); EF Cultural Travel BV v. Zefer Corp., 318 F.3d 58 (1st Cir. 2003) (affirming preliminary injunction). A subsequent court mused that the First Circuit in *EF Cultural Travel v. Explorica* had used a standard of "loss" that was too permissive because it was based on a prior version of the statute. *See* Cenveo Corp. v. Celumsolutions Software GMBH & Co., 504 F. Supp. 2d 574 (D. Minn. 2007). The CFAA now defines "loss" as "any reasonable cost to any victim, including the cost of responding to the offense, conducting a damage assessment, and restoring the data, program, system, or information to its condition prior to the offense, and any revenue lost, cost incurred, or other consequential damages incurred because of interruption of service." 18 U.S.C. § 1030(e)(11).

204. Southwest Airlines Co. v. Farechase, Inc., 318 F. Supp. 2d 435, 439–40 (N.D. Tex. 2004) (holding that when the defendant exceeded a website's terms and conditions of use prohibiting the use of "any deep-link, page-scrape, robot, spider or other automatic device, program, algorithm or methodology" the defendant's conduct was sufficient to maintain a cause of action for breach of the CFAA).

205. *See, e.g.*, NCMIC Finance Corp. v. Artino, 638 F. Supp. 2d 1042 (S.D. Iowa 2009); Southwest Airlines Co. v. Farechase, Inc., 318 F. Supp. 2d at 439–40.

206. *See* CVENT Inc. v. Eventbrite Inc., Dist. Court, E.D. Va. 2010 (No. 1:10-cv-00481) (LMB/IDD), available at http://scholar.google.com/scholar_case?case=17918858846316974173&hl=en; United States v. Drew, 259 F.R.D. 449, 467 (C.D. Cal. 2009) ("In sum, if any conscious breach of a website's terms of service is held to be sufficient by itself to constitute intentionally accessing a computer without authorization or in excess of authorization, the result will be that section 1030(a)(2)(C) becomes a law that affords too much discretion to the police and too little notice to citizens who wish to use the Internet.").

207. Electronic Communications Privacy Act of 1986, Pub. L. No. 99-508, 100 Stat. 1848 (codified as amended in 18 U.S.C. §§ 2510–2522 (the Wiretap Act), §§ 2701–2711 (the Stored Communications Act), §§ 3121–3127 (the Pen Register statute)).

208. 18 U.S.C. § 2510(12) (exceptions to the definition are listed in subsections 12(A)–12(D)).

1. Wiretap Act

Title 1 of the ECPA, more commonly known as the Wiretap Act, deals with wire and electronic communications in transit, but not in storage.[209] The Wiretap Act prohibits interception of any "wire, oral, or electronic communication"[210] for which there is a reasonable expectation of privacy.[211] Violators can face criminal penalties, including imprisonment.[212] The Wiretap Act also creates a private right of action in favor of any person whose wire or electronic communications have been unlawfully intercepted.[213] In appropriate cases, a private litigant can recover punitive damages.[214]

An organization or individual does not violate the Wiretap Act if one of the parties to the communication consented to the interception in advance, so long as the interception was not undertaken to commit a criminal or tortious act in violation of federal or state law.[215] Furthermore, organizations or individuals do not violate the Wiretap Act when they, or their duly authorized agents, intercept the wire or electronic communications of a computer trespasser, so long as the owner or operator of the subject computer authorizes the interception and the interception does not acquire communications other than those transmitted to or from the computer trespasser.[216]

The Wiretap Act also provides procedures that the government must follow to conduct authorized surveillance and prohibits the use of unlawfully obtained intercepts as evidence at trial.[217]

Courts have differed in their interpretation of the fundamental concept in the Wiretap Act of what it means to "intercept" an electronic communication. Under the majority view, embraced by the Third, Fifth, Ninth, and Eleventh Circuits, courts have held that the Wiretap Act does not apply to stored electronic communications (such as e-mails), no matter how brief the storage, and/or that an "intercept" must be contemporaneous with transmission or caught "in flight" in order to violate the act.[218] Thus, under the majority view, "interception" does not include the acquisition of undelivered electronic mail in a service provider's computer.[219] Nor does unauthorized access to a private, personal, and password-protected website violate the Wiretap Act since accessing data in storage does not constitute a contemporaneous intercept.[220] Similarly, a court subscribing to the majority view held that surreptitious copying and forwarding of e-mails was

209. Fraser v. Nationwide Mut. Ins. Co., 352 F.3d 107 (3d Cir. 2003) (holding that the act covered e-mail in transit, but not e-mail in storage); Deirdre K. Mulligan, *Reasonable Expectations in Electronic Communications: A Critical Perspective on the Electronic Communications Privacy Act*, 72 Geo. Wash. L. Rev. 1557, 1566 (2004).

210. 18 U.S.C. § 2511.

211. 18 U.S.C. § 2510.

212. 18 U.S.C. § 2511.

213. 18 U.S.C. § 2520.

214. *Id.*

215. 18 U.S.C. § 2511(2)(c), (2)(d).

216. 18 U.S.C. § 2511(2)(i).

217. 18 U.S.C. §§ 2511(2), 2517; 18 U.S.C. § 2515.

218. *Fraser*, 352 F.3d at 113; Steve Jackson Games, Inc. v. United States Secret Service, 36 F.3d 457 (5th Cir. 1994); Konop v. Hawaiian Airlines, 302 F.3d 868, 878 (9th Cir. 2002); United States v. Steiger, 318 F.3d 1039 (11th Cir. 2003).

219. Steve Jackson Games, Inc. v. United States Secret Service, 36 F.3d 457 (5th Cir. 1994).

220. Konop v. Hawaiian Airlines, 302 F.3d 868, 878 (9th Cir. 2002).

only possible in one particular case because the subject e-mails were in "electronic storage" on the server, and so the Wiretap Act did not apply.[221]

Under the minority view, however, espoused by the First and Seventh Circuits, the definition of "intercept" is broader and applies not only to communications in pure transit but also to e-mails in "transient electronic storage that is intrinsic to the communication process."[222] It is from this perspective that the Seventh Circuit has extended the reach of the Wiretap Act to undelivered communications residing in RAM on an e-mail server, even when interception does not occur contemporaneously.[223] Due to the differing approaches, resolving the question of whether a particular acquisition of an electronic communication violates the Wiretap Act may depend, in significant part, on which Circuit's decisional law applies.[224] Indeed, with respect to ECPA as a whole, determinations regarding governing law can be outcome determinative.[225]

It should be further noted that the decisional law involving the Wiretap Act is extensive and covers a number of diverse but important issues that are either collateral to, or not specifically addressed by, the statute. For example, courts have held that the placement of "cookies" on an end-user's hard drive does not violate the Wiretap Act.[226] In one instance, an end-user alleged that a third-party advertiser had used a combination of cookies and "GIF tags" (also known as web beacons) to intercept the end-user's communications with a host website. The court found, however, that the website had authorized the advertiser's use of the subject cookies, GIF tags, and other software/objects and had thereby "consented" under 18 U.S.C. § 2511(2)(d) to the subsequent, alleged interception of communications between the website and the end-user, precluding liability on the part of the advertiser under the Wiretap Act.[227]

In another case involving cookies, however, the First Circuit reversed a trial court's finding that a third-party vendor had obtained "consent" from website operators, observing that "a reviewing court must inquire into the *dimensions of the consent* and then ascertain whether the interception exceeded those boundaries."[228] The First Circuit found, in the particular case before it, that the third-party vendor had collected information such as names, addresses, telephone numbers, e-mail addresses, dates of birth, gender, insurance status, medical conditions, and medications, and that the websites had not authorized the collection of such information.[229] The First Circuit then remanded

---

221. Bunnell v. MPAA, 567 F. Supp. 2d 1148 (C.D. Cal. 2007).

222. United States v. Councilman, 418 F.3d 67, 85 (1st Cir. 2005) (en banc); *see also* United States v. Szymuszkiewicz, No. 10-1347 (7th Cir. Sept. 9, 2010).

223. United States v. Szymuszkiewicz, No. 10-1347 (7th Cir. Sept. 9, 2010).

224. The difference in interpretation boils down to a fundamental disagreement on how to parse the statutory definition of "electronic communication" under the ECPA. *See, e.g.,* Konop v. Hawaiian Airlines, 302 F.3d at 877–78; United States v. Szymuszkiewicz, No. 10-1347 (7th Cir. Sept. 9, 2010).

225. *See* United States v. Weaver, 636 F. Supp. 2d 769, 772–73 (C.D. Ill. 2009) (rejecting reliance on Ninth Circuit's decision in Theofel v. Farey-Jones, 359 F.3d 1066, 1075 (9th Cir. 2004)).

226. *See In re* Doubleclick Inc. Privacy Litigation, 154 F. Supp. 2d 497 (S.D.N.Y. 2001); *In re* Intuit Privacy Litigation, 138 F. Supp. 2d 1272 (C.D.C.A. 2001).

227. *In re* Doubleclick Inc. Privacy Litigation, 154 F. Supp. 2d at 514–19.

228. *In re* Pharmatrak, Inc. Privacy Litigation, 329 F.3d 9, 19–20 (1st Cir. 2003) (emphasis in the original).

229. *Id.* at 15.

the matter for a determination of whether the interceptions at issue had been "intentional" within the meaning of 18 U.S.C. § 2511(1).[230]

One commentator suggests that, in the case of communications surrounding popular modes of web communication, the Wiretap Act most likely protects Internet-based communications that have a reasonable right to privacy, such as IP (VoIP) telephone communications like Skype or private instant messages between two individuals, while messages in chat rooms or social networking websites may not have such protection.[231]

2. *Pen Register Act*

The Pen Register statute deals with data relating solely to the dialing, routing, addressing, or signaling involved in a wire or electronic communication.[232] The statute prohibits any person from installing or using a pen register or trap device without first obtaining a court order.[233] A violation of the statute is punishable by fines and imprisonment.[234] The data covered by the Pen Register statute enjoys substantially less protection under the Fourth Amendment prohibition against unreasonable government search and seizure because it does not involve the content of the covered communications.[235] Law enforcement officers or prosecutors need only state that the covered data may be relevant to an investigation to secure court authorization for a pen register.[236]

3. *Stored Communications Act*

Unlike the Wiretap Act or the Pen Register statute, the Stored Communications Act (SCA) governs privacy and disclosure of stored wire and electronic communications.[237] The SCA prohibits the intentional and unauthorized access by third parties of any wire or electronic communication while it is in "electronic storage" in a facility or system through which an "electronic communication service" (ECS) is provided.[238] An ECS is "any service which provides to users thereof the ability to send or receive wire or electronic communications" and includes entities such as ISPs.[239] The SCA provides for criminal penalties against violators as well as a private right of action in which an aggrieved plaintiff may, in certain circumstances, recover punitive damages.[240] More-

---

230. *Id.* at 22–23.

231. Nicholas Matlach, *Who Let the Katz Out? How the ECPA and SCA Fail to Apply to Modern Digital Communications and How Returning to the Principles in* Katz v. United States *Will Fix It*, 18 CommLaw Conspectus 421 (2009–2010).

232. 18 U.S.C. § 3127(3).

233. 18 U.S.C. § 3121.

234. 18 U.S.C. § 3121.

235. Smith v. Maryland, 442 U.S. 745 (1979). The *Smith* Court held that no reasonable expectation of privacy existed in the telephone numbers persons dialed because the number information was voluntarily turned over to the third-party telephone company. Consequently, gathering information regarding the telephone numbers a person dials was not considered a search under the Fourth Amendment and did not require a warrant issued by a judge.

236. 18 U.S.C. § 3123.

237. 18 U.S.C. §§ 2702–2703; *see* Orin S. Kerr, *A User's Guide to the Stored Communications Act, and a Legislator's Guide to Amending It*, 72 Geo. Wash. L. Rev. 1208–43 (2004); Quon v. Arch Wireless Operating Co., 529 F.3d 892 (9th Cir. 2008), *rev'd, sub nom,* on other grounds, 130 S. Ct. 2619, 2010 WL 2400087 (June 17, 2010).

238. 18 U.S.C. § 2701.

239. 18 U.S.C. § 2510(15).

240. 18 U.S.C. § 2701–2707.

over, a violation of the SCA that is undertaken for purposes of commercial advantage, malicious destruction or damage, private commercial gain, or in furtherance of any criminal or tortious act is a federal felony punishable by fines and imprisonment.[241]

The SCA also requires any entity that qualifies as an ECS or a "remote computing service" (RCS) to refrain from the unauthorized disclosure of stored communications,[242] though the restrictions differ. The SCA prohibits providers classified as ECSs from "knowingly divulg[ing] . . . contents" of files residing in intermediate "electronic storage incidental to the communication" or in "storage for backup protection."[243] An RCS, on the other hand, is a computing service that provides to the public "computer storage or processing services by means of an electronic communications system" and includes such entities as web-hosting services or ISPs when they provide e-mail storage.[244] SCA rules prevent RCS entities from disclosing the contents of communications held in long-term storage "carried or maintained on that service."[245]

Distinguishing between an ECS and RCS provider can be difficult. An e-mail provider may be both an ECS and an RCS. For e-mail that recipients have not yet opened and read, courts may view the e-mail provider as "undisputedly an ECS"[246] and messages are in electronic storage because "they fall within the definition of 'temporary, intermediate storage'" under Section 2510(17)(A). Once users open and retain their e-mail messages on the provider's e-mail system, some courts have held that e-mail providers become RCS systems supplying storage services under Section 2702(a)(2).[247]

The Ninth Circuit ruled that pager services fall under the category of ECS and that archived messages were for "backup" and not the long-term storage which would have converted them to RCS providers.[248] When, however, the city of Detroit accessed text messages Skytel provided as an ECS through a database Skytel maintained of sent messages, Skytel's pager service did transform itself into an RCS.[249]

YouTube, the video posting web service, falls under the category of RCS because it provides storage services for posted videos.[250] Social networking sites, such as Facebook and MySpace, have been held by at least one court to fall under the RCS rules because they provide similar storage for personal comments and "wall" postings.[251]

Importantly, a non-ISP-like entity—such as a typical corporation that is hosting its own e-mail system—may be treated differently after e-mails are read and not become an RCS after its corporate e-mails are read, as it is not providing these services to the

241. 18 U.S.C. § 2701.

242. 18 U.S.C. § 2702.

243. 18 U.S.C. §§ 2702(a)(1), 2703(a).

244. 18 U.S.C. § 2711(2).

245. 18 U.S.C. §§ 2702(a)(2), 2703(b).

246. *See, e.g.*, Theofel v. Farey Jones, 359 F.3d 1066, 1070 (9th Cir. 2004).

247. Crispin v. Audigier, Inc., No. CV 09-09509 MMM JEMx (C.D. Cal. May 26, 2010). *See also* United States v. Weaver, 636 F. Supp. 2d 769 (C.D. Ill. 2009).

248. *Quon* at 902–903.

249. Flagg v. City of Detroit, 252 F.R.D. 346, 362–63 (E.D. Mich. 2008).

250. Viacom International Inc. v. YouTube Inc., 253 F.R.D. 256 (S.D.N.Y 2008).

251. *Crispin*, slip op. at 34.

public. Opened e-mails residing on a laptop may not be protected by the SCA.[252] The potential implication for employer monitoring of the employment-related conduct of employees is that the inspection of opened e-mails on company-owned laptops may not be prohibited by the SCA. It is possible, however, that more stringent state law requirements may render such conduct actionable by the employee, depending on the facts of the case.[253] These rules are very dynamic and require in-depth analysis by the organization's lawyers.

There are important exceptions to the SCA's prohibitions that enable law enforcement agencies to obtain stored communications. Whether disclosure of stored communications requires a warrant or merely a subpoena often depends on the length of time that the communication has been stored and whether it has been previously accessed or opened.[254] A substantial amount of decisional law exists on the topic as well as conflicts between the courts of appeals on the issue of when a warrant is required.[255] For example, in a recent case, the Sixth Circuit held that emails are protected by the Fourth Amendment and so a warrant (instead of an administrative subpoena or court order as allowed under the SCA in certain circumstances) is required for the government to access a defendant's emails held by a service provider and "any SCA provisions to the contrary are unconstitutional."[256] The act also limits how ISPs might permissibly voluntarily disclose such information to the government.[257]

Given the complexity of the ECPA's requirements, including the different approaches taken by the various circuits on key issues of interpretation, the question remains as to what steps an organization may take in order to avoid running afoul of the statute. Getting compliance right is important. Insurers will deny coverage for violations of the ECPA based on common policy exclusions that bar coverage for the willful violation of a penal statute. Such denials have been upheld by the courts.[258]

The polestar for achieving compliance—which cuts across jurisdictions and issues—is consent, notice, and authorization.[259] The difference between compliance and breach often turns not on the technology in question but, rather, on the extent to which the defendant obtained the consent or authorization of employees, customers, or others to engage in the practice that is the subject of suit. Organizations are well advised to

---

252. See 18 U.S.C. § 2702(a); Hilderman v. Teksci, Inc., 551 F. Supp. 2d 1183 (S.D. Cal. 2008); Dyer v. Northwest Airlines Corp., 334 F. Supp. 2d 1196 (D.N.D. 2004).

253. *See, e.g.*, Stengart v. Loving Care Agency, 973 A.2d 390, 398–99 (N.J. App. Div. 2009) (observing that, under New Jersey law, "an employer's rules and policies must be reasonable to be enforced . . . . Stated another way, to gain enforcement in our courts, the regulated conduct should concern the terms of employment and reasonably further the legitimate business interests of the employer.").

254. 18 U.S.C. § 2703(a).

255. *See, e.g.*, *Theofel*.

256. *U.S. v. Warshak*, Case Nos. 08-3997/4085/4087/4212/4429; 09-3176 (6th Cir. Dec. 2010).

257. 18 U.S.C. § 2702.

258. National Fire Ins. Co. of Hartford v. NWM-Oklahoma, LLC, Inc., 546 F. Supp. 2d 1238 (W.D. Okla. 2008).

259. *See, e.g.*, United States v. Ziegler (9th Cir. 2007) (holding that an employer that (1) prohibited personal use of its computer system, (2) put employees on actual notice of that fact, and (3) maintained and exercised complete administrative access to such system, could consent to a law enforcement search of an employee's hard drive on his workplace computer without his consent).

effectuate actual notice, in advance, that would reasonably alert potential plaintiffs of the organization's practices. The best way to achieve consent, authorization, and notice is through well-articulated, formal policies followed by the organization. When an organization deals with third-party vendors who provide network-based services, it is important to expressly delimit the vendor's scope of work in order to enshrine the organization's expectations regarding ECPA compliance in the organization's working relationships with third parties.

C. USA PATRIOT and Homeland Security Acts

1. USA PATRIOT Act

Congress enacted the Uniting and Strengthening America by Providing Appropriate Tools Required to Intercept and Obstruct Terrorism Act (PATRIOT Act) to facilitate the surveillance and investigation of terrorist activities by giving law enforcement agencies broader powers to track, prevent, and combat terrorism in the wake of the September 11, 2001, attacks.[260] The PATRIOT Act largely amended several preexisting laws, including the CFAA and the ECPA, discussed earlier, and broadly amended other areas of the law to achieve its objectives, including immigration, money laundering, jurisdictional matters, and the legal use of electronic surveillance by government agencies. Although the PATRIOT Act does not create specific security obligations for organizations, it empowers the federal government to use more aggressive measures in combating information security attacks.

In particular, the PATRIOT Act made significant changes to preexisting National Security Letter (NSL) provisions of several other statutes. These provisions allow certain executive branch officials, without prior judicial oversight, to require a private party to provide certain information for national security purposes, such as under the ECPA.[261] In addition, the PATRIOT Act expands the scope of the Bank Secrecy Act, which requires covered institutions to develop and implement anti-money-laundering programs.[262] Previously, only financial institutions were required to have such programs. The amendment extends these requirements to several other types of industries, including law firms, if they engage in certain types of covered activities, most notably real estate closings and settlements. The PATRIOT Act also requires the U.S. Treasury Secretary to establish regulations to carry out the requirements of Section 326 of the act, which provides that each covered entity must develop and implement reasonable procedures for (1) verifying the identity of any person (including non-U.S. persons) who wishes to open an account; (2) maintaining copies of the records used to verify the person's name, address, and any other identifying information; and (3) determining if the person is on any list provided to the institution of known or suspected terrorists or terrorist organizations.[263]

---

260. U.S.A.P.A.T.R.I.O.T. Act (PATRIOT Act), Pub. L. No. 107-56, 115 Stat. 272 (Oct. 26, 2001).

261. 18 U.S.C. § 2709.

262. *See* PATRIOT Act, tit. III, § 311, Pub. L. No. 107-56, 115 Stat. 272 (codified at 31 U.S.C. § 5318A); *see* 31 C.F.R. pt. 103.

263. *See* PATRIOT Act, tit. III, § 326, Pub. L. No. 107-56, 115 Stat. 272; 31 C.F.R. 103.121.

2. *Homeland Security Act*

Section 201 of the Homeland Security Act assigns the Department of Homeland Security responsibility for information analysis and infrastructure protection, including: (1) receiving and analyzing law enforcement information and intelligence; (2) assessing vulnerabilities of key resources and critical infrastructure; (3) integrating intelligence analyses and vulnerability assessments to identify and prioritize protective measures; (4) developing a comprehensive national plan for securing key resources and critical infrastructure; (5) taking the necessary measures to protect those key resources and infrastructure; (6) providing security and public threat advisories, and warnings to state and local governments and the private sector, as well as advice about appropriate protective actions and countermeasures; and (7) reviewing and recommending improvements to policies and procedures for sharing domestic security intelligence among and with federal, state, and local governments.[264] The Homeland Security Act itself does not create particular rules for the prosecution of information security attacks or impose liability for lax information security.

The department's cyber security division has created the United States Computer Emergency Readiness Team (US-CERT) to coordinate the defense and response to attacks on information systems.[265] The US-CERT provides valuable warning information for organizations. Moreover, the US-CERT and the department generally have engaged in industry outreach to identify significant vulnerabilities and attacks and to coordinate the response to such attacks. The US-CERT uses these partnerships with the private-sector security vendors, other federal agencies, universities, and Information Sharing and Analysis Centers (ISACs) to help support corporate, governmental, and other computer security incident response teams. Such efforts have become particularly significant with respect to Advanced Persistent Threats (APTs) that appear highly coordinated and often require an equally coordinated response. Litigation of these issues remains rare, although several companies have considered the intrusions by such threats to be sufficiently material as to merit disclosure in their federal securities filings.

D. International Cybercrime Initiatives

The global nature of cybercrime is undeniable. The sheer scope of the problem has led many to conclude that the nature of the threat implicates national security concerns. A policy review commissioned by the U.S. government concluded that "[a] growing array of state and non-state actors such as terrorists and international criminal groups are targeting U.S. citizens, commerce, critical infrastructure, and government. These actors have the ability to compromise, steal, change, or completely destroy information."[266]

Efforts to prosecute international crimes have proven difficult. The hurdles for law enforcement include: navigating conflicting criminal laws of different countries; con-

---

264. Homeland Security Act of 2002, tit. II, § 201, Pub. L. No. 107-296, 16 Stat. 2135 (Nov. 25, 2002).

265. *See* Department of Homeland Security, Office of Inspector General, *U.S. Computer Emergency Readiness Team Makes Progress in Securing Cyberspace, but Challenges Remain* (June 2010), http://www.dhs.gov/xoig/assets/mgmtrpts/OIG_10-94_Jun10.pdf.

266. *Cyberspace Policy Review, Assuring a Trusted and Resilient Information and Communications Infrastructure* (2009) at 1, 20, http://www.whitehouse.gov/assets/documents/Cyberspace_Policy_Review_final.pdf.

ducting investigations across borders and jurisdictions; and collecting evidence. Not only is the relevant evidence usually of a highly technical nature, it may also be dispersed globally across various networks. National law enforcement agencies increasingly engage in extensive collaboration with their foreign counterparts in the investigation and prosecution of these cases.[267]

Various organizations are engaged in international cybercrime and cyber-security initiatives, such as the Group of Eight (G-8), the Asia-Pacific Economic Cooperation (APEC) forum, the Organization of American States (OAS), the Organization for Economic Cooperation and Development (OECD), the Council of Europe, the European Union, and the United Nations.[268] Several of these are addressed next.

1. G-8 Subgroup on High-Tech Crime

Originally, the purpose of this subgroup was to enhance the ability of countries belonging to the G-8 to investigate and prosecute cybercrime. Its mission has evolved, however, so that it now works with third-world countries to combat terrorism and to protect critical information infrastructures.[269] The subgroup maintains an emergency "always-on" network of contacts for cybercrime emergencies and an international Critical Information Infrastructure Protection Directory.[270] The subgroup was also involved in the negotiation of widely accepted principles to combat high-tech crime that were subsequently adopted by the G-8 Justice and Home Affairs Ministers, endorsed by G-8 Heads of State, and recognized by various jurisdictions.[271] Countries are represented in the subgroup by multidisciplinary delegations that include cybercrime investigators and prosecutors, and experts on legal systems, forensic analysis, and international cooperation agreements.[272]

2. European Union (EU) Work on Cybercrime

In February 2005, the EU adopted a Council Framework Decision on Attacks Against Information Systems. This decision, binding on all member states, seeks to harmonize cybercrime laws by identifying the categories of conduct that should be outlawed.[273]

On June 15, 2010, Europol, the EU's criminal intelligence agency, created the European Union Cybercrime Task Force.[274] As part of Europol's anti-cybercrime efforts, especially in the area of organized crime, Europol coordinates the European CyberCrime

---

267. Computer Crime & Intellectual Property Section, U.S. Dept. of Justice, *International Aspects of Computer Crime* (outline), http://www.justice.gov/criminal/cybercrime/intl.html.

268. *Cyberspace Policy Review* (2009), *supra*, at 20.

269. Meeting of G-8 Justice and Home Affairs Ministers, Washington, DC, May 11, 2004, http://www.justice.gov/criminal/cybercrime/g82004/g8_background.html.

270. *Id.*

271. *Id.*

272. *Id.*

273. Europa Summaries of EU Legislation (noting the adoption of "Council Framework Decision 2005/222/JHA of 24 February 2005 on attacks against information systems"), http://europa.eu/legislation_summaries/justice_freedom_security/fight_against_organised_crime/l33193_en.htm.

274. EUROPOL, European Union Cybercrime Task Force, http://www.europol.europa.eu/index.asp?page=news&news=pr100622.htm.

Platform (ECCP) to facilitate the collection, exchange, and analysis of intelligence; the Internet Crime Reporting Online System (I-CROSS) to catalog cybercrime events; and the Analysis Work File (AWF) to identify active criminal organizations and target them for concerted action by the law enforcement authorities of member states.[275]

3. Council of Europe Convention on Cybercrime

The Convention on Cybercrime is a multilateral treaty signed by more than 30 countries in 2001 and requires signatory nations to create the basic legal infrastructure required to address cybercrime and to commit to assisting other nations in investigating and prosecuting cyber criminals. It requires parties to establish laws against cybercrime, to ensure that their law enforcement officials have the necessary procedural authorities to investigate and prosecute cybercrime offenses effectively, and to provide international cooperation to other parties in the fight against computer-related crime.[276]

The international response to cybercrime continues to evolve to meet the threat. The current trend of integration, increased cooperation, and harmonization of laws is likely to continue for the foreseeable future.

---

275. House of Lords European Union Committee, Protecting Europe Against Large-Scale Cyber Attacks, 5th Report of Session 2009-10, H.L. Paper 68 (March 30, 2010) at 125–26.

276. *See Convention on Cybercrime,* http://conventions.coe.int/Treaty/EN/Treaties/Html/185.htm.

CHAPTER 4

Information Risk Management

Information risk management (IRM) is a framework that attempts to reduce the legal and business risks involved in protecting information. IRM addresses the statutory and regulatory requirements covered in Chapter 2 and the potential legal liabilities covered in Chapter 3. IRM establishes a strategic approach to information security and privacy plus electronic discovery, records management, and the handling of electronic transactions and other documents by focusing on electronic information during its lifecycle within the organization. This focus ties together information security and privacy practice, legal and regulatory compliance and risk assessment, treatment, monitoring, and review.

To utilize IRM, a risk assessment is first performed on the in-scope information assets. This assessment involves identifying the threats to information assets and the vulnerabilities in their protection. After these risks are identified, they must be assessed for business impact and the possibility of occurrence, resulting in a priority ranking of risks that is incorporated into the risk treatment process. Risk treatment decisions are then made and implemented, and risks must be continually monitored and reviewed. This chapter starts with the need for a risk management program and then discusses the risk assessment process, including threat modeling, the types of threats, the foreseeability of threats and attacks, and the varied approaches to risk analysis. The risk treatment types are presented next, including the cost of controls and two of the risk treatments—retaining risk and sharing/transferring risk. In addition, the concept of the legal defensibility of the choices made when selecting risk treatments is explained. The actual information security controls are covered in detail in Chapter 5.

What Global Executives Need to Know

- Risk assessment results for all areas of the organization affected by information security and privacy
- Cost-benefit analysis of the risk treatment options selecting information security and privacy controls
- Information security and privacy risks that are being shared/transferred through insurance or outsourcing and those that are being retained inside the organization

- The amount of residual risk that is accepted by the organization
- The degree of penetration of risk management methodologies throughout the organization and leadership involvement in the risk management process

4.1 THE NEED FOR RISK MANAGEMENT

Effective information risk management is an ongoing process to determine the level of risk acceptable to the organization. While a one-time risk analysis may address the present environment, it will not benefit the organization when circumstances change. Ultimately, the goal of a risk management program is to enable efficient use of resources to reduce risk. To do so requires ongoing reexamination of the threat environment to identify and update the risk landscape. Once the risks are identified, the risk management program focuses on reducing the risks to an acceptable level. A one-time risk analysis can for a time reduce risk; however, it cannot provide the continuous analysis needed to maintain the acceptable level of risk.

There are several drivers for an organization to implement a risk management program. One driver is changes to the regulatory environment, as governments become increasingly focused on risk. Risk management programs assist in demonstrating the effectiveness of internal controls and may be statutorily mandated. A second driver is contractual provisions covering sensitive information that mandate that the parties adopt a risk management program.

Federal regulations in a variety of areas require that organizations assess and control risk. Section 501(b) of the Gramm-Leach-Bliley Act (GLBA)[1] requires financial institutions to assess and control risks present within their organizations. The Federal Information Security Management Act (FISMA)[2] states that federal agencies must assess risk and apply policies and procedures based on that risk. Under the EU Safe Harbor Privacy Principles issued by the U.S. Department of Commerce,[3] organizations must take reasonable precautions to protect personal information; one method to achieve this protection is a risk management program. A risk management-based approach should align itself with Article 17 of the EU directive,[4] which calls for a risk management process by EU members. Another example of federal regulation is the HITECH Act,[5] which mandates annual privacy and security risk assessments. A number of additional regulations exist that either mandate or can be effectively complied with through the use of risk management programs. And increasingly U.S. state privacy laws[6] now list the components of risk management programs.

---

1. 15 U.S.C. § 6801 *et seq.*
2. 44 U.S.C. § 3541 *et seq.*
3. The current Safe Harbor guide is available at http://www.export.gov/.
4. Directive 95/46/EC of the European Parliament and of the Council is available at http://eur-lex.europa.eu/LexUriServ/LexUriServ.do?uri=CELEX:31995L0046:EN:HTML.
5. Pub. L. No. 111-5, 123 Stat. 226 (2009).
6. *See* 201 Mass. Code Regs. 17.00.

Many contracts contain clauses that address risk management. Section 6.1 of the Payment Card Industry's Data Security Standard[7] requires those handling card data to apply a risk management process in determining the criticality of computer systems patches. This requirement is to ensure that the most critical systems receive security patches ahead of less-sensitive systems, thereby reducing the risk of a vulnerable system exposing sensitive data. Beyond standards such as the PCI-DSS, organizations often include clauses to ensure that business partners, customers, service providers, and any other third party handling sensitive information adopt sufficient risk management processes.

4.2 RISK ASSESSMENT

Risk assessments comprise a number of discrete activities. These activities include the identification and classification of the in-scope information assets, identification of the threats to these information assets, identification of any vulnerabilities in the information asset safeguards, and an analysis of the business impacts of the threats' successfully exploiting vulnerabilities and the probability of doing so. Risk assessment should result in a prioritized ranking of the risks based on their likelihood of occurrence and magnitude of business impact, which feeds into the next phase, the choice of risk treatments.

A. Threat Modeling

"Threat modeling" is a term frequently used in the information security community. Although there are many definitions of this concept, threat modeling may be most simply defined as a way to present security threats in a structured, hypothetical environment that is then used to determine solutions.

The terms "threat modeling" and "risk assessment" are sometimes used interchangeably. Threat modeling systems are structured risk assessments.[8] Threat modeling focuses on assets, an attacker, and the means through which an attacker carries out an attack.[9] It is important that the team conducting the threat modeling use consistent language and definitions. Terms that are typically defined in a threat modeling exercise include "attacker," "asset," "attack path," "threat," "risk," and "vulnerability." All these terms are defined later in this chapter.

There are several approaches to threat modeling. Threat modeling has evolved over time from merely reactive to a more defensive, or preemptive, approach. A defensive approach is proactive, and it helps organizations identify threats and create plans to avoid these identified threats. The three general approaches to threat modeling are the following:

- *Asset-focused* approach: In an asset-focused approach, an organization focuses on its information assets and how they might be vulnerable to information security threats. This approach asks: "How do we protect this resource?"

---

7. The latest PCI-DSS is available at https://www.pcisecuritystandards.org/.
8. Maura A. Van Der Linden, Testing Code Security (2007).
9. *Id.*

- *Attacker-focused* approach: In an attacker-focused approach, an organization focuses on how attackers might try to access an organization's information technology (IT) systems and resources. This approach asks: "How will an attacker try to harm this resource?"
- *Design-focused* approach: In a design-focused approach, an organization focuses on the design of an organization's IT systems and resources. This approach asks: "How can the system be designed to resist threats?"

In principle, threat modeling is not complicated. It can be as simple an exercise as writing down an organization's assets and articulating how an attacker can threaten that asset (in the cyber security sense), then deciding what to do if things go wrong. To gain a comprehensive understanding of both the value of the asset and the proposed threats, an organization needs a representative number of its stakeholders to build and review the threat model. Members of the threat modeling team should include high-ranking business executives; data owners and custodians; technical executives such as a Chief Information Officer (CIO), Chief Information Security Officer (CISO), and Chief Privacy Officer (CPO): information security professionals: users of the in-scope information assets: third parties such as customers or partners: and appropriate external information security consultants.[10]

Threat models can be written documents or visual representations such as pictures, charts, and graphs. Written threat models are common yet do not always allow a contributor to easily comprehend how a change in one area of the model might affect other areas. A visual representation allows contributors to focus on specific objectives and determine what level of action is required for the most positive outcome.

Having a good team to build a threat model is only part of the process. After the model is developed, the next step is to apply risk management principles. Every threat and vulnerability has a cost of failure and every solution an implementation cost. The goal of any organization is to minimize both, while ensuring that the appropriate threats are addressed. As the cost of a threat rises, so too does the cost of security management. An organization must therefore manage its resources accordingly. A threat model combined with risk management principles ensures that an organization does not spend more money responding to or mitigating a potential threat than the actual cost of the realized threat. A robust collaborative threat model defines a road map for meeting challenges as they arise.

Threat modeling must be a dynamic and continuously evolving process.[11] Ultimately, it can save an organization time and money by controlling information security and privacy costs. However, this saving is possible only if the model is continuously revisited and updated over time. As the model matures it becomes an accurate representation of an organization's threat landscape and ultimately leads to rational, legally defensible risk management decisions that are appropriately cost effective.

---

10. The sampling should include both security professionals and non-security professionals able to contribute to the security of the system by their knowledge of how security and usability affect operations.

11. *See* Microsoft Corporation, *Improving Web Application Security: Threats and Countermeasures*, June 2003, *available at* http://msdn.microsoft.com/en-us/library/ff648644.aspx.

B. Types of Threats

A threat is any potential for an entity to exploit a vulnerability or otherwise cause harm to an information system. The cause of a threat may be human or natural, technological or environmental. Data breach laws have focused attention on the significant increase in the number of breaches in recent years. For example, reported data breaches in the United States rose almost 50 percent from 425 reported incidents in 2007 to 656 in 2008[12] and were on the rise again in 2010.[13] U.S. federal government agencies have experienced an increase of more than 200 percent in security incidents putting sensitive data at risk in the last several years.[14] Behind the statistics is a complex picture of heightened threats carried out by highly trained and motivated criminals targeting valuable corporate and government assets. These attacks utilize increasingly sophisticated schemes to exploit vulnerabilities in critical infrastructure.

In today's digital world threats to information systems exist everywhere a computer, server, laptop, smart phone, thumb drive, or other electronic device operates.[15] The proliferation of mobile devices and wireless technology that enable mobile commerce (m-commerce) and the expanding array of applications for them present many points of vulnerability in the flow of sensitive data. The presence of unencrypted data on easily lost mobile devices presents a particular threat. Electronic records are not the only problem—examples of lax security include threats to paper documents as well. Many data breaches occur when documents containing personal information are simply thrown into the trash, rather than being properly destroyed.

The following is a brief description of the various types of intentional and unintentional information security threats an organization may face.

1. Threats Based on Intentional Conduct

Individuals may commit intentional acts, such as a deliberate attack, or unintentional acts, such as negligence or error.[16] According to the U.S. National Institute of Standards and Technology (NIST), deliberate attacks by individuals fall into two categories:[17]

- Malicious attempts to gain unauthorized access to an IT system (e.g., via password guessing) to compromise system and data integrity, availability, or confidentiality
- A benign, but nonetheless purposeful, attempt to circumvent system security (e.g., a Trojan horse program written by an employee to bypass system security in order to facilitate his legitimate work)

---

12. *See* Identity Theft Resource Center, *2008 ITRC Breach Report, available at* http://www.idtheftcenter.org.

13. *See* Identity Theft Resource Center, *Data Breaches: A Black Hole, available at* http://www.idtheftcenter.org. The actual number of reported data breaches in the United States actually fell in 2009 but as this article and others on the site explain, this drop is due to a number of reasons for nondisclosure of data breaches to the public.

14. General Accounting Office, *Information Security Agencies Continue to Report Progress, but Need to Mitigate Persistent Weaknesses* (2009).

15. *See* US-CERT, Home Network Security, *available at* http://www.us-cert.gov/reading_room/home-network-security/.

16. *See* National Institute of Standards and Technology (NIST), Risk Management Guide for Information Technology Systems, Special Publication 800-30 (July 2002), *available at* http://csrc.nist.gov/publications/nistpubs/800-30/sp800-30.pdf.

17. *See id.* at 13.

The wide variety of threats involving intentional conduct illustrates the need for every organization to conduct a risk assessment to identify the threats to particular systems and develop a comprehensive information security program to combat these threats.

2. *Common Attackers*

a. Hackers

Broadly defined, hacking involves either intentionally accessing a computer without authorization or exceeding one's authorization. Hackers responsible for massive data breaches, such as the Heartland and TJX incidents, have shown increasing sophistication in their targeting of organizations handling vast amounts of sensitive personal information as well as major businesses and government agencies comprising the critical national infrastructure. Hacking encompasses a wide variety of intrusions into information systems. Motivations for hacking attacks range from financial gain—theft of valuable personal data such as Social Security numbers and credit card numbers that can be used for identity theft and fraud—to corporate espionage to compromising government targets. Hackers may also be motivated by the challenge, ego, curiosity, or in the case of insiders, revenge.

Hacker attacks have become increasingly sophisticated and damaging. For example, in 2010 an intrusion affecting 75,000 computer systems at nearly 2,500 companies was discovered.[18] Named the Kneber botnet, this exploit targeted proprietary corporate data, e-mails, credit card transaction data, and login credentials at companies and Internet service providers in 196 countries.[19] The Kneber botnet is believed to be run by a criminal group based in Eastern Europe using sophisticated command and control methods to infiltrate target companies, harvest login credentials, and use them to attack further systems. In late 2010, arrests were made in the United States, the United Kingdom, and the Ukraine over the Zeus botnet, which was an attempt to steal $220 million by placing this malware on the PCs of users and then stealing their banking information sufficient to log in and steal their funds.[20]

Advanced Persistent Threats (APTs) are among the most serious types of attackers because their focus is espionage. Often originating in Asia-Pacific countries, they employ zero-day exploits and social engineering techniques against company employees to breach networks. Antivirus and intrusion detection programs rarely detect them. Through the intrusions, hackers gain a foothold into a company's network, sometimes for years, even after a company has discovered them and taken corrective measures.[21] Zero-day exploits are covered in more detail later in this chapter.

---

18. *See* NetWitness.com, "NetWitness Discovers Massive ZeuS Compromise, "Kneber Botnet" Targets Corporate Networks and Credentials," Feb. 18, 2010, *available at* http://www.netwitness.com/resources/pressreleases/feb182010.aspx.

19. *See* Ellen Nakashima, *Large Worldwide Cyber Attack Is Uncovered*, WASH. POST, Jan. 18, 2010, at 1.

20. *See* ZDNet UK, *FBI Stresses International Co-operation in Zeus Arrests, available at* http://www.zdnet.co.uk/news/security-management/2010/10/04/fbi-stresses-international-co-operation-in-zeus-arrests-40090386/.

21. *See* Kevin Mandia, M-Trends, Jan. 27, 2010 (registration required), *available at* http://www.mandiant.com/products/services/m-trends; Kelly Jackson Higgins, "Anatomy of a Targeted, Persistent Attack: Seven Stages of the Advanced Persistent Threat Attack," *Dark Reading*, Jan. 27, 2010, *available at* http://www.darkreading.com/database_security/security/attacks/showArticle.jhtml?articleID=222600139.

b. Organized Crime

Attacks can be carried out by members of criminal organizations, often utilizing corruption and violence. The various criminal organizations may have differing motivations, including economic espionage, theft, and sabotage. According to the FBI, an "international hacking ring" breached the payment card processor RBS WorldPay and stole $9 million from ATMs around the world.[22]

c. Insider Attacks

These are attacks against an organization by current or former employees. The motivation of the employee may range from financial gain (theft of trade secrets or other valuable information) to revenge for perceived wrongs. Malicious insiders pose a serious threat, accounting for a third of the data breaches in recent years. Abuse of system administrative privilege and management failures, such as not suspending access by terminated employees, have led to a number of data breaches. In one of the most publicized insider cases, a Bank of New York Mellon computer technician working in the bank's information technology department stole information on 2,000 bank employees and opened bank and brokerage accounts in their names. He then used the purloined employee information to steal more than $1.1 million from charities, nonprofit groups, and other entities.[23] The employee pleaded guilty to grand larceny, money laundering, and computer tampering.

d. Attacks by Service Providers and Other Third Parties

These attacks involve abuse of otherwise authorized access to an organization's networks and information. Third parties often provide critical services to an organization that involve sensitive information. The misappropriation or misuse of that information can cause considerable damage. These attacks are often motivated by financial gain but sometimes may be based on a dispute between the parties, as in the case of the service provider who placed a time bomb in one of the periodic software updates disabling the client's software on a designated date.[24]

e. State-Sponsored Espionage

This threat concerns spying attacks conducted to gain access to sensitive or valuable information for economic, national policy, or military information. The number of cyber attacks against the U.S. government has been rising sharply. Many of these are believed to come from state or state-sponsored entities. During 2008, for example, there were more than 50,000 cyber attacks against the U.S. Department of Defense (DoD).[25]

---

22. *See* Gordon Snow, Federal Bureau of Investigation, Statement before the House Judiciary Subcommittee on Crime, Terrorism, and Homeland Security, July 28, 2010, *available at* http://www.fbi.gov/congress/congress10/snow072810.htm.

23. *See* Press Release, District Attorney New York County, District Attorney Vance Announces Guilty Plea in Massive Identity Theft Scam (July 1, 2010), *available at* http://manhattanda.org/whatsnew/press/2010-07-01.shtml.

24. North Texas Preventive Imaging, LLC v. Eisenberg, 1 996 U.S. Dist. LEXIS 19990 (C.D. Cal. Aug. 19, 1996).

25. *See* 2009 Report to Congress of the U.S.-China Economic and Security Review Commission, 111th Congress, First Session, November 2009, *available at* http://www.uscc.gov/annual_report/2009/annual_report_full_09.pdf.

f. Industrial Espionage

These spying attacks are conducted by competitors to gain access to sensitive or valuable information. In January 2010, Google announced that it had been the victim of a targeted attack and identified over 34 additional organizations that had also been breached. The attack is believed to have originated in China and used botnets to access victim networks and steal confidential business systems and information.[26] According to news reports, the hackers stole from Google "source code for a password system that controls access to almost all of the company's web services."[27]

3. *Common Attack Tools*

a. Malware

Software that is put onto a user's device without her or his knowledge and consent falls under the general category of malware. Malware, although it may be involved in less than a majority of the data breaches, is present in almost every data record that is compromised.[28] There are a number of different variations, such as the following:

- *Malicious code:* Any software or code developed for the purpose of compromising or harming information assets without the owner's informed consent is called malicious code.[29] Malicious code is meant to attack, destroy, or malevolently modify information on the victim organization's information systems.
- *Viruses:* "A virus is a program or programming code that replicates by being copied or initiating its copying to another program, computer boot sector or document. Viruses can be transmitted as attachments to an e-mail note or in a downloaded file, or be present on a diskette or CD."[30] The most well publicized viruses include I Love You (overwrote picture files, stole passwords, and sent them to a remote location), Nimda (spread by e-mail on Windows machines), and Melissa (propagated in the form of an e-mail message containing an infected Word document as an attachment).[31]
- *Worms:* "A worm is a self-replicating virus that does not alter files but resides in active memory and duplicates itself. Worms use parts of an operating system that are automatic and usually invisible to the user. It is common for worms to be noticed only when their uncontrolled replication consumes system

---

26. *See* Damballa, *The Command Structure of the Aurora Botnet*, *available at* http://www.damballa.com/downloads/r_pubs/Aurora_Botnet_Command_Structure.pdf.

27. Ellen Nakashima, *Google Hackers Duped Company Personnel to Penetrate Networks*, WASH. POST (April 21, 2010), at A15.

28. *2010 Data Breach Investigations Report*, Verizon and U.S. Secret Service (hereafter "Data Breach Report,") p. 23. Malware was involved in 38% of the data breaches the respective parties were involved with in 2009 but 94% of records affected involved malware.

29. *Id.* at 22.

30. TechTarget, Inc., "Virus" definition, *available at* http://searchsecurity.techtarget.com/sDefinition/ 0,,sid14_gci213306,00.html.

31. CERT® Advisory CA-2000-04 Love Letter Worm, *available at* http://www.cert.org/advisories/CA-2000-04.html; CERT® Advisory CA-2001-26 Nimda Worm, *available at* http://www.cert.org/advisories/CA-2001-26.html; CERT® Advisory CA-1999-04 Melissa Macro Virus, *available at* http://www.cert.org/advisories/CA-1999-04.html.

resources, slowing or halting other tasks."[32] In 1988, Robert Morris, Jr., a graduate student at Cornell, wrote an experimental, self-replicating, self-propagating program called a worm and injected it into the Internet. The program took advantage of a bug in a Unix program, and replicated and reinfected machines at a much faster rate than Morris had anticipated, causing computers at many sites, including universities, military installations, and medical research facilities, to crash. Morris was convicted of violating the Computer Fraud and Abuse Act.[33] More recently, the sophisticated W32.Stuxnet worm was the first known attack targeted at critical infrastructure. Stuxnet reprogrammed programmable logic controllers, sabotaging the industrial controls systems of certain types of manufactured systems, all the while hiding its tracks, while utilizing a "vast array of components to increase their chances of success. This includes zero-day exploits, a Windows rootkit, the first ever PLC rootkit, antivirus evasion, techniques, complex process injection and hooking code, network infection routines, peer-to-peer updates, and a command and control interface."[34]

- *Trojan horses:* A Trojan horse is a 'back door' into a computer system. A hacker may hide malicious or harmful code inside another program, video, or game. Once a trojan is installed, a hacker could have access to all the files on a hard drive, a system's e-mail, or even to create messages that pop up on the screen. Trojans are often used to enable even more serious attacks. A well-known Trojan is Sub-Seven, which comes in two parts: a client part and a server part. The client is used by the hacker to connect to the victim's machine. Once the server.exe is installed on the victim's machine the hacker has full access to the victim's machine.[35] In October 2010 the FBI arrested 20 persons in an international cybercrime network involved in a bank fraud scheme. The attack is attributed to the "Zeus Trojan" malware, which allegedly allowed hackers to get into victim accounts from thousands of miles away, compromising dozens of individual and business accounts in the United States and transferring more than $3 million under false identities.[36]
- *Malicious scripts:* These are malicious codes embedded in a website or other interactive system meant to do harm to those who access that system. Often these scripts are delivered through a compromised website with the goal of infecting the systems of those who visit the site.

b. Social Engineering

The use of social skills to obtain insider knowledge, passwords, or PINs to gain unauthorized access to systems or physical locations is called social engineering. Social engi-

32. *Id.*, "Worm" definition, *available at* http://searchsecurity.techtarget.com/sDefinition/0,,sid14_gci213386,00.html.

33. *Available at* http://ethics.csc.ncsu.edu/abuse/wvt/worm/.

34. *W-32 Stuxnet Dossier*, Symantec Security Response, ver 1.3 (Nov. 2010).

35. Intrusion Detection FAQ: SubSeven Trojan v 1.1, *available at* http://www.sans.org/security-resources/idfaq/subseven.php.

36. Federal Bureau of Investigation, *Cyber Banking Fraud: Global Partnerships Lead to Major Arrests* (Oct. 1, 2010), *available at* http://www.fbi.gov/news/stories/2010/october/cyber-banking-fraud/cyber-bankingfraud/?searchterm=trojan%20zeus.

neering occurs when an attacker convinces an insider to share his or her password. The attacker then uses the password to impersonate the insider. This type of attack is a growing threat, and more than a quarter of reported cases may now utilize social engineering, over twice as much as the previous year.[37] Much of the newest malware is being deployed through social engineering schemes or through third-party applications on social networking sites like Facebook (but by no means limited to them), often in the form of suggested plug-ins, games, and new friend requests.[38]

- *Phishing:* A subset of social engineering whereby the attacker uses carefully crafted e-mail or other messages to pose as a trusted figure known to the target. The Google breach discussed earlier was considered particularly troublesome for the companies involved because the hackers used social engineering and phishing techniques to trick company officials into opening e-mail attachments or links to a malicious website that subsequently led to downloading and installing malware.

c. Physical Security Breaches

These are intrusions into physical locations within an organization's facility or "dumpster diving" for paper records or other media in an organization's garbage, recycling bins, shredding bins, or other disposal sites. The motivation for these breaches may include reconnaissance or preparation for later attacks, theft of equipment or trade secrets, or mere vandalism. This includes consent decrees reached by the FTC with various defendants in the dumping of consumer records. For example, in one case 40 boxes of consumer information, including copies of driver's licenses, credit cards, and consumer reports, were found in a dumpster outside one of the former offices of a mortgage brokerage company.[39] Theft of equipment is common, such as the theft of the portable media device holding information on students with federal loans and the breach of more than 3.3 million records.[40]

d. Eavesdropping

This tool is an attack to intercept and capture information communicated on a network or displayed by a computer. Attackers may use standard network tools called "sniffers" to intercept unencrypted traffic and attempt to harvest sensitive information. The eavesdropping may not be detected by the victims. Another form of eavesdropping involves the interception of Radio Frequency (RF) signals emanating from computer screens or terminals and using the signals to display the information appearing on such screens or terminals. Several of the massive data breaches, including Heartland, Hannaford, and TJX, were the result of hackers using malware designed to harvest payment card data as it moved across company networks.

---

37. Data Breach Report at 32.

38. Steven R. Chabinsky, Federal Bureau of Investigation, Remarks at the GovSec/FOSE Conference, Washington, D.C. (March 23, 2010), *available at* http://www2.fbi.gov/pressrel/speeches/chabinsky032310.htm.

39. Federal Trade Commission v. Gregory Navone (D. Nev.), FTC File No. 072 3067.

40. *See* http://www.crn.com/slide-shows/security/225700255/top-10-data-breaches-of-2010-so-far.htm?pgno=2.

e. Injection Attack

This attack technique is used to exploit website vulnerabilities. A common attack is SQL[41] injection, a process in which a hacker adds extra SQL code commands to a web page request. "Vulnerable web applications process the extra SQL commands, which then cause the web application to leak additional information, such as user credentials, which can be used to log into the targeted application."[42] This technique can allow an attacker not only to steal data from a database but also to modify and delete data and leave behind eavesdropping software, as previously described. Many of the recent massive data breaches were started with SQL injection attacks to gain initial access to the systems of the corporations. This list of data breaches is long, including Heartland, Hannaford Bros., 7-Eleven Inc., TJX Companies, Dave & Buster's, BJ's Wholesale Club, OfficeMax, Boston Market, Barnes & Noble, Sports Authority, Forever 21, and DSW.[43] Over 30 million e-mail addresses were exposed during such an attack on social network RockYou.[44] Experts believe injection attacks to be the most serious security risk to web applications.[45]

f. Denial of Service

A denial-of-service (DOS) attack seeks to prevent normal function of a system by occupying the system's resources and rendering them unavailable for normal use. A more sophisticated version of a DOS attack involves an attacker using hundreds or even thousands of computers to launch a coordinated attack against a target. This is known as a "distributed denial of service" (DDoS) attack. These attacks normally involve flooding of a website with unwanted traffic. These range from the attack on Twitter[46] and the attack on Georgian sites during its conflict with Russia[47] to the attack on a law firm in the United Kingdom.[48] Launched in March 2010, the IM DDoS botnet is a commercial service for delivering distributed denial of service (DDoS) attacks against any desired target.[49] Operated by a criminal organization in China, it is a publicly available service that allows anyone to establish an online account, input the domain(s) they wish to attack, and pay for the service.

---

41. Sequential Query Language (SQL) is a database computer language. Databases are fundamental components of web applications. They enable web applications to store data, preferences, and content elements. Web applications use SQL to interact with databases to dynamically build customized data views for each user.

42. *See* Angela Moscaritolo, *"NASA Sites Hacked Via SQL Injection," quoting Gunter Ollmann, VP of Research at security firm Damballa*, SC MAGAZINE (Dec. 7, 2009), *available at* http://www.scmagazineus.com/nasa-sites-hacked-via-sql-injection/article/159181/.

43. COMPUTERWORLD, accessible at http://www.computerworld.com.au/article/315418/sql_injection_attacks_led_massive_data_breaches/.

44. *See* http://www.pcworld.com/article/185664/rockyou_sued_over_data_breach.html.

45. *See* Angela Moscaritolo, *Injection Tops List of Web Application Security Risks* SC MAGAZINE (April 19, 2010), *available at* http://www.scmagazineus.com/injection-tops-list-of-web-application-security-risks/printarticle/168304.

46. *See* http://blog.twitter.com/2009/08/denial-of-service-attack.html.

47. *See* http://www.zdnet.com/blog/security/coordinated-russia-vs-georgia-cyber-attack-in-progress/1670.

48. *See* http://www.bbc.co.uk/news/technology-11434809.

49. Damballa, a security firm that specializes in tracking botnets and their criminal operations, announced its discovery of the new IM DDoS botnet on September 13, 2010. *The IMDDOS Botnet: Discovery and Analysis*, Damballa Threat Research, *available at* http://www.damballa.com/downloads/r_pubs/Damballa_Report_imDDOS.pdf.

g. Relay Attack

A relay attack involves an attacker taking control of a chain of computer systems used to channel or "relay" the attack from system to system in order to mask the true origin of the attack. Relay attacks now also comprise man in the middle attacks, in which wireless communications are intercepted between, say, a card and a card reader that do not come into contact and the intercepting party is able, by utilizing the intercepted authentication sequence, to convince the remote reader of its authenticity.

h. Spoofing

In spoofing, attackers falsely assume the identity of a person or system. E-mail headers are commonly altered to appear as if they came from a trusted individual, but Media Access Code (MAC) addresses, domain names, and even Internet Protocol (IP) addresses can also be "spoofed."[50] Content can also be spoofed, as in the story about Twitter spoofing a story about the health of a leading figure in the digital entertainment field.[51]

4. Threats Based on Accidental, Inadvertent, or Natural Events

a. Human Error

People make mistakes, and these mistakes may cause an information system to operate incorrectly or leave an organization vulnerable. Errors include typographical errors, failures to follow security procedures, incompetence, and mistakes in judgment. Hundreds of data breaches over the past four years were caused by human error; it accounted for 27.5 percent of the data breaches reported in 2009.[52] One example is the Health Net case in which a portable drive containing unencrypted protected health information was lost, eventually leading to charges against the company for violation of HIPAA/HITECH.[53] Another case involved the loss of unencrypted backup tapes and the potential exposure of the personal information of more than 12 million people.[54]

b. Bugs and Defects

These are hardware and software flaws not intentionally created that cause malfunctions or create vulnerabilities to attack.

c. Accidents

Various kinds of accidents may affect information systems, including fires, water-pipe breaks, physical damage to computer equipment, the erasure of media by exposure to magnetic fields, and accidental deletion of information.

---

50. Gregory Kruck, *Spoofing—A Look at an Evolving Threat*, J. COMPUTER INFO. SYSTEMS (Fall 2006), available at http://www.allbusiness.com/marketing-advertising/direct-marketing-direct-mail/4107802-1.html.

51. *See* http://www.wired.com/epicenter/2009/01/wiredcom-imagev/.

52. Identity Theft Resource Center, *Breaches 2009—Data Breaches: The Insanity Continues*, available at http://www.idtheftcenter.org/artman2/publish/lib_survey/Breaches_2009.shtml.

53. *See* http://www.informationweek.com/news/healthcare/security-privacy/showArticle.jhtml?articleID=222600681.

54. http://www.reuters.com/article/idUSN2834717120080828.

d. Disruption of Infrastructure Services

Outages of water, heating, air conditioning, gas, or electricity; fiber-optic cable cuts; phone line breakage; and similar events may prevent the smooth operation of information systems and render security precautions ineffective.

e. Natural Disasters

Earthquakes, hurricanes, lightning, floods, fires, and the like may harm security measures enacted to protect the organization's information systems.

There are some helpful tools that organizations can utilize when evaluating the vulnerabilities that their systems may be exposed to in cyberspace. One example is a checklist provided by the U.S. Cyber Consequences Unit. The checklist details vulnerabilities that have been accumulated based on the collective experience of several U.S. government organizations and includes questions to uncover vulnerabilities that could lead to data breach.[55]

C. Foreseeability of Threats and Attacks

One of the key challenges of risk assessment is to account for reasonably foreseeable threat agents and events. This notion of foreseeability evokes a particular set of challenges around generating accurate and precise probability estimates more easily understood in the context of risk as broken into its respective components.

Risk can generally be divided into two components: loss event frequency and loss magnitude.[56] Loss magnitude is an estimate of the financial impact of a threat, whereas loss event frequency is an estimate of the frequency, within a time frame, that a threat action will result in a loss. It is the loss event frequency that is the focus of foreseeability.

Loss event frequency also has two components: threat event frequency and vulnerability. Threat event frequency measures the frequency of contact that threats have with an asset and the probability that a threat that has made contact will act against that asset. Taken altogether, threat event frequency is defined as the probable frequency, within a given time frame, that a threat will act in a manner that may result in loss.

Vulnerability in loss event frequency is used in a very specific context. Instead of the traditional use of "vulnerabilities" (plural) to describe various weaknesses in a system, "vulnerability" (singular) pertains to the probability that a threat action will result in a loss (i.e., how vulnerable an asset is to attack). Vulnerability is further broken into two components: threat capability and resistance strength. Threat capability provides a ranged estimate of the likely attacker's competency (e.g., amateur hackers versus skilled professionals) while resistance strength estimates the degree of protection afforded a given asset (literally, just how resistant an asset is to attack in general).

The notion of foreseeability pertains to the ability, during analyses, to reasonably anticipate a menace agent acting against a specific asset. Put into risk analysis terms,

55. *US-CCU Cyber-Security Check List* (2007).

56. The definition of risk and its respective components is directly taken from the Factor Analysis of Information Risk (FAIR) framework. For more information on FAIR, please see http://fairwiki.riskmanagementinsight.com/.

foreseeability describes the ability to assert that given threats exist and the ability to properly gauge resistance strength in an inclusive manner based on reasonable assumptions of the threat landscape.

Some of the controversy over estimating loss event frequency has to do with the ability to reasonably estimate a few factors: contact frequency, probability of action, and threat capability. Arguments are made that there is not presently enough data available about known threats to successfully estimate the probability that a threat agent will make contact, the probability that it will initiate action, or what its capabilities might be.

In decision theory, data is generally put into three categories: *knowns*, *known unknowns*, and *unknown unknowns*. In plain English, these categories equate to things we know, things we know that we don't know, and the remaining universe of things that we don't yet realize that we don't know. This issue of what is known is daunting, but nevertheless ties directly into the overall question of foreseeability. For example, we know that there are other planets in the universe (a known). We know that we do not know if life exists on these planets (a known unknown). But there is undoubtedly much about the universe that we are unable to yet imagine (the unknown unknowns).

Many of the issues of estimating probability can be addressed through the methods.[57] These can produce accurate probability estimates, although the precision of those estimates (i.e., their "narrowness") may vary widely. For example, if it is known that threat agents exist, then it is possible to say that there is between a 0 and 100 percent probability that a threat will result in an attack. This estimate is deemed accurate because the actual probability of attack will have to fall in this range. However, the precision of this estimate is very low, mandating the use of statistical methodologies such as *certain distributions* to properly describe both accuracy and precision.

1. Zero-Day Threats

In the context of electronic systems a *zero-day,* or *"0-day,"* threat is one that remains unknown to those responsible for defending against it. The term "zero-day" is a bit of a misnomer in that it represents a class of attacks that may or may not be widely known, but are certainly known to someone, somewhere. The typical zero-day attack is one that exploits a weakness that has not been disclosed to those responsible for maintaining the system or application under attack. An individual attack is an unknown unknown, but zero-day attacks as a class are not.

As to foreseeability, zero-day threats represent a potential wrinkle in performing a risk analysis. Zero-day exploits are perfect examples of unknown unknowns and present unique challenges to risk analysis assessment. After all, how can an analysis be performed for an unknown unknown? Fortunately, while it is not necessarily possible to foresee unknown unknowns, it is foreseeable that zero-day attacks will occur, and it is then possible to provide a reasonably accurate, if not overly precise, estimate of the probability of such an attack and its eventual impact (loss magnitude).

57. Douglas W. Hubbard, How to Measure Anything: Finding the Value of Intangibles in Business (Wiley, 2010).

An example of how defense against zero-day threats can play out in real life is shown in a study of "resilient and survivable networks" (ResiliNets).[58] In the doctrine of resiliency and survivability, focus is split between defensibility and recoverability. With the increasing prevalence of zero-day threats, it is only possible to implement defenses to a reasonable degree (based on risk analysis). The rest of the focus in protecting an asset must then switch to optimizing recovery. The objective of recoverability is continuity despite degraded conditions rather than allowing a single event to result in cessation of operation. The foreseeability of zero-day attacks therefore impacts both pre- and post-attack planning.

2. *Foreseeability and Legal Defensibility*

Risk analysis is an important part of an organization's decision-making process, but foreseeability introduces a degree of uncertainty which may in turn create questions about the reasonableness of a given decision. Ultimately, decision-making processes must be defensible when subjected to legal scrutiny. If a decision is based on a risk analysis that does not adequately consider reasonably foreseeable threats, including zero-day attacks, the ability of the organization to defend its decisions is weakened, resulting in legal exposure and financial impact.

It is thus imperative to maintain an understanding of what is and is not reasonably foreseeable as part of an overall risk management strategy. All classes of known attacks should be included, as should placeholders for zero-day attacks and other unknown unknowns. It is also important to revisit decisions as new information is gathered. Over time it is expected that case law will develop and provide a deeper foundation for understanding what is and is not reasonably foreseeable. In the end, foreseeability is a balance of ongoing risk analysis and existing legal precedent.

D. Approaches to Risk Analysis

The risk analysis phase of risk assessment is typically split into two distinct areas: quantitative and qualitative. In recent years a third area, evidence-based risk management, has also emerged. Each of these areas has a place and purpose within the broader landscape of IRM. Today, quantitative risk assessment is generally preferred over qualitative risk assessment, while evidence-based risk management encompasses all forms of assessment.

1. *Quantitative Risk Assessment*

The objective of quantitative risk assessment is to provide a numbers-based analysis of risk factors that accounts for fuzziness in estimated probabilities and impacts. The Factor Analysis of Information Risk (FAIR) methodology[59] is currently seen as the leading example of the quantitative approach. The upside to quantitative methodologies is that they provide a consistent, numerical basis for measuring information risk factors. The downside is that quantitative risk assessments' calculations rely on estimates (typically from subject-matter experts) that have a degree of fuzziness. Fortunately modern sta-

58. For more information on ResiliNets, please visit the ResiliNets Wiki maintained by the University of Kansas and Lancaster University, available online at https://wiki.ittc.ku.edu/resilinets/Main_Page.

59. For more information, please see http://fairwiki.riskmanagementinsight.com/.

tistical methods like Bayes[60] and Monte Carlo[61] enable an assessor to account for the degree of precision and confidence behind the estimates.

2. *Qualitative Risk Assessment*

In contrast, qualitative risk assessment is not based on estimating numerical values for threats, organizational vulnerability, or the primary or secondary impact to the business. Qualitative risk assessment may include a pseudo-quantitative numerical system, but it is not based on estimations or calculations. This methodology is often used in quick assessments to provide a simple ranking of identified threats or weaknesses. The downside is that the assessed risk rating may have no direct relevance to the affected organization. For example, a standard risk-rating rubric may be quickly applied to the results of a security assessment. In such a scenario, a given vulnerability called "critical," "high," "medium," or "low" may be misleading absent contextualization. For instance, a risk generally labeled critical for an online system is probably not critical in the context of an off-line, or stand-alone, system.

3. *Evidence-Based Risk Management*

Evidence-based risk management provides a method for including assessment results from both quantitative and qualitative methodologies through use of weighting and prioritization. In this manner, both quantitative and qualitative methodologies contribute to an overall information risk management strategy. The key is ensuring the results of each methodology are properly contextualized and categorizing according to the quality of the inputted data.

Where possible, quantitative risk analysis methods should be used, though this does not diminish the usefulness of a qualitative analysis. The emergence of evidence-based risk management makes a qualitative cost-benefit feasible, though less desirable than quantitative methods. Regulatory compliance provides a ready example of a case in which a qualitative assessment may be suitable. Consider a scenario in which an organization is statutorily required to produce security policies or face a steep fine. In this scenario, most organizations will rightly determine that deploying security policies is more beneficial than taking a chance on getting fined and suffering a negative impact to reputation. Moreover, this analysis would likely conclude that in both cases the organization would incur the cost of deploying security policies, but in the latter case it would also incur the cost of fines on top of the deployment costs.

4.3 RISK TREATMENT

A number of strategies can be employed when managing risk factors that have already been assessed. All rely on input from a qualified risk assessment. Information security professionals traditionally refer to four approaches, or *treatments*, for managing identified risk factors:

- *Avoidance:* Not performing the activity that generates the risk.
- *Reduction (through use of controls):* Where possible and cost-effective, a risk factor can be reduced or even eliminated through the use of preventive, detec-

60. For more information, please see https://secure.wikimedia.org/wikipedia/en/wiki/Bayesian_probability.
61. For more information, please see https://secure.wikimedia.org/wikipedia/en/wiki/Monte_Carlo_method.

tive, or corrective controls. The cost of such controls is discussed later in this chapter, and the actual controls are covered in Chapter 5.

- *Sharing/Transfer:* If reduction is not feasible, it may be possible to share the risk factor with a third party via outsourcing or insurance. Often referred to as risk transfer, the transferor actually retains the ultimate risk of liability (e.g., if the transferee goes out of business). This is discussed later in this chapter.
- *Retention:* It may not be cost-effective or feasible to reduce or transfer/share a risk factor. It will then be necessary to retain or *self-insure* that risk. This approach is discussed later in this chapter.

In all cases it is necessary to thoroughly document risk management decisions, recording the assessed risk and the rationale for how it will be treated. After all these decisions are made on identified risk factors, what remains is the residual risk that the organization takes on as a matter of course. Every organization has some sort of residual risk related to information security and privacy because not all risk can be cost-effectively eliminated. Acceptance of the commensurate level of residual risk should be an active decision process by the appropriate levels within the organization.

A. Legal Defensibility

The risk treatment decisions should be based also on analysis of their defensibility in the legal and regulatory arenas, and before audiences of an organization's customers, shareholders, leadership, and the public at large. Legal defensibility means that security controls, individually and as a whole, must be responsive to what is laid out in statutes, regulations, and contracts. This may be for controls that satisfy specific provisions on, for example, encryption or data destruction or for the sum of all controls and other security and risk procedures that demonstrate a "reasonable" security program has been implemented and maintained. Legal defensibility requires the legal arguments to be built when the risk assessment and risk treatment processes are being performed, not later when the data breach has occurred. Legal defensibility analysis is a core IRM strategy and a significant area in which legal counsel and information security technologists need to work closely with business executives.

Planning for legal defensibility takes into account a large number of legal considerations, requiring extensive information security and privacy knowledge plus litigation-related expertise, including at least the following:

- General and/or specific information security and privacy requirements in statutes/regulations, contracts, or common law, including arguments for and against the applicability of such legal requirements (these are discussed in Chapters 2 and 3)
- How judges and juries interpret such statutes/regulations and the common law (e.g., what information do courts look at to interpret an ambiguous provision of a regulation?)
- The existence of common law duties, including the use of risk in determining whether a legal duty to provide reasonable information security and privacy controls exists and has been met and an understanding of the elements of such duties and how they are proved or defended in court

- The strategies of the other party's attorneys and how they construct arguments in the information security and privacy breach or other liability context and in general
- Litigation strategy, procedure, leverage points, and risk, including an understanding of the discovery, motion to dismiss, motion for summary judgment, and trial phases of an action
- How regulators interpret the statutes discussed earlier and undertake regulatory actions (discussed in Chapters 2 and 3)
- The importance of risk, industry standards, and general security standards (discussed in Chapters 5 and 6) under the law
- The use of contracts to legally bind service providers and other third parties storing, processing, or transmitting information on behalf of the organization (discussed in Chapter 3)
- The importance and use of attorney-client privilege (discussed in Chapter 3)
- The significance and impact of expert testimony
- Document retention and preservation and the impact of electronic discovery and electronic evidence on legal proceedings and legal risk (briefly discussed in Chapters 6 and 7)

In the private sector, information management risk factors are governance issues owned by the board of directors. This is particularly true in the context of publicly traded companies or heavily regulated industries such as health and financial services. Virtualization, cloud computing, and social media add new dimensions to the risk management challenges. As such, legal counsel, risk management, internal audit, and information security professionals need to advise business executives of both the actual and potential costs involved with the assessment, creation, deployment, enforcement, and audit of IRM policies.

Examination of each step in the process not only prepares a company for potential losses but also helps decision makers make better-informed decisions. Absent a well-founded risk assessment, a proposed course of action may look good on paper, but not in practice. The risk management process and resulting safeguards may add substantial costs to any information technology project, but integrating information security controls after the fact can prove more costly. Decisions on whether to adhere strictly to risk management practices and risk remediation measures are ultimately business decisions requiring consideration of both the costs and the ultimate value to the organization of the proposed action.

B. The Cost of Security Controls

Despite the constant drumbeat of the necessity of information security and privacy precautions, an appropriate risk management strategy is largely dependent on the nature of an organization. While heavily regulated industries like financial services, health care, and energy are statutorily bound to a certain level of security safeguards that cannot be waived, many other organizations have more flexibility. Moreover, many organizations that use the Internet only for promotional purposes and basic services (e.g., e-mail) could argue that firewalls, security monitoring services, and full-time security staff are unnecessary. Nonetheless, the implementation of some level of security practices is important to all organizations. Quality information security practices can increase customer confidence, improve profitability, and provide the basis for preventing significant losses or damage. It is, however, important to balance the cost of those practices against the benefit to the organization.

Information security requires a focus on people, processes, and technology. It is the responsibility of every person employed by or having a relationship with the organization. Accounting for this participation makes calculating costs difficult. For example, the time it takes for an employee to remember and type his or her username and password and to log on and off each time he or she leaves the computer is a cost to the organization in the form of lost productivity. Such costs often are hidden at the time of implementation but are inevitably captured in the organization's bottom line. By clearly identifying these staff costs before proceeding with a security plan, managers can more wisely apply appropriate safeguards for an organization's financial capabilities and risk profile and thereby avoid costly surprises.

Organizations may be tempted to reduce the cost-benefit analysis to a basic return on investment (ROI) computation. Unfortunately, to do so would belie the fact that security safeguards are inherently expenses that are oriented toward reducing overall risk exposure rather than investments that can be measured for growth. Security safeguards are not generally sources of new or increased revenue, but rather provide mechanisms to reduce operational expenses. Being able to capitalize the costs of security safeguards does not mean that those costs are investments. As such, calculating ROI is an inappropriate step in evaluating safeguards.

Instead, cost-effectiveness and cost-efficiency provide more reasonable measures of the value of information security expenditures. Beyond the goal of reducing the overall risk exposure for the organization, information security and privacy measures can be evaluated in terms of how effectively they reduce the vulnerability of an asset to an attack, as well as how well they improve operational efficiencies. For example, implementing an organization-wide identity and access management solution can streamline overall user management, reducing support and maintenance costs while boosting productivity (positive cost-efficiency impact). At the same time, this solution may also dramatically reduce the ability of an attacker to compromise accounts, which in turn protects assets impacted by these improved access controls (positive cost-effectiveness impact).

In the context of a formal quantitative risk analysis, there are typically two key components: loss event frequency and loss magnitude (discussed earlier). During this analysis, a given asset is evaluated for its overall resistance to attacks in order to estimate its overall vulnerability to attack. On the other side of the equation is the financial impact associated with lost productivity, response costs, replacement costs, loss of competitive advantage, incurred fines and judgments, and damaged reputation. From the perspective of a strict risk-based cost-benefit analysis, there must first be an estimate of the degree of risk afflicting an asset in a given threat scenario (represented in real dollar estimates), and then an evaluation of security safeguards in terms of how well they reduce that risk. As such, cost-effectiveness tends to be the primary benefit in the cost-benefit analysis, with cost-efficiencies providing a potential secondary benefit.

Regardless of the efforts engaged to reduce risk factors afflicting an organization, there will always be residual risk that must be managed since running a business necessitates taking risks. It is thus important to accurately assess the degree to which an asset is at risk, the costs associated with mitigation of that risk, and the extent of residual exposure. Ultimately, the risk management strategy must be evaluated in light of a cost-benefit analysis of security practices and safeguards. Clearly, an information security program that costs more to implement and maintain than the organization has in available revenue is not an option. An information security and privacy program that does not reduce major security threats is also not effective.

Increasingly, several factors point toward increasing probability of loss from information security failures. The growing complexity of information systems, along with the accelerating rate of technological change, means that inadvertent errors and interruptions will have broader impacts than in the past. An ever-increasing number of businesses have moved critical business functions to digital environments. These business functions now take place online with their most valuable information stored electronically. The world's financial institutions have long handled transactions and money transfers electronically, but digital technology has brought online commerce to the masses. The emergence of digital technology provides increasing incentives for cybercrime. To counter these growing threats, governments issue increasingly complex regulations and businesses utilize contractual provisions mandating tighter security controls. Violations of these regulations and contractual provisions often carry penalties, fines, and specific liability for failure to provide required security protections. Violations of these regulations and contracts, along with heightened awareness and the rising security expectations of the general public, increase the likelihood that financial losses will result from failures to secure sensitive information.

It is important to recognize that the obligation to protect sensitive information is a risk management decision. Management must identify and quantify expected losses to conduct a realistic cost-benefit analysis of the protection alternatives. This analysis should consider both the short- and long-term costs of implementing and maintaining the protection solution, and then compare those costs to the protection program's its effectiveness in reducing the risk of loss. The ultimate goal is to provide reasonable protection at an acceptable cost.

C. Risk Retention

All business decisions involve some degree of risk. Organizations can choose to retain that risk or attempt to mitigate it. When an organization retains a risk, it makes a decision to do nothing about a particular risk. Retaining a risk is a business decision. An organization may choose to retain a certain risk because mitigating it by using security safeguards is more costly than having this risk realized. An organization may also be forced to retain a risk that it cannot insure against or for which it does not have the financial resources to cover on its own. The reality of operating a business is that there will always be unavoidable risks that, if realized, could threaten to bankrupt the organization.

Some organizations are able to purchase insurance to cover the costs of potential information security risks. Insurance policies often do not cover all possible losses and liabilities that an organization may sustain. If an organization does not use insurance or other contractual relationships to shift risk to a third party, then that organization must plan to absorb the impact of these risks, in effect self-insuring against them.

Organizations may self-insure for loss in two ways. The first is through active self-insurance. In an active self-insurance scenario, an organization accepts a particular risk and prepares for it to be realized. This is done by setting aside funds to cover the potential loss and liability or by creating a "captive" insurance carrier subsidiary to insure the parent's risks. This notion of active self-insurance assumes that the organization has sufficient funds to cover the potential loss. All organizations self-insure to some extent;

however, organizations that choose this option must consider the tax implications. It may be difficult to write off the cost of maintaining a reserve fund as a business expense. Captive insurance may address this issue, but it can be complicated.

The alternative is passive self-insurance. When an organization retains risks passively it does not set aside funds to cover the potential loss. If the loss occurs, the organization must cover it using whatever resources are available at the time. Most organizations purchase insurance for the larger unpredictable or catastrophic risks and passively self-insure smaller, manageable risks. Determining which risks to actively insure and which to passively self-insure is a business decision. An organization's directors and officers must make these decisions in accordance with their fiduciary duty.

Both active and passive approaches have their role in an organization's risk management program. Their use depends on the circumstances of the threats and vulnerabilities that the organization faces. The importance of the information or systems at stake is a key consideration, as are the cost and effectiveness of information security controls. Where a particular threat poses a remote chance of insignificant harm, and the cost of controls and active self-insurance is high, an organization may appropriately choose passive measures. As the risk of substantial harm increases, active measures become more cost-effective. New insurance products appear regularly, requiring organizations to periodically review their active versus passive self-insurance policies.

D. Risk Sharing/Transfer—Insurance

Standard insurance policies normally cover bodily injury and damage to tangible property—not loss of intangible data. For example, a California appellate court determined that a first-party property policy did not cover the loss of stored computer data not accompanied by the loss or destruction of the storage medium.[62] Although courts have issued decisions on both sides of the "intangible property" issue of whether property and general liability (GL) policies do cover data loss,[63] the standard ISO (Insurance Services Office) forms now expressly exclude coverage for losses based on electronic data. Specifically, in 2001, ISO amended the definition of property damage in the standard GL policy[64] to expressly state that "electronic data is not tangible property." And, in 2004, ISO added an exclusion[65] that eliminates coverage for "[d]amages arising out of the loss of, loss of use of, damage to, corruption of, inability to access, or inability to manipulate electronic data."

But new products are available to address intangible data issues such as data breach. For example, network security and privacy (NSAP) insurance is a relatively new product that covers the expenses (forensics costs to investigate the breach, breach notification, call center, credit monitoring, legal, liability settlements, and, if available, fines or penalties) incurred as a result of a data breach event. Assuming that policyholders continue to face legal uncertainty when applying standard insurance to a data breach, the most effective method may be to transfer that risk to specific NSAP insurance coverage.

62. Ward Gen. Ins. Services, Inc. v. The Employers Fire Ins. Co., 114 Cal. App. 4th 548, 7 Cal. Rptr. 3d 844 (Cal. App. 2003).

63. *Compare Ward Gen. Ins. Services, Inc. with* Lambrecht & Associates, Inc. v. State Farm Lloyds, 119 S.W. 3d 16 (Tex. App. 2003).

64. ISO Form CG 00 01 10 01.

65. Exclusion p to ISO Form CG 00 01 12 04.

NSAP policies should be broadly triggered by the compromising of sensitive information. The trigger will be pulled regardless of whether the information was compromised via social engineering, direct attack by an external entity, or the acts of rogue employees or independent contractors. There should be full coverage for regulatory defense, fines, and penalties. Companies buying this specialty insurance should also be covered for the violation of any privacy statute, including breach notification laws, including mitigation-related expenses such as credit monitoring, call center, crisis management, compliance with notice laws, and other related expenses.

It is standard to have exclusions in an NSAP insurance policy that eliminate coverage for certain intentional conduct such as:

- Criminal, fraudulent, or malicious acts of the insured
- Discriminatory employment practices
- Misappropriation of a trade secret
- Wrongful acts that lead to expected or intended injury

The key issue when negotiating an NSAP insurance contract is ensuring that coverage remains intact even if a rogue employee is the originator of the intentional act. For example, an exclusion that bars recovery based on criminal acts of the insured—including its employees—is unacceptable. Most NSAP insurers understand this requirement and have been quite flexible in providing terms suiting the needs of businesses.

Not all NSAP insurers provide coverage for regulatory defense or the fines and penalties arising from a regulatory investigation. Some take the position that such coverage is void as against public policy—no matter the jurisdiction. Other insurers provide such insurance on a sub-limit basis—for example, a $5 million policy with a $1 million sub-limit for regulatory defense. Such defense coverage should include legal and related expenses incurred during the investigation. Some insurers also provide coverage for fines and penalties. Whether or not such coverage is void as against public policy should not preclude a company from seeking the coverage. Even if such a bar exists, there are likely situations when it would not apply.

Pricing terms are currently driven by the industry sector and revenue of the applicant. For example, a large health care provider tends to pay more per million of coverage than retailers even though retailer breaches get significant press. Another area that impacts pricing is the risk controls and practices put in place by the applicant. Insurers want to ensure that certain "basic" protocols, such as the encryption of data at rest, are in place prior to providing coverage. Not having the right controls will impact pricing, availability of limits, and the size of any deductible. When negotiating price, NSAP insurers are also very interested in past claim activity. A prior privacy incident will not preclude obtaining the insurance so long as the insurer is comfortable that the incident is not easily replicated or that the cause has been effectively remediated. Simply put, NSAP insurers want to ensure corrective measures have been put in place to prevent similar claims.

Organizations should seek out an insurer that will act as a business partner over and above mere coverage. For example, the NSAP insurer should be willing to participate in the risk management process. And it should be willing to use its market strength and network connection to find cost-effective providers to meet the pre-and post-breach needs of the organization.

CHAPTER 5

Information Security and Privacy Controls

There are a number of sources for the information security and privacy controls organizations implement. National and state laws and regulations provide for both general and specific controls, as do certain industry group standards, all of which were discussed in Chapter 2. Other controls come from control frameworks established by international and national standards bodies, independent information security or privacy associations, or industry associations. Organizations adopt these control frameworks to comply with statutory, regulatory, or contractual requirements or on a voluntary basis for reasons of competitive advantage and business and legal risk reduction.

The chapter begins with those controls mandated by statute or regulation and then discusses various control frameworks. Given the outsized impact of cryptography on the confidentiality and integrity of data and the authentication of users in the vast open environment of the Internet, this topic is covered in depth, including the legal relationships in public key infrastructures, management of keys and encryption standards for data at rest, in use, and in transit. Identity management, in the Internet environment, takes on an even more critical role, and so it is also covered in significant depth, including a discussion of the legal issues surrounding it. The chapter then presents seven other major categories of information security and privacy controls. Controls are further covered in Chapter 6, which includes examples of best practice policies that guide the selection of these types of controls, and in Chapter 7, which discusses additional controls for the new and emerging technologies.

What Global Executives Need to Know

- The information security and privacy controls that are mandated by statute or regulation and how the organization maintains compliance with those statutes and regulations
- The information security and privacy control framework utilized by the organization and why it was selected
- The breadth of use and algorithm lifespan for encryption of the secret, confidential, and personal data held by the organization

- How the organization addresses identity management in the open Internet environment
- The degree of implementation of the major control categories throughout the organization

5.1 CONTROLS FROM STATUTES AND REGULATIONS

Although the enactment of statutes and regulations involving information security and privacy controls has been somewhat uneven across the world, there are nevertheless three broad approaches that regulators use to either encourage or mandate information security and privacy safeguards. These approaches are: breach notice, generic security standards, and specific security measures. In each case, the approach focuses on efforts to protect the confidentiality of personal information.

A. Breach Notice Laws

On one end of the spectrum are the breach notice laws. These laws have been adopted by almost all states and territories in the United States[1] as well as the EU.[2] Typical breach notice laws require "data owners" to provide notice to individuals whose personal information may have been exposed due to a security breach. While these laws do not mandate specific controls, they create incentives for organizations to implement security measures. For example, a number of breach notice laws enacted by the U.S. states have an encryption "safe harbor." If the exposed personal information was encrypted at the time of a security breach, the data owner may not have an obligation to provide notice to relevant individuals under the state law.

More generally, breach notice laws may have a "sunshine" effect. By requiring organizations to provide notice to impacted individuals, breach notice laws expose organizations with poor security measures. In order to avoid this public scrutiny and potential loss of customers and reputation, some organizations may implement better security measures in order to avoid a security breach. This incentive is enhanced based on the potential for costly litigation that may arise after notice of a security breach. This topic is covered in more detail in Chapter 2.

B. Generic Security Standards

Another approach concerning legally mandated controls found in both U.S. and international data privacy laws involves establishing a generic standard for security. Rather than (or in addition to) mandating specific security controls or the use of specific tech-

1. *See* http://www.ncsl.org/IssuesResearch/TelecommunicationsInformationTechnologySecurityBreachNotificationLaws/tabid/13489/Default.aspx.

2. *See* European Union Directive 2009/136/EC of the European Parliament and of the Council, 2009 O.J. (L 337) 11; *see also* Personal Information Protection Amendment Act, S.A. 2009 (c. 50) (Alberta), http://www.assembly.ab.ca/ISYS/LADDAR_files/docs/bills/bill/legislature_27/session_2/20090210_bill-054.pdf.

nologies to prevent data security breaches, these laws require "reasonable,"[3] "adequate,"[4] "appropriate,"[5] or "comprehensive"[6] security controls.

While these laws may not set forth the specific controls needed to achieve the generic security standard, they often identify certain risk factors and other considerations that regulated entities should evaluate when determining which specific security measures to implement. For example, under the Gramm-Leach-Bliley Act (GLBA) regulating the financial industry, regulated entities must maintain a security program that includes administrative, technical, and physical safeguards that are "appropriate to [the] size and complexity [of the regulated entity], the nature and scope of [the regulated entity's] activities, and the sensitivity of any customer information at issue."[7] In some statutes, the financial resources of the organization may also be listed as an explicit factor impacting the types of security measures an organization must deploy.[8]

Beyond the legal text of the statute or the regulation in question, other information may be available to inform organizations as to which controls are necessary to satisfy a particular generic standard. Some regulators release guidance documents that may recommend particular controls to achieve regulatory compliance. The Office for Civil Rights of the U.S. Department of Health and Human Services has issued a series of documents providing guidance on complying with HIPAA's security requirements.[9] In another example, the Federal Financial Institution Examination Council (FFIEC) has released a publication that suggests that multifactor authentication may be necessary to secure online banking systems.[10]

C. Specific Security Standards

Some information security laws expressly mandate the implementation of specific security controls or technologies to prevent data security breaches. In some cases, these statutes may impose a generic security standard and also mandate specific controls. The following table outlines U.S. examples of specific security controls that are mandated by particular laws. Note that this table is not intended to be exhaustive and is included for the purpose of providing examples of laws that require specific controls. It does not show all the controls that are legally mandated nor does it list all the laws that include such mandates. Laws dictating controls in non-U.S. countries were covered in Chapter 2.

---

3. NEV. REV. STAT. § 603A.010 *et seq.* (2009).
4. Sarbanes-Oxley Act of 2002, Pub. L. No. 107-204 (July 30, 2002), 116 Stat. 745, codified at 15 U.S.C. § 7201 *et seq.* (2009).
5. European Union Directive 95/46/EC of the European Parliament and of the Council, 1995 O.J. (L 281) 31.
6. 16 C.F.R. § 314.3 (2010).
7. 16 C.F.R. § 314.3 (2010).
8. 201 MASS. CODE REGS. 17.03 (2009) ("Duty to Protect and Standards for Protecting Personal Information").
9. *See* http://www.hhs.gov/ocr/privacy/hipaa/administrative/securityrule/securityruleguidance.html.
10. *See, e.g.,* Authentication in an Internet Banking Environment (Federal Financial Institutions Examination Council) http://www.ffiec.gov/pdf/authentication_guidance.pdf.

Information Security Controls	***U.S. Laws/Regulations***
Written information security program/policy	Massachusetts' Personal Information Protection Law[11]
	GLB Safeguards Rule[12]
Encryption	Massachusetts' Personal Information Protection Law[13]
	Nevada's Security of Personal Information Law[14]
Data disposal	Nevada's Security of Personal Information Law[15]
	HIPAA's Security Rule[16]
	Wisconsin Stat. § 134.97[17]
Training	Massachusetts' Personal Information Protection Law[18]
	GLB Safeguards Rule[19]
	HIPAA's Security Rule[20]
PCI Data Security Standard	Nevada's Security of Personal Information Law[21]
Employee responsible for security	Massachusetts' Personal Information Protection Law[22]
	GLB Safeguards Rule[23]
	HIPAA's Security Rule[24]
Risk assessment	Massachusetts' Personal Information Protection Law[25]
	GLB Safeguards Rule[26]
	HIPAA's Security Rule[27]

11. 201 MASS. CODE REGS. 17.03 (2009).
12. 16 C.F.R. § 314.3 (2010).
13. 201 MASS. CODE REGS. 17.03 (2009).
14. NEV. REV. STAT. § 603A.010 *et seq.* (2009).
15. *Id.*
16. 45 C.F.R. pts. 160, 162, 164 (2009).
17. WIS. STAT. § 134.97 (2010).
18. 201 MASS. CODE REGS. 17.03 (2009).
19. 16 C.F.R. § 314.3 (2010).
20. 45 C.F.R. pts. 160, 162, 164 (2009).
21. NEV. REV. STAT. § 603A.010 *et seq.* (2009).
22. 201 MASS. CODE REGS. 17.03 (2009).
23. 16 C.F.R. § 314.3 (2010).
24. 45 C.F.R. pts. 160, 162, 164 (2009).
25. 201 MASS. CODE REGS. 17.03 (2009).
26. 16 C.F.R. § 314.3 (2010).
27. 45 C.F.R. pts. 160, 162, 164 (2009).

Information Security Controls	*U.S. Laws/Regulations*
User authentication controls	Massachusetts' Personal Information Protection Law[28]
	HIPAA's Security Rule[29]
Least access/minimum necessary use	HIPAA's Security Rule[30]
System monitoring (detection of unauthorized access/use of systems)	Massachusetts' Personal Information Protection Law[31]
	GLB Safeguards Rule[32]
Antivirus/malware protection software	Massachusetts' Personal Information Protection Law[33]
Service provider security management	Massachusetts' Personal Information Protection Law[34]
	GLB Safeguards Rule[35]
	HIPAA's Security Rule[36]

5.2 CONTROL FRAMEWORKS

An information security control framework is a system designed and implemented to manage risk within an enterprise. The term denotes "a means of managing risk, including policies, procedures, guidelines, practices or organizational structures, which can be of an administrative, technical, management, or legal nature."[37]

Information security control frameworks may be prescriptive frameworks, guidelines, best practices, or hybrid models. The frameworks are commonly organized around "control objectives" or families of controls and the supporting controls themselves. Control frameworks not only help ensure that the enterprise is secure but also enable audit and regulatory compliance.

Some frameworks have originated within international bodies like the International Organization for Standardization (ISO) and within national bodies such as the National Institute of Standards and Technology (NIST). Others originated with government and

28. 201 Mass. Code Regs. 17.03 (2009).
29. 45 C.F.R. pts. 160, 162, 164 (2009).
30. 45 C.F.R. pts. 160, 162, 164 (2009).
31. 201 Mass. Code Regs. 17.03 (2009).
32. 16 C.F.R. § 314.3 (2010).
33. 201 Mass. Code Regs. 17.03 (2009).
34. 201 Mass. Code Regs. 17.03 (2009).
35. 16 C.F.R. § 314.3 (2010).
36. 45 C.F.R. pts. 160, 162, 164 (2009).
37. ISO/IEC 27002:2005, *Information Technology—Security Techniques—Code of Practice for Information Security Management,* at 1.

within specific industries like health care. The result today is a number of control frameworks that can help secure the enterprise, each with a slightly different emphasis.

A major distinction among frameworks is the nature of information that the framework is designed to secure. Frameworks developed by standards groups like ISO and NIST can be used to protect electronic information. The ITIL framework, developed originally by the Central Computer and Telecommunications Agency within the United Kingdom, is a process-oriented framework that has security controls based primarily on the ISO standard, but also focuses on the use of service level agreements (SLAs) to achieve security objectives. Frameworks developed under specific legislation such as HIPAA/HITECH are designed to protect the information defined within that legislation—in the case of HIPAA/HITECH, protected health information (PHI). In certain instances, specific industry groups have developed frameworks for use by their members. Such is the origin of the PCI Data Security Standard (PCI-DSS), developed by members of the payment card industry and designed to help secure cardholder information. PCI was discussed in detail in Chapter 2.

Individual controls are often grouped by type. Within HIPAA, controls are classified as administrative, physical, and technical. NIST, in NIST 800-53, groups controls into "classes" that include technical, operational, and management controls. An organization that needs to comply with multiple frameworks will usually obtain or create a control "crosswalk" that maps individual controls from one framework to another. In this way, duplicative effort is reduced.

Other frameworks such as COBIT (Control Objectives for Information and Related Technology) organize controls into yet additional categories. COBIT defines an "entity level control" to be a control that applies to the entire organization. An example would be overall risk assessment. Controls applying to a specific business process would be designated "activity level controls." IT controls supporting the entire business are known as IT General Controls (ITGC). The last category is "application controls," which support a specific business process at the application level.

In practice, a business will implement a control framework depending on customer security requirements, regulatory requirements, and overall risk profile. The following table summarizes some control frameworks and their applicability. The first five will be discussed further in the following sections. Some of the frameworks (e.g., ISO 27001) focus on information security, but others (e.g., COBIT and ITIL) include controls that cover a broader range of subject matter.

Framework	*Description*
ISO 27001/02	The leading international information security standard.
NIST 800-53	A control framework required by U.S. government agencies. It is also used by organizations doing business with U.S. government agencies.
COBIT	A broad-ranging control framework for IT governance. Often used as the basis for SOX 404 audits (described in Chapter 6).

Framework	Description
FFIEC IT Handbook	Booklets that include processes and controls for examinations of financial companies.
BITS AUP	A set of agreed-upon procedures for vendors providing services to financial companies.
PCI-DSS	A prescriptive framework of IT security controls. Compliance is required for PCI certification.
HIPAA/HITECH	A framework required by all businesses and government agencies working with protected health information.
ITIL (IT Infrastructure Library)	A set of best practices books on effective and efficient IT processes. It includes information security controls.

A. ISO/IEC 27000 Series

The ISO and the International Electrotechnical Commission (IEC) have created a number of information security standards within the ISO 27000 series of standards.[38] They include:

- ISO/IEC 27000:2009, *Information Technology—Security Techniques—Information Security Management Systems—Overview and Vocabulary*
- ISO/IEC 27001:2005, *Information Technology—Security Techniques—Information Security Management Systems—Requirements*
- ISO/IEC 27002:2005, *Information Technology—Security Techniques—Code of Practice for Information Security Management*
- ISO/IEC 27003:2010, *Information Technology—Security Techniques—Information Security Management Systems Implementation Guidance*
- ISO/IEC 27004:2009, *Information Technology—Security Techniques—Information Security Management—Measurement*
- ISO/IEC 27005:2008, *Information Technology—Security Techniques—Information Security Risk Management*
- ISO/IEC 27006:2007, *Information Technology—Security Techniques—Requirements for Bodies Providing Audit and Certification of Information Security Management Systems*
- ISO/IEC 27011:2008, *Information Technology—Security Techniques—Information Security Management Guidelines for Telecommunications Organizations Based on ISO/IEC 27002*

When discussing information security and privacy controls, two of these standards are essential. The first is ISO 27001, which is the standard against which an organization's

38. The ISO/IEC standards are available for purchase from the International Organization for Standardization's website at: http://www.iso.org.

information security management system (ISMS) can be certified. It uses a risk-based approach to establishing, implementing, operating, monitoring, and maintaining an organization's ISMS. ISO 27001 will be discussed further in the section on audit and certification in Chapter 6.

The second essential standard is ISO 27002,[39] which provides guidance on selecting controls for an organization's ISMS, following the risk assessment process. It defines a control as the "means of managing risk, including policies, procedures, guidelines, practices or organizational structures, which can be of administrative, technical, management, or legal nature." The ISO's ISMS framework outlines reiterative cycles for continuous improvement based on the "Plan, Do, Check, Act" (PDCA) model.[40]

The following are relevant information security controls sections of this standard:

- **Security Policy:** Sets the guidance for the organization's use of information security.
- **Organizing Information Security:** Includes management's commitment to information security, organizational allocation of responsibility for information security, independent reviews of information security, and handling external party security.
- **Asset Management:** Includes an inventory of information assets, classification according to each asset's "value, legal requirements, sensitivity, and criticality," and handling.
- **Human Resources Security:** Prior to, during, and upon termination of employment.
- **Physical and Environmental Security:** Includes equipment and physical site controls, including disposal of equipment.
- **Communications and Operations Management:** Includes change management; separation of duties; separation of development and production environments; managing third parties; capacity planning; malware; backups; network security; media handling; e-mail, voice, video, and EDI (electronic data interchange) systems; e-commerce systems; and monitoring.
- **Access Control:** Access to systems and applications, remote access, and user authentication and responsibilities.
- **Information Systems Acquisition, Development, and Maintenance:** Input, processing, and output controls; encryption and key management; change control; technical vulnerability assessments.
- **Information Security Incident Management:** Reporting and response to incidents and weaknesses.
- **Business Continuity Management:** Risk assessment, development, implementation, and testing of business continuity plans.
- **Compliance:** Complying with legal requirements, including privacy of personal information, with the organization's information security policy, and with audit needs.

---

39. ISO/IEC 27002:2005 was formerly known as ISO/IEC 17799.

40. Dr. W. Edwards Deming was a pioneer in quality control. He built on the work of others and popularized the PDCA model.

B. NIST 800 Series

NIST created the 800 series special publications (SP) to promote sound information security practices for federal information systems under the Federal Information Security Management Act (FISMA).[41] NIST 800-53[42] is important to companies doing business with the U.S. federal government because it states minimum information security requirements for federal information systems. NIST 800-53 is supplemented by NIST 800-53A,[43] which contains more specific security controls. It also suggests methodologies for assessing the implementation of such controls.

NIST 800-37 Rev. 1 includes processes to assess and address risks, evaluate controls, and revisit their effectiveness as part of a recurring system authorization process that usually occurs as part of a three-year cycle. This new approach is a fundamental change from FISMA's old Certification and Accreditation approach. This publication states that it

> transforms the traditional Certification and Accreditation (C&A) process into the six-step Risk Management Framework (RMF). The revised process emphasizes: (i) building information security capabilities into federal information systems through the application of state-of-the-practice management, operational, and technical security controls; (ii) maintaining awareness of the security state of information systems on an ongoing basis though enhanced monitoring processes; and (iii) providing essential information to senior leaders to facilitate decisions regarding the acceptance of risk to organizational operations and assets.[44]

There is a growing movement in the information security field to create frameworks and approaches that are internationally consistent. This approach makes it easier for both U.S. and international organizations to more effectively meet a growing body of rules and legislation. NIST recognizes this trend as well. NIST 800-39, which deals with risk and controls, will change significantly as its next version will attempt to harmonize NIST 800-53 with ISO/IEC 27001 in order to develop a more consistent approach to managing organizational information security risk both internationally and in the United States.[45]

C. COBIT

The Control Objectives for Information and Related Technology (COBIT) is ISACA's enterprise governance of IT framework. Released by the IT Governance Institute (ITGI), a nonprofit, independent research organization established by ISACA, COBIT is an

41. Federal Information Security Management Act, Title III of the E-Government Act of 2002, Pub. L. 107-347, 116 Stat. 2899, codified at 44 U.S.C. §§ 3541–3549 (2010).

42. NIST SP 800-53 Rev. 3, *Recommended Security Controls for Federal Information Systems and Organizations* (2010).

43. NIST SP 800-53A Rev. 1, *Guide for Assessing the Security Controls in Federal Information Systems and Organizations* (2010).

44. NIST SP 800-37 Rev. 1, *Guide for Applying the Risk Management Framework to Federal Information Systems: A Security Life Cycle Approach*, pp. 1–2, http://csrc.nist.gov/publications/nistpubs/800-37-rev1/sp800-37-rev1-final.pdf.

45. *See* NIST, *Managing Risk from Information Systems: An Organizational Perspective*, NIST SP 800-39, Draft (April 2008), http://csrc.nist.gov/publications/PubsSPs.html, and NIST SP 800-53 Rev. 3 App. H, which provides a map to cross-walk between the ISO and NIST sets of security controls.

international set of generally accepted IT control objectives for day-to-day use by business managers, as well as by security, control, and audit practitioners.[46] The framework is currently organized into three levels:

- IT Processes (4)
- Control Objectives (44)
- Control Practices (300+)

The "Deliver and Support IT Process" contains a control objective, "Ensure Systems Security," that includes the following control practices:

- Management of IT Security
- IT Security Plan
- Identity Management
- User Account Management
- Security Testing, Surveillance, and Monitoring
- Security Incident Definition
- Protection of Security Technology
- Cryptographic Key Management
- Malicious Software Prevention, Detection, and Correction
- Network Security
- Exchange of Sensitive Data

COBIT is most commonly used in setting IT control objectives and defining and then auditing controls, so it is further discussed in the section on audit and certification in Chapter 6. COBIT has been mapped to other information technology and information security standards including those from NIST, ITIL, FFIEC, and ISO.[47]

D. Financial—FFIEC, BITS

The financial services sector falls under a complex web of U.S. federal and state regulations designed to govern operations and the protection of customer information. At the highest level, the Board of Governors of the Federal Reserve System sets the overall monetary policy of the United States.[48] The Federal Reserve maintains a set of regulations often referred to colloquially as "Regs" that are then followed by a letter of the alphabet.[49] For example, the Truth in Lending Act[50] is referred to as "Reg Z." These federal regulations govern a range of banking activities.

The activities of a financial services company determine which regulatory body provides oversight. A bank will often fall under several regulatory programs. Different federal agencies regulate banks offering traditional checking and savings accounts depending on the nature of the bank charter. Nationally chartered banks fall under

46. *See* ISACA, "COBIT Framework for IT Governance and Control," *available at* http://www.isaca.org/Knowledge-Center/cobit/Pages/Overview.aspx.

47. *See* http://www.isaca.org/Knowledge-Center/cobit/Pages/Downloads.aspx.

48. *See* Board of Governors of the Federal Reserve System, http://www.federalreserve.gov/.

49. *See* Board of Governors of the Federal Reserve System, listing of regulations, http://www.federalreserve.gov/bankinforeg/reglisting.htm.

50. 12 C.F.R. pt. 226.

the Federal Deposit Insurance Corporation (FDIC) and the Office of the Comptroller for Currency (OCC). Credit unions and state chartered banks fall under the review of the National Credit Union Administration (NCUA). The FDIC insures deposits held in traditional personal checking and savings accounts. The Securities and Exchange Commission (SEC) governs financial institutions involved in trading.

The Federal Financial Institutions Examination Council (FFIEC) is an interagency council that assists with uniform principles, standards, and reporting for the examination of financial institutions.[51] The FFIEC IT Handbook InfoBase provides examination guidance in 11 booklets on topics that include business continuity planning, online banking, auditing, and payment systems.[52] The booklets provide guidance on the expectations of the regulatory agencies that perform on-site reviews of financial services companies, so that the financial institutions may appropriately prepare for these examinations. The Information Security booklet includes sets of information security controls and processes that financial institutions will be required to implement and effectively operate to ensure confidentiality, integrity, and availability of information and to be able to successfully pass these reviews by regulatory agencies.[53]

On the private-sector side, financial institutions have joined together in a consortium to support their shared goals. BITS (formerly the Banking Industry Technology Secretariat) was formed in 1996.[54] It includes members from the 100 largest U.S. financial institutions. BITS members collaborate to protect the security, privacy, and integrity of financial transactions. This nonprofit group has a number of initiatives, including a shared assessment program of agreed-upon procedures (AUP) for vendors providing services to financial companies. It relies heavily on controls from ISO 27002 controls and global privacy directives. BITS also facilitates interactions with federal agencies including the FFIEC.

5.3 CRYPTOGRAPHIC CONTROLS

A. Public Key Infrastructure

1. Sources of Law

The implementation of information security at the network level is often enabled by a public key infrastructure (PKI). PKI refers to the institutions and technological processes involved in the use of digital certificates. In the United States, one of the primary uses of PKI is to authenticate which website owner is paired with which public key.[55] This PKI-based authentication serves as the foundation for secure communication over the Internet using Transport Layer Security (TLS) and the Secure Sockets Layer (SSL). TLS and SSL are cryptographic protocols that create an encrypted tunnel intended to

51. *See* Federal Financial Institutions Examination Council (FFIEC), http://www.ffiec.gov/.

52. *See* FFIEC Information Technology Examination Handbook, http://www.ffiec.gov/ffiecinfobase/html_pages/it_01.html.

53. *See* FFIEC Information Technology Examination Handbook, Information Security (July 2006).

54. *See* BITS, Financial Services Roundtable, http://www.bits.org/index.html.

55. *See* Niels Ferguson & Bruce Schneier, Cryptography Engineering: Design Principles and Practical Applications 275 (2010).

render Internet traffic unreadable in transit by third parties that might intercept it.[56] TLS and SSL are extensively used to protect most e-commerce transactions and other confidential communications occurring over the Internet.[57]

PKI, in addition to its technological foundations, rests on a series of institutional and legal relationships that exist among four kinds of parties: the certificate authority (CA), the owners/operators of websites, the sponsors of the major Internet browsers, and end-users.[58] When a CA is trusted by one of the sponsors of the major Internet browsers, it is referred to as a "Root CA" relative to that browser. Root CAs issue digital certificates to the sponsors of the major Internet browsers as well as to the operators of various websites.[59] A certificate issued to a website indicates that the owner of the website owns a particular public key.[60] When an end-user attempts to access a secure channel on a website that has purchased a digital certificate from a Root CA, the end-user's browser will authenticate that the website owns the public key. The purpose of this process is to verify the identity of the website. PKI is also used, on certain occasions, to do the reverse—to verify the identity of the end-user.

The U.S. federal government and the states have taken a minimalist approach with respect to regulating the relationships among the four basic PKI parties involved in the authentication process.[61] With limited exceptions, the relationships among the PKI parties are not currently governed by federal or state statutes and regulations.[62] As a result, these relationships are governed primarily by private law.[63]

Setting the stage for the parties' rights and responsibilities is a complex backdrop of institutional and technological norms that govern the issuance and use of digital certificates. These norms consist largely of the recommendations and proposals issued by various standards-setting organizations and professional associations such as the International Telecommunications Union (ITU), the American National Standards Institute (ANSI), the Internet Engineering Task Force (IETF), the American Institute of Certified

---

56. *See id.* at 218.

57. *See id.* at 218.

58. *See generally,* American Institute of Certified Public Accountants (AICPA) and Canadian Institute of Chartered Accountants, AICPA/CICA WEBTRUST PROGRAM FOR CERTIFICATION AUTHORITIES (2000), www.webtrust.org/certauth_fin.htm. It should be noted that the Certificate Authority function is often splintered among "Registration Authorities" and "Subordinate CAs." *Id.* at 15.

59. *See* Internet Engineering Task Force, *Request for Comment 5280* (May 2008), http://www.ietf.org/rfc/rfc5280.txt.

60. *See* FERGUSON & SCHNEIER, *supra* note 55, at 218.

61. *See* Jane K. Winn & Mariana C. Silveira, *Secured Transactions and Electronic Commerce Law: Diverging Perspectives in North and South America,* 16 MICH. ST. J. INT'L L. 239, 249–55 (2007) (noting the minimalist approach by the United States regarding PKI in the specific context of digital signatures).

62. *See id.*

63. The countervailing movement, which sought explicit regulatory norms and technology-specific mandates, has petered out. For example, in 2006, the vanguard state for PKI regulation, Utah, repealed its Digital Signature Act of 1995, which purported to set norms for the conduct of certain CAs. *See* UTAH CODE, § 46-3-101. A partial and narrow exception to the minimalist approach on the federal level would be the Part 11 regulations of the United States Food and Drug Administration (FDA), which, although containing some PKI requirements, only have industry-specific application. *See* 21 C.F.R. § 11.1 *et seq.* The Federal Financial Institutions Examination Council (FFIEC) has issued some limited PKI guidelines, but it has not addressed the legal rights and responsibilities of the PKI parties to one another.

Public Accountants (AICPA), the Canadian Institute of Chartered Accountants (CICA), and the CA/Browser Forum.

The explicit terms and conditions of the legal relationships among the PKI parties are driven in significant part by documents issued by the CA. For example, the website owner purchases the CA's certificates subject to a subscriber agreement. Detailed guidelines for the content of subscriber agreements are set forth in the "WebTrust" program materials.[64] CAs also generally post exemplar subscriber agreements on their websites. These agreements many times purport to limit the CA's liability, disclaim warranties, establish the rights and responsibilities of the parties, and require that the website owner indemnify the CA for certain categories of third-party claims.

A CA will also often post a document known as a certification practice statement (CPS) on its website.[65] The CPS describes the business practices regarding the CA's issuance of digital certificates. The terms of the CPS will also typically seek to limit the liability of the CA and further set forth the responsibilities of the PKI parties.

A CA will often post a document on its website entitled relying party Agreement. This document purports to define the relationship between the CA and the end-user. Like the subscriber agreement, the relying party agreement generally contains, among other things, a sweeping limitation on the CA's liability, a disclaimer of warranties, and an indemnity provision. The main difference, however, between a subscriber and a relying party agreement is that the subscriber agreement is generally executed by the parties whose conduct the agreement purports to govern, while a relying party agreement appears to lack a mechanism for assent by end-users. At present, there appear to be no published court decisions addressing whether relying party agreements are actually enforceable against end-users. The question of whether these documents will actually control the legal rights of the end-user in the event of a dispute remains open.

As the volume of business conducted over the Internet continues to grow, the need for transparency and more formalized legal arrangements regarding the end-user's reliance on PKI will likely increase.

2. The Need to Verify Certificate Authorities

Secure business communications rely on the PKI model described in the previous section. This process involves the authentication of the parties involved in the communication by third party Certificate Authorities (CAs). While some CAs may be well-known and easily trusted, others may be unknown or may involve CAs that organizations may not want to be part of their network of trust for secure communications. As such, it is necessary for lawyers and technologists to work together to actively determine all of the CAs that the organization will trust, instead of passively accepting that all CAs are worthy of trust. This starts with understanding the models of trust used by end-user Internet browsers when accessing websites.

The major Internet browsers all currently use the Certificate Authority Trust Model ("CA Trust Model") to verify the identity of websites on behalf of end-users. Unfor-

64. *See supra* note 4; *WebTrust for Certification Authorities—Extended Validation Audit Criteria version 1.1* (CICA 2008), *available at* http://www.webtrust.org/.

65. *See supra* note 32, at 20.

tunately, the CA Trust Model appears to be flawed, leaving it vulnerable to attack in various ways. These attacks include "man-in-the-middle" wiretap exploits that enable a party to read encrypted communications, as well as "phishing" attacks using imposter servers.[66] Although select companies have taken steps to not utilize the CA Trust Model for business-to-business communications and the U.S. government aims to move beyond this Model at some point in the future, the vast majority of all encrypted Internet communications still rely upon it as a matter of course.[67]

Most encrypted communications taking place over the Internet use special transport protocols that operate largely out-of-sight known as "SSL" or "TLS" (Secure Sockets Layer and Transport Layer Security) (collectively, "SSL"). When an end-user tries to establish a secure connection using SSL, his or her browser will attempt to authenticate the identity of the destination website. For example, when an end-user wishes to access his or her account at "Amazon.com" using SSL, the end-user's browser will try and authenticate that the server representing itself as being operated by Amazon.com is telling the truth. The major Internet browsers perform this authentication process by using "digital certificates."

CAs issue digital certificates to websites as well as to the sponsors of the major Internet browsers. When an end-user seeks to establish a secure connection with a website, the end-user's browser attempts to match one of its CA-issued certificates with one of the website's CA-issued certificates. If the match is successful, the browser will then establish a secure connection. This requires that all parties are able to trust the CA.

There are at least three major problems with the CA Trust Model. First, there is a staggering number of CAs. The major browsers each trust more than 100 CAs by default.[68] Globally, there are in excess of 600 CAs and growing.[69] There may be far too many for an organization to completely be able to vet and trust. These CAs consist of commercial and quasi-governmental entities from all over the globe. A significant number of CAs are either controlled by, or closely associated with, governments or organizations one may not want verifying who is who for the purpose of carrying out confidential communications. For example, one CA that is also a telecom carrier reportedly used digital certificates to insert, on a wide scale, wiretap software on mobile devices under the guise of a required service upgrade.[70] The presence of potential bad actor CAs is a cause for concern under the CA Trust Model, because any CA that is officially trusted by another CA which is trusted by the major browsers will then automatically also be trusted by those brows-

---

66. *See* Steve Gibson, Security Now, Episode 243 "Subverted SSL," *available at* thisweekintech.com/sn243.

67. Certain pharmaceutical companies have implemented their own authentication infrastructure, "Safe BioPharma" in lieu of the CA Trust Model, *available at* http://www.safe-biopharma.org/infocenter.htm. The U.S. government has announced its "National Strategy for Trusted Identities in Cyberspace" that would replace the CA Trust Model with alternative institutions, hardware, software, and authentication processes. *See* National Strategy for Trusted Identities in Cyberspace (July 10, 2010).

68. Christopher Soghoian and Sid Stamm, "*Certified Lies: Detecting and Defeating Government Interception Attacks Against SSL*" (2010).

69. *See* http://www.eff.org/observatory, which includes a map of known CAs.

70. Danny O'Brien, *The Internet's Secret Back Door*, SLATE (August 27, 2010).

ers.[71] Under the CA Trust Model, one must not only trust the hundreds of CAs recognized by the major browsers, but also the CAs that are simply trusted by other CAs.

The second problem with the CA Trust Model is that legitimate CAs have issued digital certificates that were improperly configured or issued digital certificates without even checking to see if the entities requesting the digital certificates were who they said they were. For example, a Web researcher unaffiliated with Mozilla (the sponsor of the Firefox browser) suspected that a particular CA was performing little or no confirmation of a subscriber's identity or the actual ownership of a given domain name prior to issuing SSL certificates. When the researcher requested that the CA issue him an SSL certificate for *mozilla.com,* the CA reportedly issued the certificate with "no questions asked, no verification checks done, no control validation, no subscriber agreement presented, nothing."[72]

The third problem with the CA Trust Model is that it allows *any* of the hundreds of CAs to issue bogus, yet technically valid, digital certificates for *any* website on the web. This means that any CA can issue an SSL certificate for "XYZ Bank Corp" to HackerAttacker.com. If an end-user's browser already recognizes the issuing CA as trusted (either by default, or by being trusted by another CA), then the end-user's browser will treat the bogus certificate as if it were valid and rely upon it to perform authentication. This is true even though XYZ Bank Corp never purchased its SSL certificates from the issuing CA and has no affiliation or connection to the issuing CA. This also means that the attacker can attempt to obtain such a bogus certificate from the least scrupulous or secure CA, regardless of which CA is the issuer of the legitimate XYZ Bank Corp SSL certificates.

There are two types of risks that an organization must address in its use of digital certificates. In the first type where the organization acts as an end-user, the risk consists of possible man-in-the-middle and phishing attacks that enable data breach, loss of trade secrets, and wiretapping. To address this, corporate counsel, working with technologists, needs to determine which outside organizations can be trusted. This involves assessing the criminal and regulatory background of the CAs, analyzing affiliations with state actors and quasi-governmental entities, and determining the governing law that controls the CAs' conduct. The goal is for the organization to configure its browser platform so as to trust as few CAs as possible, and to "untrust" those CAs deemed to be unnecessary or untrustworthy. Technologists should explore the use of various plug-ins and software add-ons to assist in the detection of CA irregularities and CA-based attacks. Organizations should also engage a CA in dialogue regarding the CA's practices, both with respect to adherence to best practices, and also to address the issue of whether, or to what extent, the CA trusts other CAs.

The second type of risk is when the organization is an owner or operator of a website that offers secure connections to customers, clients, and the browsing public. The risk is that either the organization's selection of a CA (from which it purchases digital certifi-

---

71. *Id.*

72. *See* https://blog.startcom.org, as quoted in *The 'Certificate Authority' Trust Model for SSL: A Defective Foundation for Encrypted Web Traffic and a Legal Quagmire,* Steven B. Roosa and Stephen Schultze, THE INTELLECTUAL PROPERTY & TECHNOLOGY LAW JOURNAL, Vol. 22 No. 11 (Nov. 2010).

cates) might put customers or clients at risk, or that the organization's failure to apprise customers and clients of the use of digital certificates might create unnecessary exposure for the organization in the event of an exploit. The organization should maintain a written policy regarding how it will determine which digital certificates to purchase and which criteria it will employ for selecting a CA (or CAs). The organization should also review its own website's terms and conditions of use to ensure that they account for the fact that third-party digital certificates are used in authentication.

B. Key Management

Keys are basically electronic codes used by mathematical algorithms to achieve specific outcomes, such as encryption, decryption, or authenticating a user.[73] Key management is the process of ensuring the following:

- *Generation:* Keys must be unique, created securely, and sufficiently strong (usually in terms of length) to meet their intended purpose.
- *Assignment:* Keys must be assigned properly and conveyed securely to their legitimate owners.
- *Control:* Keys must be properly controlled by their owners so that others cannot gain access to, or control over, them.
- *Updates:* Keys should be periodically changed to reduce the likelihood of their being compromised.
- *Revocation:* A key must be revoked (i.e., rendered useless or at least ineffective) if it is stolen or otherwise compromised.

The mechanisms used to achieve these goals will vary depending on whether a key is asymmetric or symmetric. Asymmetric keys are used in public key technology, where two keys are created having a specific mathematical relationship such that what one key does, the other key, and only the other key, undoes. Using a physical analogy, if one key locks a door, only the other key can unlock it. Symmetric keys, by contrast, are akin to the keys with which most people are familiar—namely, the same key both locks and unlocks a door. Key management of asymmetric keys uses a PKI meeting ISO X.509 standards. Key management of symmetric keys typically uses a Key Distribution Center, which keeps copies of keys and parcels them out in a secure fashion to users (human or devices) and may conform to emerging technologies, practices, and standards.

Key management mechanisms also vary depending on whether a key is ephemeral or persistent. An ephemeral key is generated, for example, when two parties wish to communicate securely. They may generate keys to encrypt then decrypt information solely for a single communication. Once the parties have finished passing information between them and their communication is complete, the keys become useless and may be destroyed. Conversely, if information is to be encrypted for persistent use, such as protecting stored data, then the keys will not be destroyed. Instead, these keys need to be persistent so that the information can be decrypted and read later as needed.

---

73. For comprehensive best practices regarding key management and design recommendations, see NIST, Computer Security Division, Computer Security Resource Center, Key Management, http://csrc.nist.gov/groups/ST/toolkit/key_management.html.

Management of persistent keys is thus much more complex than the management of ephemeral ones, and involves ensuring that: (a) such keys are revealed only to authorized parties—in other words, the entities desiring access must prove who they are (as described earlier in the identity section) before obtaining the keys or being allowed to use the keys; (b) keys are periodically changed (sometimes called "rolled over") to reduce the likelihood that they may be compromised (the longer a key is used, the greater the risk that it can be deduced or compromised; this is also true of physical keys such as the keys used to lock one's house); and (c) there is a mechanism to mark keys that have been compromised or "revoked" so all affected parties are aware that those keys are no longer trustworthy.

In addition, software to create and control "key-chains" can facilitate the access by authorized parties to the relevant persistent keys. Powerful encryption techniques that protect such key-chains are necessary to avoid blanket disclosure of keys; however, concatenated encryption can help to mitigate such possibilities. Further, matching a needed key to a designated decryption step is best handled by bundling the requisite connective information with the item requiring the decryption step, but still requiring other key-related information to access the encrypted key. Capabilities such as this are available as embedded capabilities in various software components, whether end applications or infrastructure. Emerging standards in key management include the Organization for the Advancement of Structured Information Standards (OASIS) Key Management Interoperability Protocol (KMIP)[74] and the IEEE P1619.3 key management standard for stored data.[75]

C. Encryption

The need for encryption has increased parallel to the increased movement of data outside controlled environments. The use of the Internet in all its forms, the vast increase in the use of outsourcing, and many new types of mobile technology mean that an organization's data may need to be protected at all times in all locations. Several key questions must be addressed in creating a cryptographic system that deploys encryption:[76]

- How sensitive is my information, and which encryption algorithms and key lengths are recommended to protect it?
- What is the difference between data at rest, data in transit, and data in use, and what should be done to protect this data?
- What are the key business, information security, and privacy risks, and what can be done to mitigate them?

---

74. OASIS, *Key Management Interoperability Protocol (KMIP)—Addressing the Need for Standardization in Enterprise Key Management* v1.0 (2009).

75. IEEE 1619.3 *Standard for Key Management Infrastructure for Cryptographic Protection of Stored Data* (2007).

76. The term "cryptography" is broader than "encryption" in that it also includes at least digital signatures. For purposes here, the terms may be used interchangeably.

1. The Shelf Life of Cryptosystems

"The floor of history is littered with the shards of broken cryptosystems."[77] When the Data Encryption Standard (DES) was first introduced in 1976, claims were made that it would take a personal computer millions of years to break it. Yet in 1998, the Electronic Frontier Foundation built a special purpose machine (nicknamed "Deep Crack") for less than $250,000 that performed a brute force search of the 56-bit DES key to break a challenge cipher, and completed the task on July 17, 1998, in only 56 hours. This convinced the world that single DES was not sufficiently secure, and although the federal government reaffirmed DES as a federal standard in October of that year, the standard was amended to recommend the use of triple-DES.

Today, NIST is recommending that the use of triple-DES be phased out and that it should not be used for data that must be protected beyond 2030. The message should be clear: Anything that is invented by humans is likely to be broken, sooner or later, given enough resources. It is therefore prudent to consider cryptosystems as having a certain shelf life.

The key questions facing business executives are, how long does their sensitive information need to be protected? and what algorithms and key sizes are recommended? The answers depend on the kind of information.

- **Financial Reports.** Corporate quarterly earnings reports for a public company are generally very closely held until they are published, but after that date, no one cares, as the information becomes public knowledge. So any kind of cryptography that is sufficient to withstand the demonstrated attacks of today is good enough. Practically speaking, RSA-1024 and triple-DES would suffice.
- **Credit/Debit Card Numbers.** Credit and debit card numbers need to be protected until the expiration date on the card, after which a new card is issued. So payment card processing information typically needs to be secure for three to five years. RSA-2048 and Triple-DES or AES-128 would be sufficient, at least at present.
- **Military Plans.** Secret military plans may need to be protected until the attack commences, but in other cases, especially those that involve intelligence sources and methods and long-term strategic plans, may need to be protected for 30 to 50 years, and perhaps longer in cases involving the identities of covert agents. The NSA-defined "Suite B" algorithms come in two strengths, for simplicity and interoperability. AES-128 with ECC-256 and SHA-256 is considered adequate to protect data labeled secret, whereas AES-256, ECC-384, and SHA-384 are considered strong enough to protect even top secret compartmented information—in both cases, when used in an NSA-approved implementation.
- **Other Data.** Some data needs to be protected for even longer periods. Personally identifiable information (PII), including Social Security numbers, witness protection records, sealed adoption records, census data, and sealed court records may need to be protected for as long as a person could reasonably be alive, which could mean as long as 110 years for a newborn.

---

77. David Kahn, The Codebreakers—The Story of Secret Writing (1974), the preeminent book on the history of cryptography.

- **Protected Health Information.** An even longer period will be required for protected health information, according to the Notice of Proposed Rule Making that was announced by the Department of Health and Human Services on July 14, 2010. The relevant rule specifies that health records must be protected for a period of 50 years after the death of the affected individual. So in the case of the newborn, we are talking about as much as 160+ years, or until the year 2170!

It should be obvious that no one's crystal ball extends out as far as 160 years, at least with any real degree of confidence. One website attempts to extrapolate how long various algorithms and key lengths will be secure.[78] It can be used to compute the key sizes that are considered necessary to resist exhaustive search attacks and other known approaches to breaking cryptographic algorithms and specific key sizes.

As can be seen from that website, as well as recommendations from NIST and other agencies around the world, RSA-2048 and triple-DES are nearing their end of life and should not be relied on to protect information past the year 2030. Fortunately, the introduction of elliptic curve cryptography (ECC) in 1985 has yielded new public-key algorithms based on the discrete logarithm problem.[79] Although mathematically more complex than RSA, ECC uses significantly smaller key sizes and faster operations for an equivalent level of security.

The various authorities all agree that AES-256 should be secure for the "foreseeable future," or somewhere around the year 2282. The higher strength Suite B algorithms and key sizes approved by the U.S. government to protect even top secret information use AES-256, in combination with elliptic curve cryptography with P-384 keys. It is predicted that ECC P-384 keys should resist attack until the year 2186, or 176 years from now—a value that easily covers even the 160+ year requirement. A couple of decades from now, however, we may need to migrate to the stronger ECC P-521 keys.

Cryptographers tend to divide the various data protection problems into three classes: data at rest, data in transit, and data in use, depending on the mobility of the data and where it is stored: at rest, in transit, and in use.

2. *Data at Rest Protection*

Data at rest refers to data that is written to a permanent storage medium (e.g., a hard disk). The primary risk to be addressed is the possibility that the device containing the data is lost or stolen and potentially could be accessed by someone else. The usual defense against this threat is the use of full disk encryption, typically software-based. Several cautions should be noted in regard to these software-based systems.

First, because they operate seamlessly and essentially invisibly, all the data written to the disk is automatically encrypted. By the same token, all data read from the disk is decrypted equally automatically, whether the read operation was initiated by the user or by some virus or malware applications. As a result, full disk encryption only

78. *See* www.keylength.com. This estimate is based on the formulas of Dr. Arjen Lenstra, a highly regarded crypto-mathematician. In addition, the website summarizes the recommendations by other groups.

79. Certicom has an interactive tutorial about ECC on its website, http://www.certicom.com/index.php/ecc-tutorial.

protects the data once the machine has been powered down. If the computer normally operates 24/7, either because it is a server or because the user never turns off the power to the client machine, full disk encryption accomplishes almost nothing at all. A thief can steal the machine, leaving it powered on and running on batteries, and gain full access to the data. There have even been cases in which an entire rack-mounted server was stolen, including the uninterruptible power supply used to keep it running during a power outage!

Second, without the use of some kind of a hardware security chip or token, the keys used to perform the encryption are at best merely obfuscated within the operating system. Various applications can be used to attack these keys through a dictionary lookup attack, assuming the user has not used a lengthy, pseudo-random password or passphrase as the key.

Third, none of the full disk encryption products provides any form of integrity protection to the stored, encrypted data. If a single uncorrected read-error occurs on the disk, the usual form of encryption will magnify that problem, and at a minimum make the 128-bit block in which the error occurred complete gibberish. Some modes of operation will extend the error through the remainder of the sector and perhaps beyond.

Several of the common modes of operation are not recommended for use with static, fixed-length sector applications.[80] The recommended mode of operation for sector-based disk or media encryption is the XTS-AES mode, originally standardized under IEEE P-1619 and later accepted as NIST standard SP 800-38E.[81]

Fourth, if the user forgets the password required to unlock the disk encryption, then the data may be essentially unrecoverable.

The usual way of solving this problem is to centrally generate all the keys or passwords and keep a record of them, or to generate the keys on the device and then export them, using a form of key escrow. Neither of these two techniques is particularly recommended, both because they tend to give too much power to a system administrator and because the repository of such keys or passwords becomes a lucrative "honeypot" to an attacker.

Instead, the recommended solution is to use hardware-based encryption, where the AES-256 disk encryption keys are generated securely in hardware and then "wrapped" (encrypted) in a public key of a Recovery Agent, preferably using ECC. That Recovery Agent should also be implemented in a hardware device, but one that could easily be locked in a safe or bank vault, under the control of multiple senior individuals. In addition, it is possible to encrypt the information file-by-file, allowing the data to be backed up securely to multiple locations, and at the same time, the file format includes a digital signature covering both the plaintext and the ciphertext. This technology has been approved by the U.S. government to protect tactical data at the secret level, and its adoption by the armed forces of Canada, Australia, and the United Kingdom is presently under way.

---

80. *Cf.* http://en.wikipedia.org/wiki/Disk_encryption_theory.

81. For more on modes of operation, see Robert Jueneman, *Full Disk Encryption—An In-Depth Look*, INFO. SEC. & PRIVACY NEWS (newsl. ABA Sec. Sci. & Tech. L.), Volume 2, Issue 1 (Winter 2011).

3. Data in Transit Protection

Protecting data in transit primarily means dealing with the threat of eavesdropping on communications between point A and point B. In today's digital environment, this effort isn't quite as simple as it used to be. And the long-distance, Internet communications are even more difficult to intercept, as they typically involve tapping a buried fiber-optic cable or intercepting a microwave signal or de-multiplexing a T3 communications line. This is all easy enough for a large carrier or a foreign intelligence agency, but it is beyond the capabilities of most amateurs or criminals.

The same is not true of the endpoints of the link, however. As at least one retailer discovered (discussed in Chapter 1), it is all too easy to intercept Wi-Fi communications between a point of sale terminal and a server, and it is equally easy for someone in the IT organization to tap the LAN connections to individual desktop or laptop computers.

The usual defense against such attacks involves a virtual private network (VPN), which typically uses a protocol called IPSec to encrypt the connection on a machine-to-machine level, or, at a higher level in the architectural stack, to use Secure Sockets Layer (SSL) or its successor protocol, Transport Layer Security (TLS). These protocols typically (but not necessarily) operate between a client-level browser and a server and provide an encrypted communication. The usual form is the common *https* connection to a company server (e.g., Amazon), which uses a public-key-based authentication mechanism, with a certificate that can be validated against a trusted root. In this case, only the server is authenticated by SSL or TLS. If the user needs to be authenticated, a username and password are often used, despite the well-known limitations of such mechanisms. But all popular browsers also support the use of *mutual* authentication, where the users authenticate themselves to the server using their own private keys and certificates, while the servers authenticate themselves to the users the same way.

It is possible to use both IPSec and SSL/TLS in combination, and this approach has some advantages. The IPSec connection secures the "tunnel" between the enterprise network and the user, so that no one can log on to the enterprise network without authentication. The SSL or TLS session can then be used to provide an additional level of security between the user's browser and the specific server, thereby securing the connection even within the corporate network.

Most IPSec protocols presently run in software, at least at the client end of the link, although there are a few hardware devices that are used outboard of the host computer to provide hardware-based encryption.

The SSL/TLS protocols are almost invariably implemented in software at the client end, even though most implementations are capable of using smart cards or other security devices to perform the public-key operations required for mutual authentication. At the server's end, both hardware and software approaches are used, with high-volume sites generally opting for the use of relatively expensive, high-performance hardware crypto-accelerators.

Because Windows XP does not support ECC, most IPSec and SSL/TSL connections are still using RSA, with either triple-DES or AES. However, the newer servers, including Microsoft Windows Server 2008, Apache, and others, are capable of negotiating the protocol to be used and can support ECC and AES, assuming the client supports it. Users are therefore encouraged to use the latest operating system releases and to enable

TLS (and disable SSL 2.0 and 3.0, unless this causes problems with certain websites) and to consult with their IT department as to how to enable both AES-256 and ECC P-384 for the best possible link or session encryption.

It should be clear, however, that neither IPSec nor SSL/TLS is a cure-all. They protect the bits on the wire, but once they arrive at the server (or are returned to the client machine), the bits may "fall on the floor" unless Data at Rest protection or other measures are in place. For this reason, the same kind of file-by-file encryption mentioned earlier can be used to provide a much stronger level of protection, both while the data is in transit and while it is at rest. And those devices that utilize file-by-file encryption also provide very strong integrity and nonrepudiation, which neither full disk encryption nor IPSec link encryption nor TLS session encryption provides.[82]

In addition, both IPSec and SSL/TLS are potentially vulnerable to a man-in-the-middle attack. If someone can impersonate the credentials of the real server, he or she may be able to intercept the incoming connection, decrypt it, then re-encrypt it and forward it on to the designated recipient. Such an attack would involve both the impersonation of the server's certificate and the diversion of the traffic, which would be difficult for a hacker or criminal enterprise to carry out, but it would not be beyond the means of a rogue Internet service provider or an intelligence agency. The best defense against this type of attack is to limit the list of trusted root certificates to those you really trust and delete the rest. See the discussion above on the need to verify CAs.

4. *Encrypted E-mail Protection*

End-to-end, desktop-to-desktop encryption provides an additional solution for both data at rest and data in transit protection. The standard in this area, Secure/Multimedia Internet Mail Extension (S/MIME) is supported by all popular e-mail programs used on desktop and laptop computers, and in addition has been extended to work on handheld devices and smart phones, such as the Blackberry. The S/MIME protocol uses a symmetric key algorithm (triple-DES or AES) in combination with a unique message encryption key and a unique initialization vector to encrypt each message. That message encryption key is then "wrapped" (encrypted) using a key encrypting key that is unique per originator/recipient pair.[83]

In contrast to link encryption protocols and most (but not all) disk encryption protocols, S/MIME was intended from the outset to support secure information sharing between and among multiple individuals. In practice, the originator obtains the public key of the various recipients, either by direct e-mail transmission, or by downloading them from a certificate server. The message encryption key for the particular message is then encrypted in a unique key encryption key derived from each recipient's public key, and the wrapped keys are then included in the message header. Each recipient of the

82. A new Suite B compliant IPSec protocol is beginning to be deployed, which uses AES-256 in combination with a mild integrity scheme called Galois Counter Mode. This does provide link-level (but not end-to-end) integrity, but without any form of nonrepudiation.

83. Key encrypting keys are derived from one of several possible public key transport or key agreement algorithms, including RSA; the DoD's Key Exchange Algorithm (KEA), which is based on a Diffie-Hellman key agreement; and most recently, EC Diffie-Hellman, the ECC variant of Diffie-Hellman.

message can then find the blob that was encrypted using his or her public key, use their private key to decrypt the key encryption key, then decrypt the message encryption key, and finally decrypt the message itself. In order to provide a degree of certainty that the designated recipients really are who they appear to be, conventional PKI techniques are used to authenticate a user's public key. Unlike disk encryption, which provides data at rest protection; and link encryption, which provides data in transit protection; S/MIME messages are protected both during transmission and storage.

Another valuable S/MIME feature missing from full disk encryption and link encryption solutions is a provision for integrity control and technical non-repudiation, through the optional inclusion of a digital signature of the originator on each message. Normally, before the message is encrypted, it is hashed and then digitally signed. In most cases, the hash function that is used is the now-deprecated SHA-1, and the digital signature is typically RSA-1024 or RSA-2048.[84] *Assuming* that only the originator knows or has effective control over the private signature key, it is mathematically provable that only that private key could have signed the message, and therefore, only the originator could have caused the message to be signed.[85]

E-mail encryption protects the confidentiality and integrity/nonrepudiation of the message and any attached files, and that protection is maintained as the e-mail messages are stored, either on the e-mail server, or when downloaded and saved on the user's computer. Note that the originator's digital signature applied to a message that includes an attachment does not provide proof of origin of the attachment itself, which could have been created by anyone. It only proves that the originator was the person who forwarded the attachment.

Because each message is encrypted in a unique message encryption key, e-mail encryption is less vulnerable to a wholesale compromise of a single symmetric key than full disk encryption or link encryption protocols. On the other hand, if a user's private key should be compromised somehow, all of the messages encrypted in that key would effectively be compromised, whether the particular user was the originator or a recipient. This risk can be mitigated by the use of a high-assurance hardware token to generate and store the private keys, and by the issuance of a new certificate based on a new public/private key pair every year or so.

---

84. E-mail clients capable of handling AES, SHA-2, and ECC are now widely available, but to date there are serious interoperability problems with them, caused by the fact that Microsoft's Windows XP does not support ECC. Although a user who has an RSA-1024 key can communicate with some degree of security with a user who has an RSA-2048 key, no interoperability is possible between a user who has only an RSA key and a user who only has an ECC key pair, and in fact Alice and Bob must use the same key strength in order to communicate when using ECC keys. To date, little has been done within the industry to ameliorate this serious interoperability problem by supporting multiple certificate types and negotiating which algorithms and key strengths to use. This is a particularly severe problem when attempting to communicate securely across organizational boundaries.

85. This assumption is only true so long as the strength of the keys used is sufficient to defy cryptanalysis for the information life of the data to be protected, whether by encryption and/or a digital signature. RSA-1024 is deprecated today, and RSA-2048 is only expected to be secure until 2030, but ECC with P-384 keys is expected to be secure until around 2186. This is particularly important in the area of health care, because the Interim Breech Notification Rule released by HHS (July 14, 2010) calls for Protected Health Information to be maintained securely for the duration of the patient's lifetime plus 50 years. In the case of a newborn baby who might live to be 110, that requires 160 years of protection!

It should be noted that the implied binding between an individual's public/private key pair and their *role*, as indicated by their organizational affiliation and even their name in their X.509 certificate, is not eternal. People can change jobs or be reassigned to a different organizational unit within a particular enterprise, where they may not longer have the same responsibilities. For that reason, if the user's certificate is to be relied on to connote the originator's *authority*, as opposed to their mere *identity*, it is important that the certificate be validated as up-to-date, and not revoked or suspended, at the time or reliance. Certificate Revocation Lists or the Online Certificate Status Protocol can be used to confirm the status of a user's certificate, both before relying it before sending sensitive information to that individual, and likewise, before relying on that individual's digital signature to convey authority. Users should also be aware that these mechanisms do not provide any notice of *prior* revocation, once the validity period has expired.

5. Data in Use Protection

Assuming that adequate Data at Rest and Data in Transit protection is provided, the question then remains as to how to protect data while it is actually in use (i.e., decrypted and in memory).

There are two different issues here. The first is how to protect the data from another, unauthorized user that may be sharing the computer, particularly in the case of a server or a "cloud" computer. In the best of all worlds, this level of protection would be provided by hardware encryption at the bus or memory level, so that all the data would be encrypted at all times, and any attempt by one user to spy on the process of another user would be defeated cryptographically. That capability would be wonderful, but no such general-purpose computing hardware is available.

The next best solution is to use a combination of hardware and the operating system that performs memory mapping in such a way that one user is not able to ascertain the memory addresses of another user's memory, and therefore cannot conveniently access such data (although it may be possible to sweep through all memory looking for random data (e.g., keys)). Some hardware platforms, and some operating systems, attempt to provide this kind of separation, with varying degrees of success. Consult the hardware manufacturer for further details.

The second, and probably more important issue, is what happens once a legitimate user has decrypted the data—what can he or she do with it then? This can lead to what we call a data leakage or *data containment* problem.

If the user is allowed to copy the decrypted data to another flash drive, iPod, or even a recordable CD or DVD, the data could be out the door in minutes. This is allegedly how thousands of classified documents were sent to Wikileaks in 2010. Likewise, if the user is allowed to send unencrypted data (or even encrypted data) to a friend outside the enterprise, or to post it to an external website or file server, the data is gone. A user's motivation to leak data could be multifaceted. The user could be a whistle-blower, whether misguided or not. The user could be someone who is leaking confidential or even classified information to an accomplice, perhaps in a foreign country, either for classical espionage or to divulge confidential information and intellectual property for monetary or other gain. Or the user could leak data through simple carelessness, which may then be compounded when the user plugs the memory device into his or her own computer, and a virus captures it and "phones home."

Various software solutions exist to solve these problems. Most use some form of a "filter driver" that is installed in the OS under system administrator control and serves to block all information (except, perhaps, properly encrypted information) from being read from or written to removable mass storage devices. Even those kinds of mechanisms can be defeated if the "properly encrypted" paradigm is not enforced, such that the user is not allowed to transmit even encrypted information outside the confines of the enterprise. Requiring that the software be installed or configured by the system administrator means that the user cannot simply walk up to any computer, including one in the hotel lobby or other public place, plug in a device, and start using it. Some people view that requirement as an absolutely essential level of control, while others consider it an intolerable infringement on their ability to get their work done efficiently. The issue comes down to security versus convenience. But inconvenience is generally a minor nuisance, while a security compromise can have very long-term and expensive consequences. In general, the data leakage or containment problem is a digital rights management problem, and solutions are still evolving.

6. Data Security Risks and Mitigation

Data security risks fall into two general categories—the risk that highly sensitive information is disclosed (or potentially disclosed) that directly damages the enterprise (e.g., the disclosure of valuable intellectual property); and the risk that customer/client/patient data is disclosed that is considered protected information under federal or state laws.

The first case may be relatively innocuous, depending on whether the apparent loss of control over the data (e.g., a lost laptop) actually materializes as a data compromise. If it does, then the questions are, how valuable was the information? and did it fall into the hands of someone who could actually make use of it?

The second case may involve information that by itself may have relatively little or no economic value if lost, but is considered protected information under the law. One sub-case would be the inadvertent disclosure or potential disclosure of personally identifiable information, such as Social Security numbers, credit card numbers, and the like. Beginning with the landmark California SB-1386 law and later extended to many other states and federal law, such disclosures generally require notification to the customer and may require the provision of ongoing credit monitoring and other service expenses. In addition to the actual expense, there is the cost of the ensuing adverse publicity, loss of customer goodwill, and a potential loss in the valuation of the company's stock.

A second sub-case would be the potential disclosure of a patient's protected health information to anyone who was not authorized to receive such information. Such a case is treated as a serious infraction under HIPAA/HITECH. The Department of Health and Human Services has issued regulations concerning the breach of such confidentiality requirements, and several of the state attorneys general have filed lawsuits against violators, with fines in the millions of dollars for the more egregious cases.

Generally, the use of encryption provides a legal "safe harbor" in such instances. Although the use of encryption is not specifically required to protect such information, if encryption is used, that provides a very significant defense against the need to publish the fact that the information was lost or stolen. Although the cost of encrypting all the sensitive information might at first seem considerable, that cost must be weighed against the possible economic losses if a data compromise event actually occurs, not to mention the moral and reputational costs.

7. Independent Evaluations

Regardless of the strength of the algorithm and the associated keys, the security they provide is merely illusory if the keys are not generated, protected, and managed properly. This is a rather difficult problem. The best solution to the problem of managing keys properly is to rely on an evaluation by an independent, well-qualified laboratory, against a recognized set of security standards. In the United States and Canada, this function is provided by the Cryptographic Module Validation Program (CMVP), which is jointly administered by NIST and the Canadian Security Establishment (CSE) and makes use of a number of certified commercial laboratories to validate cryptographic modules against the current Federal Information Processing Standard, FIPS 140-2.

FIPS 140-2 validation is required for all unclassified U.S. government cryptographic applications and is often required by policy for various state and local governments and commercial enterprises. Unfortunately, although FIPS validation may be required, many procuring agencies fail to understand the significant differences between the various levels of validation or to specify the required level, thereby encouraging a cost-driven, race-to-the-bottom approach:

- *FIPS 140-2 Level 1* is a relatively low-assurance certification that basically confirms that the algorithms are implemented correctly, but not much else. It is typically used for software-based implementations. It is considered rather easily penetrated.
- *FIPS 140-2 Level 2* is a step up from Level 1 in complexity and assurance. It is typically used for relatively low-cost, low-assurance hardware products. It provides tamper-evidence, but the hardware module can be penetrated rather easily if it is lost or stolen.
- *FIPS 140-2 Level 3* is a significant step up from Level 2, and it is difficult to achieve. In many respects, Level 3 represents the "sweet spot" in terms of relatively high assurance versus reasonable cost. The Level 3 products are universally hardware-based. Level 3 is physically tamper-resistant and offers much stronger internal protection, but it is still not completely bulletproof. Various drilling, milling, acid, and high-temperature melting attacks are still possible, which might expose the keys.
- *FIPS 140-2 Level 4* is the highest level and is rarely sought or awarded. The device or system under test is expected to resist virtually any conceivable attack and still be secure, or at least fail-secure. Level 4 devices are normally used in applications where cost is of little or no concern (because of the small number of devices required), yet the security should be of the highest order.

8. Recommendations

Organizations should consider the following recommendations regarding encryption:

- **Algorithms/Key Lengths.** Use sufficiently strong algorithms and key lengths to protect sensitive data, taking into account how long the information must be protected. RSA and triple-DES are nearing their end-of-life, and ECC and AES are strongly recommended in their stead.

- **Integrity/Nonrepudiation.** Do not ignore the need for integrity and nonrepudiation, which can be provided only by using a strong modern hash function (e.g., SHA-384) and an equally strong digital signature mechanism such as ECDSA.
- **No Silver Bullet.** There is no single silver-bullet solution. Full disk encryption provides protection only when the computer is turned off, and link encryption by itself doesn't prevent interception at the endpoints. Data in Use protection is also very important, and especially so if shared resources are involved, such as with cloud computing, or if the users may not be completely trustworthy.
- **Independent Review.** Cryptography, like brain surgery, is not a game for amateurs, and even the professionals can make mistakes. It is essential that all cryptographic products be reviewed by competent, independent authorities. The gold standard in this area is the CMVP.
- **Hardware-based.** Although software-based cryptographic products have their place, if the computer is lost or stolen, the keys can generally be recovered and the data compromised. Hardware-based FIPS 140-3 Level 3 encryption products are therefore recommended as the sweet spot, providing the maximum security at a reasonable cost.

9. Government Restrictions on Encryption

In 2010, various countries, including India, Indonesia, Lebanon, Saudi Arabia, and the United Arab Emirates, have threatened to impose restrictions on the use of encryption and encryption products, most notably the popular BlackBerry smart phone, unless some accommodation is provided to allow them to access these encrypted communications on demand.[86, 87] Because one of the key features of that phone is the ability to restrict access to private communications, even by (or perhaps especially by) various foreign governments and other groups, this has shaped up as a rather epic battle, and as yet there is no definitive conclusion. In addition to threatening to block encrypted BlackBerry services, Indian officials were seeking access to encrypted data sent by popular Internet services such as Gmail, Skype, and even the virtual private networks used to log on remotely to corporate computer systems.[88]

The governments in question claim to need this access in order to combat terrorism (or child pornography, drug dealing, or money laundering). But the business community is pushing back hard, claiming that if organizations cannot be assured of the security of their communications, they simply won't travel to or do business within those countries. Corporate outsourcing to foreign countries of data handling responsibilities, such as processing medical records or handling confidential research projects, poses an

86. "The Ongoing Battle Between India and Research in Motion," http://knowledge.wharton.upenn.edu/arabic/article.cfm?articleId=2549, October 19, 2010.

87. "Blackberry Bans Suggest a Scary Precedent: Crypto Wars Again?" https://www.eff.org/deeplinks/2010/08/blackberry-bans-suggest-scary-precedent, August 4, 2010.

88. "Blackberry Buys Time in India; Google, Skype Next?" http://spectrum.ieee.org/riskfactor/telecom/internet/blackberry-buys-time-in-india-google-skype-next, September 1, 2010.

especially difficult risk of data compromise, and if their confidentiality is threatened, the clients may simply withdraw from that country, thereby putting a countervailing economic pressure on those governments.

The U.S. government has also been calling for new laws to give greater power to law enforcement to intercept encrypted communications, just as the CALEA Act gives them the power to remotely wiretap telephone communications.[89] Although the proposed regulations are not yet finalized, according to sources, any company doing business in the United States could not create or sell an encrypted communication system without having a way for the government to order the company to decrypt it.[90]

This government push was initiated in the 1990s, when the FBI and NSA argued that national security would be endangered if they did not have the means of breaking encrypted traffic. At the time, the exportation of encryption with keys that were stronger than 40 bits was prohibited, even in the form of source code and mathematical papers. The Arms Export Control Act and the International Traffic in Arms Regulations (ITAR) required anyone wanting to publish such information to submit his or her ideas to the government for review, to register as an arms dealer, and to apply for and obtain from the government a license to publish such ideas. Failure to do so would result in severe civil and criminal penalties. Professor Daniel J. Bernstein believed that this was a violation of his First Amendment rights and sued the government, and was sponsored in that effort by the Electronic Frontier Foundation.

In December 1996, the Commerce Department issued new Export Administration Regulations (EAR) controlling most encryption items, and the same items were removed from control under the ITAR.[91] In 1997, Bernstein challenged the constitutionality of the EAR. In 1999, the Ninth Circuit Court of Appeals ruled that such restrictions were unconstitutional.[92] The Ninth Circuit subsequently ordered that the case be reheard en banc and withdrew its May 6, 1999 opinion. On September 16, 1999, before the Ninth Circuit had an opportunity to hear the matter en banc, the Clinton Administration announced plans to make significant changes to the EAR and did so throughout 2000. Bernstein continued to argue that the EAR interfered strongly with his planned scientific activities, and the case was remanded to the district court.[93] Eventually, the government realized that this policy was merely encouraging the development of stronger cryptography abroad, while at the same time limiting the ability of U.S. citizens and companies to protect their own data. Recent revisions to the EAR have significantly eased (but not erased) the rules regarding the export of cryptography.[94]

---

89. Communications Assistance for Law Enforcement Act of 1994 (CALEA), Pub. L. No. 103-414, 108 Stat. 4279.

90. "U.S. Tries to Make It Easier to Wiretap the Internet," http://www.nytimes.com/2010/09/27/us/27wiretap.html, September 27, 2010.

91. *See* 61 Fed. Reg. 68572 (1996).

92. "Bernstein v. United States Department of Justice," https://www.eff.org/cases/bernstein-v-us-dept-justice, a particularly useful chronology of the case.

93. https://www.eff.org/files/filenode/bernstein/20020107_amended_complaint.pdf.

94. 15 C.F.R. pts. 730, 734, 738, et al. Encryption Export Controls: Revision of License Exception ENC and Mass Market Eligibility, Submission Procedures, Reporting Requirements, License Application Requirements, and Addition of Note 4 to Category 5, Part 2; Interim Final Rule, June 25, 2010, http://www.access.gpo.gov/bis/fedreg/pdf/75fr36481.pdf.

But perhaps more importantly, knowledgeable cryptographers have always argued that the only way to provide on-demand access by the government to encrypted communications is to build in some kind of a trapdoor and that such trapdoors are inevitably broken by hackers (or by adversarial governments). The recent disclosure of the master key used to protect BluRay disks,[95] the earlier breaking of the DCSS system for protecting DVDs,[96] and the cracking of the Clipper chip[97,98] would all seem to provide ample evidence that such technological solutions may inevitably be subject to compromise.

The Fourth Amendment of the U.S. Constitution states:

> The right of the people to be secure in their persons, houses, papers, and effects, against unreasonable searches and seizures, shall not be violated, and no Warrants shall issue, but upon probable cause, supported by Oath or affirmation, and particularly describing the place to be searched, and the persons or things to be seized.[99]

Not surprisingly, with the invention of the microphone, the telephone, and the dictograph recorder, it became possible to "eavesdrop" with much greater secrecy and expediency.[100]

The government may be required to have a warrant to seize encrypted documents or communications, if they were stored or communicated in such a way as to have a reasonable expectation of privacy.[101] But if the information is communicated in public, whether via a radio signal (e.g., WiMax or a satellite) or on a publicly accessible website, then no warrant is needed to intercept the information, and in any case, no warrant would be required to decrypt the intercepted (encrypted) communications. The reason is that the Fourth Amendment regulates *access*, not understanding. No matter how unlikely it is that the government will successfully decrypt a ciphertext, the Fourth Amendment offers no protection if the decryption succeeds. The reasoning is similar to the reassembly of shredded documents, the recovery of deleted files, and the translation of foreign languages.[102]

There is also an ongoing controversy as to whether someone can be compelled to disclose the password or key that is used to encrypt a document or message. A U.S magistrate judge ruled that prosecutors cannot force a criminal defendant accused of having illegal images on his hard drive to divulge his PGP (Pretty Good Privacy) passphrase.[103] It is unclear if this case will be appealed.

---

95. "HDCP Master Key Confirmed; Blu-ray Content Vulnerable," http://www.pcmag.com/article2/0,2817,2369280,00.asp, Sept. 16, 2010.

96. "DeCSS," http://en.wikipedia.org/wiki/DeCSS.

97. "Encrypting History at the NSA," Matt Blaze, http://www.crypto.com/blog/mcconnell_clipper/, Feb. 27, 2008.

98. "Protocol Failure in the Escrowed Encryption Standard." Matt Blase, http://www.crypto.com/papers/eesproto.pdf, Aug. 20, 1994.

99. "U.S Constitution: Fourth Amendment," http://caselaw.lp.findlaw.com/data/constitution/amendment04/.

100. "Electronic Surveillance and the Fourth Amendment," http://caselaw.lp.findlaw.com/data/constitution/amendment04/05.html#1.

101. "Electronic Communications Privacy Act," http://www.answers.com/topic/electronic-communications-privacy-act.

102. Orin S. Kerr, *The Fourth Amendment in Cyberspace: Can Encryption Create a Reasonable Expectation of Privacy?* 33 Conn. L. Rev., 503 (2001).

103. *In re* Boucher, U.S. District Court for the District of Vermont, 2007 WL 4246473 (Nov. 29, 2009). Cf. http://www.volokh.com/files/Boucher.pdf.

In the United Kingdom, however, failure to turn over an encryption key upon demand is in itself a violation of law, and at least three people have been convicted to date. When police found that one defendant's computer was secured using strong (ish) encryption and demanded his password, the defendant told the police that he could not remember it: it was somewhere between 40 and 50 characters long.[104] He had not written it down and was prosecuted for failing to provide the necessary information within the time allowed. The court was told that it was ridiculous that anyone would create a password of as many as 50 characters and not write it down. And that was the basis of the conviction. So organizations and their employees, at least in this jurisdiction, may need to write down passwords or use something that is easily guessed, or face the possible legal consequences.[105]

5.4 IDENTITY MANAGEMENT AND AUTHORIZATION

In this age of the Internet, social networks, and mobile computing and the related issues of phishing, hacking, social engineering, and identity theft discussed in Chapter 4, the answer to the question, "who are you?" becomes critical. On the Internet, without the benefit of face-to-face personal contact, authenticating the identity of the remote party is of the utmost importance. It plays a key role in fighting identity fraud, is essential to establishing the trust necessary to facilitate electronic transactions of all types, and in many cases has become a legal obligation.

Verifying the identity of a person or entity that seeks remote access to a corporate system, that authors an electronic communication, or that signs an electronic document is the domain of what has also come to be called "identity management." It is increasingly playing a critical role in online commerce. The OECD has noted that

> [e]lectronic authentication provides a level of assurance as to whether someone or something is who or what it claims to be in a digital environment. Thus, electronic authentication plays a key role in the establishment of trust relationships for electronic commerce, electronic government and many other social interactions. It is also an essential component of any strategy to protect information systems and networks, financial data, personal information and other assets from unauthorized access or identity theft. Electronic authentication is therefore essential for establishing accountability on line.[106]

Identity management is also a critical building block of information security. It forms the basis for most types of access control and for establishing accountability online.

104. A completely random password consisting of characters on a conventional U.S. keyboard contains 6.5 bits of entropy per character. A natural language passphrase is considered to have approximately 3.3 bits of entropy per character. To be equal in strength to AES-256, a random password would therefore have to contain over 39 characters, and a more easily memorizable passphrase would have to contain more than 77 characters.

105. "The Risk Professional: If You Can't Remember Your Computer Passwords, You Go to Jail," http://chiefofficers.net/888333888/cms/index.php/news/management/risk_professional/the_risk_professional_if_you_can_t_remember_your_computer_passwords_you_go_to_jail (Oct. 18, 2010).

106. Organisation for Economic Co-operation and Development (OECD) *Recommendation on Electronic Authentication and OECD Guidance for Electronic Authentication*, June 2007, at p. 7; *available at* http://www.oecd.org/dataoecd/32/45/38921342.pdf.

Thus, it contributes to the protection of privacy by reducing the risks of unauthorized access to personal information, data breaches, and identity theft.

At the same time, however, the need to identify persons seeking online access is complicating life for individual users and consumers (who must remember or track numerous user IDs and passwords) and is becoming increasingly costly for organizations that must identify and authenticate the ever-growing number of persons and entities with whom they deal electronically. In addition, it increases privacy risks to the individuals being identified, especially as more and more entities collect and exchange an ever-increasing amount of personal data from and about such individuals, all in the name of identity management.

One approach to address the challenges of identity management in the distributed computing world of the Internet, including the cloud computing model, is the concept of federated identity management. It allows businesses to, in effect, outsource the identification and authentication processes to a third party, and eases the burden on users and consumers by allowing them to use a single sign-on.

A. Identification, Authentication, and Authorization

The identification and authentication processes form the foundation of identity management. Although the term "identity management" is relatively new, the concept is not. In fact, the underlying processes have been in use for many generations in the noncomputing environment. Passports, driver's licenses, library cards, and employee ID cards are all common examples of what might be referred to as identity management systems.

While there are many definitions and numerous approaches to identity management,[107] it essentially involves two fundamental processes: (1) the process of identifying a person (identification), and (2) the process of later verifying that a particular person claiming to be that previously identified person is, in fact, such person (authentication). Once an individual's identity is successfully authenticated, a third process, referred to as "authorization," is used by the business relying on the authentication to determine what rights and privileges are accorded to such person (e.g., whether such person should be granted access to a database, a bar, an airport boarding area, etc.).

A simple and familiar example of a basic identity management process is the case of the employee who logs into his or her employer's network using a user ID and password. Before a company allows a person to access its internal network, that person must be properly identified in a manner appropriate for the transaction (e.g., as an employee with certain authority), and then that identity must be authenticated at the time of each transaction. Employees are identified by their employer, and an identity credential containing (or consisting of) a unique identifier (typically a user ID) and other relevant

107. The OECD defines identity management (IdM) as "the set of rules, procedures and technical components that implement an organisation's policy related to the establishment, use and exchange of digital identity information for the purpose of accessing services or resources. Effective IdM policies safeguard digital identity information throughout its life cycle—from enrolment to revocation—while maximising the potential benefits of its use, including across domains to deliver joined-up services over the Internet." OECD Working Party on Information Security and Privacy, The Role of Digital Identity Management in the Internet Economy: A Primer for Policy Makers, DSTI/ICCP/REG(2008)10/FINAL (June 11, 2009), at p. 4, *available at* http://www.oecd.org/dataoecd/55/48/43091476.pdf.

information attributes is created and stored on the company's computer system. A secret (in this case, a password) is then used to link the employee to the identity credential. Thereafter, when the employee wants to remotely access the company's network, he or she can be authenticated by using the password in an authentication protocol. The authentication protocol allows the employee to demonstrate to the employer that he or she has or knows the secret, and thus, is the person previously identified.

1. Identification

The *identification* process is designed to answer the question, Who are you? It involves associating one or more *attributes*[108] (e.g., name, height, birth date, SSN, employer, home address, passport number) with a person in order to identify and define that individual to the level sufficient for the contemplated purpose. Sometimes called "identity proofing," "identity vetting," or "enrolment," this process is usually a one-time event. It typically involves the collection of personal information about the person to be identified, and often relies on a patchwork of documents from birth certificates and Social Security cards to driver's licenses and passports.[109] The personal information may be collected directly from the person being identified, as well as from third-party sources (e.g., government agencies, credit agencies, public record databases, etc.). Note that the attributes may be permanent (e.g., date of birth) or temporary (e.g., current employer), inherited (e.g., DNA), acquired (e.g., educational degrees), or assigned (e.g., employee number).

At the end of the identification process, a person's identity is typically represented by data in a paper or electronic document referred to as an identity *credential*. A credential is data that is used to authenticate the claimed digital identity or attributes of a person.[110] In the physical world, the identity credential may be a driver's license, a passport, a library card, or an employee identification card. In the online world the identity credential may be as simple as a user ID or as complex as a cryptographically based digital certificate. (Examples of digital credentials include: an electronic signature, a password, a verified bank card number, a digital certificate, or a biometric template.)

Electronic identity credentials typically contain a unique *identifier* (such as name, user ID, account number, Social Security number, etc.) along with the relevant attributes that describe or define the person to the level necessary for the purpose at hand (e.g., address, title, gender, status, date of birth, credit score, medical information, etc.). In addition, identity credentials are often associated with an *authenticator* (also called a *token*) possessed and controlled by the person identified in the credential. The token ensures that the credential can be reliably associated with the specific person about whom it relates. The token can be digital information, such as a secret known only to

---

108. Personal information concerning a specific category or characteristic of a given identity, such as name, address, age, gender, title, salary, health, net worth, driver's license number, Social Security number, etc.

109. Industry Advisory Council Transition Study Group, *Identity and Access Management* (Dec. 9, 2008), at p. 4, *available at* www.actgov.org/knowledgebank/studies/Documents/Transition%20Study%20Group%20Papers/Identity%20and%20Access%20Management,%20IAC,%2012-9-2008.pdf.

110. OECD Guidance for Electronic Authentication (2007), at p. 12, *available at* http://www.oecd.org/dataoecd/32/45/38921342.pdf.

the individual (e.g., a password), or a physical object such as a smartcard or ATM card. The token and credential may then be used in subsequent authentication events.

With respect to both of the dimensions of identification, the nature of the process is critical. Before someone relies on an identity that is based on the results of an identification process, they need to be able to trust both that the process is appropriate for the task and that it was accurately conducted. Likewise, following completion of the identification process, the continuing security of the data and the authenticating token is also a critical concern. If a new photo can be pasted into a driver's license, or if a password is lost or stolen, an identity thief can successfully claim to be the person identified by the credential created during the identification process.

2. Authentication

When a person presents an identity credential (such as by using a user ID on a corporate network or presenting a driver's license at an airport), claims to be the individual identified in the credential, and seeks to exercise a right or privilege granted to the individual named in the credential (e.g., to access the network or a sensitive database, to board a plane, etc.), an *authentication* process is used to determine whether that person is, in fact, who he or she claims to be.[111] In other words, once someone makes a declaration of who he or she is, authentication is designed to answer the question, okay, how can you prove it? In essence, it is the process of establishing confidence in a person's claimed identity.

Typical legal definitions of authentication include: "the corroboration that a person is the one claimed,"[112] "utilizing digital credentials to assure the identity of users and validate their access,"[113] and "a procedure for checking a user's identity."[114] It is a transaction-specific event that involves verifying that the person trying to engage in the transaction really is the person who was previously identified and authorized for the transaction.

There are a variety of technologies and methodologies to authenticate individuals. These methods include the use of passwords, personal identification numbers (PINs), digital certificates using a public key infrastructure (PKI), physical devices such as smart cards, one-time passwords, USB plug-ins or other types of tokens, transaction profile scripts, biometric identification, and others.[115]

In all cases, however, authentication is essentially performed by cross-checking a claimed identity against one or more authenticators, often referred to as tokens, that are associated with or linked to that identity. An authenticator (or token) typically consists of one of the following *factors*:

---

111. *See* Fed. R. Evid. 901(a). *See also* Federal Trade Commission Report, "Security in Numbers: SSNs and ID Theft" (FTC, Dec. 2008), at p. 6, *available at* http://www.ftc.gov/opa/2008/12/ssnreport.shtm.

112. HIPAA Security Regulations, 45 C.F.R. § 164.304.

113. Homeland Security Act of 2002 § 1001(b), amending 44 U.S.C. § 3532(b)(1)(D).

114. Spain, Royal Decree 1720/2007 of 21 December, Which Approves The Regulation Implementing Organic Law 15/1999, of 13 December, on the Protection of Personal Data, Article 5(2)(b).

115. Federal Financial Institutions Examination Council (FFIEC), "Authentication in an Internet Banking Environment," Oct. 12, 2005, at p. 2, *available at* http://www.ffiec.gov/pdf/authentication_guidance.pdf [hereinafter FFIEC Guidance].

- something the person *knows* (e.g., a secret such as a PIN, password, or other secret code)[116]
- something the person *possesses* (e.g., a cryptographic key, an ATM card, a smart card, a driver's license, or other physical token)
- something the person *is* (e.g., a biometric characteristic,[117] such as a fingerprint or retinal pattern)

For example, when someone presents a driver's license, the biometric characteristic that comprises his face (something he "is") can be compared to the picture embedded in the license, and if they match, the person's claimed identity (e.g., name, age, etc., as stated on the license) is authenticated. Likewise, in the online environment, when an employee logs in to the company network, her password (something she "knows") is checked against the password associated with her identity credentials stored on the company's server, and if they match, the employee's claimed identity (represented by the identifier known as a user ID) is authenticated.

Authentication processes may require one or more of these factors. The online use of a password is *single-factor authentication* (i.e., something the user knows), whereas an ATM transaction requires *two-factor authentication*—that is, something the user possesses (the ATM card) combined with something the user knows (the PIN number).[118] Properly designed and implemented multifactor authentication methods typically are more difficult to compromise than single-factor systems. As a result, they are more reliable indicators of authentication and stronger fraud deterrents.

3. Authorization

Once a user has successfully authenticated himself or herself to a system, an *authorization* process controls what the user is allowed to access and use. It addresses the question, what can I do? In other words, authentication of identity is not just an end in itself, but rather a process used to authorize some type of grant of rights or privileges (e.g., to access and use certain system resources), to facilitate a transaction or decision, or to satisfy an evidentiary obligation. For example:

- With respect to *computer systems and networks*, authentication is often used for access control—for example, to determine who is seeking access in order to ensure that only authorized persons are given the right to access a database of sensitive personal information or the right to transfer funds out of a bank

116. The use of a user name or user ID, coupled with a secret string of characters such as a password or PIN, is one of the most common authentication methods. The security provided by user IDs and passwords depends, of course, on the password being kept a secret.

117. A biometric identifier measures an individual's unique physical characteristic or behavior and compares it to a stored digital template to authenticate the individual. Thus, it represents "something the user is." Commonly used biometrics include a person's voice, fingerprint, hand or face geometry, the iris or retina in an eye, or the way the person signs a document or enters keyboard strokes. The security of a biometric identifier rests on the ability of the digitally stored characteristic to relate to only one individual in a defined population.

118. FFIEC Guidance, at p. 3.

account. As such, it can play a critical role in protecting the privacy and confidentiality of data stored on corporate networks.[119]

- With respect to *electronic communications*, authentication of identity can be used to assure the recipient of a message that the sender is who he or she (or it) claims to be so that the recipient can determine whether to proceed with the transaction. For example, when a bank receives an electronic payment order from a customer directing that money be paid to a third party, the bank must be able to verify the source of the request and ensure that it is not dealing with an impostor. This is a critical defense against identity theft.
- With respect to *electronically signed records*, authentication might be used to verify the identity of the signer. Someone seeking to enforce an electronic promissory note, for example, must be able to authenticate the identity of the signer. In this case, it serves an important evidentiary function.

In all cases, note that there is a clear difference between identification and authentication. *Identification* is the process of verifying a person's identity to a level sufficient for the intended purpose (such as during the hiring process or an account origination process) and usually occurs once. *Authentication* is the process of confirming that a person presenting himself or herself as a previously identified person entitled to certain rights and privileges is, in fact, that person (such as when a person attempts to gain access to an online system) and typically occurs at the time of each transaction.

B. Federated Identity Management

Traditionally, each business entity and government agency has handled its own identity management. For example, a company would identify each of its employees and customers, and then assign each of them a unique identifier (typically a user ID) tied to an internal identity credential, and associate an authenticator or token (typically a password) to that user ID and identity credential, so that those persons could be authenticated for remote network access. Only two parties are involved in this type of identity management process—the business and the individual to be granted access.

Today, however, businesses and government agencies increasingly want to: (1) use third parties to handle the difficult and often expensive tasks involved in identity management, particularly in situations involving high volume or one-off transactions, or (2) leverage the identification and authentication previously done by a related business (e.g., a hotel and car rental company might want to rely on an airline's identification of a traveler). In addition, users, overloaded with user IDs and passwords, are looking for a one-stop option. A three-party identity management model, known as *federated identity management*, offers a promising solution for dealing with the cost and complexity of addressing these identity management problems.

Under a federated identity model, a business relies on an identification process performed, and identity information provided, by a third party. The goal is to facilitate

119. That is, it helps to keep out unauthorized persons. It does not, however, prevent authorized persons from misusing their access rights, although it does help provide an audit trail that can detect misuse of such data by identifying who accessed the compromised data.

the secure exchange of identity credentials between organizations—that is, to enable the portability of identity information across different systems and entities. Thus the model "allows individuals to use the same user name, password, or other personal identification to sign on to the networks of more than one enterprise in order to conduct transactions."[120]

1. The General Process

While there are many different approaches to federated identity management, and the technical details and specifications of each approach can become quite complex, the following oversimplified summary of the process will help to put the legal issues in perspective:

- A business or a government agency (the *relying party*) wants to (1) authenticate the identity of a particular person (the *subject*), and (2) obtain certain information about the subject (an *identity assertion*) before it allows the subject to access its system or enter into a proposed business transaction. The subject may, for example, be a customer seeking access to the relying party's network, a person seeking to enter into an online contract with the relying party, or someone seeking to access his or her financial account with the relying party. The information the relying party needs may be the subject's account number, Social Security number, address, or membership status.
- To provide the required identity information and facilitate the authentication process, a third party (called the *identity provider*) must have previously identified the subject and issued a digital identity credential to facilitate authentication of the subject. The identity provider will then be asked to make an identity assertion about the subject that contains the requested information.
- At the time of the transaction, the subject is first authenticated by the identity provider[121] and then the identity assertion is communicated to the relying party (by either the subject or the identity provider, depending on the system involved), the relying party validates the identity assertion to ensure that it is authentic and not revoked, and then relies on it to obtain the necessary information in order to grant access to a network or proceed with the proposed transaction.

A very common off-line example of this federated identity process (although it was never intended as such) is the way we currently issue and use driver's licenses. Obtain-

120. Liberty Alliance Project, Liberty Identity Assurance Framework, Version 1.1 at p. 119 (2008), *available at* http://www.projectliberty.org/resource_center/specifications/liberty_alliance_identity_assurance_framework_iaf_1_1_specification_and_associated_read_me_first_1_0_white_paper.

121. Authentication can occur in various ways: the relying party can initiate an authentication request to the identity provider the subject designates when logged on to a relying party, or the subject can first authenticate at an identity provider and then access a relying party. In either case, the technology enables single sign-on in which the identity provider authenticates the subject, thus allowing her access to protected resources at a relying party. Susan Landau, Hubert Le Van Gong, and Robin Wilton, "Achieving Privacy in a Federated Identity Management System" (2009) at § 1.1, *available at* http://research.sun.com/people/slandau/Achieving_Privacy.pdf.

ing a driver's license begins with an in-person identification process conducted by a state's Department of Motor Vehicles (the identity provider), whereby selected identifying information (or attributes) about a person, such as name, address, date of birth, height, weight, and eye color, are collected and verified. Following testing of eyesight and driving competence, the process culminates with the issuance of a driver's license (an identity credential) that identifies the individual with a unique driver's license number (the identifier), contains some of the identity attributes about the individual that were collected during the identification process (identity assertions), and includes a photograph of the person named in the license that was taken at the time the license was issued. The photograph functions as an authenticator—that is, it is used to tie the person to the identity credential.

The person obtaining that license may later present it to a relying party (such as a TSA agent at an airport or the bartender at a bar), claiming to be the person with the identity attributes stated on the driver's license. That third party will then attempt to verify that the person standing in front of him is the same person identified in the license by comparing the photo on the license to the person before him—that is, he will attempt to authenticate the claimed identity asserted by that person. If successful, he will typically be willing to rely on the data stated in the identity credential (the identity assertions) for purposes of a transaction with such person. The bartender, for example, will rely on the identity assertion regarding age stated in the license to determine whether to serve alcohol to the license holder; the TSA agent will rely on the identity assertion regarding the name stated in the license for purposes of determining whether such person is the same as the person named in the airline boarding pass, and thus entitled to enter the boarding area.

2. *Online Examples*

In the traditional two-party identity management system, the identity provider and the relying party are the same entity. For example, a business will identify its employees and issue them user IDs and passwords so that the employees can access the company's network. In that case, the company fills the role of the identity provider as well as the role of the relying party.

On the other hand, when that same business provides a link (via the company intranet) to a third party managing the retirement accounts for its employees, and its employees are able to access their retirement accounts without entering an additional user ID and password, a federated approach to identity management is in place. In that scenario, the company acts as the identity provider (i.e., it identifies its employees and authenticates them when they sign on to the company network at work), and the third-party manager of the retirement accounts is the relying party. It relies on the identity assertions made by the company to allow the company's employees (who have signed on to the company network) to have seamless access to their benefit accounts.

Another example of a federated identity arrangement (in a closed system) is the typical ATM transaction whereby an individual with an account at Bank A wants to obtain cash from an ATM machine operated by Bank B (with whom he has no relationship). The individual signs on to Bank B's ATM network using his ATM card and password from Bank A. Through the ATM network, Bank B contacts Bank A to determine whether the individual is a valid customer of Bank A, to have Bank A authenticate the identity of the individual (i.e., did he enter the correct password), and to obtain certain identity information about the individual from Bank A (e.g., whether his account has funds sufficient to cover the requested withdrawal, and the balance in his account so Bank B can print it on the transaction receipt).

C. Legal Risks in Identity Management

The legal risks in an identity management system are all centered on issues raised by the collection, verification, use, communication, and security of personal information. But they are not all strictly privacy issues. Rather, they tend to fall into the following four categories:

- Privacy risk
- Identification and Authentication risk
- Liability risk
- Performance risk

These risks apply in both two-party (nonfederated) and three-party (federated) systems. This section will focus on federated systems but for those utilizing two-party identity management systems, the identity provider and relying party roles may be combined and certain risks could possibly be reduced or eliminated. Each of these four risks affect all the roles in a federated system (subjects, identity providers, and relying parties), although perhaps in different ways. Thus, each role may well have potentially conflicting needs and goals with respect to addressing these risks.

1. Privacy Risk

By its nature, any form of federated identity management involves the collection (by an identity provider) and disclosure (to a relying party) of personal information about a subject. Thus, "the foundational issue in approaching any [identity management] system is personal information—how it is collected, stored, shared, and used."[122] Moreover, by its nature, federated identity management "presents a new challenge to privacy," in that transfers of personal information routinely occur between organizations as well as between the individual and an organization and may frequently cross industry sectors and jurisdictional boundaries in the process.[123]

For subjects, protecting the privacy and security of their personal information is a primary concern. At the same time, however, the other roles have needs that potentially conflict with the subject's privacy rights. For identity providers, the right to collect, process, and exchange this personal information is critical to the identity services they provide, and thus, they have a major interest in ensuring their continued ability to do so. Likewise, relying parties often need the ability to receive, process, and use at least some of this information for the transaction they are entering into with the subject.

---

122. Office of Science and Technology Policy (OSTP), National Science and Technology Council (NSTC), Subcommittee on Biometrics and Identity Management, "Identity Management Task Force Report 2008," (Sept. 2008) at p. 16, *available at* http://www.ostp.gov/galleries/NSTC%20Reports/IdMReport%20Final.pdf.

123. Privacy Commissioner of Ontario Paper: Information and Privacy Commissioner of Ontario, "The New Federated Privacy Impact Assessment (F-PIA): Building Privacy and Trust-enabled Federation" (Jan. 2009), at pp. 7, 13, *available at* http://www.ipc.on.ca/images/Resources/F-PIA_2.pdf.

The privacy risk for subjects focuses on the protection and use of their personal information by identity providers, relying parties, and other third parties, the resulting possibility of inappropriate use, disclosure, and compromise, and the harms that may result, such as identity theft, unauthorized account access, embarrassment, and the like. And this risk relates not only to the information provided by the subjects but also to information about the subjects collected from third parties, as well as metadata and transaction data about subjects generated as a result of their online activities.

To benefit from participation in a federated identity system, subjects must disclose personal information and thus expose it to risk. Yet a vital part of maintaining their confidence in the process is ensuring that the personal information that identity providers collect about subjects during the identification process, and disclose to relying parties during the authentication processes, is verified, maintained in an accurate and up-to-date form, kept private, not shared with third parties, and not misused or exposed to unauthorized individuals, such as identity thieves, as discussed later in the Privacy controls section.

For identity providers and relying parties, the privacy risk involves navigating the challenges of compliance obligations and restrictions that might inhibit their ability to achieve their goals. Laws and regulations may restrict their collection and use of personal information as well as impose a variety of obligations to protect the information.[124] In addition, restrictions on cross-border transfers and other forms of use or sharing of such information may have an impact. Failure to address these obligations may result in penalties and fines, as well as potential liability for any harms suffered by the subjects themselves.

Identity providers and relying parties are also concerned about obtaining (or retaining) the rights necessary to do what is required to satisfy their obligations in the identification and authentication processes (as well as their right to use the personal information for other related, or unrelated, business purposes). At the same time, they are also concerned about limiting their liability exposure in the event of a misuse or breach of the personal information in their possession. This is often a difficult balancing act in an identity management context, as collecting and holding too much personal data may expose them to disproportionate liability or an excessive burden of compliance; at the same time, collecting too little personal data can itself lead to liability exposure in certain contexts, such as money laundering or providing health care services.

Part of the solution for all parties may well lie in establishing a set of rules that govern the privacy and security of that personal information (and allocating the related liability risks) in a manner acceptable for all participants.

2. *Identification and Authentication Risk*

If personal information is the foundation of any identity management system, the use of that information to identify the correct person, and the exchange of that information between organizations, for the purposes of remote authentication of identity and the related communication of identity assertions, is clearly the goal of identity management.

124. This includes, e.g., GLB, HIPAA, state data security laws, etc., as well as the data protection laws in other countries, including the EU, Argentina, Australia, Canada, Hong Kong, Japan, and South Korea.

Without the ability to accurately identify individuals and remotely and reliably authenticate that identity and provide appropriate identity assertions, the trust necessary for online transactions is missing. Thus, the success of the identification and authentication process and the reliability of the identity assertion are key concerns both for relying parties (who need to know who they are dealing with) and for subjects (who want to be sure that they are able to complete an online transaction and that identity thieves are not).

For subjects the authentication risk is both a business concern (will I be able to complete this online transaction, access this database, etc.?), and a privacy concern (will someone be able to use my identity to successfully complete this transaction in my name?). For identity providers, the identification and authentication risks relate to the possibility that faulty identification or authentication processes will result in an improper identification and subsequent harm to the relying party and/or the subject, with the consequence that the identity provider will be liable for the damages incurred.

For relying parties, identification and authentication risks are both a liability concern (focused on the losses they will suffer if they rely on an inappropriate authentication or identity assertion) and a legal compliance obligation. From a liability perspective, the relying party needs the assurance or trust necessary to enter into a particular online transaction, as well as some level of confidence that it can prove the identity of the other party in court if that becomes necessary. At the same time, however, laws and regulations increasingly impose on businesses a duty to identify and authenticate the persons with whom they deal remotely. Thus, for many relying parties, identity management has become a legal obligation.

In many cases, the obligation is imposed by law or regulation. The FFIEC Guidance makes clear that "[f]inancial institutions offering Internet-based products and services to their customers should use effective methods to authenticate the identity of customers using those products and services."[125] Expanding on the rationale for this requirement, the FFIEC points out that

> [a]n effective authentication system is necessary for compliance with requirements to safeguard customer information,[126] to prevent money laundering and terrorist financing,[127] to reduce fraud, to inhibit identity theft, and to promote the legal enforceability of their electronic agreements and transactions. The risks of doing business with unauthorized or incorrectly identified persons in an Internet banking environment can

125. FFIEC Guidance, at p. 1. Other countries, such as Singapore, have also adopted similar requirements. Monetary Authority of Singapore, Circular No. SRD TR 02/2005, 25 November 2005.

126. "The Interagency Guidelines Establishing Information Security Standards that implement section 501(b) of the Gramm–Leach–Bliley Act, 15 USC 6801, require banks and savings associations to safeguard the information of persons who obtain or have obtained a financial product or service to be used primarily for personal, family or household purposes, with whom the institution has a continuing relationship. Credit unions are subject to a similar rule." FFIEC Guidance, at fn. 3.

127. "The regulations implementing section 326 of the USA PATRIOT Act, 31 USC § 5318(l), require banks, savings associations and credit unions to verify the identity of customers opening new accounts. See 31 CFR 103.121; 12 CFR 21.21 (OCC); 12 CFR 563.177 (OTS); 12 CFR 326.8 (FDIC); 12 CFR 208.63 (state member banks), 12 CFR 211.5(m) (Edge or agreement corporation or any branch or subsidiary thereof), 12 CFR 211.24(j) (uninsured branch, an agency, or a representative office of a foreign financial institution operating in the United States (FRB); and 12 CFR Part 748.2 (NCUA)." FFIEC Guidance, at fn. 4.

result in financial loss and reputation damage through fraud, disclosure of customer information, corruption of data, or unenforceable agreements.[128]

The FFIEC's reference to "requirements to safeguard customer information" identifies another key source of authentication requirements. That is, the many laws and regulations that impose on a company a duty to provide reasonable security for its data[129] typically include (expressly or impliedly) an obligation to properly authenticate persons seeking to access its data, networks, or services. In addition to the GLB security regulations referenced by the FFIEC,[130] other examples of the express duty to authenticate include:

- the HIPAA security regulations, which require covered entities to "implement procedures to verify that a person or entity seeking access to electronic protected health information is the one claimed"[131]
- state information security laws, such as Massachusetts, which requires the use of "secure user authentication protocols" and "secure access control measures," and California, which requires "reasonable security procedures and practices . . . to protect the personal information from unauthorized access"[132]
- the FTC Identity Theft Red Flags Rules, which require most financial institutions and creditors in all sectors to develop and implement a written Identity Theft Prevention Program that includes reasonable policies and procedures for detecting, preventing, and mitigating identity theft in connection with existing accounts or the opening of new accounts[133]
- the FCC Order addressing the problem of pretexting, which imposes specific authentication requirements on telephone and wireless carriers to protect personal telephone records from unauthorized disclosure[134]
- the Homeland Security Act, which requires "utilizing digital credentials to assure the identity of users and validate their access," and "protecting information and information systems from unauthorized access"[135]

---

128. FFIEC Guidance, at p. 2.

129. *See generally* Thomas J. Smedinghoff, "The State of Information Security Law: A Focus on the Key Legal Trends," 37 EDPACS, The EDP Audit, Control, and Security Newsletter (Jan.–Feb. 2008), Nos. 1–2, http://ssrn.com/abstract=1114246.

130. GLBA Security Regulations, 12 C.F.R. pt. 30, app. B, at pt. III.C(1)(a) (OCC), 12 C.F.R. pt. 208, app. D (Federal Reserve System), 12 C.F.R. pt. 364, app. B (FDIC), 12 C.F.R. pt. 568 (Office of Thrift Supervision), and 16 C.F.R. pt. 314 (FTC).

131. HIPAA Security Regulations, 45 C.F.R. § 164.312(d).

132. *See, e.g.*, CAL. CIV. CODE § 1798.81.5(b); Mass., Standards for the Protection of Personal Information of Residents of the Commonwealth, 201 CMR 17.04.

133. 16 C.F.R. pt. 681.

134. *See* FCC Order re Pretexting, 2 April 2007—In the Matter of Implementation of the Telecommunications Act of 1996: Telecommunications Carriers' Use of Customer Proprietary Network Information and Other Customer Information IP-Enabled Services, CC Docket No. 96-115, WC Docket No. 04-36, 2 April 2007, at ¶¶ 13–25, *available at* http://hraunfoss.fcc.gov/edocs_public/attachmatch/FCC-07-22A1.pdf.

135. Homeland Security Act of 2002 § 1001(b), amending 44 U.S.C. § 3532(b)(1)(D), and § 301(b)(1) amending 44 U.S.C. § 3542(b)(1) ("'information security' means protecting information and information systems from unauthorized access").

- Homeland Security Presidential Directive 12, which mandates the development of a federal standard for secure and reliable forms of identification issued by the federal government to its employees and contractors (including contractor employees) and requires the use of identification by federal employees and contractors that meets the standard in gaining physical access to federally controlled facilities and logical access to federally controlled information systems[136]
- numerous data protection laws in other countries that impose similar requirements[137]

The FTC has also begun to use FTC Act Section 5 to enforce identity management obligations. In the wake of the well-publicized security breach at ChoicePoint, the FTC brought a complaint alleging that "ChoicePoint has not employed reasonable and appropriate measures to secure the personal information it collects for sale to its subscribers, including reasonable policies and procedures to: (1) verify or authenticate the identities and qualifications of prospective subscribers; or (2) monitor or otherwise identify unauthorized subscriber activity."[138] Specifically, the FTC alleged that "ChoicePoint failed to detect [false credentials and other misrepresentations] because it had not implemented reasonable procedures to verify or authenticate the identities and qualifications of prospective subscribers."[139]

Similarly, in the case of *United States v. Rental Research Services, Inc.*,[140] the FTC alleged that a consumer reporting agency failed to employ reasonable and appropriate security policies and procedures to "verify or authenticate the identities and qualifications of prospective subscribers"[141] and that, as a result, it sold at least 318 credit reports to identity thieves. This practice, the FTC asserted, was "an unfair act or practice" in violation of Section 5 of the FTC Act, as well as the FCRA.[142] In addition, the FTC has recommended "that Congress consider establishing national consumer authentication standards covering all private sector entities that maintain consumer accounts." These standards, the FTC indicated, "should require private sector entities to create a writ-

136. Homeland Security Presidential Directive 12: Policy for a Common Identification Standard for Federal Employees and Contractors, *available at* http://www.dhs.gov/xabout/laws/gc_1217616624097.shtm.

137. *See, e.g.*, Italy, Personal Data Protection Code, § 34(a) and (b) and Annex B, §§ 1–13; Poland, Regulation of April 29, 2004, § 5.2 and Attachment A (Basic Security Measures) § II.2; Spain, Royal Decree 1720/2007, Articles 93 and 98 (basic-level and medium-level security measures).

138. United States v. ChoicePoint, Inc. (Stipulated Final Judgment, FTC File No. 052 3069, N.D. Ga. Jan. 26, 2006), Complaint at ¶ 25, *available at* http://www.ftc.gov/os/caselist/choicepoint/choicepoint.htm.

139. *Id.*, Complaint at ¶ 13.

140. United States v. Rental Research Services, Inc., FTC File No. 072 3228, D. Minn. (Stipulated Final Judgment, March 5, 2009) (settlement of allegations that its lack of reasonable client identification procedures and adequate data security safeguards resulted in the sale of credit reports to identity thieves), *available at* http://www.ftc.gov/os/caselist/0723228.

141. United States v. Rental Research Services, Inc., FTC File No. 072 3228, Complaint at ¶¶ 28–29, *available at* http://www.ftc.gov/os/caselist/0723228/090305rrscmpt.pdf.

142. *Id.*, at ¶ 29.

ten program that establishes reasonable procedures to authenticate new or existing customers."[143]

In other cases, courts are finding a common law duty. For example, in *Wolfe v. MBNA America Bank*[144] the court held that, under Tennessee negligence law, where "the injury resulting from the negligent issuance of a credit card is foreseeable and preventable, . . . Defendant has a duty to verify the authenticity and accuracy of a credit account application before issuing a credit card."[145] "[T]his duty to verify," the court held, "requires Defendant to implement reasonable and cost-effective verification methods that can prevent criminals, in some instances, from obtaining a credit card with a stolen identity."[146]

Another example of authentication risk can also be seen in the decision in *Kerr v. Dillard Store Services, Inc.*, a case involving the enforceability of an electronic signature. There the court refused to attribute an electronic signature to the plaintiff because the authentication process could be easily circumvented, raising legitimate doubts as to who actually signed the electronic record.[147]

3. *Liability Risk*

Things that can go wrong in a federated identity management operation typically result from faulty identification, faulty authentication, inadequate security for or misuse of personal data, or failure to follow appropriate procedures. They can lead to two primary harms. First, a relying party and/or a subject may suffer damages when the relying party acts (a) in reliance on a false identity credential or identity assertion that it thought was valid (e.g., by granting access to, or entering into an unauthorized transaction with, an impostor), or (b) fails to act in reliance on a valid identity credential that it mistakenly believes to be false. Second, a subject may suffer damages when (a) his or her personal information is misused or compromised by the identity provider or a relying party or other third party to whom it has been disclosed, or (b) when the subject is improperly denied access or the ability to conduct a transaction he or she is otherwise entitled to do.

A primary concern of all participants in any identity federation is determining who will bear the risks associated with these problems and their consequences. For example:

- What is the liability of the subject for providing false identity information during the identity proofing process or for failing to protect the password or key necessary to initiate an authentication process? Does the subject bear the risk of losses due to identity theft facilitated by his or her own negligent actions in the identity management system?

---

143. Federal Trade Commission Report, "Security in Numbers: SSNs and ID Theft" (FTC, Dec. 2008), at p. 6, *available at* http://www.ftc.gov/opa/2008/12/ssnreport.shtm.

144. Wolfe v. MBNA America Bank, 485 F. Supp. 2d 874, 882 (W.D. Tenn. 2007).

145. 485 F. Supp. 2d at 882.

146. *Id.*

147. Kerr v. Dillard Store Services, Inc., 2009 U.S. Dist. LEXIS 11792 (D. Kan. Feb. 17, 2009) (court declined to attribute an electronic signature to an employee because her employer failed to provide adequate security for its intranet passwords).

- What is the liability of the identity provider for failing to follow proper identification procedures that result in an incorrect identity assertion? For failing to revoke the validity of a token on notice of compromise? For misusing or failing to adequately protect the subject's personal information?
- What is the liability of the relying party for relying on a fraudulent assertion (e.g., in the case of identity theft, especially in a case where it could have determined that the assertion was false)? For misusing or failing to adequately protect the subject's personal information?

Numerous statutory, common law, and contract theories have been advanced to identify, define, and clarify the source and scope of such potential liabilities.[148] For the identity provider, the primary focus from a liability perspective is on the tort of negligent misrepresentation and contract actions for breach of express or implied warranty regarding the accuracy of the information provided. In addition, a potential source of liability for an identity provider or relying party may arise through the application of provisions contained in privacy and data security legislation and regulations. Yet at the end of the day, the legal risks remain somewhat uncertain.

In many respects, federated identity management is a business model for which the law has not yet had time to adapt. By issuing digital credentials that verify identity, an identity provider is, in essence, engaged in the business of an information provider. Moreover, the identity provider understands that the information it provides is intended to be relied upon by parties to a commercial transaction. It is this aspect of reliance that is critical. Both the identity provider that issues an identity assertion and the subject that participates in the process do so with the intention that it will be used by third parties to verify identity and engage in business transactions. Thus, an identity provider risks potential liability to relying parties, subjects, and victims (a class of persons in whose names credentials or identity assertions are improperly issued by the identity provider). At the same time, the relying party (and often the subject) is on the front line in bearing the losses and other harms that flow from inaccurate authentication of identity.

All participants in a federated identity system have an interest in fairly allocating, in advance, the risk of liability that flows from participation in the process. Without addressing how that liability should be allocated or who is in the best position to bear the risks, suffice it to say that there may be a clear benefit to some legal certainty with respect to this issue. As identity management processes are used for increasingly significant transactions and the risks to the parties increase accordingly, the benefits to all parties of addressing those risks up front, as well as mitigating those risks (to the extent possible) by requiring performance of specific obligations by each participant role, are significant.

148. *See* Thomas J. Smedinghoff, "Certification Authority Liability Analysis" (study for the American Bankers Association, discussing potential liability risks of an identity provider operating as a certification authority), *available at* http://www.wildman.com/resources/articles-pdf/ca-liability-analysis.pdf.

4. *Performance Risk*

For each participant, obtaining the benefits of a federated identity system, and effectively controlling each of the foregoing risks, depend on each of the other roles properly performing certain basic obligations that are fundamental to the concept of federated identity management. The failure of any participant to perform its obligations could lead to substantial harm to others in the federation. In fact, mere concern about the performance of another participant could be fatal to the system. Quite simply, a federated identity model will not function properly and the various participants will not be able to rely on it for online transactions unless each participant has an appropriate degree of confidence or trust that all other participants will adequately perform certain basic responsibilities.

The fundamental responsibilities of each role include the following:

Subject: The conduct of the subject can directly affect the validity of the identification and authentication processes. Thus, to ensure accurate and reliable processes, the subject must:

- Provide accurate information to the identity provider during the identification process (e.g., not omit or misrepresent any material fact, or otherwise engage in any identity fraud);
- Prevent the unauthorized use of any token (e.g., a password, PIN, key, etc.) that is issued or registered to the subject for purposes of the authentication process (e.g., to keep such token confidential and to take reasonable steps to prevent others from gaining access and using it to commit fraud); and
- Notify the identity provider if such token is lost or compromised (so that the identity provider can take steps to prevent the thief from successfully using it to commit identity fraud).

Identity Provider: The identity provider is primarily responsible for the validity and integrity of the identification process and the resulting identity credential, the accuracy of the identity assertions, and the privacy and security of the subject's personal information in its control. Thus, it must:

- Properly and accurately identify subjects and, where appropriate, use reasonable procedures to detect omissions or misrepresentations by the subject;
- Ensure that all identity assertions are accurately based on current valid information that is properly authenticated (e.g., an employer should not issue an identity assertion for a terminated employee);
- Comply with disclosed policies, practices, and procedures for the identification and authentication processes (so that relying parties can identify assurance levels and determine the level of trust they should have in the resulting authentication and identity assertions);
- Provide to the subject a capability to revoke tokens or identity credentials (to limit identity theft opportunities in the event that the subject's token is compromised or the subject no longer wants to participate); and
- Protect the privacy and security of a subject's personal information in accordance with disclosed policies, practices, and procedures and in accordance with applicable law.

Relying Party: The relying party must ensure that its reliance on the identification and authentication processes is reasonable under the circumstances and that its use of the subject's personal information is appropriate. Specifically, the relying party must:

- Properly authenticate credentials and any identity assertions before relying on them (e.g., by analogy, compare a claimant's face to the picture on the driver's license before relying on the data in the license);
- Limit its use and reliance on an identity assertion as appropriate for the circumstances (e.g., credentials issued with a low assurance level, such as a library card, should not be relied upon in situations requiring a very high assurance level, such as access to a sensitive nuclear facility); and
- Protect the privacy and security of the subject's personal data and restrict its use of that data in accordance with disclosed policies, practices, and procedures and in accordance with applicable law.

Unless each participant has confidence that the other participants will properly perform their obligations, the identity federation is of little value. Thus, there is a need to clearly define the obligations of each role and to utilize a mechanism (statutory, contractual, and/or technological) to provide some assurance that the participants in each role will perform their obligations and to provide some remedy if someone does not.

5.5 OTHER MAJOR CONTROL CATEGORIES

Numerous types of controls are required to implement an information security and privacy system. The following does not present every category of controls, attempting only to highlight those control categories of increasing significance based on changing business, legal, and technical needs and risks. But that presentation should not imply that any control categories not described here are not important. For example, data backups, systems change management controls, and application systems development lifecycle (SDLC) controls (separate testing environments; separate test data; quality checks; separation of duties for developers, testers, promoters, and approvers) are essential to managing risk and safeguarding organizational assets. Change management, backups, and SDLC should be well established in every organization by now and so do not require the additional emphasis of those control categories described next.

A. Network and Computer Security

Network and computer security threats are perhaps the most visible and publicized information security threats. The networks and computer systems must be safeguarded from threats to protect the information that is stored and processed by these systems. Computer security deals with securing a computer's operating system, applications, and access to individual workstations. Network security addresses protecting data while it is transmitted across networks and securing networks from intrusion and unauthorized access.[149] For both, information security and privacy controls are used to protect an

149. *See* Warwick Ford & Michael Baum, Secure Electronic Commerce 94 (2001).

organization's information technology resources from harm and its information from exposure. These controls can be used in a preventive, detective, or corrective manner.

Network-based security controls can help limit the exposure of computer systems to attackers, thus reducing the attack surface. However, at some point computer systems must generally be exposed to other systems, whether servers providing web services to the Internet or users' workstations being part of a shared network environment. As such, it is imperative that network and computer security controls be considered and implemented that address the following principles:

- *Access Control:* Authentication and authorization mechanisms should be implemented to ensure that only authorized users have access to protected resources. This principle was introduced in the preceding section on identification, authentication, and authorization.
- *Reduced Exposure:* Use of mechanisms like firewalls and operating system "hardening" help reduce the degree to which systems and data are available to attackers for compromise or exploitation.
- *Separation:* The principle of least privilege should be employed whenever possible, even for internal resources. Many major data breaches have been the result of inadequate separation of systems or environments that results in a less-secured environment being compromised on the way to compromising a more-secured environment.
- *Defensibility:* Reasonable measures should be undertaken to defend systems and networks against attack. These measures may include hardening operating systems, implementing local and network firewalls, patching systems in a timely manner, deploying antivirus to workstations, and making use of other network-based technologies (e.g., SSL, VPN, IDS/IPS) to further protect against attack.
- *Monitoring:* Network-based logging and monitoring, such as with Security Information and Event Management (SIEM) systems, should be leveraged to the greatest extent possible. Network and computer systems should generate event logs that help monitor access to systems, networks, applications, and data to help aggregate and correlate the events toward a greater understanding of active threats.

1. Computer Security Controls

Several controls can be implemented with computer systems. The degree to which these controls are selected and used will depend on the purpose and degree of exposure of the system, along with the expected sensitivity of data handled therein. The following controls should be considered the minimum currently acceptable:

a. System Hardening

The term "hardening" is derived from military lingo and refers to efforts to make a target less susceptible to attack. Hardening in the context of computer security pertains to disabling services that are not needed, removing or disabling default accounts, changing default passwords, removing unneeded software, and minimizing user access to only files and applications needed to perform job responsibilities. Many organizations will build standard operating system (OS) images to ensure consistent deployment throughout the enterprise. These images should be hardened prior to deployment.

b. Patching

Keeping systems fully patched is one of the most important practices that one can cite. There are automated methods for keeping systems current on all major operating systems, allowing for controlled provisioning of software updates.

c. Reasonably Strong Authentication

All systems should require a reasonable degree of strong authentication. At a minimum this control should equate to a username and password. Traditionally, a password adhering to complexity rules that require a minimum length plus the use of uppercase and lowercase letters, numbers, and non-alphanumeric characters has been advocated. These principles are still useful, though increasingly the length of a password (12+ characters) may be more than adequate to cause users to create a password that is not guessable. A strong authentication control also typically requires that passwords be changed on a regular basis and will lock out or disable an account when five or more failed logins have occurred within a certain period of time (usually 15 minutes).

d. Antivirus

As a good practice, almost all systems should deploy antivirus. Antivirus systems should be evaluated based on their overall effectiveness in protecting against both exploits and payloads, as well as for the manageability within the enterprise environment. Large deployments should have central management and logging/reporting capabilities to ensure that software continues to run and is kept current and that potential infections are flagged and addressed accordingly.

It is important to also understand the limits of certain antivirus protection software. In the most recent testing performed by a leading laboratory, the consumer anti-malware products tested showed that there should be no expectation that these products are 100 percent successful.[150] Of the products tested, the success at blocking malware ranged from 54 to 90 percent, meaning that "cybercriminals have between a 10%–45% chance of getting past your AV with Web Malware."[151] Blocking of exploits was even worse, ranging from 3 to 75 percent. And the cybercriminals seem to be improving more quickly, as the products' ability to block these attacks decreased from the prior year. As such, it is vital to know which vendors are keeping current and have the most recently tested capabilities to block the malware and exploits discussed in Chapter 4.

e. Secure Remote Access

TELNET should never be used for remote access as it is inherently insecure (with the exception of Kerberos-enabled TELNET, which at least protects credentials during authentication). Likewise, FTP should also be eschewed in favor of more secure protocols. Secure Shell (SSH) version 1 should also be disabled as it has been broken in

---

150. NSS Labs, *Consumer Anti-Malware Products Group Test Report* (2010).
151. *Id.*, p. 1.

the past. Instead, SSH version 2 and Secure FTP (SFTP) or Secure Copy (SCP) should generally be relied upon for remote access, at least at the command line. For graphical remote access, solutions may use SSH as the underlying communication protocol, or the use of modern protocols like Virtual Network Computing (VNC) or Remote Desktop Protocol (RDP) can be leveraged as long as security properties (e.g., SSL) are enabled.

f. Local Firewall

All major OS distributions now come with local firewall capabilities. While the general utility of these tools may be debated, they are better than full exposure to a network and should thus be enabled. All major operating systems have software firewalls that should be enabled.

g. User Education, Training, and Awareness

One of the most effective ways to secure a computer system is to increase user competency and awareness. The more users understand the impact of their actions, the more likely it will be that they will make better choices. It is thus imperative that users be given the opportunity to become better educated and trained so as to improve their awareness of what can come from their actions.

Beyond these basic practices, there are a number of other control areas to take into consideration, including:

h. Local IDS

Intrusion detection systems (IDSs) have traditionally been deployed as network security controls, but they are also increasingly available for computer systems. Key servers should have IDSs deployed, and deploying these tools to workstations is also within reason (especially for mobile users). An IDS provides a mechanism for detecting network-based attack patterns, minimally to report the attack and with the potential capability to prevent the attack from succeeding (by way of intrusion prevention systems, or IPSs).

i. Web Application Firewall (WAF)

One fairly new tool for protecting applications is a server-based tool called a web application firewall. A WAF is an application proxy firewall that resides on the server rather than the network and can provide protection to services like web servers and applications.

j. Remove Local Administrator Access

Wherever possible, user and service accounts should not have administrative rights unless required to perform a function. Enablement tools exist today for all major operating systems to facilitate limited administrator-level access to perform certain functions without providing full carte blanche access.

2. *Network Security Controls*

Network-based threats are perhaps the most visible and publicized information security threats. Network security deals with how networked systems and their underlying infrastructure are secured from these threats. These systems typically must be secured to protect the confidentiality and integrity of information contained therein, as well as to provide safeguards that guarantee availability. Network security addresses protecting data while it is transmitted across networks, as well as securing networks from intrusion and unauthorized access. In practice, network security encompasses information security controls that are used to protect an organization's information technology resources from harm and its information from exposure.

At a minimum, the following security technologies should be implemented in almost all environments:

a. Firewalls

The answer to most network security questions is typically, "Deploy a firewall." In ancient realms there were three types of firewalls, but today it is really only necessary to consider two: stateful inspection and proxy. Stateful inspection firewalls are mainstream and very common, and derive their name from their ability to monitor the state of network connections (primarily TCP, which is stateful, rather than UDP, which is stateless, though some pseudo-state can be established). Proxy firewalls, most often seen now as web application firewalls deployed on servers, don't simply pass approved packets, but in fact terminate connections on the firewall and create a new connection out to the endpoint. A firewall should generally be chosen over basic router access control lists, though use of an integrated router plus firewall is typically adequate in most environments as long as internal routing data is not exposed.

b. SSL/TLS

Secure Sockets Layer (SSL) and Transport Layer Security (TLS) provide transport encryption for network-based communication. SSL versions 1 and 2 are deprecated due to security weaknesses. SSL version 3 or the most recent 1.x version of TLS is preferred. SSL/TLS makes use of public key infrastructure by creating public/private certificate pairs that are validated by third parties. Any Internet-based communication involving sensitive data (e.g., username, password, credit card data, e-PHI, PII) should use transport-layer encryption, which will most frequently leverage SSL/TLS.

c. Network Segmentation

All networked environments containing more than a few endpoints should use network segmentation. Segmentation means dividing a network into separate zones to limit the spread of a threat through the networked environment. The term "DMZ" has historically been associated with this concept, though it's a somewhat antiquated notion because production environments should also be segregated. At a minimum, there should be separate network segments for office LAN workstations, office LAN servers, and production servers. Additional zones may separate various production environments (web servers, databases, cardholder data environment(s), etc.). The access control (firewall) rules separating these zones should assume a "default deny" stance that explicitly allows only those services that are deemed necessary to perform specified functions.

In addition to the minimum practices just described, the following practices should be considered if not absolutely deployed:

d. VPN (IPSec and SSL)

Virtual private networks (VPNs) provide secure remote access to networked environments. There are several uses, such as connecting two remote data centers over public networks or providing secure remote file server access for users. A VPN may use the IPSec

Security Extensions or SSL/TLS. The specific type chosen will depend on use and should be discussed with an appropriate network security professional in order to optimally meet the needs of the business.

e. IDS/IPS

Intrusion detection systems and intrusion prevention systems have been developed to provide signature-based detection of network-based threats/attacks. These systems have significant limits (being signature-based), but can still perform a useful function. Some standards may require the deployment of an IDS/IPS despite the limited effectiveness.

f. DLP

Data loss prevention (or data leak prevention) systems have been developed to provide smarter monitoring of data in motion, data at rest, and data in use. Solutions can exist in a variety of places, such as actively monitoring data traversing the network (data in transit), data that has been stored on systems (data at rest), and data that is currently being processed through systems (data in use). It is still unclear whether DLP has long-term viability, but the technology is potentially promising and should be considered, at least in limited-use cases. In certain situations, DLP is now being integrated with traditional outbound web filtering products to provide a more effective method for blocking unapproved dispersion of sensitive data.

g. SSL Acceleration

SSL accelerators can help speed the use of SSL/TLS for high-traffic web properties. They can also be used to proxy SSL connections to provide insight into otherwise-encrypted network communication. These tools can be implemented in coordination with other network monitoring tools, such as IDS/IPS and network forensics, to help regain visibility into network traffic within the local network that has been lost thanks in large part to increased use of SSL/TLS for transport encryption.

h. Network Forensics

An emerging niche tool market is that of network forensics. As data and processing move out of local data centers into cloud computing environments, so does the ability to perform forensic analysis on those servers. Instead, network forensics allows for full packet capture and analysis that can provide a much more effective analysis of network traffic, including monitoring for various attacks, as well as data leakage. These tools have become reasonably mature in recent years and represent a potentially useful capability for analyzing the kinds of traffic and data that are flowing through the network. Combined with SSL accelerators (proxies), these tools can have a much more complete view into network traffic to provide an even more complete analysis. These tools also typically integrate with SIEM systems to help facilitate more effective monitoring, alerting, and response.

B. Physical Security

Physical security focuses primarily on the protection of people, physical infrastructure, equipment, and hardware, or the use of physical means to protect valuable resources such as people, information, and equipment.[152] Physical security goes beyond locked doors and cabinets. It includes security cameras, barriers through landscaping, gates, guards, traps, and so on as well as environmental controls such as fire and smoke alarms and earthquake and flood protections, plus procedures to keep mobile equipment secured. All these controls are designed to limit or deny access to unauthorized persons and to protect employees, valuable data, and equipment.

Physical security also includes training employees to remain alert, recognize suspicious persons or activity, and be aware of their surroundings and property, including while they are outside work or traveling. Theft of laptops and loss of backup tapes are common causes of data breach—indeed, more common than intrusion by hackers. Physical security, much more so than other types of security, requires training. For example, piggybacking, in which an employee swipes his or her badge to enter a space and another person walks in behind without swiping his or her own badge (assuming the person has one) is a security concern. Training employees on proper physical security practices and how to prevent or avoid bad practices, as well as how to optimize the use of existing procedures, will enhance overall information security effectiveness.

Because the requirements for physical and environmental security controls have been around since the days of the earliest data centers, the principles of protecting the physical premises and preparing for environmental threats (e.g., fire, flood, earthquake, power loss) where the most expensive information assets are located are well established in almost all organizations. What has changed with the vast increase in the number of users accessing networks remotely is the location of those users and access devices. Theft protection/recovery devices and enhanced user awareness in conjunction with principles explained elsewhere in this chapter, such as encryption, provide appropriate physical security controls for mobile employees. And given the increasing need to protect data, equipment disposal procedures must be enhanced to prevent data leakage when equipment is removed from service. The impact of mobile computing and cloud computing on physical security is further discussed in Chapter 7.

C. Personnel Security

People store, access, and use data. An organization can have excellent physical security controls, but those controls may be defeated by a single negligent or malicious employee. Except in the area of national security and the military, personnel security tends to be the most critical yet overlooked component of information security. Risky or malevolent behavior in a technically secure environment can still lead to breaches in confidentiality, integrity, and availability. While an unaware employee can be as dangerous as a malicious one, a malicious employee with unrestricted access and intimate knowledge of internal systems and their vulnerabilities might be the most dangerous threat. Thus, good person-

152. *See generally,* Lawrence Fennelly, Effective Physical Security, 3d ed. (2003); Search Security and Tech Target (Dec. 15, 2005), http://searchsecurity.techtarget.com/sDefinition/0,,sid14_gci1150976,00.html.

nel processes that cover hiring, training, employment, and post-employment transition are essential in reducing the information security risk from human conduct.[153]

1. *Preemployment Screening*

An organization should implement controls to ensure that it is hiring both competent and trustworthy employees. The organization should have a procedure to investigate applicants to ensure that a job candidate is qualified and that the candidate has not misrepresented his or her qualifications. Personnel controls at the hiring stage include: (1) job descriptions requiring applicants to be trustworthy and possess necessary skills, (2) background checks that cover civil, criminal, credit, and educational history, and (3) a follow-up on background check results and on character references, previous experience, and other available resources (e.g., an Internet search may reveal comments, personal interests, and photos associated with the applicant's professional and social networks).

One critical issue to consider is the organization's Consent, Authorization, Waiver, and Release for Background Check document. How long ago was it updated? Does it authorize periodic checks during employment? Does it cover current applicable local and national law? For instance, most such forms in the United States will address the Fair Credit Reporting Act[154] (when an employer obtains a consumer credit report), but does the organization's background check authorization form cover other laws? Some character and professional references may not speak freely if they do not have immunity from defamation. Some laws provide for a waiver and release of civil liability in such situations. Other laws[155] may, however, grant additional rights to the job applicant. Thus, a thorough review of the potential legal issues implicated by the organization's background check authorization form is highly recommended.

2. *Orientation and Continuous Training*

Once the employee is hired, he or she should be given training and retraining on an organization's information security and privacy policies and procedures. Prior to accessing the organization's information systems, employees should sign: (1) a confidentiality agreement, (2) an acknowledgment that they received and understood the organization's information security and privacy policies and practices, and (3) a system access agreement (e.g., acceptable and authorized uses versus unacceptable or unauthorized uses of system resources).

The information security and privacy policy should be sufficiently broad so as to cover certain activity after hours, away from work, and when using personal resources. For example, conduct on social networking sites may facilitate social engineering attacks. However, such policies should also be reasonably drawn and reviewed by qualified coun-

---

153. For an overview of this area, see Jeffrey M. Stanton & Kathryn R. Stam, The Visible Employee: Using Workplace Monitoring and Surveillance to Protect Information Assets—Without Compromising Employee Privacy or Trust (2006).

154. Fair Credit Reporting Act, Pub. L. 91-508, 84 Stat. 1114 (Oct. 26, 1970), codified at 15 U.S.C. § 1681 *et seq.* (2010).

155. *See* Cal. Civ. Code § 1786.22 (Investigative Consumer Reporting Agencies Act).

sel to ensure compliance with applicable law, relative to the rights of employees.[156] The security policy acknowledgment should remind the employee of the disciplinary process for violations of policies or practices (e.g., oral warnings followed by written warnings followed by punishment). These documents can be combined as a signature page in the employee handbook or an information security handbook, but separating them out can help emphasize the organization's high priority on information security and privacy.

Monitoring employee use of company computers and communications systems can be an important part of an employer's information and security policy. Indeed, a failure to engage in some degree of monitoring may, in certain circumstances, even give rise to legal liability for failure to monitor.[157] However, it is also true that employer monitoring of employees can go too far and infringe on an employee's rights.[158] To the extent employee monitoring is included as part of an employer's information security and privacy policy, it is important for that policy to be spelled out in detail and acknowledged in advance in writing by employees. It is also critical to seek out professional advice in both crafting and executing the policy to ensure that it does not violate applicable law. An overly broad policy or one that is poorly executed may result in legal liability for the employer.[159]

Continuous information security training results in continuous improvements in the security posture of the organization. Information security and privacy concepts can be reinforced through regular communications. Ongoing security-awareness training in the kinds of threats and vulnerabilities facing the organization will sensitize employees to guard against various kinds of attacks and to identify, monitor, and report system or process vulnerabilities. For example, a good information security policy directive is this: "It is your responsibility to note and report any observed or suspected security weak-

---

156. *See* Konop v. Hawaiian Airlines, Inc., 302 F.3d 868 (9th Cir. 2002) (summary judgment denied to employer in litigation where employee alleged that employer unlawfully accessed and disclosed information from employee's private website); Pure Power Boot Camp v. Warrior Fitness Boot Camp, 587 F. Supp. 2d 548 (S.D.N.Y. 2008) (holding that employer's access of employee's personal e-mails maintained by an outside electronic communications service provider violated the Stored Communications Act).

157. *See* Doe v. XYC Corporation, 887 A.2d 1156 (N.J. App. Div. 2005) (the appellate court allowed a mother's lawsuit to proceed, which alleged that her husband's employer was liable for the husband's use of a workplace computer to access pornography and send nude photographs of the mother's daughter to a child porn site).

158. Various courts have rejected the blanket proposition that the employer's ownership of its computer systems, standing alone, is determinative of an employee's rights (or the employer's rights) relative to the employee's personal e-mails. *See, e.g.*, Stengart v. Loving Care Agency, 973 A.2d 390, 398–99 (N.J. App. Div. 2009) (observing that, under New Jersey law, "an employer's rules and policies must be reasonable to be enforced . . . . Stated another way, to gain enforcement in our courts, the regulated conduct should concern the terms of employment and reasonably further the legitimate business interests of the employer."); Thyroff v. Nationwide Mut. Ins. Co., 864 N.E.2d 1272, 1278 (N.Y. 2007) (New York's Court of Appeals held that an employee's breach of a company policy with regard to the use of its computers does not justify the company's claim of ownership of the employee's personal communications and information); *but see* United States v. Ziegler (9th Cir. 2007) (holding that an employer that (1) prohibited personal use of its computer system, (2) put employees on actual notice of that fact, and (3) maintained and exercised complete administrative access to such system could consent to a law enforcement search of an employee's hard drive on his workplace computer without his consent).

159. Watkins v. L.M. Berry & Co., 704 F.2d 577 (11th Cir. 1983) (in a suit by an employee alleging that the employer's conduct under its monitoring policy violated the federal Wiretap Act, the Court of Appeals for the 11th Circuit reversed the district court's grant of summary judgment in favor of the employer and remanded to the district court for further proceedings).

nesses in systems or services." Employees who are proactive at reporting threats, vulnerabilities, or system malfunctions may be able to assist management in closing those gaps in information security.

3. *Access Controls*

Personnel controls should also minimize the possibility of corruption by limiting an employee's access to only those areas that are necessary to the job function. In addition, employees should be restricted in their access so that the potential impact on the organization of a single careless or malicious employee is minimized. This restriction can be accomplished by classifying the kinds of information that the employee "needs to know" and then storing information in containers (file folders, databases, etc.) that are secured by authentication mechanisms that enforce the classification and minimize the degree of internal access. Broad, unrestricted access increases the risk of accidental damage to or loss of control over the information.

4. *Post-Employment*

Special termination procedures should be in place for employees leaving the organization. Termination controls include return of assets, collecting keys, and removing access to or deactivating accounts. A separation checklist is essential for ensuring that the employee and the organization have completed all termination tasks. The checklist also will help management review with the employee important provisions from the confidentiality agreement and remind him or her of security obligations and responsibilities that survive termination.

5. *Visitors and Contractors*

Organizations should have procedures for the supervision of visitors, contractors, and other persons who might temporarily have physical access to systems or logical access to information. Many regulated sectors such as health care and finance are now required to perform due diligence checks on vendors and temporary employees. The guidance provided earlier for employees should also be applicable for these nonemployees.

D. Application Security

Information security is often described as an effort to achieve "defense in depth." That description means that there are many layers to achieving a secure environment, starting with the device (such as a laptop or mobile PDA) and including the network that the device uses to communicate with remote servers and the applications running on those servers. Most security professionals today believe that while security vulnerabilities exist in all the layers, the most significant ones reside within the applications. This is true because applications are diverse, and the standards that apply to their design are not as prescriptive as those used for networks, which are based largely on international or vendor standards.

The threat against applications is both internal and external. People within an enterprise (malicious insiders), some of whom have accounts on the network or on the very applications themselves, can attack applications. People outside the enterprise (hackers or criminals) can attack applications over the Internet. While proper application security defends against both types of threats, external threats are usually easier to defend against.

Application vulnerabilities can be used as launching points for broader attacks against other applications, devices, or the network itself. All of this makes it critically important that applications be developed, installed, and maintained with security in mind. Given the complexity of the topic, it is useful to divide application security into these key elements:

- Establishing security requirements
- Designing the application to meet security requirements
- Specifying a conformant application configuration in production
- Testing and periodically scanning the production application

1. Key Elements of Application Security[160]

Applications are designed to accomplish tasks. To do so, they must fit within a network architecture, allow authorized users to take specified actions, create and maintain logs of such actions, and interact with other applications and services (such as databases). These requirements must be documented and must cover security considerations to ensure that only authorized users are permitted access, and then only to take permissible actions. The information being processed, managed, or stored by the application must be kept under proper control.

These considerations become the security "design requirements" for the application. They include ensuring that user passwords are securely stored, regulatory requirements (e.g., SOX, HIPAA, Safe Harbor, GLB) are met, and user authentication to the application is accomplished securely. Security requirements are normally defined in the beginning of a software development lifecycle (a disciplined, multistep process designed to ensure that the preparation of software follows a logical, consistent progression and garners appropriate sign-offs at each step).

Once the security requirements are specified, they must be built into the application. For example, if a security design requirement states that passwords used by the application must be changed periodically, the application design needs to allow such changes. Similarly, if communication between the user (at the endpoint, e.g., a laptop) and the application (on a remote server) needs to be kept confidential, then the communication path between the laptop and the server must be encrypted and the identity of the endpoints must be authenticated. These steps are often called "security engineering," which means the engineering necessary to ensure security requirements are addressed as part of application development.

In designing and implementing an application, designers must decide how to configure it in order to ensure that it will be secure once it begins operation. Application programs present many choices. There are user configuration choices available in the Preferences section or through the Tools or Options tabs. There are also even more significant installation configuration options. These options are established at the time the application is installed on the laptop, desktop, or server. They are usually transparent or

160. For application security generally, see, e.g., GARY MCGRAW, SOFTWARE SECURITY: BUILDING SECURITY IN (2006), and MICHAEL HOWARD, THE SECURITY DEVELOPMENT LIFECYCLE: SDL—A PROCESS FOR DEVELOPING DEMONSTRABLY MORE SECURE SOFTWARE (2006).

invisible to the user—that is, the user does not see them and has no opportunity to set them. The application owners established them.

Both types of configuration flexibility need to be "locked down" from a security standpoint, by specifying a standard configuration of security settings and then implementing that configuration in a fashion that cannot be altered except by those who have authority to do so. The unauthorized ability to override security configuration settings is a key mechanism used to defeat application security.

Once the properly configured application has been designed and is ready for production, its security behavior must be tested and verified. This is the final step prior to production to prove that the application actually meets its security requirements. The testing at this stage usually involves vulnerability scans (looking for known weaknesses) and penetration tests (looking for how well the application can resist a focused attack). Vulnerability scanning is usually done with automated tools and requires a moderate level of testing skill. Penetration testing, by contrast, is typically done by highly skilled technical personnel.

After the application is placed into production, it must be periodically checked and tested to ensure that its configuration is not deviating from the selected standards. It also must be checked to ensure that it is being patched to correct vulnerabilities that may have been identified after the start of production. Automated tools usually perform these functions.

2. *Additional Areas of Concern*

Applications are like any other user—they need to have accounts and passwords to access other applications and services. How applications store and manage the information needed for this purpose is of particular concern. For example, if an application needs to access a database, the application is issued its own database account and password for that access. Usually this password is held in a configuration file within the application and written to the hard drive of the server on which the application is installed.

The vulnerability presented by this situation is that anyone who has authorization to access that server hard drive may be able to see that file and obtain the password. There are often many individuals who have such elevated privileges (e.g., system or database administrators). Thus, these credentials must be properly protected against compromise, such as by storing them in an encrypted file or ensuring that the number of people who can access the file is limited, with all access to the file recorded.

Logging application activity is another area of concern. One of the first steps in any investigation of potentially abnormal behavior is reviewing system or application logs. Logs represent a record of what transpired on a system or in an application (i.e., what actions the application took, what human actions were taken on the application, the grant or revocation of account privileges, and successful—or failed—login attempts). Logs may be incomplete and, in some cases, susceptible to alteration. There are sophisticated techniques available to preclude unauthorized alteration, but many applications do not employ them. This concern reinforces the first, critical element of application security: what were the security design requirements for application logging, and how well were they implemented?

When being audited, the issue of separation of duties in user and administrative accounts will arise. While improper segregation of duties may entail security risks in theory, it is not always the case in practical application. Consider two scenarios that illustrate the dichotomy:

- A person holding an account with elevated privileges on a server that also hosts an application also has an account within the application itself. This situation could pose a security vulnerability because the individual has the ability to adjust the configuration of the application or alter log files, as well as take actions (such as executing transactions) within the application.
- A person holding a normal user account in an application is given a second user account that is allowed to approve actions initiated by the first account. A classic example of this scenario is someone holding both an accounts receivable role and an accounts payable role. In essence, the user is given overt permission to do things that may allow fraudulent behavior. However, the user has no ability to change system or application configuration or to use his or her privileges to circumvent security controls.

In order for application security to be achieved, it must be addressed during the entire lifecycle of the application, beginning with the design stage through and including the administration of user privileges. The change management process, including module promotion and testing criteria, is vital to ensure inappropriate code is not introduced into applications during authorized revisions.

E. Incident Management

While operating their information security management system, organizations must be able to respond to security incidents. This response means not only reacting to an incident that has already occurred but also working proactively to note any vulnerabilities that could lead to future incidents. In responding to incidents, the organization's management needs to ensure that the incident is contained, quarantined, eradicated if possible, and monitored and that affected systems are recovered based on preestablished procedures. Immediate efforts should be made to discover the cause, classify the incident so that appropriate resources are involved, collect appropriate evidence, report the incident to appropriate stakeholders, and review the incident with appropriate technical and management resources so that the organization learns from each such incident and that all necessary follow-up actions occur.

There are variety of tools, techniques, and procedures that information security incident management relies upon, including the controls in the sections discussed earlier. Review of system, network, security, application, and audit trail logs across all these functions; specialized monitoring tools including intrusion detection systems, firewalls, and malware detectors; and reporting by users are all sources of security incident reporting. Those involved in security incident management must be aware of what is occurring with other related processes, such as application change management, systems change management (including patching and automated changes/downloads), and capacity planning. Clearly defined escalation procedures should exist (supported by process flow documents), with both predefined escalation criteria (e.g., time, severity, data or process criticality, customer impact) and responsible individuals at each escalation level. All security incidents should eventually be closed and the information gained added to the organization's knowledge base to prevent recurrence of the same or similar incidents.

For assistance is designing or improving an incident management set of controls, the NIST has published a guide that takes an organization through the listed steps of an incident, from preparation for incidents to detection and analysis of incidents to containment and eradication to recovery and what should be done to follow up after the incident.[161]

Some metrics to measure an incident management program by include:

- Total number of reported and detected incidents
- Average time to respond and resolve an incident
- Total number of incidents successfully resolved
- Total number of employees receiving security awareness training
- Total damage from reported and detected incidents
- Total savings from potential damage from incidents resolved

Two specialized cases of incident management are disasters, where predefined and previously tested business continuity plans and disaster recovery plans must be invoked, and data breaches, which also require predefined and hopefully previously tested procedures. Response to a data breach, including forensic techniques, is discussed in Chapter 6. The legal obligations of business continuity were discussed in Chapter 2. What follows are the planning and control aspects of business continuity.

F. Business Continuity

Business continuity involves the ability of an organization to keep its data and systems available in the event of a disaster or failure. The event can be a natural disaster, a pandemic, terrorism, other malicious acts, unintentional acts, or the failure of power sources, other utilities, hardware, software, or network resources. It is often paired with disaster recovery, which involves the rebuilding of facilities and system capability after the disaster. As such, they may run in parallel or may run sequentially but to the end-users, business continuity is the key activity in terms of availability. Business continuity planning (BCP) looks at the risks of disasters and the business impacts of each and then designs preventive and reactive controls, much as is done for the information security and privacy risks. When disasters strike, confidential, secret, personally identifiable, or sensitive data may be exposed, and business continuity plans must take into account how to protect this information when potentially using a different business continuity infrastructure.

1. RTO/RPO

BCP incorporates the concepts of recovery time objective (RTO) and recovery point objective (RPO). RTO is the maximum amount of time after a disaster that a system and its data must be available to users, while RPO is the point of data and system consistency to which the recovery should occur (i.e., the maximum amount of allowable data loss). The business impact analysis developed in the risk assessment process for information security and privacy is extended here to cover the impact of the loss of business processes. These impacts feed into the risk assessment of business continuity threats and

161. NIST SP 800-61 Rev. 1, *Computer Security Incident Handling Guide* (2008).

vulnerabilities, prioritized after determining the likelihood of occurrence. Risk management determines the composition of the key proactive and reactive actions in the BCP, followed by risk monitoring and review.

2. Key Attributes

Several key activities must be incorporated into the BCP. These include:

- Setting of scope for BCP activities
- Procedures for declaration of an emergency
- Predefined roles and responsibilities, including secondary and tertiary resources
- Call lists and escalation criteria
- Communications plan, including with external emergency personnel
- Evacuation plans
- Scenario creation for the impact of each type of failure and disaster
- Priority order for recovering each information resource based on scenarios
- Acquisition of secondary processing site and equipment and determination of the most appropriate type of site (cold, warm, hot)
- Design, implementation, and testing of failover and redundancy in hardware, software, and network capabilities
- Data backup, mirroring, off-site storage and retrieval, and transaction commit/rollback logging and system checkpointing
- Remote access/office capabilities in case of loss of organization business facilities
- Procedures for acquiring end-user and system hardware and software in case of disaster
- Testing of BCP, including on paper and using real facilities
- Training of all involved parties
- Reassessing BCP on a regular basis to analyze new risks

3. Standards

No single international standard exists in this area; rather, several address this evolving field. ISO has released its initial guideline as ISO/PAS 22399,[162] based on best practices from leading countries, with the follow-up expected in 2011.[163] The most influential standard globally is the British Standards Institution's BS 25999.[164] The leading standard in the United States is NFPA 1600.[165] Other countries such as Canada, Japan, Singapore, Israel, and Australia have their own national standards. There is also national legislation in several countries, including countries as geographically diverse as the United Kingdom, South Africa, New Zealand and South Korea, that

162. ISO 22399: 2007, *Societal Security—Guideline for Incident Preparedness and Operational Continuity Management.*

163. ISO/CD 22301, *Societal Security—Preparedness and Continuity Management Systems—Requirements.*

164. British Standards Institution, BS25999-1: 2006, *Code of Practice for Business Continuity Management* and BS25999-2: 2007, *Specification for Business Continuity Management.*

165. NFPA Standard 1600 on Disaster/Emergency Management and Business Continuity Programs.

addresses disaster preparation and management, as was discussed in Chapter 2. But much more significant are regulations for covered entities in regulated industries such as finance and energy, spelling out the need and procedures for responding to disasters. For example, FFIEC has its own handbook on BCP,[166] and NIST has released a guide for contingency planning.[167]

For BCP and information security and privacy, the organization must try to ensure that:

- Failure of any hardware, software, or network resource or the cumulative effect of a disaster does not impact the information security and privacy controls;
- Controls on business continuity hardware, software, and networks implement the same or equivalent information security and privacy controls as under the normal mode of operations;
- The legal consequences of any disaster or failure are included in the risk assessment and disaster response activities;
- The BCP is in compliance with all applicable statutes, regulations, and standards; and
- Legal and information security technologists are involved in the creation, testing, and review of the BCP.

G. Privacy

Beyond the information security controls are a series of controls implemented to comply with privacy requirements. These controls are highly dependent on the privacy statutes for all jurisdictions where the organization does business but should include at least the following privacy policies, both in print and disseminated internally to the organization and on each applicable website.

1. *Privacy Policies*

Privacy policy: The privacy policy should include how the organization collects and uses the consumer's personally identifiable information; the nature of information collected, including site navigation; the use of technologies like cookies and beacons; security controls; restrictions on third-party and affiliate disclosures; whom to contact for questions about the website; and how notification of changes to the policies is carried out.

Web-based privacy policy: The privacy policy should be posted on each website (and always linkable from each page) that is used to collect information from consumers for purposes of e-commerce, social networking, or other types of websites. It should also explain how links to third-party sites affect the privacy policy. See Chapter 6 for further discussion of a best practices policy.

166. FFIEC, IT Examination Handbook—*Business Continuity Planning* (2008).
167. NIST SP 800-34 Rev. 1, *Contingency Planning Guide for Federal Information Systems* (2010).

2. Privacy Controls

The privacy controls should include at least the following:

- Privacy notices, including online posting of notices
- Documentation of ownership, location, media, and all steps in the personal data privacy lifecycle: collection, storage, usage, sharing, transferring to 3P, retention, and destruction
- The stated purposes of collection and use of personally identifiable and sensitive data
- The sources/origins of collected data, including third parties, website URLs and IP addresses, web beacons, widgets and cookies, and GPS/location-based services
- Personal and sensitive data retention periods and disposal/destruction methodologies
- Understanding of and limitations on the roles and locations of any user of the collected personal or sensitive data
- Transfers to and processing by third parties and restrictions thereof (e.g., sale to third parties)
- Data subject approvals as required, such as for secondary uses, use of sensitive data, etc.
- Data subject access and correction controls, including how to verify the data subject is who he or she claims to be
- Visible accountability to data subjects, including maintenance of the privacy policy and program
- Contractual clauses mandating protection of data, confidential and personal, belonging to the organization and its customers and employees
- Controls affecting what minors can do and view online
- Privacy awareness education and in-depth training for anyone involved with personal information collection, storage, use, and destruction
- Data breach procedures and data subject notification procedures, including statutory requirements in each applicable jurisdiction

CHAPTER 6

Information Security and Privacy Best Practices

When designing and implementing the information security and privacy program described in Chapters 4 and 5, it is critical to benchmark against the best practices in this discipline. Best practices should be understood as the minimum aspirations for an organization's policies, procedures, and controls. Due to the unique requirements of individual organizations and their differing geographies, industries, and clients, no one set of best practices will govern the ultimate selections by any organization. But any variances from accepted best practices should be justified and documented. This chapter begins with some best practices that should be appropriate for almost any organization's information security and privacy policies. It then discusses in more detail a best practice approach to responding to a data breach, including working with external resources. After the best practice policies and controls have been implemented, their effectiveness must be assessed and reported to external stakeholders. So the final section of the chapter discusses information security, privacy, and website audits and certifications.

What Global Executives Need to Know

- How the organization's information security and privacy policies compare to best practices
- The compliance of the organization's website privacy policies with the statutes and regulations in all countries where the organization has customers
- The organization's plan to respond to data breach in all locations where it collects, uses, or stores personal data
- The types of information security and privacy audits the organization undergoes and the key findings from these reports
- The status of the organization's pursuit of information security and privacy certifications and trustmarks

6.1 INFORMATION SECURITY AND PRIVACY POLICIES

The policies listed in this section illustrate many of the key provisions in best practice information security and privacy policies. The direction set by these policies will lead to the controls covered in depth in Chapter 5. As such, the policies related to some of those controls will not be repeated here, but can be easily abstracted from the discussion in the previous chapter. Although stated as separate policies in this discussion, for documentation, presentation, and training purposes, these policies may be consolidated into a single information security and privacy policy, with many subpolicies included.

A. Policies Involving Business Judgment

These information security and privacy policies require significant input from senior leadership of the organization. The nature and implementation of these policies may vary radically from one organization to another. Decisions on the most appropriate design of these policies will involve input from a variety of departments and require executive oversight to ensure organization-wide acceptance and follow-through.

1. Top-Level Information Security and Privacy Policy

The purpose of a written information security and privacy policy is to demonstrate the organization's commitment to information security and privacy. The policy therefore not only should be approved by the highest-level leadership possible but must be communicated and practiced from the top. It must apply to all members of the organization, including all those external parties who interact with the organization. An individual should be designated to head the organization's information security and privacy efforts. This individual must be empowered to make decisions quickly when necessary to safeguard systems or data. This policy should articulate the complexity of information security and privacy and the need for all policy-level changes to be vetted by legal counsel. The policy should be reviewed on a regular basis—no less than annually—and revised accordingly.

The policy should also describe the roles of the various stakeholders in the information security and privacy program. These stakeholders include executive management, the owners of information, the users of information, the business departments, internal audit, and the information security and privacy departments. Executive management must meet regularly to review the state of information security and privacy in the organization, make decisions about any identified information security and privacy risks, and allocate sufficient resources to be able to carry out these responsibilities.

2. Risk Management Program

All organizations must adopt a risk management program, as described in Chapter 4. The goal of the risk management program is to provide the information necessary for the organization's leadership to make the business decisions necessary to reduce risk. In short, the program identifies and quantifies those risks faced by the organization and provides cost-benefit analysis of potential mitigation options. A risk-management program provides the risk-weighted analysis upon which to base risk reduction, retention, transfer/sharing, and avoidance decisions.

3. Acceptable Use Policy

An acceptable use policy provides guidance to employees and leaders by outlining how the organization's information systems are to be used, in the workplace and remotely. The policy should also specifically describe which uses are strictly prohibited. A typical acceptable use policy will state that information systems provided by the company (1) shall be used only for business purposes; (2) shall not be used to harass, discriminate against, or defame others; (3) shall not be accessed by unauthorized persons; (4) shall not be used to access pornographic material; and (5) shall not be used to violate or aid in the violation of intellectual property rights.

The recent Supreme Court decision on the use of an organization's information devices by its public sector employees should provide employers with sufficient foundation to perform reasonable audits covering the use of corporate assets by employees but in all cases organizations should make it clear in their written policies and in awareness training that is the organization's intent to monitor and audit their employees' use of all corporate information assets.[1]

Acceptable use policies should not be overly restrictive, as this can create problems, and should therefore be approached pragmatically. As employees are expected to abide by such policies, a clear distinction must be made between productivity and security measures. It should also be made clear that the objective is risk-weighted security, not simply employee monitoring. Personal uses such as web surfing, even when performed on an employee's personal time, can open computer systems to innumerable Internet-based threats. Where an organization does allow personal use of an organization's information assets, employees should be provided with appropriate tools and training to ensure that all such use is performed under appropriate safeguards.

Acceptable use policies must address use of the Internet, including the downloading of files and all types of software (nonapproved and approved) and the proper usage of company and external blogs, use of the organization's e-mail and other communication systems, use of personal e-mail systems from work locations or on work equipment, access to inappropriate or disallowed websites, and the use of social networking and messaging services. While the employee's access to these services may utilize a personal account, if done on corporate equipment or corporate time or if it can be linked back to the organization, then express limits must be stated and disseminated to all users.

Restrictive acceptable use policies should not be undertaken lightly. Many employees, particularly tech-savvy young employees, will react negatively to limitations on how they communicate. A boilerplate "no personal use" policy is rarely effective and often foments an "us versus them" culture whereby employees take steps to hide evidence of personal uses. The adoption of liberal, flexible, acceptable policies is therefore a defensible business decision.

4. Access Compartmentalization

No person should be given access to sensitive data or information systems beyond that needed for his or her role. Strictly hierarchical access-granting structures should

---

1. City of Ontario, Cal. v. Quon, 130 S. Ct. 2619 (June 2010).

be avoided, as seniority within an organization does not warrant greater access. Lateral compartmentalization protects systems from accidental interference by unqualified persons and reduces the damage done if security devices such as encryption keys fall into the wrong hands. This policy even applies to executives operating outside their organizational responsibilities.

The scope of an employee's clearance should be defined by his or her day-to-day needs, not by the theoretical limits of that employee's job description. For example, an employee may on occasion make emergency repairs to a critical system. The employee would of course need access to that system, but this temporary need does not mean that the employee requires 24/7 access. When the occasional emergency occurs, the employee can then be granted temporary access or be directly supervised as a guest.

Guests, if they are to be given access to organization resources, should never be allowed access to sensitive information, and their access should always be granted with a preset termination date.

5. Communications Monitoring Policy

Organizations must decide whether they have a business interest in monitoring electronic communications. Communications monitoring, particularly of customer communications, may also have negative business consequences. A hotel might provide Internet access to patrons, but many patrons would react negatively to warnings that the websites they visit while in their rooms were being monitored. The technological systems for monitoring can themselves be subject to abuse, particularly by those wishing to blackmail or spy upon others. Use of the monitoring system must therefore itself be subject to monitoring. Given these complexities, organizations must carefully decide whether they have an actual business interest in the adoption of a monitoring policy.

Communications monitoring may run afoul of wiretap legislation (discussed in Chapter 3). Other safe harbor legislation may also protect organizations from liability where they choose not to engage in monitoring. Organizations must therefore consult legal counsel regarding any changes to communications monitoring policies.

The communications monitoring policy ensures that users realize and affirm that communications via company equipment may be monitored. Organizations should adopt such a policy regardless of whether they presently engage in active monitoring.

If an organization has a business need to monitor e-mail or other forms of digital communication, it must clearly disclose to employees, business partners, customers, and other communicators who access the organization's equipment that such access constitutes express consent to monitoring. This policy must be outlined and disclosed to the user prior to use of the equipment. The user should be required to acknowledge that he or she is aware of any monitoring policy prior to accessing the equipment, and such acknowledgment should be recorded if possible.

Although communication equipment and the electronic data generated by or stored within that equipment are generally considered the property of the organization, various statutes prohibit the monitoring of wire and electronic communications unless some exception applies. Consequently, an employer generally may not monitor the use of the equipment, including e-mail, unless it does so to protect an organization's assets or obtains the consent of the individual parties to such communications. The statutes are discussed in Chapter 2.

Monitoring can take many forms, but may involve verbatim recording of communications. This action presents privacy and security concerns. Access to intercepted communications must be restricted to a similar degree as the communications themselves. For instance, allowing IT auditors to intercept communications involving the organization's legal counsel may impact attorney-client privilege. It may be that some intercepted activity, particularly communications either to or from an attorney, should never be subject to verbatim monitoring.

6. Breach Reporting

Security breaches must be planned for. Employees should be encouraged to report any unusual activity, regardless of whether they believe a breach has occurred. Something as innocuous as a sluggish computer may be evidence of a major security breach. There are three forms of breach, each requiring a different protocol:

- *Breaks from policy or established routine:* Such events are the lowest form of breach and may or may not present a security risk. Leaders should note them and, where appropriate, pass the information along to the risk management team for further evaluation. Any incident involving sensitive data must be reported.
- *Detected breaches:* Any incident involving unauthorized access to information systems containing sensitive data, or any other breach of security protocols, must be reported to both risk management and legal counsel. Risk management will determine the extent of the breach, and legal counsel whether breach notification obligations have been triggered.
- *Potential vulnerabilities or undetectable breaches of system security:* An undetectable breach is one that, if it had occurred in the past, would not have been detected. So-called zero-day vulnerabilities (discussed in Chapter 4) are typical in that while the vulnerability has existed for some time, it has only recently become known to the organization. All such vulnerabilities require immediate investigation by the risk management team, regardless of whether any actual breach has been detected. The risk management team will then report its findings to both legal counsel and leadership.

Response to data breach is discussed in more detail later in this chapter.

7. Outsourcing

Before outsourcing any activity involving sensitive information, organizations must consult qualified legal counsel. Many jurisdictions now regulate how organizations handle personal and sensitive information. Regardless of legal obligations, every organization considering outsourcing should ensure that the contracted provider enforces equivalently robust security policies and practices. Any agreement should carefully delineate responsibilities, risks, and liabilities borne by the organization and those borne by the service provider. Organizations should strive to monitor and supervise the provider's personnel and periodically audit the provider's performance. The organization should maintain contingency plans in the event that the provider is no longer able to perform.

"Equivalently robust" requires line-item comparison of the information security and privacy policies. The two organizations may have equivalent general policies and may even be certified by the same organizations, but that is not enough. The outside organization must maintain equivalent or higher standards in every respect. Any deficiency in the external organization, should it result in a breach, will defeat any notion of equivalence. If the organization has determined that 256-bit encryption is the required minimum for its data, outsourcing to an external organization using 128-bit encryption would increase its risk, regardless of whether 128-bit encryption would normally be considered sufficient. Each standard and control utilized by the external organization must be clearly understood.

Outsourcing, especially to vendors operating outside the organization's country, introduces new security issues. The movement of data to and from the external organization will normally occur via the Internet, necessitating encryption. The external organization may be subject to a very different legal regime in the other country. Many governments are not burdened by the same warrant requirements prior to accessing electronic information as may be used domestically. Intellectual property and contract rights also differ greatly around the globe. Additionally, any information regarding governments, defense, or other high technology may be subject to export limitations. Therefore legal counsel, including international legal counsel, must be consulted prior to the outsourcing of any sensitive information across national boundaries.

8. Document Retention

An effective document retention policy (DRP) will address which documents need to be retained, the purpose for which they are to be retained, and stated retention periods. The DRP should also outline a system for identifying whether any alterations have been made to a document, including any associated metadata, while in storage. If changes are to be permitted, the DRP should describe who is permitted to make such changes and outline a method to record what, how, and when changes are made. Normally this verification is accomplished through a combination of digital signatures and hashing. The DRP should describe a method and schedule for the effective destruction of documents that need no longer be retained. Such documents should be destroyed as soon as practicable. Permanent storage should be considered only where required by law, regulations, or other rules governing the organization.

9. Other

A policy should describe how change control is practiced in all aspects of the organization's hardware, software, and network resources, including those done by third-party providers. The software development lifecycle and the promotion process must also be described in a policy. The separation of duties must be shown between those with the ability to change applications and systems and those who own and act as custodians for data. No developer or systems administrator should have the ability to initiate and approve his or her own changes into production. And commitment to third-party verifications, such as external information security audits and network and application penetration testing and vulnerability analyses, should be part of the organization's policy.

B. Technical Policies

Technical policies cover areas that, while still important, are more technical in nature. The specifics of each will be less a matter of business judgment and more of technological expertise. Senior leadership must still oversee and approve these policies, but will normally rely on expert opinion as to their design, implementation, and effectiveness.

1. Encryption

The proper use of encryption technology is a cornerstone of information security. Encryption protects data from being read by unauthorized persons. Many organizations are subject to legal or contractual requirements that certain data remain encrypted. Above and beyond these, an organization's encryption policy should demand that all data be encrypted whenever possible. The policy should address three distinct areas:

- *Data at rest:* Data that is stored on media is considered "at rest" in that it is not moving through a network. This data should always be encrypted in a manner that protects it should the media containing it be lost or stolen.
- *Data in transit:* Data or other communications moving across a network must remain properly encrypted if the network through which it moves is in any way accessible by persons not authorized to read the data. All sensitive information transitioning the Internet must be encrypted.
- *Data in use:* There are times when data simply cannot be encrypted. Data displayed on a computer screen or on printed paper cannot be encrypted and simultaneously be readable. Similarly, data stored on Random Access Memory modules with computer systems cannot be easily encrypted. The encryption policy should anticipate these situations. Encryption cannot answer every security threat. It may be necessary that some data never be displayed outside a physically secured environment.

The appropriate method of encryption will depend on the circumstances. See Chapter 5 for an in-depth discussion of which method to use in each circumstance.

2. Wireless Communications

Given the increasing prevalence of mobile devices, all organizations must adopt a wireless communications policy regardless of whether they plan on using wireless technology. All communications transitioning to a wireless connection must be treated as transitioning a publicly accessible medium. Communications containing sensitive information must therefore be encrypted, but the risk of eavesdropping is so great that all wireless communications should probably be encrypted.

All wireless transmissions that may contain sensitive information should, over and above TLS, be encrypted via Wi-Fi Protected Access 2.0 (WPA2) or better. Wired Equivalent Privacy (WEP) should not be used under any circumstances, as it is an easy target for cracking. The encryption keys used should be treated as the most important passwords. They should be computationally very complex (16 characters or more), subject to extensive wordlist testing, and changed monthly.

All employees using wireless technologies must be trained in their safe use. Where public wireless networks are used (i.e., the cellular networks) it may not be possible to implement wanted encryption protocols. Employees must recognize such situations and restrict their activities appropriately.

3. Password Policy

Memorized passwords are by far the most common method of authentication used. Organizations should adopt a password policy suited to their particular security needs and the attacks to which the password may be subject. Longer passwords using a wider range of characters are computationally more complex and are therefore less subject to guessing, "brute force," or dictionary attacks. They are therefore considered more secure, but complex passwords are more difficult for humans to remember. Passwords that are too short are insecure, too long and users start writing them down on notepads which are eventually lost or stolen, defeating the purpose of the password.

Passwords should be altered periodically. This alteration will reduce the useful life of any copied or stolen password but if done too often will cause users to either simplify their passwords or write them down. Organizations should realize that a compromised password will be misused within hours if not minutes. Forcing users to renew their passwords on even a daily basis will not prevent this. The renewal period should therefore be based on the password's susceptibility to attack or theft and the importance of the authentication for which it is used. Renewal of important passwords should require authorization from multiple persons.

All new passwords should be checked against lists of commonly used passwords. Many such wordlists are available commercially. A good list will contain hundreds of millions of words.

4. Authentication of Persons

There is no single best practice for authentication of persons. The degree of rigor applied to any particular authentication should vary depending on the nature of the privileges granted by that authentication. For instance, an authentication procedure prior to permitting a person access to sensitive customer information should be more rigorous than that used in deciding whether to allow access to the company cafeteria. Organizations should establish specific written policies outlining both general procedures and specific requirements for access to crucial systems or information.

There are three primary methods of authenticating physical persons:

- *Something they know*, typically a secret password.
- *Something they have* or an object they possess, such as an employee badge or security token. The reliability of this method depends on the reliability of the authentication process prior to the issuance of the object and the chances that the object has been copied or stolen.
- *Something they are* or a physical measurement (e.g., a fingerprint). Often referred to as "biometrics," this form of authentication runs the gamut from the ability of a security guard to recognize a face to an electronic scan of the person's retinal blood vessels.

The three approaches are normally combined. For access to critical systems or locations, a person may have a password, a smart card or other token, and an employee badge with a picture. But no matter how many credentials are used, they are no more reliable than the process behind them. Therefore it is vitally important to thoroughly vet everyone prior to issuing them any sort of security credential. See Chapter 5 for an in-depth discussion of authentication.

5. *Authentication of Network Actors or Information Systems*

Authentication of persons within computer networks presents unique difficulties. Without face-to-face interaction, persons must be identified via possession of passwords, codes, or other data. Biometrics aren't a realistic option, but cryptographic tokens such as smart cards are still useful. The greater challenge is authentication of nonhuman network actors. Websites and other network locations can be faked or "spoofed" in an effort to acquire sensitive information.

The answer to this problem involves third-party authentication via digital certificates. Certificates are digital tokens that allow their holder to prove that it is what it claims to be. For instance, a bank's website will have a certificate issued to that bank by a certificate authority whose digital signature is integrated into the certificate. Those accessing the website can trust that the website is under the control of the bank because they trust the certificate authority. In such situations the user's web browser software will indicate that the connection is both trusted and encrypted. The entire system has been integrated into the TLS cryptographic standard. Any transmission of sensitive information between systems across a public network should utilize TLS or a similar certificate-based protocol. Organizations should also outline which certificate authorities are to be trusted and ensure that their systems are configured appropriately.

6. *Authentication of Electronic Communications*

As with persons, data itself must be authenticated prior to being allowed access to information systems. The standard technique involves the use of digital signatures. These tools, through the cryptographic methods discussed in Chapter 5, allow the recipient of data to verify the identity of the sender and detect whether the data has been altered in transit. All important data, even if not encrypted, should be accompanied by a digital signature. This is especially true for e-mail. All employees using e-mail or similar methods should be trained in the safe use of digital signatures.

7. *Disaster Recovery Policies*

Disaster recovery and business continuity policies should be broad enough to encompass any number of disasters that might realistically befall the organization, from natural disasters that may physically destroy equipment to denial-of-service attacks that may restrict access to networks. These policies should include measures to ensure that crucial information is backed up on alternative equipment, preferably off-site, so that business may continue despite the loss of one facility or set of equipment.

Disasters take many forms. Natural disasters are one, but more common are criminal actions or widespread hardware failures. Disaster and continuity plans are equally useful if an office is robbed of equipment or if the cooling system for the server room fails. A complete plan will also anticipate software failures such new zero-day vulnerabilities that can render software temporarily unreliable. Well-prepared organizations should be capable of moving to alternative software platforms as easily as they move to alternative hardware.

Disaster recovery policies should also anticipate the need to quickly abandon facilities. Floodwaters can rise in a matter of hours, and security guards cannot be expected to remain at their stations. In such situations, systems must be in place to remove, encrypt, or even destroy sensitive information prior to abandonment.

8. *Employee Termination*

Organizations must establish procedures to ensure that terminated employees have no access to secure information or secure areas. They should return all keys, access devices, and other tokens permitting access to physical locations or computer systems. Any user accounts and passwords for network access should be disabled. Organizations should also secure the return of critical property given to terminated employees, such as laptops.

Once the decision to terminate an employee has been made, the organization should move quickly to terminate the employee's access to critical or sensitive information prior to the employee learning of his or her termination. The former employee should then be treated as a guest. All further access to information systems, such as to retrieve personal files, should be strictly supervised. All memory devices, especially flash drives, should be either inspected or destroyed prior to leaving with the employee.

These procedures are equally applicable to the termination of business relationships with business partners, customers, contractors, or any other third parties who may have access to information systems.

9. *Intrusion Detection*

Organizations should make use of and maintain intrusion detection systems, network-monitoring software, and security assessment tools to detect attempts to penetrate the organization's networks. Organizations can either employ qualified personnel or outsource the process to a qualified security firm. The best approach is to do both.

Once an intrusion is detected, the organization must be capable of immediate action to identify an incident, contain any damage, and properly preserve evidence.

Organizations should perform periodic network penetration, or "pen," testing to determine whether their networks are vulnerable to attack. Such testing is most effective when both inside and outside personnel participate in planning and execution.

10. *Patching*

Software developers regularly release patches to update their application or systems software. These patches involve the installation of new software code, often without opportunity for security testing. Patching must therefore not be taken casually. The organization's technology team should remain alert to patch-related announcements and verify the authenticity of patches prior to installing them. Only qualified IT personnel should be allowed to install software patches. All major patches and all patches to critical systems should be recorded.

11. Anti-Phishing

Employees should be trained to be alert for social engineering attacks. Employees should be able to recognize suspicious e-mails or other communications asking for passwords or other private information. Such e-mails should never be responded to, but instead reported to the organization's information security team.

12. Malware

If applicable, organizations should obtain, install, and regularly update antivirus software for workstations and servers and all access devices to the extent possible with rapidly emerging technologies. The extent of and/or necessity for this protection will depend on the nature of the software running on each device and on known and unknown vulnerabilities and threats.

13. Elimination of Unnecessary Software Processes

Organizations should harden their operating systems, other software, and hardware using industry-recognized guidelines. For instance, organizations should remove or turn off unnecessary software services and applications, some of which may be turned on by default. The fewer the number of applications on a system, the easier it is to maintain its security.

14. Physical Security

All information systems are valuable, regardless of whether they contain sensitive information. All hardware devices should, at a minimum, be locked or otherwise protected from physical manipulation by nonauthorized persons. Critical systems should be behind locked doors manned by human security guards where necessary. Guests or other third parties in such areas should be heavily supervised by persons knowledgeable enough to detect suspicious behavior. Guests entering or leaving should be searched, both to deter theft and to guard against listening devices.

C. Website Privacy Policies

Organizations should have privacy policies posted on each customer-facing website, either because such posting is mandated by law or for reasons of business competitive advantage. These policies must include requirements from privacy statutes for all jurisdictions and industries that the organization operates within (as discussed in Chapter 2). For example, organizations operating websites in the United States involved with financial consumers must comply with the privacy policy set forth under GLBA. Those dealing with children must comply with the privacy policies dictated by COPPA, and those dealing commercially with California residents have a California state statute to comply with. The sum of such applicable statutes can serve as a minimum best practice for website privacy policies.

Website privacy policies explain an organization's policy with respect to use and disclosure of personal information collected from the user. In general, a privacy policy will address what type of information is collected, why it is collected, how it is used, and under what circumstances, if any, the information will be disclosed to third parties. In addition, a privacy policy will frequently explain whether cookies, web beacons, and similar devices are placed on a user's computer and, if so, why.[2]

It is also important that the privacy policy consider what happens if an organization were to go out of business or become bankrupt. In a recent case,[3] the potential sale of the names and personal information gathered from a bankrupt firm's website drew a letter from the FTC, stating that the sale or transfer of sensitive personal information to a new owner that occurs as part of a bankruptcy proceeding must be in accordance with the privacy policy of the bankrupt entity.[4] Otherwise the sale would be considered a deceptive or unfair business practice, in violation of section 5 of the FTC Act, as this company's privacy policy had stated that they would never transfer such information. The FTC Act is discussed in Chapter 2.

1. COPPA

Under COPPA, the website must post a link to its privacy policy on its home page and on every other page where personal information is collected. The link must be clear, prominent, and distinguishable from other links on the site. The notice itself must be clear and understandable and include the following information:

- the name and contact information of the operator of the website who is collecting or maintaining children's personal information obtained from the site;
- the kinds of information collected from children and how the information is collected (i.e., directly from the children or through cookies);
- how the website operator uses the information;
- whether the information is disclosed to third parties and, if so, the kinds of businesses to which information is disclosed and the general purpose for which the information is used;
- whether these third parties have agreed to any confidentiality or security of the information;
- the option to consent to the collection but not the disclosure of information to third parties;
- a disclosure that the website operator cannot require a child to disclose more information than is reasonably necessary to participate in an activity as a condition of participation; and
- the procedures to be followed by parents in reviewing a child's personal information, requesting that some be deleted, and refusing to allow any further collection or use of the child's information.[5]

A separate notice for parents must advise that the parents' consent is required for the collection, use, and disclosure of information and must explain how that consent is to be

---

2. Frequently, a privacy policy will explain that a cookie is used to enhance a user's experience on the website by recognizing the user and adding greater functionality for recognized users.

3. Letter from FTC's Bureau of Consumer Protection regarding XY brand name personal information (July 1, 2010).

4. *See* 11 USC § 363(b).

5. 16 C.F.R. pt. 312. *See* http://www.ftc.gov/ogc/coppa1.pdf.

given by the parents. A new notice and consent are required to be sent to parents when any material changes in the collection, use, or disclosure of information occur.

2. GLBA

GLBA also requires a privacy policy for consumers.[6] The privacy policy must disclose the categories of third parties to whom personal information will be disclosed, the policies and practices of the institution of disclosing personal information of people who are no longer customers, types of personal information collected, and the institution's confidentiality and security policies.[7] This privacy policy must be provided when a relationship with a consumer is established.[8] To facilitate the creation of privacy policies under GLBA, the FTC and other federal regulatory agencies released a final rule amending the GLBA privacy rules in late 2009.

The Final Model Privacy Form can be used by financial institutions to describe their privacy policies and how consumers can opt out of letting their information be disseminated to unaffiliated third parties. This form is not required, but its proper use will allow compliance (safe harbor) with the obligations for initial and annual notice to the consumer on disclosure of his or her nonpublic personal information and for opt-out procedures to prevent the sharing of his or her information with unaffiliated third parties. There are three versions of the model form, allowing opt-out by mail, opt-out by telephone/online, or no opt-out option. The existing sample clauses are no longer the approved safe harbor for compliance after December 31, 2010.

3. State Law

California's Online Privacy Protection Act[9] imposes privacy obligations on any "operator" of a website or online service if the website or online service has a commercial purpose and is accessed or used by a California resident. "Operator" is defined as "any person or entity that owns a Web site located on the Internet or an online service that collects and maintains personally identifiable information from a consumer residing in California who uses or visits the Web site or online service if the Web site or online service is operated for commercial purposes." The law mandates the use of a privacy policy that may be accessed from each website page and that contains the following information:

- the effective date of the policy;
- a list of the categories of personally identifiable information collected by the operator from consumers who use or access the website and a list of the types of third parties to whom the operator discloses such information;
- an explanation of how the operator will notify users if the privacy policy is materially changed; and

---

6. 15 U.S.C. §§ 6801–6809.

7. 15 U.S.C. § 6803(a).

8. Consumers include people who have applied for loans or used automated teller machines but have not used the institution for any further services.

9. Cal. Bus. & Prof. Code §§ 22575–22579.

- an explanation of how users may review and change their personally identifiable information—if the operator allows such review and changes—or a statement that the operator does not permit such review and changes.

6.2 RESPONSE TO DATA BREACH

Data breach can result in loss of intellectual property, employee personal and sensitive data, customer data held by the organization, or other corporate confidential or secret information. It can result in reputational harm; loss of business revenue and profit; loss of competitiveness; loss of employee, partner, or client confidence; and noncompliance with statutes, regulations, and standards. Regardless of what is breached, when any information is disclosed, modified, or lost due to a data breach, the organization must respond swiftly and effectively to the incident.

A. Incident Response Plan

Even organizations with a well-managed information security and privacy program must rigorously prepare for such a breach event. The incident response plan must include:

- Initiating of the computer incident response team (CIRT), whose members were selected based on the appropriate skill sets;
- Rapid assessment of the data breach activity to determine the type of incident and extent of its damage;
- Appropriate breach containment activities; and
- Guidelines for involving other parties, including law enforcement and officials requiring notification under data breach laws.

The CIRT should be a group within an organization that has various skills including technology officers (CTO, CISO), IT and information security staff, human resources staff, communications staff, and corporate counsel. Each CIRT member brings his or her area of expertise to ensure that the organization is properly responding to an incident. For the CIRT to be effective, it must have authorization to act quickly, in areas such as declaring, prioritizing, and escalating incidents, taking systems and networks off-line, contacting other parties, and deploying external resources. Reacting quickly to an incident requires an initial understanding of the incident and the extent of damage that was or may be caused by it.

B. Responding to an Incident

The assessment of incoming reports about the incident includes prioritization of incidents and verification about the nature of the incident. This assessment will help the business understand the balance of focus on remediation (i.e., preventing further damage to systems) and investigation (i.e., preserving evidence in order to track down the attacker). Companies should strive to both remediate and investigate—processes that often complement and enhance each other. In any situation, the incident must be fully documented while attempting to maintain the confidentiality of the information that was breached.

If an occurring incident has a detrimental effect on a business, one of the key steps is to identify and isolate the affected systems from the network without altering its files (i.e., not powering off the system, logging into it, or deleting any files). If an ongoing incident does not have an immediate business impact and information from monitoring the incident can assist with an investigation, it may be best to closely watch the activity. In any case, the incident investigation must stay active until the root cause is understood and the incident can be reviewed, appropriate remedial actions taken, and the episode officially closed. To create such procedures, organizations could, for example, start with the series of questionnaires ISACA developed to facilitate the evaluation of the internal controls necessary when responding to cyber incidents[10] and NIST SP 800-61 on security incident handling.[11]

The CIRT should decide whether to monitor or resolve the issue and may involve the assistance of law enforcement in this decision. In general, in determining when to contact law enforcement, companies should report incidents that are malicious and have a real and substantial impact on the organization or activity that is noteworthy as defined by the CIRT. Law enforcement should be contacted if an incident appears to involve criminal activity, indicated by any of the following events:

- An unauthorized user has logged on to the system, including root access;
- A heavy volume of packets has bombarded the system in a short period of time (from the same or varied sources) evidencing a denial-of-service attack;
- An incidence of social engineering has led to security breach;
- Continuous network scanning or probing is occurring;
- A demonstrated exploit of a public-facing website or web application has taken place; or
- The attack appears to be aimed at critical information or areas of the network affecting critical infrastructure.

Once an organization has decided to involve law enforcement in the activity, determining the proper agency can be complex. The Department of Justice's Computer Crime and Intellectual Property Section has compiled a useful table that lists the type of crime and the corresponding appropriate federal investigative law enforcement agencies.[12] In addition, *CIO* magazine, in conjunction with the U.S. Secret Service and the FBI, has issued response and reporting guidelines that list federal law enforcement agencies and their areas of responsibility, along with the local offices to contact in the event of an information security attack or breach.[13]

Reporting of an incident requires a careful analysis. Reporting to law enforcement or other agencies is often very difficult for companies because of fear of negative publicity. Not reporting, however, undermines general deterrence of computer crime, which leaves all networks much less secure. In addition to the benefit of deterring cybercrime, many state laws and contractual obligations require that certain breaches be reported. But there are also legal requirements to report to avoid civil or even criminal sanctions.

10. ISACA, *Cybercrime: Incident Response and Digital Forensics,* Internal Control Questionnaires (2005).
11. NIST SP 800-61 Rev 1, *Computer Security Incident Handling Guide* (2008).
12. Available at http://www.cybercrime.gov/reporting.htm.
13. Available at http://www.cio.com/research/security/incident_response.pdf.

Almost all U.S. states and many countries require some sort of notification after data breaches, especially when the data is not encrypted, is of a personally identifiable or sensitive nature, and affects the records of more than a stated number of individuals. Regulated companies should check with their regulator to determine if they have a duty to report incidents and to whom they should report, as such duties often will be industry-specific. For example, a financial institution may be required to complete a Suspicious Activity Report (SAR) and file the signed form with the Financial Crimes Enforcement Network (FinCEN).

If the cyber incident results in the unauthorized disclosure of unsecured[14] individually identifiable health information and is also a security breach[15] as defined in the HITECH Act,[16] HIPAA-covered entities are required to give notice of breach. Payment card brands such as Visa and MasterCard also have specific reporting requirements for retail merchants that suffer a data breach. In addition, some cyber insurance policies (discussed in Chapter 4) require the insured to report security incidents to law enforcement before a claim can be paid under the policy. Therefore, if the insured desires the loss to be covered under the policy, the incident must be reported to law enforcement.[17]

C. Digital Forensics

An investigation into a security incident must be carefully conducted in order to ensure quality evidence and admissibility in court. "A basic tenet of evidence handling is to maintain the item of evidence in its original state and to thoroughly document access to the item as well as the reason and process associated with any changes."[18] In order to preserve evidence in its original state, a proper forensic examination must occur, potentially including digital forensics.

Digital forensics is the application of scientific methods and techniques to recover data from electronic media. Digital forensics investigators can collect and analyze digitally stored information to show where, when, and how the incident occurred. The key to any forensic investigation is to gather the data in a forensically sound manner, using appropriate forensic protocols. The digital media must be copied or imaged in a way that preserves the original data and results in a complete snapshot. The forensic imaging

14. "Unsecured" means "not rendered unusable, unreadable or indecipherable to unauthorized individuals through the use of a technology or methodology specified by the Secretary of the Department of Health and Human Services." *See also* HHS Guidance at http://www.hhs.gov/ocr/privacy/hipaa/administrative/breachnotificationrule/brguidance.html.

15. "Breach" means "an impermissible use or disclosure . . . that compromises the security or privacy of the protected health information such that the use or disclosure poses a significant risk of financial, reputational, or other harm to the affected individual," with a few specified exceptions. State laws that are inconsistent with the HITECH Act notice of breach requirements are preempted by federal law, without regard to those exceptions. In other words, once it has been determined that there has been a "breach" under federal law, inconsistent state notice of breach laws are preempted. On the Web, go to http://www.hhs.gov/ocr/privacy/hipaa/administrative/breachnotificationrule/ for HIPAA breach notification requirements.

16. Subtitle D of Division A of the American Reinvestment and Recovery Act of 2009, Section 13402.

17. For a more detailed analysis of data breaches, *see* Lucy L. Thomson, Data Breach and Encryption Handbook (American Bar Association 2011).

18. Network Reliability and Interoperability Council, NRIC FG1B Best Practice Appendices, Appendix X (f), June 3, 2003, *available at* http://www.nric.org/fg/charter_vi/fg1/RECOM_FG1B_Combined_Appendices_FINAL_3-6-03_1.doc.

system must not alter the original data in any way. The data must be collected in a manner that maintains the authenticity and integrity of the data existing at the time of the incident, to the extent possible. The process used for collection of the data must be documented, and the chain of custody of the data must be complete and fully documented.

Understanding which data is relevant to the incident and where the data resides is critical to the investigation. Relevant data may be located on servers, desktops, laptops, or even USB devices, PDAs, and home computers.

In the event of a lawsuit involving digital evidence, location, collection, and preservation of the evidence are critical for both plaintiff and defendant.[19] Failure to preserve evidence may result in sanctions for spoliation. Digital evidence is often collected, processed, and authenticated at trial using hardware and software supplied by vendors. Because these forensic tools often play a critical role in how digital evidence is collected, processed, and authenticated in court, the reliability of these products is of the utmost importance.

It should be noted that the work of a digital forensics investigator is different from that of the corporate IT professional who is responsible for the day-to-day operations of the company's system. Although the CIRT should be involved in the forensic investigation to determine the scope of the incident and the appropriate method for restoration of service, digital forensics requires specialized knowledge and protocols. For assistance in building forensic capabilities, NIST has created SP 800-86.[20]

D. Public-Private Partnerships

The CIRT often can work with local or national law enforcement to ensure that a proper investigation is completed. This type of public-private partnership is not unusual in the information security arena. National, state, and local governments offer opportunities for private organizations to work collaboratively to improve information security. In many cases, the primary emphasis of these partnerships is on protecting the nation's critical infrastructure (e.g., transportation, power, food, health) or preventing crime (e.g., protection from computer fraud or data theft). The government also invites private party participation in setting standards and defining best practices.

One of the most well-known public-private partnerships in the information security arena in the United States is Infragard. The FBI hosts Infragard, through which law enforcement, corporations, and academia exchange information about threats and attacks on the nation's critical infrastructure. Infragard began as a project of a single FBI field office in 1996 and grew to a nationwide activity. In 2003, Infragard's parent organization, the National Information Protection Center, was transferred to the newly created Department of Homeland Security.[21] The FBI retained Infragard by refocusing its emphasis on the crimes—terrorism and cybercrime—under the FBI's jurisdiction.

The Department of Homeland Security hosts multiple public-private programs that address different aspects of information security. These programs include Sector

19. *See generally* George Paul & Bruce Nearon, The Discovery Revolution (American Bar Association 2006), and George L. Paul, Foundations of Digital Evidence (American Bar Association 2008).

20. NIST, SP 800-86, *Guide to Integrating Forensic Techniques into Incident Response* (2006).

21. 6 U.S.C. § 121(g)(1) (2003).

Coordinating Councils focused on Critical Infrastructure/Key Resources[22] and the U.S.-Computer Emergency Response Team (US-CERT), which collects information and educates nonprofessionals about computer and cyber security threats and vulnerabilities.

Although public-private partnerships have become a critical element of information security and privacy, attorneys need to research and inform their clients if there are potential legal issues associated with sharing information with government entities. For example, Congress explicitly included a protection[23] for companies sharing trade secrets with the Department of Homeland Security in relation to critical infrastructure protection, but many programs do not have such explicit legal authority.

Private corporations also may find themselves encouraged or even required to adopt a government directive if the corporation is working with a government entity. For example, the Personal Identity Verification (PIV) standard[24] was created in response to a 2004 White House order[25] to standardize identity credentials for federal employees and contractors and was to be used to support both physical and logical access. That order was followed by the Personal Identity Verification—Interoperable (PIV-I)[26] standard released in 2009 to address the challenges for interoperating across organizations—federal, state, local, and private. Some corporations are mandated to adopt the standard as a result of their federal contractor status, and others are encouraged to adopt it to facilitate their work as first responders or as part of the nation's critical infrastructure. It has been proposed that eventually the standard be expanded to support private-sector secure transactions and that a public-private partnership help establish the initiative.[27]

6.3 AUDIT AND CERTIFICATION

After the information security and privacy controls have been designed and implemented and staff appropriately trained, the effectiveness of the controls must be monitored, measured, reviewed and remediated, and reported to the interested stakeholders, including existing and potential customers, shareholders, creditors, and executive leadership. Whether to comply with regulatory requirements or to promote competitive differentiators, organizations pursue a variety of audit opinions and certifications that cover information security and privacy. Depending on the audience, the type of assurance or certification sought, and the nature of the controls, these opinions and certifications can be categorized as follows:

- Information Security Certification: ISO 27001, U.S. government
- Information Security Assurance: SAS 70/ISAE 3402, SOX

---

22. *Cf.* Homeland Security Presidential Directive 7 (HSPD-7) and the National Infrastructure Protection Plan (NIPP).

23. 6 U.S.C. § 133.

24. Federal Information Processing Standard (FIPS) 201.

25. "Policy for a Common Identification Standard for Federal Employees and Contractors," Homeland Security Presidential Directive 12 (Aug. 27, 2004).

26. "Personal Identity Verification Interoperability for Non-Federal Issuers," Federal CIO Council (May 2009).

27. Written testimony of Vivek Kundra, Federal Chief Information Officer, before the House Committee on Oversight and Government Reform Subcommittee Government Management, Organization, and Procurement (March 24, 2010) (referencing the establishment of the National Strategy for Secure Online Transactions).

- Privacy Assurance: GAPP, Privacy audit
- Privacy Certification: National/regional standards
- Website Certification/Assurance: WebTrust, trustmarks

A. ISO 27001

The ISO 27001 information security standard describes the components of an adequate information security management system. The specific controls for the information security management program are contained in a related standard, ISO 27002. Metrics for the information management security system and controls are covered in ISO 27004. The risk management and assessment process to identify controls for external or internal threats and internal vulnerabilities is under ISO 27005. Certification is sought under ISO 27001, which may involve these other ISO standards.

As discussed in Chapter 1, there are three significant parts of an information security program. The first part is the information security and privacy policy, whereby a corporation's executives document their support of and participation in the protection of organizational, employee, and customer data. The high-level security direction is laid out here, as well as the standards for acceptable usage of corporate assets, physical as well as informational. The written information security and privacy policy is then disseminated to all employees and awareness training held. Some best practices for these policies were described earlier in this chapter. The second part of an information security program is the risk management program, which documents the information assets a corporation has and assesses the threats to those assets from either external (e.g., viruses) or internal (e.g., employee theft) sources, the vulnerabilities in practices and systems, and the exploits possible for the interaction of the threats and vulnerabilities. Decisions are then made on how to respond to each of these risks, including creating controls, outsourcing the risk, or accepting the risk. This process was described in Chapter 4. The third part of the information security program is the controls discussed in Chapter 5, which must be designed, tested, and implemented and then monitored, measured, reviewed, and revised as appropriate. The ISO 27002 controls are grouped into technical, administrative, and physical categories, including the separation of duties, periodic reviews by management and auditors, physical access limits to facilities, virus software, access controls on applications and file systems, change management processes, backups, limits on wireless and mobile device usage, encryption, training, monitoring, incident management, and operational tasks.

To bestow certification, the certifier will examine the design of the controls and interview the organization's management and employees to determine the organization's commitment to information security in the normal course of operations. It is essential to show both that management has a deep commitment to information security and that information security is embedded in what the organization does on a daily basis in all major processes and not viewed as some external process taken up periodically. After providing suggested remediations, the certifier will return to review the implementation of those remediations and to determine if the controls as designed and implemented are working effectively. Keeping records of control activities is essential. If the policies, procedures, and controls described in the standard are appropriately implemented, maintained, monitored, reviewed, and revised and if the organization's commitment is demonstrated, ISO certification will then be granted.

B. U.S. Federal Government

Under the Federal Information Security Management Act (FISMA) of 2002, U.S. federal agencies are required to implement and report on effective information security controls. This process includes "periodic testing and evaluation of the effectiveness of information security policies, procedures, and practices." The law designates the Director of the Office of Management and Budget to oversee the implementation of this and other information security requirements for federal civilian agencies, the Secretary of Defense for Defense Department systems, and the Director of Central Intelligence for the CIA. NIST, in coordination with the National Security Agency (NSA), is responsible for providing more detailed guidance in defining and implementing the security controls described in FISMA. Additionally, OMB Circular A-130, Appendix III, and subsequent annual FISMA reporting guidance requires agencies to authorize processing on a system-by-system basis, defining a system as "an interconnected set of information resources under the same direct management control which shares common functionality."[28]

These systems are subdivided into general support systems and major applications, but agencies have flexibility in what constitutes a system. It is ultimately up to the agency head or his or her designee to accept the risk for each information system in use at the agency. In furtherance of this process, NIST has proposed and OMB has endorsed a Risk Management Framework for the ongoing information security protection of each federal system. The defense and intelligence communities have a similar process, and there is ongoing work to consolidate these processes into a single risk management process for the federal government. Consequently, the NIST process is the focus, which will likely absorb the processes from the defense and intelligence communities with some minor changes. The steps in the framework and the related standards are as follows:

1. Categorize the information system—FIPS 199/SP 800-60
2. Select the security controls—FIPS 200/SP 800-53
3. Implement the security controls—SP 800-70[29]
4. Assess the security controls—SP 800-53A
5. Authorize the information system—SP 800-37
6. Monitor security state—SP 800-37/SP 800-53

The first step, highlighted in Federal Information Processing Standard (FIPS) 199, is to categorize a system.[30] Under FIPS 199 guidance and more detailed guidance found in

---

28. OMB Circular A-130, Appendix III, http://www.whitehouse.gov/omb/circulars_a130_a130appendix_iii/.

29. NIST SP 800-70 Rev. 1, *National Checklist Program for IT Products—Guidelines for Checklist Users and Developers* (2009).

30. FIPS Publication 199, *Standards for Security Categorization of Federal Information and Information Systems* (2004).

NIST Special Publication (SP) 800-60,[31] agencies are to select the types of information that are found in the system and use the guidance to determine whether that information falls into a low-, medium-, or high-impact category. Using that impact category, agencies are to select the controls relevant to that system. Under FIPS 200,[32] the control framework and associated impact levels specified in NIST SP 800-53[33] are mandatory. However, there is consensus that some flexibility exists where certain controls are not feasible or where other compensating controls are used. SP 800-53 offers agencies a fair amount of latitude as to how the controls are to be implemented on specific platforms.

For more detailed guidance, NIST has developed a variety of platform and application-specific guidance documents. Some, such as the Federal Desktop Core Configuration, have been made mandatory by OMB. The Defense Information Systems Agency (DISA) offers a wide range of Security Technical Implementation Guides (STIGs) that are frequently used by both the public and private sectors as examples of sound, albeit very stringent, security controls to implement at a very granular level. Following implementation, controls are typically documented in a System Security Plan (SSP) that is described in NIST SP 800-18.[34] At minimum, agencies are to describe how the controls in SP 800-53 are being implemented. Ideally, detailed information should be included so that an auditor can readily verify whether the controls are in fact implemented. However, in most cases, agencies simply parrot the language from SP 800-53 and leave it to the interpretation of the person assessing the system to determine whether a particular configuration setting adequately satisfies the control requirements. That assessment process is described in NIST SP 800-53A,[35] which breaks down the SP 800-53 controls into a series of test steps to be performed. It is also expected that supplemental guidance such as DISA STIGs and platform-specific NIST guidance be used to confirm that the controls are implemented and effective.

The next step is officially the certification and accreditation (C&A) step that is spelled out in NIST SP 800-37.[36] This step is largely a paperwork exercise once a system is assessed. It is here that the assessment team formally delivers its assessment report. Usually this assessment is done on behalf of the CIO, who generates a letter to the accrediting authority indicating the state of the security controls and provides a recommendation as to whether the system is sufficiently secure so as to allow it to begin or continue operating. Based on that recommendation, the system owner, who, under FISMA, is effectively acting on behalf of the agency head, generates an accreditation letter or, in the Defense Department context, an authorization to operate. Under traditional C&A guidance, this authorization must be renewed at least every three years, and under FISMA, the system must undergo some assessment on an annual basis. At this

31. NIST SP 800-60 Vol. 1, Rev. 1, *Guide for Mapping Types of Information and Information Systems to Security Categories* (2008).

32. FIPS Publication 200, *Minimum Security Requirements for Federal Information and Information Systems* (2006).

33. NIST SP 800-53 Rev. 3, *Recommended Security Controls for Federal Information Systems* (2009).

34. NIST SP 800-18 Rev. 1, *Guide for Developing Security Plans for Federal Information Systems* (2008).

35. NIST SP 800-53A Rev. 1, *Guide for Assessing the Security Controls in Federal Information Systems* (2010).

36. NIST SP 800-37 Rev. 1, *Guide for the Security Certification and Accreditation of Federal Information Systems* (2010).

point, any deficiencies are also noted and a Plan of Action and Milestones (POA&M) is generated to track the findings. The status of any high- or medium-risk findings needs to be reported to OMB as part of the annual reporting process. The current trend is to implement a process described in SP 800-37 called continuous monitoring, which will ultimately rely on automated tools to verify controls on an ongoing basis making formal assessments less onerous. OMB mandates continuous monitoring and automated reporting in its latest FISMA reporting guidance.[37] Some agencies are scrapping their traditional C&A process that relies on doing exhaustive assessments every three years and instead are relying on the use of automated tools on an ongoing basis to ensure compliance. While reauthorization every three years is still required under OMB Circular A-130, that process would usually only involve packaging the already generated automated reports with the required certification and accreditation letters.

C. SAS 70/ISAE 3402

The AICPA's Statement on Auditing Standards (SAS) 70 auditing standard (or local national equivalents such as those in the United Kingdom, Japan, and Canada) is a methodology for auditing the internal controls of a third-party outsourcing vendor. This older standard is now being replaced by the International Auditing and Assurance Standards Board's (IAASB) International Standard on Assurance Engagements (ISAE) 3402.[38] It is commonly used in SOX audits for assessing the internal controls—in this case, information security and privacy—relevant and material to outsourcing entities' financial reporting. Although frequently utilized for reporting on internal controls of service organizations for any purpose, such as confidentiality, availability, and integrity of the user entity's information, these standards are strictly only for internal controls over financial reporting.

Unlike an ISO 27001 certification, there is no predescribed set of policies, procedures, and controls to check the service organization's controls against. Rather, it is up to the service auditor's judgment. Management of the service organization creates a description of the outsourcing services provided to users and how the services are performed, including the controls utilized. The result of the attestation engagement is based on the judgment of the auditor about the design and effectiveness of the controls in scope (management determines which controls or organizational groups are in scope). The ISAE 3403 standard does now require that management of the service organization provide a written assertion of the fairness of their description of their system and control design and (if in scope) control effectiveness.

The reports (and examination procedures to produce the reports) can be one of two types. Type I reports examine only the design of the controls. Type II reports examine both control design and effectiveness over a period of time (at least six months), including the description of the tests used by the auditor. To perform this engagement, the

---

37. OMB Memorandum M-10-15 (2010).

38. SAS 70 is being replaced in the United States by SAS *Audit Considerations Relating to an Entity Using a Service Organization* and Statement on Standards for Attestation Engagement (SSAE) 16 *Reporting on Controls at a Service Organization*. SSAE 16 is based on the IAASB's ISAE 3402.

service auditor will visit the service organization to examine the control objectives and control design, interview the control users and management, review applicable documentation, and perform appropriate control testing (if a Type II report). The resulting Service Auditor's Report contains the auditor's conclusion as to the adequacy of controls and lists the control objectives, the controls tested, and the results of testing as well as, under ISAE 3402, the conclusion on management's assertions. The reports are used by organizations that outsource and their auditors when preparing the organization's financial statement audits. Strictly speaking, these reports are not intended for use by potential customers of service organizations, only by existing customers and their auditors.

D. SOX

In reaction to the Enron and WorldCom scandals and other financial frauds, the Sarbanes-Oxley Act (SOX) was passed in 2002. The intention of SOX is to stop fraudulent financial and accounting practices. Indirectly, SOX has had far-reaching impacts on information security practices.

As a consequence of SOX, the Securities and Exchange Commission (SEC) has issued guidance directing how corporations report on internal control over financial reporting (ICFR).[39] ICFR is a process that a corporation uses to ensure that its financial reports are prepared in a proper manner. The SEC guidance states that "management's annual assessment of the effectiveness of ICFR must be made in accordance with a suitable control framework's definition of internal control." In a footnote, the SEC gives examples of suitable frameworks, such as the ones developed by the Committee of Sponsoring Organizations of the Treadway Commission (COSO), the Canadian Institute of Chartered Accountants (CICA) Criteria of Control (CoCo),[40] and the Internal Control: Guidance for Directors on the Combined Code (The Turnbull Report)[41] from the Institute of Chartered Accountants in England. The COSO framework is the one most commonly cited in 10-K reports filed with the SEC.

1. COSO

Five professional organizations formed COSO in 1985 to study the causal factors leading to fraudulent financial reporting.[42] COSO's recommendations are primarily directed at public companies and their independent auditors. COSO published its primary work,

39. 17 C.F.R. pt. 241 (2010).

40. For a discussion of CoCo, see http://www.mcgill.ca/internalaudit/tools/coco; to purchase CoCo, see https://www.knotia.ca/kStore/Catalogue/ProductPricing.cfm?productID=16.

41. The Turnbull Report, available at http://www.frc.org.uk/corporate/internalcontrol.cfm.

42. *See* Committee of Sponsoring Organizations of the Treadway Commission, "About Us," http://www.coso.org/aboutus.htm.

Integrated Control—Integrated Framework, in 1992.[43] The initial components of the framework were:[44]

- Control environment
- Risk assessment
- Control activities
- Information and communication
- Monitoring

While information technology (IT) security falls within the framework's control activities and monitoring components, COSO's output is high level and has limited direct impact on IT security.

2. *Public Company Accounting Oversight Board (PCAOB)*

SOX established the PCAOB as a private-sector, nonprofit corporation to oversee the auditors of public companies.[45] It protects investors and the public interest by promoting informative, fair, and independent audit reports. Many of COSO's recommendations were incorporated into SOX and the work of the PCAOB.

For companies subject to SEC regulation under U.S. law, the PCAOB has the authority to set standards for auditors who attest to an organization's financial statements and to management's statement of internal control.[46] SOX also requires that management describe those controls.[47] In 2007, the PCAOB issued Auditing Standard No. 5.[48] It states:

> As part of evaluating the period-end financial reporting process, the auditor should assess—
>
> - Inputs, procedures performed, and outputs of the processes the company uses to produce its annual and quarterly financial statements;
> - The extent of information technology ("IT") involvement in the period-end financial reporting process.[49]

In short, IT controls—including IT security controls—are included in the independent auditor's evaluation. "The use of IT . . . affects the fundamental manner in which transactions are initiated, recorded, processed, and reported."[50] The PCAOB, as well as the AICPA, however, give minimal guidance on what types of controls are meaningful in an IT environment.

---

43. *See* Committee of Sponsoring Organizations of the Treadway Commission, "Guidance on Internal Control," http://www.coso.org/IC.htm.

44. The framework has since been expanded to eight components and rechristened the *Enterprise Risk Management (ERM) Integrated Framework* (2004).

45. 15 U.S.C. § 7211 (2010).

46. 15 U.S.C. § 7213 (2010).

47. 15 U.S.C. § 7262 (2010) (this section is commonly known as "Sec. 404, Management Assessment of Internal Controls").

48. Public Company Accounting Oversight Board, Auditing Standard No. 5, *An Audit of Internal Control Over Financial Reporting That Is Integrated with an Audit of Financial Statements*, July 27, 2007, http://pcaobus.org/Standards/Auditing/Pages/Auditing_Standard_5.aspx#introduction.

49. *Id.*, ¶ 27.

50. PCAOB AU Section 319, *Consideration of Internal Control in a Financial Statement Audit*, http://pcaobus.org/Standards/Auditing/Pages/AU319.aspx.

3. COBIT

As discussed in Chapter 5, COBIT is ISACA's enterprise governance of IT framework. In the IT controls aspects of SOX and similar internal controls audits, COBIT audit techniques may be the preferred choice. ISACA has developed a number of tools to assist in these audits, including the Information Technology Assurance Framework (ITAF) that provides guidelines, terminology, tools, techniques, and general performance and reporting standards for IT audits. One of the tools is the Information Security Management Audit/Assurance Program. This program starts with an evaluation of the 11 areas under the COBIT IT process DS5, *Ensure systems security*, from the Deliver and Support (DS) domain and ends with an evaluation of the maturity level of the COBIT control framework, using an approach derived from the software development maturity model defined by the Software Engineering Institute (SEI) of Carnegie Mellon University.[51]

E. GAPP

A privacy audit compares an organization's actual privacy practices against a known benchmark, such as national statutes or regional frameworks. Because the privacy principles in these statutes are often at a high level, to derive a detailed audit approach, the AICPA's/CICA's *Generally Accepted Privacy Principles* (GAPP) can be used. A combination of the GAPP plus any additional domestic statute-specific provisions can address privacy compliance requirements in each of the organization's jurisdictions. The AICPA and CICA allow privacy practitioners to provide either privacy advisory services or privacy audit examination services. The audit services can be performed either on management's assertion that they maintained effective controls over the privacy of personal information in accordance with their privacy notice and GAPP or directly on the subject matter of the privacy controls and privacy notice.

The GAPP document includes a table with measurement criteria for each principle, illustrative controls and procedures, and additional considerations. This table can be used both proactively when setting up the privacy controls and then during the audit itself to measure actual operational compliance of the controls and procedures with GAPP.

F. IT Audit/Assurance—Privacy Guidelines

Because most data is now electronically stored, the privacy audit could fall within the realm of an IT audit, so ISACA's IT audit and assurance standards and guidelines may be appropriate. Guideline 31 on privacy[52] deals with how to apply privacy to an IS audit. There are a number of useful features in this guideline. One is a checklist of 21 questions that allows comparison of the differences between the privacy laws in each country. Another is a list of key controls, in the areas of media reuse, training, access controls, maintenance, data integrity, physical access, and risk assessments. There is also a list of considerations for the protection of personal information, covering some of the following areas: privacy management, risk assessment, security audit, professional secrecy, physical security, confi-

51. ISACA, *IT Assurance Guide: Using COBIT*, Appendix VII—Maturity Model for Internal Control (2007).
52. ISACA, *IT Audit and Assurance Guidelines—G31 Privacy* (2005).

dentiality, integrity, availability, security measures, security toward external partners, and awareness and training sessions.

The audit itself requires that the IT auditor determine the existence of the following: a privacy policy, privacy officer, data controller, training and awareness plans in relation to privacy, privacy complaint management process, regime of privacy audits conducted against the privacy legislation, and privacy requirements for outsourcers and contractors. The auditor is required to undertake a privacy impact analysis and produce an audit report. The report should document the results of the privacy review, outline the scope and objectives, and provide a summary of the types of data and information collected, stored, and used by the organization. The report should include information on the privacy-related risks that the organization faces and a summary of the risk reduction measures or privacy protection strategies that exist. Weaknesses identified in the privacy review because of missing or inadequate controls should be brought to the attention of both information owners and management responsible for privacy. Any material weaknesses should be addressed immediately. The IT auditors should include appropriate recommendations for stronger privacy controls.

G. Privacy Certifications

Privacy certifications are typically country or regional programs that organizations use for business competitive advantage. The United States is not currently an international leader in this area. Two leading examples are the EU's EuroPriSe and Japan's Privacy Mark.

1. Japan

Japan's Privacy Mark is a voluntary scheme under which businesses can achieve certification for their personal data protection systems. Developed by the Japan Information Processing Development Corporation (JIPDEC) in 1998, the plan requires an independent certifier to verify compliance with the Japan Industrial Standard (JIS) Q 15001 (2006). The objectives of the program are to enhance consumer awareness of personal information protection through display of the Privacy Mark symbol and to promote appropriate handling of personal information through enhanced credibility for business operators. In the certification process, the certifier will first review the applicant's documents off-site then come onsite to further review documents, perform interviews, investigate the privacy-related procedures, and provide suggested remediations. After the material remediations are resolved, the Privacy Mark can be granted to the applicant, who may then display it prominently on the company's website, envelopes, letters, contracts, and business cards. The requirements are to establish, implement, maintain, and improve a personal information protection management system, including policies, organizations, inventories, risk assessments, plans, implementations, audits, and reviews.

2. Europe

The European Privacy Seal (EuroPriSe) allows organizations that do business in the EU to demonstrate privacy compliance for IT products and services in sales to both consumers and governments. EU-backed and involving nine data protection authorities in the region, the audit of the products and services is against European Data Protection privacy and information security regulations. The process uses two phases, beginning with an evaluation by independent qualified IT and legal experts and followed by a verification process by the accredited certification body. The products include both hardware and software, and the services include any type of electronic commerce, search engines, and data centers. The experts are qualified only after they have proven their proficiency through working experience in IT and have passed a demanding test demonstrating a profound knowledge of privacy and data protection.

H. Trustmarks

Trustmarks are used by website operators, often those involved in electronic commerce, to demonstrate a certain degree of recognition and integrity in the operation of the website and the use of the consumer's information. The trustmarks can signify any of the following about the website:

- Use of appropriate encryption for its consumer transactions
- Adherence to appropriate privacy standards
- Compliance with periodic security audits and vulnerability assessments
- Qualification as a legitimate business[53]

1. *Global Alliances*

Most of the companies providing the trustmark services are private companies, some nonprofit and others for profit. Efforts have been made to create regional and global alliances of trustmark operators to provide an assurance level that works on the same geographic span as the Internet. The Global Trustmark Alliance included members from Europe, North America, and Asia, including the Asia-Pacific Trustmark Alliance, which allows its trustmark operators to act as "APEC privacy accreditation service providers" using the APEC Privacy Framework and so deal with market demand for privacy assurance services. The Global Trustmark Alliance also includes the Better Business Bureau in the United States, which offers BBBOnLine as a trustmark program. In Europe, the Alliance includes the Trust UK program, E-comtrust, Eurochambres, and the Federation of European Direct and Interactive Marketing.

2. *WebTrust*

The AICPA and CICA have a program called WebTrust for websites. This program is based on the AICPA/CICA Trust Principles and Criteria, as follows:[54]

- *Security:* The system is protected against unauthorized access (both physical and logical).
- *Availability:* The system is available for operation and use as committed or agreed.

53. *Trust Marks: What's Behind the Label Counts*, Yankee Group Research, Inc. (2009).
54. *Trust Services Principles and Criteria*, AICPA/CICA (2009).

- *Processing integrity:* System processing is complete, accurate, timely, and authorized.
- *Confidentiality:* Information designated as confidential is protected as committed or agreed.
- *Privacy:* Personal information is collected, used, retained, disclosed, and destroyed in conformity with the commitments in the entity's privacy notice and with criteria set forth in generally accepted privacy principles issued by the AICPA and CICA.

This program covers policies, communications, procedures, and monitoring. The WebTrust family of branded assurance services includes the following, applied in the context of an e-commerce system:

- *WebTrust Online Privacy:* The scope of the assurance engagement includes the relevant online privacy principles and criteria.
- *WebTrust Consumer Protection:* The scope of the assurance engagement includes both the processing integrity and relevant online privacy principles and criteria.
- *WebTrust:* The scope of the assurance engagement includes one or more combinations of the principles and criteria not anticipated above.
- *WebTrust for Certification Authorities:* The scope of the assurance engagement includes the principles and related criteria unique to certification authorities.[55]

55. *See* www.webtrust.org.

CHAPTER 7

New and Emerging Technologies

New and emerging technologies represent significant challenges in managing an organization's information security and privacy risk and control structures. Often new technologies will upset an existing way of doing business—for example, exploding consumer use of the Internet has reshaped commerce and social interaction. If controls are not already in place, organizations must develop them for managing these technologies as they enter the organization's environment, whether planned for or not. Use of new and emerging technologies may be revealed during business or IT planning, risk assessments, procurement, change management, monitoring, audits, or when providing end-user support to employees. A number of new technologies have arisen and become an integral part of organizations in recent years, and others will continue to emerge. This chapter provides insights into addressing some of these new and emerging technologies that now or will soon impact information security and privacy risks and controls. The topics covered are social networking, cloud computing, mobile computing, storage technologies, offensive cyber activity, and critical infrastructure/control systems.

What Global Executives Need to Know

- The penetration and impacts of social networking on the organization's information security and privacy program
- The scope of current and planned use of cloud computing by the organization
- The penetration and impacts of mobile computing on the organization's information security and privacy program
- The impact of storage technologies on the organization's information security and privacy program and the use of offensive cyber activity by the organization
- The impact of governmental initiatives supporting critical infrastructure on the organization's information security and privacy program

7.1 SOCIAL NETWORKING

Social networking by definition focuses on building and reflecting personal and social relations among people who share common interests, causes, or goals. A social networking site (SNS) is an online service that attracts a community of users and provides them a variety of tools for posting personal data and creating user-generated content directed to a given user's interests and personal life, providing a means for users to socially interact over the Internet through e-mail, instant messaging, websites, or other resources. In so doing, SNS allow users to share ideas, activities, recommendations, personal information, and interests within their individual networks, as opposed to an online community that is focused on individuals rather than groups.

As of June 2010, 22 percent of all time spent online was social (i.e., messaging, commenting, blogging, and sharing).[1] For the first time ever, social network or blog sites were visited by three-quarters of global consumers who go online.[2] In the United States alone, the total minutes spent on SNSs has increased 83 percent year-over-year each year.[3] These results are astounding for such a new medium. Facebook, the most popular SNS worldwide, only started in February 2004. Upward trends in user membership, corporate marketing, and other metrics with respect to SNSs are expected to continue.[4] A 2009 study found that the Global 100 largest companies have been strongly embracing social networking, with 65 percent having Twitter accounts, 54 percent having Facebook fan pages, 50 percent having YouTube video channels, and 33 percent having corporate blogs.[5] From a global perspective, Asian companies are most frequently involved in blogging, while Latin America, Europe, and the United States are similar in having Twitter accounts. The United States leads in Facebook fan pages, and Europe and the United States lead in the use of YouTube video channels.[6]

The issue of information security and privacy on social networks is paramount but has largely been tabled by SNSs in favor of emphasizing user growth and brand marketing. Achieving information security within the arena of social networking, though, is difficult and complicated, as users tend to overlook security risks, businesses downplay the gravity of the security issues, and owners of SNSs are somewhat conflicted by financial incentives that may run contrary to privacy and security concerns.

A. The Overlooked Issue of Security

By definition, social networks—regardless of whether they are informal networks (e.g., Facebook or Twitter) or professional networks (e.g., LinkedIn or Martindale-Hubbell Connected)—are community-based forums where the free trade of ideas and informa-

1. http://blog.nielsen.com/nielsenwire/online_mobile/social-media-accounts-for-22-percent-of-time-online/.
2. *Id.*
3. http://www.nielsen-online.com/pr/pr_090602.pdf.
4. *See* http://www.professionalexperts.net/articles.php?article_id=49; http://www.pcworld.com/business-center/article/202333/take_advantage_of_increased_time_spent_on_social_networking.html.
5. Burson-Marsteller, *The Global Social Media Check-up Insights: From the Burson-Marsteller Evidence-based Communications Group, available at* www.burson-marsteller.com/Innovation_and_insights/blogs_and_podcasts/BM_Blog/Documents/Burson-Marsteller%202010%20Global%20Social%20Media%20Check-up%20white%20paper.pdf.
6. *Id.*

tion is encouraged. From an information security and privacy standpoint, therefore, the pivotal weakness with SNSs is conversely their strength: social networks encourage open interaction among both known and loosely connected users, and, as a result, the normal social barriers against interacting with near strangers are lowered. Juxtapose this openness against the dramatic increase in cybercrime and identity theft worldwide[7] and therein lies a potential privacy epidemic.

Unsurprisingly, there have been countless reports of cyber criminals "phishing"[8] for personal information on SNSs.[9] In fact, data suggests that an increasing volume of cybercrime is now directed to Internet users on SNSs.[10] At risk is not only the personal information of the user but presumably also that of the user's employer. The tools of the trade for cyber criminals are clever and devious, such as (1) creating fake profiles of friends, (2) hacking into friends' profiles and sending messages that appear to be from a friend, and (3) e-mailing hostile computer code known as "malware,"[11] usually from an account of a "friend," that becomes activated when unwitting recipients click on the infected Internet links. Unsuspecting users on these sites run the risk of unintentionally disclosing sensitive information, including bank and financial data, highly personal information such as relationship, health, and employment information, and similar sensitive information of family and/or friends.

Up to this point, SNSs, at least informal sites, have been somewhat behind on the issue of information security:

- In January 2010, the CEO of Facebook stated at a technology conference that privacy is no longer a "social norm," as users have adapted to sharing information online over blogs and other social media and, in turn, the company has structured its privacy settings accordingly.[12] Roughly six months later, a hacker created a program that legally harvested and published personal data from over 100 million Facebook users who failed to change their privacy settings to make their profile pages unavailable to search engines.[13]
- In February 2010, shortly after the release of Google's SNS, Google Buzz, a class-action lawsuit was filed in a federal court and a complaint with the Federal Trade Commission (FTC) based on claims that Google automatically

7. *See* http://www.aim.org/guest-column/threat-of-cyber-crime-continues-to-increase/; http://gigaom.com/2010/02/10/identity-theft-on-the-rise-survey/.

8. The term "phishing" refers to online scams intended to trick users into divulging sensitive data like usernames and passwords. For more information, please see the associated Wikipedia article, available at http://en.wikipedia.org/wiki/Phishing.

9. *See* http://www.time.com/time/business/article/0,8599,1895740,00.html; http://www.informationweek.com/news/security/cybercrime/showArticle.jhtml?articleID=227701164; http://community.norton.com/t5/Ask-Marian/Social-Network-Members-Increasingly-Vulnerable-to-Phishing/ba-p/162749.

10. *See* http://www.networkworld.com/news/2009/012309-social-networking-sites-a-hotbed.html; http://www.esecurityplanet.com/features/print.php/3874206.

11. The term "malware" is used to describe malicious computer programs, such as a virus, Trojan horse, or bot. These computer programs are often destructive and can be costly to clean up. An ounce of prevention is often worth a pound of cure.

12. http://www.reuters.com/article/idUS174222527820100112.

13. *See* http://www.net-security.org/secworld.php?id=9652.

activated and generated publicly accessible lists of followers gleaned from users' Gmail accounts and Gtalk conversations.[14]

- In June 2010, Twitter, another major player in the social media landscape, agreed to settle charges by the U.S. FTC that "it deceived consumers and put their privacy at risk by failing to safeguard their personal information."[15]

B. Managing Security Risks

At this time, information security on social networks is fundamentally a behavioral issue, not a technology issue. Users, rather than the sites themselves, appear best suited to manage security risks, as it is the users who have full control and discretion over what is published, posted, tweeted, or otherwise shared via the sites and who are invited into circles of friends. Simple measures—such as refraining from publishing financial and sensitive information, using strong and unique passwords, not assuming there is any expectation of privacy on SNSs, and selecting social media friends with caution—greatly improve information security on SNSs. For businesses, managing security risks via employees can be more challenging but is necessary, as potential risks include inadvertent disclosure of sensitive enterprise information such as financial data, corporate intellectual property, and IT infrastructures. At a minimum, businesses should implement policies governing the use of social media to ensure that employees are made aware of the threats online to themselves and the enterprise through the disclosure of sensitive information.

Although social networking offers a new access point, some of the risks are not new and information security and privacy controls should already be in place. This new access point may provide ways for malware to enter the organization's network and new vectors for outside attackers to launch attacks. What may be more significant is the outbound use of social networks, where insiders, intentionally or innocently, may export corporate intellectual property and customer data outside the organization. This activity can lead not only to legal and regulatory claims but also to potential losses of competitive advantage and reputational damage. For example, if an employee known to be a member of your organization posts confidential or defamatory information of or about a customer to a SNS, the legal and reputational damage could be significant.

Even though SNSs have deemphasized information security in the past, they are not totally apathetic to users' security and privacy concerns. These sites, for example, have privacy and security safeguards, including procedures for users to adjust how others access their personal information.[16] However, the default settings for these functions—as discussed in the case of Facebook—tend to be quite permissive and require users to configure the settings to take advantage of the potential protections available, including limiting the searchability default disposition of posted information.

---

14. *See* http://www.pcworld.com/article/189712/google_hit_with_lawsuit_over_google_buzz.html.
15. *See* http://www.ftc.gov/opa/2010/06/twitter.shtm.
16. http://www.sophos.com/sophos/docs/eng/papers/sophos-security-threat-report-jan-2010-wpna.pdf; http://www.examiner.com/technology-in-san-francisco/privacy-settings-and-social-networking.

There has also been increased intensity related to information security by both public agencies and private watchdogs,[17] such as the Electronic Privacy Information Center (EPIC),[18] the entity that filed the complaint against Google Buzz. Collectively, these entities have scrutinized the SNSs' policies relating to, among other things, information security and privacy. In response, the sites have reassessed security measures in the face of potential legal calamity, monetary damages, and loss of user membership.

Certain industries, especially those that are heavily regulated, such as financial services, have taken some initial steps to address the use of social networking. For example, the Financial Industry Regulatory Authority (FINRA) issued *Guidance on Blogs and Social Networking Web Sites* for securities firms,[19] investment advisors, and brokers following previous guidance on interactive websites.[20] These firms should adapt appropriate policies and procedures, supervise employees' activities on these sites, retain records of communications through these types of sites, and monitor the content on their own sites. The Commodities Futures Trading Commission (CFTC) has approved amendments on the topic of communicating with the public regarding the use of social networking by its members.[21] These communications are now subject to the same standards as other types of communications with the public.

It is still important to realize that these issues remain fundamentally a behavioral issue, not a technology issue. Therefore, it is naive for users and businesses to disregard security risks and outsource security to SNSs, where there is no uniformity with respect to security safeguards at each site, there are constant reports of security leaks and breaches of users' profiles, and where the relevant legal landscape is in its infancy.

Social networking has become fully engrained in our societal fabric in a very short time. This new medium is still very young and immature, and questions such as legal issues regarding information security remain largely unsettled. Indeed, uniform legal standards for security on these sites—whether case driven or by statute—are still relatively nonexistent. Government action is on the horizon and is inevitable in response to a growing public awareness of the security risks, but no one can accurately predict when and to what degree. Until such government intervention occurs, it appears that the burden of security will be borne by users. Behavioral choices by users, and the businesses that employ them, offer the best safeguards against cybercrime and disclosures of sensitive information.

C. Electronic Discovery and Privacy Considerations

With the global proliferation of SNS adoption and use came privacy concerns, and at least one such site, Facebook, has become the target of a class action lawsuit alleging,

17. http://www.informationweek.com/news/government/security/showArticle.jhtml?articleID=224600656; http://epic.org/2010/10/new-social-networking-privacy.html.

18. A number of non-profit organizations have taken up the cause of privacy in recent years, with the American Civil Liberties Union (ACLU) and the Electronic Frontier Foundation (EFF) often providing leadership.

19. FINRA *Regulatory Notice 10-06*(2010).

20. *See* NASD Rule 2210(a)(5).

21. CFTC Interpretive Notice, *Use of On-Line Social Networking Groups to Communicate with the Public* (2010).

inter alia, breach of user privacy.[22] Over time, Facebook has itself taken a more proactive stance in providing its subscribers with enhanced and customizable use and access controls. Facebook's most recent privacy policy outlines what a user can limit the exposure of, completely or only to designated friends (e.g., e-mail address, personal information, posts, age, birth date, tags), and what a user cannot limit (e.g., name content shared with friends, profile information shared with others, messages to others, comments on others' posts or profiles).[23]

It should be noted that even with these modifications, however, Facebook states unequivocally that certain information cannot be blocked by users—for example, information sent to "everyone" is publicly available information, just like a user's name and connections. This information may be accessed by anyone on the Internet and associated with users. The default privacy setting for certain types of information posted on Facebook is set to "everyone."[24] However, concerns have begun to focus on the legal status of Facebook users' rights to privacy in connection with information posted by them or communicated by or between other Facebook users.

Two of the first court decisions to address these issues have called into question the legal status of Facebook users' privacy rights over information they post or communicate. While focusing on SNS user information in the context of electronic discovery, and further involving discovery from party litigants, both decisions address objections to production predicated in part on assertions of a producing party's privacy rights to his or her SNS information.

1. *E.E.O.C. v. Simply Storage Management, LLC*

In this Title VII employment action, the defendant requested "full electronic" Facebook and MySpace profiles from the plaintiffs, together with edits, changes, and profile modifications. The defendants also requested all SNS-based communications, including any multimedia (audio and video) as well as writings information, located at the plaintiffs' Facebook and MySpace pages ("and all status updates, messages, wall comments, causes joined, groups joined, activity streams, blog entries, details, blurbs, comments, and applications").[25]

The EEOC (representing the plaintiffs) asserted the standard objections that the defendants' requests were overbroad, not relevant, and unduly burdensome, arguing that such requests would also violate the defendants' privacy interests ("improperly infringe on claimants' privacy, and will harass and embarrass the claimants").[26] The court granted the defendants' motion to compel production of the plaintiffs' SNS content, determin-

22. The "Beacon" feature was introduced by Facebook in December 2007. A class action lawsuit captioned Lane et al. v. Facebook, Inc. et al., Case No. 5:08-CV-03845-RS (N.D. Cal. 2009) was filed. The complaint alleged that Beacon traded Facebook consumer information with Beacon-affiliated companies such as Hotwire.com, Fandango.com, and Zappos.com. Plaintiffs claimed, inter alia, that the introduction of the Beacon feature was made without obtaining their consent and violated their privacy rights. The case was settled after approximately eight months of litigation, with Facebook's termination of the Beacon program and contribution of $9.5 million to a privacy foundation.

23. http://www.facebook.com/policy.php.

24. *Id.*

25. E.E.O.C. v. Simply Storage Management, LLC, 2010 WL 3446105, 1 (S.D. Ind. 2010).

26. *Id.*, at p. 2.

ing that (1) SNS content was not shielded from discovery because it is locked or private; (2) SNS content must be produced when it is relevant to a claim or content in a case; and (3) where, as in this case, the plaintiffs' mental state is at issue, all SNS material "relating or referring" to the same during the relevant time period was discoverable.

While acknowledging that privacy concerns may have some importance in determining burden, oppressiveness, or harassment, the court found that expectations of privacy do not. The court pointed out that merely designating relevant material as "private" or locking it does not necessarily shield that information from discovery. "Although privacy concerns may be germane to the question of whether requested discovery is burdensome or oppressive and whether it has been sought for a proper purpose in the litigation, a person's expectation and intent that her communications be maintained as private is not a legitimate basis for shielding those communications from discovery."[27]

It is a fundamental maxim of discovery that all relevant evidence is discoverable and must be produced, subject to certain limitations. The court found in essence that where SNS information may be relevant to a party's claims or defense, the liberal standard for discovery applied to the SNS information at issue. The court interpreted the scope of relevant (to the plaintiffs' mental state) and producible evidence to include: profiles, postings, or messages (including status updates, wall comments, causes joined, groups joined, activity streams, and blog entries) and SNS applications, third-party communications, photos, and videos.

The court indicated that the plaintiffs' privacy concerns are diluted where SNS subscribers share allegedly "private information" with third parties: "The court agrees . . . that broad discovery of the claimants' SNS could reveal private information that may embarrass them. . . . [T]he court finds that this concern is outweighed by the fact that the production here would be of information that the claimants have already shared with at least one other person through private messages or a larger number of people through postings. As one judge observed, 'Facebook is not used as a means by which account holders carry on monologues with themselves.'[28]"[29]

2. *Romano v. Steelcase, Inc.*

In this personal injury action, the defendant moved for an order to show cause why it should not be granted "access" to the plaintiff's current and historical social networking accounts and information, including deleted information. The court granted the defendant's motion, holding that: (1) private information sought from the plaintiff's social networking website accounts was material and necessary for the defendant's defense; (2) the plaintiff did not have a reasonable expectation of privacy for information published on social networking websites; and (3) the defendant's need for access to the plaintiff's private information on social networking websites outweighed any privacy concerns voiced by the plaintiff.[30]

27. *Id.*
28. Leduc v. Roman, 2009 Ont. Can. LII 6838, at ¶ 31.
29. E.E.O.C. v. Simply Storage, 2010 WL 3446105, 1 (S.D. Ind. 2010). at pp. 6–7.
30. Romano v. Steelcase, Inc., 907 N.Y.S.2d 650 (N.Y. Sup. 2010).

The court explained that a plaintiff may not shield from disclosure information that is necessary to the defense of a claim. Because the plaintiff's physical condition was in controversy, material necessary to mount a defense could not be excluded from discovery. The plaintiff had asserted permanent injuries that deprived her of the ability to enjoy certain activities. The defendant asserted that the plaintiff's public Facebook and MySpace information indicated otherwise: "Plaintiff herein also claims she sustained permanent injuries as a result of the incident and that she can no longer participate in certain activities or that these injuries have affected her enjoyment of life. However, contrary to Plaintiff's claims, Steelcase contends that a review of the public portions of Plaintiff's MySpace and Facebook pages reveals that she has an active lifestyle and has traveled . . . during the time period she claims that her injuries prohibited such activity."[31]

The court then found that the information sought was both material and necessary to the defense. The discrepancy between the plaintiff's claims that she was largely housebound and bedridden and her Facebook public profile page that showed her posing for a photo outside her home prompted this comment: "In light of the fact that the public portions of Plaintiff's SNSs contain material that is contrary to her claims and deposition testimony, there is a reasonable likelihood that the private portions of her sites may contain further evidence such as information with regard to her activities and enjoyment of life, all of which are material and relevant to the defense of this action."[32]

The court held that the plaintiff had no expectation of privacy by her use of an SNS application whose very design and purpose was the dissemination of information and required production of the plaintiff's SNS information, holding: "Thus, it is reasonable to infer . . . that her private pages may contain materials and information that are relevant to her claims or that may lead to the disclosure of admissible evidence. To deny Defendant an opportunity to access these sites . . . would condone Plaintiff's attempt to hide relevant information behind self-regulated privacy settings."[33]

The court made the point that perhaps there may be no reasonable expectation of privacy in SNSs. "When Plaintiff created her Facebook and MySpace accounts, she consented to the fact that her personal information would be shared with others, notwithstanding her privacy settings. Indeed, that is the very nature and purpose of these SNSs else they would cease to exist. Since Plaintiff knew that her information may become publicly available, she cannot now claim that she had a reasonable expectation of privacy. . . . [G]iven the millions of users, '[i]n this environment, privacy is no longer grounded in reasonable expectations, but rather in some theoretical protocol better known as wishful thinking.'"[34]

Bracketing in both time and rulings on the discoverability of information on SNSs are the following two cases, the former the earliest decision of the four cases and the most protective of information on SNSs.

31. *Id.*, at 653.
32. *Id.*, at 654.
33. *Id.*, at 655.
34. *Id.*

3. *Crispin v. Christian Audigier*[35]

The defendant wanted to view the communications made by the plaintiff on the plaintiff's SNSs, Facebook and MySpace, and so subpoenaed those companies. But the court, after ruling that these SNSs were both remote computing service and electronic communication service providers under the Stored Communications Act (SCA), held that these types of entities are required not to disclose the defendant's communications via e-mail that are "inherently private." The court held that communications made available only to certain approved users on the plaintiff's Facebook wall or MySpace comments cannot be disclosed under the SCA by the sites. If the privacy settings are for public access, then the SCA does not protect those communications from discovery. This left open the possibility of a different result for a discovery request directed to the party for the same information. The SCA is covered in Chapter 3.

4. *McMillen v. Hummingbird Speedway*[36]

Defendants sought access in discovery to the plaintiff's SNSs, to ascertain whether he had made any statements contradicting his allegations of possible permanent impairment. After reviewing the public portion of his SNS and finding such statements, defendants filed a motion to compel discovery of the "private" portion. The plaintiff asked that his communications among private SNS friends be considered confidential and therefore privileged against discovery. The court reviewed the privacy policies of these SNSs, which discussed disclosures on other users' home pages, even after account deletion, disclosures for legal reasons, to avoid harm to the user or the social networking company, and disclosure to the website's operators. The court held therefore that there can be no reasonable expectation that any SNS communications would remain confidential, as there would be in, for example. an attorney-client relationship, nor is there any requirement for friendships to maintain confidentiality. The court ordered discovery of the plaintiff's relevant information on these SNSs.

D. Recommendations

The cat is out of the bag (or the genie out of the bottle or the cow out of the barn, depending on the preferred motif) with social networking. The popularity of SNSs among customers and employees requires organizations to first catch up with this wave and then get ahead of it. For those uses of social networking that went through the standard planning processes, such as a corporate blog, corresponding risk treatment options including controls should be implemented. But because many of these uses come into an organization outside the usual process, it is important to ensure that at least the following controls are in place.

1. *SNS Controls*

- **Information Security and Privacy Policy:** The information security and privacy policy addresses the extent of an organization's use of social networking, the acceptable use of organizational social networking resources by employees,

35. Crispin v. Christian Audigier, Inc. et. al., Case No. CV 09-09509 MMM-JEMx (C.D. Cal. 2010).
36. McMillen v. Hummingbird Speedway, Inc., No. 113—2010 CD (Jefferson County, PA 2010).

and the limits to use of personal social networking resources that can be in any manner associated with the organization or are used during work time.

- **Existing Controls:** Malware, intrusion detection, URL blocking, content filtering, and all applicable network control capabilities are extended to organizational social networking resources.
- **SNS Monitoring:** Monitoring of leading SNSs is done to ensure there is no inadvertent or intentional leakage of corporate or client information or improper use of intellectual property.
- **Training:** Awareness training is provided to all employees and contractors on the legal, technical, and reputational risks of improper usage of social networking, and in-depth training is provided to all IT and information security support staff to ensure that social networking controls are properly designed, implemented, measured, monitored, reviewed, remediated, and reported.
- **Legal Involvement:** The legal team is involved closely in all efforts to choose social networking policies, controls, and allowed sites, including review of privacy and information security policies of those sites and related agreements and how social networking usage may impact regulatory compliance and litigation evidence preservation issues.
- **Legal Duties:** Organizations proactively determine whether they have any legal duties to monitor SNSs and consider the potential litigation implications for privacy and electronic discovery in the organization's use and certain uses by their employees and business associates of SNSs.
- **SNS and Employment Actions:** The organization's human resources and legal departments need to work closely when an organization is planning to utilize SNSs to gather information about current and prospective employees. Information gathered about prospective employees should not include any information that could not be lawfully obtained during the interview process and should be done in a consistent manner for all candidates, including use of third parties to gather the information based on pre-existing rules. Information from the SNSs of current employees must not be used in adverse employment actions that violate section 7 of the National Labor Relations Act's[37] protection of "concerted activities," as was alleged in a recent complaint by the National Labor Relations Board, where an employee was terminated for postings on a SNS.[38]

2. *SNS Policy*

To bring all of these social networking activities into a comprehensive organizational approach, a social media policy should be created. The contents of this policy should be used to:

- **Existing Policies:** Extend social networking use to all existing policies and procedures for: protection of confidential and private information; prohibit discrimina-

37. National Labor Relations Act, 29 U.S.C. § 157.

38. American Medical Response of CT, Inc. and international Brotherhood of Teamsters, Local 443. NLRB Case No. 34-CA-12576.

tion, harassment, and obscenity; protect the reputations of the organization, its customers, employees, and business partners; and clearly state that there should be no expectation of privacy in use of SNS when using organizational resources for access.

- **Intellectual Property:** Instruct employees and subcontractors when using personal SNSs not to utilize corporate logs, trademarks, URLs, email addresses or other items identified with the organization and to make it clear that any opinions offered are their own and not the organizations (i.e. they are not authorized to speak for the organization).
- **Employee Monitoring:** Inform employees and subcontractors that it will monitor specified types of communications on SNS and which types of communications are prohibited and that it will monitor all activities necessary for compliance with this policy.
- **Endorsements:** Comply with the FTC's *Guidelines on Endorsements.*[39] These revised guidelines cover advertisements on social networks, blogs, wikis, chat rooms, discussion groups, tweets, e-mail broadcasts, virtual worlds, or other Internet sites. They spell out the required transparency and disclosure of material relationships between someone endorsing a product or service and the product maker/service provider and any compensation.
- **Ownership of Content:** Maintain the organization's ownership over all SNS content, fans/followers, features, and related intellectual property, in the event of a separation from the organization of the employee responsible for such social networking activities.

7.2 CLOUD COMPUTING

This section highlights some of the key issues of cloud computing that are covered in much greater depth in the companion book on cloud computing for lawyers.[40] The National Institute of Standards and Technology (NIST) defines cloud computing as "a model for enabling convenient, on-demand network access to a shared pool of configurable computing resources (e.g., networks, servers, storage, applications, and services) that can be rapidly provisioned and released with minimal management effort or service provider interaction."[41] The cloud model promotes availability and comprises three categories: essential characteristics, service models, and deployment models.

1. Five essential characteristics
    - On-demand self-service: by consumers for cloud services as needed
    - Broad network access: from disparate locations and device types
    - Resource pooling: the cloud service provider's (CSP's) shared storage, processing, memory, network bandwidth, and virtual machines are available to multiple clients

39. Federal Trade Commission, *Guides Concerning the Use of Endorsements and Testimonials in Advertising*, 16 CFR Part 255, (2009).

40. Thomas Shaw, Richard Santalesa, David Navetta & Peter McLaughlin, Cloud Computing—A Practical Guide for Lawyers (American Bar Association 2011).

41. NIST, *The NIST Definition of Cloud Computing*, Ver. 15 (2009).

- Rapid elasticity: resources can be rapidly scaled up and down as needed
- Measured service: resources are monitored, controlled, and metered for reporting

2. Three service models
   - Software as a Service (SaaS): customers use the CSP's infrastructure and applications
   - Platform as a Service (PaaS): customers use the CSP's application tools to create their own applications and the CSP's infrastructure
   - Infrastructure as a Service (IaaS): customers use the CSP's infrastructure

3. Four deployment models
   - Private: the customer controls the cloud infrastructure
   - Community: several customers share a cloud infrastructure
   - Public: the public shares the cloud infrastructure
   - Hybrid: a mixture of the preceding three, with the ability to load-balance between them

A. The Cloud and Information Security and Privacy

Operating in the cloud computing environment, especially when deploying nonprivate models, poses a number of new information security and privacy challenges for organizations. These challenges include (1) the interfaces to the network are publicly available and thus subject to special focus by hackers; (2) the use of hypervisors to control the multiple virtual machines that will provide customers access to the pooled resources may themselves be subject to attack; (3) confidential or sensitive personal information may be shared if not on common physical disks then in common physical memory and may remain after deletion or the cessation of service; (4) multiple subcontractors in disparate locations may provide cloud services and thus store the organization's data; (5) the rules to be followed for data protection and data breaches may be contradictory, considering the potential mobility of data across geographic and thus statutory boundaries; and (6) the sheer amount of data makes it more likely to be a target for insiders' unauthorized access.

There are additional major security issues, such as (1) the use of encryption is now more necessary than it would be if the data was all housed inside an organization's facility; (2) the management of keys becomes far more complex and subject to exposure; (3) identity management, especially when dealing with federated (single sign-on) systems, becomes complicated; (4) logging and other monitoring and tools may now be unavailable or subject to limitations due to the presence of multiple tenants using the environment; (5) vulnerability testing and penetration testing may no longer be practical given a production system shared by so many other organizations; (6) the destruction of all copies of an organization's data may be very difficult to verify upon contract termination or equipment retirement; and (7) security controls, incident management procedures, and business continuity plans must be extended and synchronized between the CSP and the organization.

B. Statutes Applicable to the Cloud

Numerous privacy and information security laws may apply in the cloud computing context. The relevant laws include, among others:

- Nonsectoral state data security laws[42]
- State encryption laws[43]
- Family Educational Rights and Privacy Act (FERPA)[44]
- Health Information Portability and Accountability Act (HIPAA) Privacy Rule[45] and Security Rule,[46] and Health Information Technology for Economic and Clinical Health Act (HITECH Act);[47]
- Fair Credit Reporting Act (FCRA) and Fair and Accurate Credit Transactions Act (FACTA) amendments,[48] including the Red Flags Rule[49]
- State breach notification laws[50]
- Uniting and Strengthening America by Providing Appropriate Tools Required to Intercept and Obstruct Terrorism Act (USA PATRIOT Act)[51]
- EU Data Protection Directive[52] and EU member country implementing legislation[53]
- Canada's Personal Information Protection and Electronic Documents Act (PIPEDA)
- Mexico's newly enacted Federal Data Protection Law[54]
- Other international laws related to information security and privacy (see Chapter 2)

---

42. *See, e.g.*, Ark. Code Ann. § 4-110-104(b); Cal. Civ. Code §§ 1798.31, 1798.81.5; Colo. Rev. Stat. Ann. § 6-1-713; Conn. HB 5658; Ky. Rev. Stat. Ann. §§ 365.720–.730; Md. Code Ann., Com. Law § 14-3503; Mass. Gen. Laws ch. 93H 201 Mass. Code Regs. 17.00–17.05; Nev. Rev. Stat. §§ 603A.210, 603A.215 (SB 227); Or. Rev. Stat. § 646A.622; R.I. Gen. Laws § 11-49.2-2; Tex. Bus. & Com. Code Ann. §§ 521.001 et seq.; Utah Code Ann. § 13-44-201; Wash. Rev. Code Ann. §§ 19.215.020–.030.

43. Mass. Gen. Laws ch. 93H and 201 Mass. Code Regs. 17.00–17.05; Nev. Rev. Stat. §§ 603A.210 and 603A.215 (SB 227).

44. 20 U.S.C. § 1232g.

45. Standards for Privacy of Individually Identifiable Health Information, 45 C.F.R. pts. 160, 164.

46. Security Standards for the Protection of Electronic Health Information, 45 C.F.R. pts. 160, 164.

47. 42 U.S.C.A. § 300jj *et seq.* and § 17901 *et seq.*

48. 15 U.S.C.A. § 1681 *et seq.*

49. 72 Fed. Reg. 63,718.

50. *See* National Conference of State Legislators, State Security Breach Notification Laws As of April 12, 2010, *available at* http://www.ncsl.org/Default.aspx?TabId=13489.

51. Public Law 107-56.

52. Directive 95/46/EC of the European Parliament and of the Council of 24 October 1995 on the protection of individuals with regard to the processing of personal data and on the free movement of such data.

53. One German state recently opined that arrangements for cloud computing that would involve personal data in the cloud outside Germany are "illegal." For more information, see "German DPA Issues Legal Opinion on Cloud Computing," *available at* http://www.huntonprivacyblog.com/2010/06/articles/european-union-1/german-dpa-issues-legal-opinion-on-cloud-computing/.

54. *Available at* http://www.dof.gob.mx/nota_detalle.php?codigo=5150631&fecha=05/07/2010.

All the stakeholders within an organization should be part of the cloud computing discussion and due diligence from the earliest stages—IT, legal, information security, compliance, privacy, all the relevant business groups, and, as necessary, vendors and customers. Information security and privacy terms are extraordinarily important in cloud computing arrangements. Customers should carefully review and revise agreements and should insist on special protections where necessary to alleviate risk.

C. Recommendations

Any organization seeking to outsource information processing into the cloud, regardless of the service or deployment models used, should consider at a minimum the following contractual provisions to help address privacy and information security concerns.

- **Scope of Information Protected:** It may make sense, from an information governance perspective, to require security for all kinds of sensitive information and systems, not just personally identifiable information (PII).
- **Definition of Security:** A good definition of "security" might include a provider's technological, physical, administrative, and procedural safeguards, including but not limited to policies, procedures, standards, controls, hardware, software, firmware, and physical security measures, the function or purpose of which is, in whole or part, to: (1) protect the confidentiality, integrity, or accessibility of information and service provider systems; (2) prevent the unauthorized use of or access to service provider systems; or (3) prevent a breach or malicious code infection of customer systems.
- **"Reasonable Security":** Most U.S. federal and state data security regulations require that a company "[take] reasonable steps to select and retain third-party service providers that are capable of maintaining appropriate security measures to protect such personal information consistent with" those regulations, and "[require] such third-party service providers by contract to implement and maintain such appropriate security measures for personal information."[55] Reasonable security should be a floor for such contracts. In addition, a provider should agree that security will be consistent with all applicable privacy and data security laws and regulations and relevant industry standards. Beyond that, a contract might also include reference to specific controls and/or standards (e.g., ISO or NIST).
- **Restrictions on Use and Disclosure of Sensitive Information:** A service provider should not use any information it receives for purposes other than carrying out the services described in the agreement. The contract should also include controls to limit a service provider's ability to share sensitive information with

55. 201 MASS. CODE REGS. 17.03(2)(f). *See also* CAL. CIV. CODE § 1798.81.5 ("[a] business that discloses personal information about a California resident pursuant to a contract with a nonaffiliated third party shall require by contract that the third party implement and maintain reasonable security procedures and practices appropriate to the nature of the information, to protect the personal information from unauthorized access, destruction, use, modification, or disclosure"); Gramm-Leach-Bliley Act Safeguards Rule, 16 C.F.R. § 314.4(d) ("[take] reasonable steps to select and retain service providers that are capable of maintaining appropriate safeguards for the customer information at issue; and . . .[require] your service providers by contract to implement and maintain such safeguards").

any service provider, subcontractor, vendor, or other third party unless it has received prior written consent from the customer or such access is specifically allowed under the agreement. Prior to sharing such information, a service provider should be required by contract to contractually impose on its own service providers, subcontractors, vendors, and other third parties the same or substantially similar duties imposed on the provider itself in the primary agreement.

- **Audit Rights:** The contract should provide a customer with the right to assess and audit the provider's security and compliance with applicable privacy and data security laws and regulations at least once per year during the term of the agreement, after any actual or reasonably suspected security breach, and if the customer has any reason to be concerned that the vendor is not providing reasonable security or is otherwise not complying with the law.
- **Definition of Security Breach:** A customer may want to define a security breach to include any actual or reasonably suspected unauthorized use of or access to service provider systems; access or theft of information; an inability to access those systems or information due to a malicious use, attack, or exploiting of information or systems; unauthorized use of information by a person for purposes of theft, fraud, or identity theft; unauthorized disclosure or alteration of information; and/or transmission of malicious code.
- **Reporting in the Event of a Breach:** Although existing U.S. state laws and the HITECH Act require vendors to notify a data owner in the event of a security breach, as defined under the applicable law(s), the contract should also spell out breach notification procedures.
- **Preservation, Return, and Secure Disposal of Information; Control and Access/Authentication:** For purposes of meeting evidence preservation requirements and discovery obligations in litigation and government investigations, it may be important for a contract to require that a vendor preserve information and provide the customer with access to the information in the form in which it is maintained in the ordinary course of business. Contracts should also provide for return and/or secure disposal of the information in accordance with the customer's directions.
- **Indemnification:** An indemnification provision for security breach incidents is critical and should cover, in addition to fees and expenses incurred in connection with claims, litigation, fines, and penalties paid to third parties, expenses associated with responding to a breach, even in the absence of a claim or lawsuit (e.g., expenses incurred: to provide notice to customers, employees, law-enforcement agencies, regulatory bodies, or other third parties; to investigate, assess, or remediate a breach; to retain a call center and/or public relations consultants; to provide credit monitoring services to individuals affected by a breach; and to respond to government investigations).
- **Limitations of Liability:** The financial risk associated with a security breach may dwarf the fees paid by a customer under the contract. In order to assess the true risk in the event of a breach, a customer must consider how many records might be implicated (including data of employees, customers, and third-party individuals who have entrusted their information to the customer). Customers should resist blanket and/or unreasonable limitations on liability proffered by vendors.

- **Compliance with Data Protection Laws:** This provision is based on laws such as the EU Data Protection Directive or similar restrictions on and/or compliance with cross-border data transfers. These compliance requirements—including the need for Safe Harbor certification, standard contractual clauses, and/or binding corporate rules—must also be addressed in cloud contracts. Different European jurisdictions have varying perspectives on the legality of cloud arrangements.

Organizations contemplating cloud computing arrangements need to carefully consider the privacy and information security risks. The RFP, due diligence, and contract negotiation processes are crucial in identifying, assessing, and addressing those risks. Where sensitive information is at issue, no organization should rush into such deals based on perceived cost savings without evaluating the risks and putting in place appropriate contractual protections. In addition, organizations should watch the developments on standardization from ISO/IEC JTC 1/SC 38, which is the international standards organization's subcommittee on interoperable distributed application platform and services, which includes web services, service oriented architecture (SOA), and cloud computing.

7.3 MOBILE COMPUTING

Mobile computing is a rapidly evolving field with rapidly evolving security issues and practices. Wireless telegraphs were first used on ships in the 1880s and pagers were first used in the 1920s, but the rapid acceleration of mobile technology began in the 1990s. Mobile devices now range from the single-function pager and cell phone to the multifunction smartphone, laptop, netbook, e-reader, and tablet, plus USB-connected devices like thumb drives and modems, infrared connections such as printers, and radio frequency devices to handle asset management. The important issues for information security and privacy, though, remain constant across all mobile devices. In order to be functional, these devices need to connect through the available pathways at any given location. This need to be sufficiently open to connect with new parties creates the risk of connecting with unintended parties. And, by the very nature of being mobile, these devices are more susceptible to loss or theft.

A. Security Issues

Most mobile devices have a beacon that allows them to find or be found by an appropriate communications system that will provide the connection to the rest of the world. Cell phones most often are matching to a cell tower, while Wi-Fi[56] devices are matching to a router or access point. When the mobile device's beacon is on, the device can connect to other devices without the owner being aware. The user often is motivated to leave the beacon on, as this makes incoming calls and messages possible. Users need to be aware that, at a minimum, traveling through life with such a device in their pocket is a constant leak of information about where they are and have been.

56. Originally an acronym for wireless fidelity, based on the IEEE 802.11 standards for wireless local area networks.

The higher risk is that the ability to intercept telephone-based communication continues to grow. While this once meant a risk of interception of telephone conversations, it now means a risk for nearly all forms of data. In 2009, the encryption algorithm of GSM[57] supporting 2G phones was hacked and publicly divulged by an encryption consultant asserting that he wished to expose the security weakness in the global mobile market.[58] Industry experts responded that the threat was not severe because the mechanics of intercepting a call were still quite difficult. At the time, GSM represented more than 80 percent of the cell phone market.[59] Israeli researchers announced a methodology for decrypting 3G transmissions in January 2010. At a security conference in August 2010, a researcher displayed the ability to simulate a cell tower, intercept a call, and route it to its intended recipient while listening in.[60] The cost of materials to accomplish this was about $1,500. While this amount is large enough to dissuade the hobby hacker, it is quite small for corporate espionage[61] or other parties with financial resources and a specific target. At that time, GSM was estimated as 90 percent of the mobile technology market.[62]

In addition to all the services just described, provided mainly by the telecommunications industry, there are technologies that support mobile computing on a much more local scale. Most common is the offer of wireless Wi-Fi connectivity (e.g., Wi-Fi) by a wide array of venues from hotels and coffee shops to cities and towns. And there is the unprotected (witting or unwitting) availability of Wi-Fi connectivity by anyone with a Wi-Fi access point without password protection. For even shorter ranges, the Bluetooth technology has become quite prevalent and facilitates a wide array of inter-device communication, such as headsets to mobile phones and running-shoe data sensors to mobile devices with data collection software. There are other less commonly used technologies, such as those that connect phones in an independent ad hoc network, which have been tested for use in crisis situations.

The most important thing to understand about security for this sort of mobile computing is that each time the device is in a new location, it is connecting through a new party with different levels of security provided. This is true not only for Wi-Fi but also for telecommunications, where the connection may actually be through a subcontracted third party. This is in stark contrast to home or office computing where the device is routinely connected via the same technology, with the same firewalls, encryption technology, and the like in place. Many locations that offer Wi-Fi do not encrypt the traffic between the laptop and the network, making all of the user's data vulnerable to exploitation by anyone nearby.[63]

---

57. An acronym for Global System for Mobile communications, originally Groupe Speciale Mobile.

58. Kevin J. O'Brien, *Cellphone Encryption Code Is Divulged*, N.Y. Times, Dec. 28, 2009, http://www.nytimes.com/2009/12/29/technology/29hack.html.

59. Global GSM Market Analysis, Summary #1, Frost & Sullivan (Sept. 21, 2009), http://www.frost.com/prod/servlet/market-insight-top.pag?Src=RSS&docid=180573024.

60. Tony Bradley, *GSM Phone Hack FAQ: What You Should Know*, PC World, Aug. 1, 2010, http://www.pcworld.com/businesscenter/article/202317/gsm_phone_hack_faq_what_you_should_know.html.

61. *Id.*

62. "GSA GSM/3G Market Update (August 2010) Highlights Continuing GSM, WCDMA Success with New Milestones in Americas, Asia," GSA (the Global mobile Suppliers Association) (Aug. 2010), http://www.gsacom.com/news/gsa_308.php4.

63. *How to Stay Safe on Public Wi-Fi Networks*, LIFEHACKER, July 1, 2010, http://lifehacker.com/5576927/how-to-stay-safe-on-public-wi+fi-networks.

Current methods to improve security in this environment include turning off file sharing, turning on firewalls, and using SSL or VPN where possible.[64] When not actively using an Internet connection, users should turn off the Wi-Fi radio as it is unnecessarily giving potential access to others. Consideration should be given to options that more explicitly expose attempts to connect or retrieve data and require a user's consent to proceed. While these measures are usually rejected by users as too time consuming, disruptive, or unintelligible, those burdens should be weighed against the value of the data being carried and the associated costs of loss. Users should be trained to weigh these same issues when deciding what to download and carry in mobile devices. Users need to be vigilant in exercising all appropriate security options and regularly checking for any newer security options.

An additional nascent threat to mobile devices is "mobile malware." This is a targeted group of viruses, Trojans, and the like built especially for mobile devices. While still relatively small, in 2010, the trend moved away from thrill-seeking hackers to for-profit criminals. For example, a media player application contained a Trojan that sent text messages to fee-associated premium numbers, surreptitiously incurring charges on a user's phone and sending the fees to the criminals.[65] To date, it appears that the same sorts of precautions apply as for nonmobile devices, including a combination of anti-malware software and user training to treat attachments, links, and e-mails with care.

The loss and theft of mobile devices represent a significant risk of data compromise. Nearly 50 percent of organizations consistently report PC theft in an annual national survey,[66] and the theft of phones and other mobile devices is on the rise. Protecting against theft begins with training users to not leave devices unattended, to be aware of surroundings when using or displaying devices (e.g., subway snatchings are frequent), and to understand the best means of securing them while unattended. When devices are in view or in use, cable locks and device leashes can be helpful; when not in use, devices should be kept out of sight and in locked spaces. Because of the risk of theft, using available software to password-protect the contents—both when booting up and taking a break—are prudent, as can be the use of data encryption solutions. More recent developments include geo-location and the ability to remotely erase the memory, providing significant assistance as soon as someone realizes the device is missing.

B. Recommendations

Because mobile computing spans a broad spectrum of devices, policies and controls must primarily be focused on these devices as a class, with any device-specific controls added as necessary. To address this class of mobile devices, at least the following policies and controls should be put in place:

- **Information Security and Privacy Policy:** The information security and privacy policy must address the extent of an organization's use of mobile networking, including which specific devices and services are allowed and which are

---

64. *Id.*

65. *Innovation: Mobile Malware Develops a Money Bug*, New Scientist. Aug. 17, 2010, http://www.newscientist.com/article/dn19321-innovation-mobile-malware-develops-a-money-bug.html.

66. 2008 CSI Computer Crime and Security Survey, Table 1 (2008), at 15, http://www.cse.msstate.edu/~cse6243/readings/CSIsurvey2008.pdf.

prohibited, the acceptable use of organizational mobile networking resources by employees, and the limits to use of personal mobile networking resources during work time using organizational information or connecting to organizational networks.

- **Transmission Controls:** Due to the problems that come from interception of the transmission of information across wireless networks, very specific controls must be designed and implemented to address wireless technologies, often based on the protocols utilized. In general, the risks associated with wireless technologies should not be allowed to introduce any new risks into the organization's main network infrastructure. Proper authentication is critical as is the control of sessions between the wireless device and the organization's network.
- **Other Controls:** Given the mobile nature of these devices, special asset management and incident response processes are required, including the ability to track them remotely, to lock them down or wipe them clean if stolen, and to audit them at the transactional level. Control of access ports on user PCs is essential to prevent data leakage. Mobile assets should be tracked through their lifecycle to retirement.
- **Training:** Awareness training must be provided to all employees and contractors on the proper use of allowed mobile devices and the legal, technical, and reputational risks of improper usage and loss of mobile networking. In-depth training must be provided to all IT and information security support staff to ensure that mobile networking controls are properly designed, implemented, measured, monitored, reviewed, remediated, and reported.
- **Legal Involvement:** The legal team must be involved closely in all efforts to design mobile networking policies, controls, and allowable devices and services, including the encryption, malware, and authentication techniques used. The potential liability from litigation, data breach notice requirements, or regulatory or statutory noncompliance should be understood proactively.

7.4 STORAGE TECHNOLOGIES

The rapid adoption of digital communications by individuals and organizations as well as increased dependence on electronic information in normal business transactions and operations place greater importance on electronically stored information (ESI). Lawyers must be prepared to handle and protect ESI as part of their litigation activities, while taking appropriate steps to protect their own digital assets from unauthorized disclosure as well as accidental or intentional corruption or destruction. It is likely that storage technologies will help lawyers meet these challenges because of their intimate relationship with data—they are the repository and potentially the last line of defense against an adversary.

At the heart of all storage technologies are either storage devices (i.e., mechanisms capable of nonvolatile data storage) or storage media (i.e., the material in a storage device on which data is recorded). Nonvolatility, or the property that data will be preserved even if normal environmental conditions are not met (such as on disks or tapes, which continue to preserve the data on them when electrical power is cut), is an attribute of all storage devices and media. Common examples include hard disk drives (HDD), optical media (CD, DVD, BD), tapes, USB (Universal Serial Bus) flash drives, memory sticks/ cards (SD, SDHC, CompactFlash), and solid state disks (SSD).

Storage technologies can also include other useful capabilities such as mechanisms that facilitate networking and sharing of storage resources, data reduction mechanisms like compression and de-duplication to reduce storage and transmittal needs, virtualization to simplify use and management of storage resources, data mirroring and replication to guard against data loss or corruption, encryption to protect the confidentiality of sensitive data, sanitization to eliminate data when it is no longer needed, search mechanisms to find data, and data retention/archive platforms to ensure data availability throughout the data lifecycle (measured in months or possibly 100 years).

A. Storage Security Issues

The Storage Networking Industry Association (SNIA)[67] has identified what it believes are the primary business drivers associated with data security and documented them in its *Introduction to Storage Security* whitepaper.[68] These business drivers are: theft prevention, prevention of unauthorized disclosure (privacy), prevention of data tampering, prevention of accidental corruption/destruction, accountability, authenticity, verifiable transactions, business continuity, and regulatory/legal compliance. Threat agents originate from both external and internal sources. The external sources include: nation states, hackers, terrorists/cyber-terrorists, organized crime, other criminal elements, and industrial competitors. Internal sources include: careless employees, poorly trained employees, disgruntled employees, and partners. This combination of business drivers and threat agents has significantly influenced the data protection and data security mechanisms included in storage technologies, which in turn influences the guidance on how these mechanisms should be used.

Some of the major security challenges for storage ecosystems are:

- Protection of storage management
- Data in-flight protection
- Data at-rest protection
- Data availability protection (redundancy, resiliency, integrity, performance)
- Data backup and recovery (disaster recovery, business continuity)
- Securing information lifecycle management or other forms of autonomous data movement

SNIA currently provides one of the most comprehensive sets of best practices for securing storage, which includes general practices for all storage- and technology-specific practices for certain categories, like network attached storage.[69] NIST provides important guidance documents as well.[70] In addition, ISO/IEC is currently studying the

67. SNIA is a registered 501(c)6 nonprofit trade association that leads the storage and information management industry in developing and promoting standards, technologies, and educational services to empower organizations in the management of information.

68. *Introduction to Storage Security—Version 2.0*, Storage Networking Industry Association, 2009, http://www.snia.org/forums/ssif/knowledge_center/white_papers.

69. *SNIA Technical Proposal, Storage Security Best Current Practices (BCPs)—Version 2.1.0*, Storage Networking Industry Association, 2008, http://www.snia.org/forums/ssif/programs/best_practices/.

70. *See, e.g.*, NIST SP 800-111, *Guide to Storage Encryption Technologies for End User Devices* (2007).

need for formal standardization of storage security, and it is likely that one or more standards will be developed.

B. Recommendations

In general, lawyers will not be directly concerned with storage security, but they may be indirectly affected because of complications associated with locating and extracting data for litigation (e.g., forensics and electronic discovery). The notable exception is that lawyers should understand that their intentional and unintentional use of storage technologies to assist in the practice of law may place their clients and themselves at risk unless they take reasonable steps to ensure that client confidentiality is maintained and that the media are sanitized or destroyed before disposition.[71]

Possible reasonable security steps include:

- Ensuring that data retention and destruction and media sanitation are part of the information security and privacy policy
- Inventorying and classifying all storage technologies that contain storage devices or other storage media as well as device and management interfaces
- Ensuring that all storage events, both transactional and management related, are monitored and logged
- Determining use of storage in fault tolerance, hot swapping, replication, business continuity planning, and disaster recovery (cold, warm, or hot)
- Taking responsibility for sanitization of the device by requiring meaningful assurances from the vendor at the intake of the device and confirmation or certification of the sanitization at the disposition of the device

The exponential growth of data is expected to continue, which will continue to push the growth of storage capacities. At the same time, organizations will seek ubiquitous access to this data, which must always be available. To cope with this glut of data and usage needs, more and more capabilities will be integrated into the storage technologies. It is reasonable to assume that more sophisticated virtualization will emerge (e.g., to support server virtualization as well as cloud computing and cloud storage), storage systems will either provide encryption or use self-encrypting media, automatic data tagging and classification of digital assets will be introduced, policy-driven autonomous data movement will be used to protect data and minimize costs, sophisticated search capabilities will help locate data assets, and data integrity and authenticity mechanisms will be commonplace. Some of these capabilities will help the legal community with the practice of law (e.g., assist with discovery and management of electronic evidence), while others will assist with data protection and data security requirements.

7.5 OFFENSIVE CYBER-ACTIVITY

The military has defined "active defense" as "[t]he employment of limited offensive action and counterattacks to deny a contested area or position to the enemy."[72] In the

71. Issues of ethical obligations have been raised in at least one state bar.

72. DoD Dictionary of Military Terms, *see* http://www.fas.org/irp/doddir/dod/jp1_02.pdf, at 4.

commercial or private sectors, "active defense" has come to mean using limited offensive means as a way of protecting oneself (i.e., attacking the hacker), or—as some may refer to it—retaliation. Perhaps no other information security topic raises more ethical and legal discussions than offensive cyber-activity. In the military cyber arena, active defense is a well-recognized theory and concept, although still complicated with numerous issues and uncertainties. In the commercial and private sectors, it is not so well known, and the ethical and legal issues appear to far outweigh any potential advantages compared to its use by the military.

While the law clearly permits the use of self-defense of one's home, no such clarity exists in cyberspace. Advantages to using active cyber-defense include the victim's ability to respond immediately, control over the situation by the victim, and no need for a victim to rely on or report the incident to anyone else such as law enforcement. Despite the advantages, there are many more disadvantages. For example, the response from a victim against an attacker could lead to an escalation—a digital "arms race"; determining attribution[73] can be difficult if not nearly impossible; and the retaliatory or defensive strike may cause more harm than the original attack and could easily impact innocent bystanders. Furthermore, legal uncertainties exist as to whether active defense as a form of self-defense would be permitted.

A. Current Landscape

Several reports and commentators have referred to the use of "all the tools of U.S. power"[74] or confronting cyber-attacks "with all available means"[75] in discussing the offensive aspects of the government's approach to cyber security. Many view these types of phrases as indirect references to offensive use of force. Other dialogue related to military use of cyber capabilities has included more direct references to "use of force,"[76] "cyber attacks," and "acts of war." Further confusing the issue are discussions that conflate cyber-espionage and cyber-attacks. For the commercial and private sectors, regardless of the terms used, an attack on their networks is just that, an attack that must be dealt with in some manner.

---

73. "Attribution" in this context refers to definitively and demonstrably identifying the attacker despite any ruses employed.

74. The Commission on Cybersecurity for the 44th Presidency recommended the creation of "a comprehensive national security strategy for cyberspace" that would include "*all the tools of U.S. power*—international engagement and diplomacy, *military planning and doctrine*, economic policy tools, and the work of the intelligence and law enforcement communities" (emphasis added). *See Securing Cyberspace for the 44th Presidency: A Report of the Commission on Cybersecurity for the 44th Presidency* at 20, December 2008, available at http://csis.org/files/media/csis/pubs/081208_securingcyberspace_44.pdf. The report also later states that "possessing an offensive capability has a deterrent effect and the absence of an offensive capability makes deterrence a hollow threat." *Id.* at 23.

75. *See* "U.S., Google and China Square Off over Internet," which included a comment by Senator Lieberman that "Google's experience should be a lesson to us all to confront this ever growing problem aggressively and *with all available means*" (emphasis added), Reuters, January 13, 2010, *available at* http://www.reuters.com/article/idUSTRE60C1TR20100113.

76. *See Cyberspace Policy Review* ("The United States needs to develop a strategy [for cybersecurity] designed to shape the international environment and bring like-minded nations together on a host of issues, including acceptable legal norms regarding territorial jurisdiction, sovereign responsibility, and *use of force*" (emphasis added) at 17, May 2009, available at http://www.whitehouse.gov/assets/documents/Cyberspace_Policy_Review_final.pdf.

As mentioned earlier, a significant lack of clarity in all areas (legal, technical, political) exists with respect to cyber-offensive activity,[77] especially with regard to attribution. This confusion has led to a significant amount of commotion over various overt acts that occur. Three poignant examples include the attack on Estonia in 2007 and Georgia in 2008 and the attack on Google (and other major U.S. technical companies) in 2010. The media sensationalized all of these situations, though the identity of the culprits is still uncertain.

One significant impediment to a well-informed public dialogue over cyber-offensive activity is the lack of clarity in the area of liability. There could be both criminal and civil repercussions if a stakeholder pursues cyber-offensive activity. At the very least with regard to criminal liability, until Congress creates a carve-out for cyber-offensive actions, many if not most types of offensive cyber actions would be violations of the Computer Fraud and Abuse Act (CFAA).[78]

B. Appropriate Legal Balance and the Path Forward

Moving toward a clearer policy position on cyber-offensive activity will require, among other things, an appropriate legal balance between the rights of the entity in the defensive position, or the victim, and the potential for cyber-offensive activity to quickly escalate out of control. An appropriate legal balance will require appropriate policy debate and development on a range of issues. As mentioned, the number one issue involves attribution. Because of the nature of Internet communications and the protocols that facilitate those communications, properly identifying an attacker can be a very difficult process. In the event that the wrong entity is identified as the attacker and a cyber-offensive attack is launched, significant liability could result. In addition to attribution, proper reporting of cyber attacks and responses to those attacks will be necessary. An appropriate legal balance related to cyber-offensive activity must also take into account the nature of the attacked target and its overall value from a community perspective. If an attacker brings down an e-commerce site, it most certainly would be an inconvenience. If an attacker incapacitated a portion of the military or brought down part of the electric grid (or any other part of the critical infrastructure), the analysis would be somewhat different.

Charting a path forward will require analysis of cyber-offensive activity through a variety of lenses, including domestic law, such as the Foreign Intelligence Surveillance Act (FISA),[79] Posse Comitatus,[80] and the CFAA and international law, such as the Law of Armed Conflict[81] and the Convention on Cybercrime.[82] Ultimately, a balance will need

77. *See* National Research Council, Technology, Policy, Law, and Ethics Regarding U.S. Acquisition and Use of Cyberattack Capabilities (The National Academies Press 2009).

78. 18 U.S.C. §§ 1030 *et seq.*

79. 50 U.S.C. §§ 1801 *et seq.*

80. 18 U.S.C. § 1385.

81. The Law of Armed Conflict (LOAC) refers to the international recognition among civilized societies that unnecessary destruction and human suffering should be avoided while still allowing war to be waged. In the United States, the DoD Law of War Program (DODD 5100.77) provides guidance for compliance with the LOAC. See http://www.pegc.us/archive/DoD/docs/DoD_Dir_5100.77.pdf.

82. The Convention on Cybercrime is a treaty that a number of countries (including the United States) have signed. It deals with a variety of issues, including lawful intercept, copyright infringement, fraud, child pornography, and computer security violations. *See* http://conventions.coe.int/treaty/en/treaties/html/185.htm.

to be struck that allows an entity under attack to respond proportionally to the attack it is facing. It is unclear whether commercial or private industry will ever be granted such authorization for a cyber-offensive response, suggesting that a focus on networked system survivability doctrine may provide a more cogent strategy for the foreseeable future.

7.6 CRITICAL INFRASTRUCTURE AND CONTROL SYSTEMS

The term "critical infrastructure" refers to assets of both physical and computer-based systems that are considered essential to the minimum operations of an economy or government. These infrastructures include crucial systems such as telecommunications and IT, power, energy, banking and finance, transportation, water systems, and emergency services (both government and private-sector).[83] Industrial control systems (ICSs) are devices and systems that are cyber-based[84] and are used throughout many infrastructures and industries to monitor, regulate, and control sensitive operational processes, some based on security, others based entirely on safety. A typical ICS collects sensor measurements as well as operational data from geographically dispersed locations, usually providing this data to an operations center for whatever company is managing that infrastructure. These devices include high-voltage relays, valve controls, motor drives, pumps, and so on and are crucial in controlling and regulating critical infrastructure functions. ICSs are more consistent and preferred over human controls because they are more reliable and can be automated.

A. Information Security and Privacy Issues

Historically, most critical infrastructures have been isolated. These infrastructures, however, have grown in scale, complexity, and interdependency. As a result, during the troubleshooting of critical infrastructure disruptions, these factors require governmental and private entities to adopt an industry-wide or cross-enterprise approach in order to identify the root cause (or causes) of infrastructure disruptions and to reinstitute services. In power systems, availability is considered the most important security objective and confidentiality the least important.

In particular, interdependencies may compromise the reliability of a given infrastructure. For example, a power company may rely on a telecommunications carrier to provide crucial services to track power consumption at remote locations of the national power grid. The telecommunications carrier may in turn be relying on the power company to provide power to keep the telephone switches within the same area operational. Should a power outage last for more than a few hours, power recovery efforts could be impeded by the lack of a working infrastructure to communicate with the field. This sit-

83. *See* U.S. Department of Homeland Security, "Critical Infrastructure and Key Resources," http://www.dhs.gov/files/programs/gc_1189168948944.shtm.

84. The U.S. government has merged IT and ICS together by calling them "cyber-based systems." *See* United States General Accounting Office, Testimony Before the Committee on Homeland Security, House of Representatives, Cybersecurity: Continued Attention Is Needed to Protect Federal Information Systems from Evolving Threats, Wednesday, June 16, 2010, GAO-10-834T, at 2, http://www.gao.gov/new.items/d10834t.pdf.

uation is considered a crossed interdependency in which both infrastructures are dependent on one another.

Another key concern is the increasing use of automated systems (not necessarily information technology). These improvements have created new vulnerabilities. Addressing these vulnerabilities necessitates a broader view that encompasses entire enterprises and sectors and requires significant public/private cooperation (further discussed in Chapter 6).

Privacy issues can be raised by using smart meter data combined with traditional information collected by utility companies, such as names, addresses, Social Security numbers, birth dates, and credit card information. Even anonymized data combined with certain patterns of use and public information could lead to re-identification. The privacy concerns include: fraud, determining personal behavior, remote surveillance, and commercial non-grid use of the collected data.

Many ICS configurations do not take security into consideration. Several reasons account for this failure, ranging from insufficient embedded computational resources to avoidance of the cost and complexity of adding extra layers of security to plant operations.

B. Government Response

Notwithstanding complexity, interdependence, and a large number of independent players, there appears to be common ground for many infrastructures to define a common language needed to coordinate both public and private policies. The National Infrastructure Advisory Council (NIAC) provides the U.S. President (through the Secretary of Homeland Security) with advice on current security issues relating to the critical infrastructure sectors and their supporting systems. One of the ongoing discussions in the NIAC relates to "critical infrastructure resiliency," which defines additional methodologies to reduce the magnitude or duration of disruptive events or incidents. The degree to which an infrastructure is considered resilient depends on how effectively its enterprise operations can absorb, adapt to, and/or recover quickly from a potentially disruptive event/incident. It also involves how quickly an infrastructure's enterprise operations can migrate their services (sometimes geographically dispersed) from one region to another while minimizing the impact of a potentially disruptive event/incident. Thus, resiliency and redundancy are gaining traction among executives as means to manage and reduce risk.

Similarly, many supply chains are global, with goods and services using multiple and differing modes of transportation throughout the world at any time. This fact must be taken into account both as a risk and also as a potentially useful tool for creating resiliency and redundancy.[85] On the specific issue of cyber-based infrastructure, the government took early steps to coordinate the protection of key IT assets and the public-private response to threats to those assets. Concurrent with OMB and CIO Council efforts during late 1997 and early 1998, the Clinton Administration developed and issued Presidential Decision Directive No. 63 (PDD-63) in response to recommendations made by the President's Commission on Critical Infrastructure Protection.

---

85. *See* Allan McDougall & Robert Radvanovsky, Transportation Systems Security 11–16 (2008).

1. Authority

The directive acknowledged computer security risk as a national security risk, addressed a range of national infrastructure protection issues, and included several provisions intended to ensure that critical federal computer-based, or cyber-based, systems are protected from attacks by our nation's enemies. It established a National Coordinator for Security, Infrastructure Protection, and Counter-Terrorism, who reports to the President through the Assistant to the President for National Security Affairs; a Critical Infrastructure Coordination Group; and a Critical Infrastructure Assurance Office (now incorporated in the Department of Homeland Security). The directive addressed federal information security by:

- requiring each federal department and agency to develop a plan for protecting its own critical infrastructure, including its cyber-based systems;
- reviewing existing federal, state, and local entities charged with information assurance tasks;
- enhancing collection and analysis of information on the foreign information warfare threat to our critical infrastructures;
- establishing a National Infrastructure Protection Center within the Federal Bureau of Investigation to facilitate and coordinate the federal government's investigation of and response to attacks on its critical infrastructures;
- assessing the federal government systems' vulnerability to interception of communications and exploitation; and
- incorporating agency infrastructure assurance functions in agency strategic planning and performance measurement frameworks.[86]

Much of this directive was incorporated into the Homeland Security Presidential Directive No. 7 (HSPD-7)[87] and includes provisions for protecting cyber-based systems, including both information systems and industrial control systems.

All of the foregoing concerns constitute a challenge to the legal community. However, several current laws do protect infrastructures holistically. Those laws include:

- Homeland Security Act of 2002,[88] introduced following September 11. This act created the U.S. Department of Homeland Security (DHS) and now represents the largest federal government reorganization since the Department of Defense was created by the National Security Act of 1947. The DHS consists of a conglomeration of several departments and organizations to help streamline internal communications and includes several organizations under the powers of the USA PATRIOT Act of 2001.[89] Among other things, the Homeland Security

86. *See* United States General Accounting Office, GAO Report to the Committee on Governmental Affairs, U.S. Senate, "Information Security: Serious Weaknesses Place Critical Federal Operations and Assets at Risk, September 1998," GAO/AIMD-98-92, at 7–8, http://www.gao.gov/archive/1998/ai98092.pdf.

87. Homeland Security Presidential Directive No. 7: Critical Infrastructure Identification, Prioritization, and Protection (HSPD-7), http://www.dhs.gov/xabout/laws/gc_1214597989952.shtm.

88. Homeland Security Act of 2002, Pub. L. No. 104-296, 116 Stat. 2135 (2002).

89. Uniting and Strengthening America by Providing Appropriate Tools Required to Intercept and Obstruct Terrorism Act (2001), Pub. L. No. 107-56, 115 Stat. 272 (Oct. 26, 2001).

Act created a new cabinet-level position of Secretary of Homeland Security. From a critical infrastructure perspective, the act provided DHS with a broad responsibility to manage risk (but with limited authority) and to share and disseminate information, while coordinating development of private-sector best practices.

- Critical Infrastructure Information Act of 2002 (as defined under Title II—Information Analysis and Infrastructure Protection, Subtitle B—Critical Infrastructure Information, Sections 211 through 215, contained within the entirety of the Homeland Security Act of 2002) provides legal protection for voluntarily provided data/information pertaining to a critical infrastructure, information (including the identity of the submitting person or entity) that is voluntarily submitted to a covered federal agency for use by that agency regarding the security of critical infrastructure and protected systems, analysis, warning, interdependency study, recovery, reconstitution, or other informational purpose, and is considered exempt from disclosure under Section 552, Title 5 U.S.C. (commonly referred to as the Freedom of Information Act, or FOIA).[90] This law provides a safe haven for infrastructure asset owners and managers to submit crucial information about their operations, thus preventing would-be attackers/terrorists from acquiring such knowledge through public methods (such as FOIA), state and local disclosure laws, and the use of civil litigation.[91]

2. Smart Grid

In February 2010, NIST put out the second draft of its *Smart Grid Cyber Security Strategy and Requirements* report.[92] The report covers cyber-security requirements and privacy concerns, among other topics, for the electrical power infrastructure in the United States. Cyber-security in the Smart Grid is more inclusive than in a typical IT-centric view, including both "power and cyber system technologies and processes in IT and power system operations and governance." To ensure confidentiality, integrity, and availability of the Smart Grid cyber infrastructure, the report states that other hardware must be included, such as "control systems, sensors, and actuators." This report was followed in August 2010 by NIST's *Guidelines for Smart Grid Cyber Security*. Developed as a public-private partnership with almost 500 representatives from private industry, the guidelines aim at a large cross-section of industry stakeholders and comprise three volumes. The first volume involves security requirements, the second deals with privacy, and the third concerns vulnerabilities and current security issues.[93]

---

90. 6 U.S.C. § 133 (2010).

91. *See* U.S. Department of Homeland Security, Protected Critical Infrastructure Information (PCII) Program, http://www.dhs.gov/files/programs/editorial_0404.shtm.

92. NIST IR 7628 (Draft), *Smart Grid Cyber Security Strategy and Requirements* (2010).

93. NIST IR 7628, *Guidelines for Smart Grid Cyber Security:* Vol. 1, *Smart Grid Cyber Security Strategy, Architecture, and High-Level Requirements;* Vol. 2, *Privacy and the Smart Grid;* Vol. 3, *Supportive Analyses and References* (2010).

CHAPTER 8

The Role of Advisors and Wrapping Up

Before concluding this review of information security and privacy, it is important to provide a context for the roles of the key information security and privacy advisors. The lawyers and the information security technologists must understand not only how they must function in their roles guiding business executives but also how they must work in tandem to ensure the organization's successful use of information security and privacy policies and practices. It is also important that the advisors not only have a view of current and historical events but also are able to look as far in the future as possible to stay ahead of changing business, legal, and technical risks. To assist with understanding these disparate requirements, this chapter opens with an explanation of the roles of lawyers and technologists. It then presents a look forward to help facilitate the organization's business planning process. The chapter and the book wrap up with some concluding thoughts.

What Global Executives Need to Know

- The roles played by lawyers in advising executives
- The roles played by technologists in advising executives and working with lawyers
- Some ideas on what the short-term future may bring for information security and privacy
- How (again) organizations can succeed in a dynamic business and legal environment by using a stable methodology to address information security and privacy
- Why (again) executives must both own and lead the risk-based response to information security and privacy requirements

8.1 THE ROLE OF LAWYERS

Lawyers play a crucial role in assisting an organization to implement information security and privacy policies and practices. The modern lawyer plays an ever more interesting and vital role—one undergoing transformation as digitalization sweeps the globe and the dynamic nature of data rapidly changes how organizations function. Today, the lawyer's job is no longer constrained to knowing just the law; it is about knowing processes and technology and shaping them to comply with laws and regulations in all subject areas and locations. Two of the lawyer's most critical roles are to manage risk and to help build defensibility into the core of an organization's information security and privacy practices.

A. The Lawyer as Risk Manager

An abundance of old, new, global, and overlapping laws and regulations challenge the lawyer working in this area. In addition, each organization has its own unique footprint and legacy infrastructure. No one solution fits all situations, and a range of factors require assessment. The lawyer must work across the organization to advise on the legal and regulatory issues and then to help identify, manage, and mitigate meaningful information risk. The lawyer advises on how to fit requirements to processes to manage risk at the right cost and achieve compliance where necessary. Perfect compliance is not always the goal, but it should be cost-effective, risk-based, and legally defensible.

For a lawyer, developing this risk management mindset is crucial for an organization trying to build defensible practices. This aspect of the lawyer's role cannot be underestimated. Risk management should be cost-effective. The utility of information should not be so encumbered as to lose its value to the organization. The lawyer's role is to aid in finding ways to balance these interests. Several core objectives should guide the lawyer in developing such practices: defensibility; cohesive, consistent decision making; and the economic advantage of a good enterprise information risk framework.

1. Defensibility

Information and information risk spread across functions and expand well beyond an organization's firewall. Soundness of practices adapted to regulatory requirements and industry issues create a baseline expectation of reasonableness and defensibility. Defensibility across information security practices requires steady awareness and a good read on the potential impact of risk and on what constitutes reasonable controls. The lawyer has to understand the regulatory landscape, the organization, its processes, its technologies, and its vendors—the who, what, why, where, and by whom of the organization's data. This fundamental knowledge allows the lawyer to create innovative solutions unique to the organization that achieve defensible, acceptable information security practices.

Lawyers should:

- partner extensively with the information security team and business units to understand the uses and impacts of technology within the business to create a defensible, consistent, and cohesive legal and regulatory posture for a firm;
- be sufficiently tech savvy to grasp the multicollinearity of data and related risk profiles as well as to articulate risk levels (e.g., risk/cost benefit) to best conform to legal and regulatory requirements; and
- be versed in data breach and enforcement cases and the vulnerabilities that materialized (i.e., facts, technology, and result) and understand what regulators expect to be reasonable and defensible and what is not so the organization's information security and privacy policies and processes can change to meet evolving standards and to weather any storms.

2. *Consistent, Cohesive Enterprise Practices*

Lawyers have to possess a critical awareness of the ubiquitous and dynamic nature of data. As they work through issues, they need to be aware of building decisions that sustain prior decisions and support in-depth practices across the enterprise. Defense in-depth is a well-known security concept that also carries over to how the lawyer must drive cohesive enterprise risk policy and make consistent data-risk decisions.

To be effective, lawyers must have a keen sense of the impact of interlocking data functionality on legal and regulatory requirements. Managing legal and regulatory risk requires knowing historical practices and then continuing to make well-integrated decisions. The lawyer also has to watch for disparate, insular, or ad hoc practices that jeopardize the defensibility of other practices and decisions. Defensibility is not a one-off but is about building a framework that demonstrates consistent and cohesive practices—depth and breadth—in the information risk profile of the organization.

3. *Economic Advantage*

Providing economic advantage has at least three prongs. The first is mitigating unnecessary expense associated with data breach, fines and penalties, and excessive litigation costs. The second is optimizing access to information stores for both compliant and innovative use and reuse, such as in data mining and expanded information utility. The third is building out risk transfer mechanisms that in turn provide greater financial and operational stability and efficiency.

B. The Lawyer as Enterprise Risk Advisor

The transformation to digital information and the ubiquitous nature of data provide endless opportunities for organizations in the Internet age. Simultaneously, they increase the requirements for lawyers whose job is to help manage and protect the organization's information assets and its financial stability. The lawyer today must understand far more than just the black-and-white letter of the law and regulation.

The lawyer's call to expertise is multidimensional. He or she needs to help manage the intersection of legal, business, and technology information risk-related issues and continually assess opportunity with the potential impact of risk to the organization. New technologies can translate into instant important economic opportunities for organizations, and the lawyer must be able to weigh the value of opportunity against legal and regulatory requirements and assess the impact on the risk profile. To truly bring value, the lawyer in this position must be comfortable working across three roles:

- legal and regulatory expert
- business and technology advisor
- enterprise risk professional

This three-pronged expertise requires good legal skills with a solid grasp of law and regulation; competence, curiosity, and know-how in business processes, enterprise objectives, and technology fundamentals; and a willingness and ability to work collectively with others to shape and guide the organization. The lawyer providing purely legal advice with little or no pragmatic value will, in the end, add expense and risk to the organization. In sum, the lawyer should be comfortable with risk and with making enterprise risk-based decisions.

1. Pragmatic Insight

Pragmatic insight is essential to the lawyer advising on how to comply with diverse legal and regulatory requirements and attempting to implement effective solutions. Legal concerns are broad but interrelated—data security, privacy, legal and regulatory retention, books and records compliance, and vendor management, to name a few. The lawyer must be familiar enough with these requirements to ensure integrity, accuracy, trustworthiness, and utility across these functions. Processes and procedures in one area must be reliable, consistent, and defensible in other areas. A lawyer has to be acutely aware of the intersection of legal and regulatory issues and the multifaceted impact of data-related decisions.

The breadth of legal issues transforming the lawyer's role in information security is illustrated next. Such practices will help establish in-depth defensibility across an organization. Adhering to many of these practices will also provide for effective risk transfer and greater financial stability when an incident occurs:[1]

- Acting as a liaison between the corporate directors and managers, who hold the fiduciary duty of care for the organization's assets, and the security specialists, who seek to protect those assets;
- Providing guidance in the drafting and implementing of the company's information security policies; ensuring compliance with those policies; and integrating privacy, data retention, and vendor requirements into such policies;
- Participating as an essential member of the incident response team for any internal or external security issues, including any legal requirement to advise law enforcement;
- Advising on product design and proprietary information from a legal and risk perspective, with an eye toward ensuring compliance with security requirements;
- Advising on public relations matters and risk mitigation in the event of a compromise;
- Understanding and developing compliance strategies for security obligations resulting from applicable statutes;
- Providing guidance and counsel on the relevant laws and cross-border jurisdictional issues and assisting with sound and defensible forensic, preservation, and e-discovery procedures;
- Monitoring developments in the law addressing negligence and other forms of liability in order to advise the organization about the current standard of care;
- Drafting agreements with third-party vendors to delineate responsibilities for ensuring security and managing the risks relating to information security; and
- Providing advice on ways to minimize contractual and other potential liability that may result from security breaches.

1. ANSI/ISA, *The Financial Management of Cyber Risk* (2010).

2. Information Security and Privacy Best Practices

To fulfill the preceding responsibilities, the lawyer must develop an understanding of the technologies employed by organizations to protect their information assets, as well as the business and legal considerations involved in designing and implementing an information security and privacy program. Communication among the lawyers, the business managers, information security, HR, IT risk, audit, and IT staff is crucial to achieve the appropriate balance of security, risk, and business productivity. The dynamic nature of information shows that boundaries are disappearing. The interconnectedness of social networked work flows and Internet-based businesses increases concern about digital diligence. Lawyers are vital partners in managing enterprise risk and information security and privacy practices.

8.2 THE ROLE OF TECHNOLOGISTS

The role of the information security and privacy technologist is both varied and diverse. On any given day, technologists are covering strategic, tactical, and operational needs. These dedicated professionals often operate in harsh environments where budgets are highly constrained, requirements are diffuse or obscure, and their primary customers are at a distinct disadvantage. Given these circumstances, the technologist must use a blended skill set that blends technical know-how with "soft skills" that enable communication and collaboration.

Technologists of many flavors also play a crucial role in assisting an organization with implementing information security and privacy policies and practices. Their responsibilities typically comprise four key categories:

- **Subject-matter expert (SME):** Because of their unique experience, technologists provide expertise regarding technical requirements, technical performance, feasibility, and other related matters. Even as the average employee becomes more technologically savvy, it is the technologist who has specific subject-matter expertise. Failing to include the technologist's perspective in developing strategies and policies and designing solutions may create discontinuity between what is desired and what can be implemented and supported. It is essential to see the information security and privacy technologist as involved in the whole information security and privacy lifecycle, starting from the initial planning discussions.
- **Competent practitioner:** Technologists are often charged with operational responsibilities that include front-line compliance with security policies. It is their duty to evaluate and execute their duties in conformance with these requirements. Thus, it is imperative that technologists be highly competent. This high premium on current competence means that technologists must continually maintain and widen their skill sets to handle new and emerging technologies through education, participation in labs, or on-the-job exposure.
- **Educator/communicator:** Most employees will not have in-depth exposure to information security and privacy issues. It is therefore the responsibility of the technologist to proactively educate others in the organization about relevant

practices and to be accessible to all employees. Communicating information security and privacy deficiencies or disconnects, a changing environment, or a threat landscape falls squarely in the realm of the technologist's duties.

- **Collaboration leader:** Education and communication tie directly into the technologist's role as a collaboration leader. Given specialized knowledge and responsibilities, the technologist must work diligently to drive collaboration across the business. Collaboration should occur in common areas within information security and privacy, such as working with corporate counsel to develop reasonable and adequate policies. This often means translating technical terms into practical language that can be understood by the other parties involved and includes working with lawyers.

The technologist's role ranges broadly from hard-core technical skills to much-needed people skills that will bridge the gap between people and technology. Through the technologist's efforts, the chasm between people's actions and the resulting consequences (intentional or unintentional) and impact (positive, negative, or neutral) can be narrowed, leading to more effective use of technology within the organization. Narrowing this gap will help improve the management of information, people, and risk. The responsibility rests with the technologists to identify such gaps and actively work to narrow them through demonstrated leadership, collaboration, proactive education, and competence.

8.3 A LOOK FORWARD

In 2007, Microsoft's chairman and its chief of research and strategy spoke at a leading information security conference about how the industry and its technologies needed to mature.[2] They compared the state of information security to the medieval fortress, focused on higher walls and deeper moats while failing to anticipate airplanes and missiles. They talked about the impact and diversity of threats as well as the need to recognize the relationships between security, privacy, and interoperability. At the time, they called the needed future capability they were envisioning "trusted computing." Since that time, significant research and development has been under way in many quarters, and the fruits of that labor will be more evident over the next few years. A broad change to technology is likely to occur and will be coincidental with significant changes in related law and regulation.

The fundamental goal of information security is to ensure that information is accessed by only the intended people (or entities) and used only in permissible ways for permissible purposes. The "medieval fortress" model is vulnerable because it focuses only on the first of those three criteria—granting access to the intended parties. Technology is now in development that can implement complex policy about all three criteria—only granting use when it is also in a permissible manner and for a permissible

2. "The Imperative to Connect: Advancing Trust in Computing," Keynote remarks by Bill Gates, Chairman, and Craig Mundie, Chief Research & Strategy Officer, Microsoft Corporation, RSA Conference (Feb. 6, 2007).

reason.[3] For example, in the past, a bank ensured that tellers could have access to certain client account information by putting the data in a separate database and having a supervisor sign a paper form allowing the individual to access that database. But banks had no means of determining why the teller was looking up a particular person at a particular time—was he or she pulling up the account of a customer at the window or looking up a neighbor while killing time between customers?[4] In addition, it is resource-intensive to create and maintain many separate databases as the means to control access and other entitlements.

In the future, the system will figure out (1) that the person seeking to access information is a teller, assigned to work for the bank as a teller at that particular moment, (2) that the person is engaged in a transaction with or about that particular customer, and (3) which data the teller may access regardless of how many different places or ways it is stored. This is the sort of technology expected to be deployed in the next several years; incremental moves toward that functionality (e.g., role-based privilege capability)[5] are already in the marketplace. Beyond the several-year window, based on work already begun, it is possible that technology also will make a determination based on the risks involved in the transaction.[6]

As the technologies are made available, law, government policy, and regulation will change as well. And, internal to organizations, information security and privacy technology implementations are expected to drive closer together, because—to a system—each is just an expression of a set of policies about who may use what data in what manner under what circumstances. This is already evidenced in the work of the Organisation for Economic Cooperation and Development (OECD). The OECD has had a privacy guidance in place since 1980[7] and information security guidelines in place since 2002.[8] Now, the organization combines information security and privacy responsibility as "comple-

---

3. *See, e.g.*, K. Krasnow Waterman & Samuel Wang, "Implementing Policy Reasoning Over Cross-Jurisdictional Data Transactions Occurring in a Decentralized Environment," IEEE International Conference on Homeland Security Technologies (Waltham, 2010); K. Krasnow Waterman, D. L. McGuinness, & L. Ding, "Selective Privacy in a Web-based World: Challenges of Representing and Inferring Context," AAAI Spring Symposium (Palo Alto, 2010); P. A. Kodeswaran, S. B. Kodeswaran, A. Joshi, & T. Finin, "Enforcing Security in Semantics Driven Policy Based Networks," Proceedings of the 24th International Conference on Data Engineering Workshops, Secure Semantic Web (2008); P. Reddivari, T. Finin, & A. Joshi, "Policy-Based Access Control for an RDF Store," Proceedings of the International Joint Conferences on Artificial Intelligence, Workshop on Semantic Web for Collaborative Knowledge Acquisition (Hyderabad, 2007).

4. It appears that this same information security practice is what made possible the political imbroglio of 2008, when two Department of State contractors were discovered to have checked the passport records of the front-running presidential candidates. K. C. Jones, *Obama, Clinton, McCain Passport Breaches Expose Human, Not Tech Weakness*, INFORMATION WEEK, Mar. 21, 2008, http://www.informationweek.com/news/global-cio/showArticle.jhtml?articleID=206905232.

5. The American National Standards Institute (ANSI) approved the InterNational Committee for Information Technology Standards (INCITS) Role Based Access Control (RBAC) standard in 2004 (ANSI INCITS 359-2004), and RBAC was considered a standard means of implementing the Sarbanes-Oxley Act, Section 404 requirement for "adequate internal control." By 2010 it was available in server and database products.

6. *See, e.g.*, R. W. McGraw, Risk-Adaptable Access Control (RAdAC), NIST Privilege (Access) Management Workshop (2009).

7. OECD "Guidelines on the Protection of Privacy and Transborder Flows of Personal Data" (1980).

8. OECD "Guidelines for the Security of Information Systems and Networks" (2002).

mentary issues at the core of our digital activities" under the Working Party for Information Security and Privacy (WPISP).[9]

As entities become increasingly able to dynamically fulfill detailed requirements for protecting the sensitive information they control or hold, law and policy will increasingly require validation of such fulfillment and assess liability for failures to accomplish it. Already, public policy discussions are under way about the meaning of and requirements for "accountability"[10]—the ability and responsibility to demonstrate that information policy requirements are being met. And legislation and regulations mentioning or implying these principles are progressing on both the domestic[11] and international[12] fronts.

Another significant change that will be driven by this technology is the ability to continue to associate policy with data after it changes hands. When sharing data beyond the original parties will not affect the protections ensuring data is used only by permitted parties in permitted ways in anticipated circumstances, trust will be increased and, as a result, new business opportunities will be realized. At the simplest level, it is likely that there will be new contract terms to express these concepts. It is also likely that these new business opportunities will produce other changes in the legal landscape that we cannot yet predict.

One significant way in which lawyers can assist this process is to actively participate in technology requirements and architecture activities. Anecdotal evidence suggests that when asked, many lines of business personnel will provide technical staff with "rules" for access that are the simplified versions put into place when systems could not handle more complexity. Those rules have been used and repeated for a sufficient period of time that many believe they are the rules in play. Lawyers are uniquely positioned to provide clarification of the differences between the rules currently in use that were created to accommodate less-powerful systems and the actual underlying rules that should now be the aspirational goals for system implementation. Lawyers, however, must recognize that accomplishment of the goal will likely be years in the making and that they should assist in the process of choosing incremental improvements that balance cost and benefit.

8.4 CONCLUDING THOUGHTS

Business executives, lawyers, and technologists can and should work together to address the issues raised by the business, legal, and technical requirements for information security and privacy. With proper planning, utilizing the methodology explained in this book, this team can lead the way for global and domestic organizations to be able to

9. OECD webpage, "What Is the Working Party for Information Security and Privacy" (2010).

10. *See, e.g.*, Accountability Project: II, Centre for Information Policy Leadership (2010) (gathering expert opinions on questions relating to how regulators would practically measure accountability, how third parties might validate the organization's accountability, and the nature and implementation of redress in an accountability approach for data breach and privacy); D. Weitzner, H. Abelson, T. Berners-Lee, J. Feigenbaum, J. Hendler, & G. Sussman, *Information Accountability*, 51(6) Communications of the ACM 82–87 (2008).

11. *See, e.g.*, H.R. 2221: Data Accountability and Trust Act, 111th Congress, 1st Session (passed by the House, Dec. 8, 2009) (requiring regulation for information brokers to facilitate the auditing or retracing of access to, or transmissions of, electronic data containing personal information).

12. *See, e.g.*, Opinion 3/2010 on the Principle of Accountability, Article 29, Data Protection Working Party, 00062/EN WP 173 (July 13, 2010) (proposing to integrate accountability into data protection regulation).

address these risks in the most comprehensive manner. Each member of this virtual team must thoroughly understand her or his role as well as how to work together to enhance the efforts of peers. The lawyers must be able to speak to the technologists in techno-speak and the technologists to the lawyers in legal-speak, and both must be able to speak the language of the CEO and other C-suite members.

As discussed, success requires understanding and responding to both the information security and privacy requirements and risks. But this understanding cannot be static; it must be regularly revised. The legal and technology worlds are nothing if not dynamic, and so the legal obligation synthesis process, the legal liability exposure process, and the risk assessment process must be regularly utilized and the impacts (and, as applicable, likelihood) of new statutes, regulations, standards, liability exposures, threats, and vulnerabilities understood and managed. The needs to comply with these rules, successfully complete audits, and maintain certifications can play a role in driving compliance, but these ongoing legal and risk reviews should also occur as a normal part of managing an organization. The risk management process will also need to be on constant lookout for changes to technologies, not only technologies that arise from the organization's own planning efforts but those that arise from what employees are using and bringing to work with them.

To move out of a reactive mode, information security and privacy should be viewed as much a proactive necessity as are new product research, marketing, competitive analyses, or new services development. That means that organizations must look forward to understand not only how their business might be changing but also how statutes and regulations in all their relevant jurisdictions across the globe might be changing and how planned and unplanned changes to business operations might impact the information security and privacy risks that the organization must address. This is a difficult and complex set of tasks to undertake, but, with the stable methodology outlined in this book and all its subcomponents properly used by well-informed and experienced legal and technology advisors, imminently doable. Most importantly, organizations must turn to the technically skilled lawyers and legally aware technologists inside and outside the organization to garner the knowledge and expertise necessary to cost-effectively minimize the business and legal risks that are an ever-present and growing part of managing the global information security and privacy programs that successfully protect corporate, employee, and customer information.

APPENDIX A

Information Security and Privacy Standards and Guidelines

A.1 STANDARDS FOR ENTERPRISE SECURITY

A. International Organization for Standardization

ISO (International Organization for Standardization) and IEC (International Electrotechnical Commission) have established Joint Technical Committee 1 (ISO/IEC JTC 1), *Information technology*, Subcommittee 27 (SC 27), *Security techniques* to develop international standards that span information security management systems (ISMS), cryptography and security mechanisms, security evaluation criteria, and security controls and services, as well as identity management and privacy technologies. The following standards and drafts[1] are worth noting:

- ISO/IEC 27000:2009 *Information technology—Security techniques—Information security management systems—Overview and vocabulary.* This standard provides an overview of information security management systems (ISMS), which form the subject of the ISMS family of standards, and defines related terms.
- ISO/IEC 27001:2005 *Information technology—Security techniques—Information security management systems—Requirements.* This standard provides requirements for establishing, implementing, operating, monitoring, reviewing, maintaining, and improving an information security management system (ISMS). It adopts a control-centric approach to the application of sound information security management principles, and it can be used by internal and external parties, including certification bodies, to assess the organization's ability to meet customer, statutory, legal, and regulatory requirements and the organization's own requirements.
- ISO/IEC 27002:2005 *Information technology—Security techniques—Information security management—Code of practice for information security manage-*

1. In addition to the documents marked as draft, the following international standards are undergoing revision: ISO/IEC 27001, ISO/IEC 27002, and ISO/IEC 27005. Also note that the titles of the draft standards may change before final publication as international standards.

ment.[2] This standard establishes guidelines and general principles for initiating, implementing, maintaining, and improving information security management in an organization. The control objectives and controls of this standard are intended to be implemented to meet the requirements identified by a risk assessment. It may also serve as a practical guideline for developing organizational security standards and effective security management practices and for building confidence in interorganizational activities.

- ISO/IEC 27003:2010 *Information technology—Security techniques—Information security management system implementation guidance.* This standard provides practical guidance in developing the implementation plan for an information security management system (ISMS) within an organization in accordance with ISO/IEC 27001:2005.
- ISO/IEC 27004:2009 *Information technology—Security techniques—Information security management—Measurements.* This standard provides guidance on the development and use of measures and measurement in order to assess the effectiveness of an implemented information security management system (ISMS) and controls or groups of controls, as specified in ISO/IEC 27001.
- ISO/IEC 27005:2008 *Information technology—Security techniques—Information security management—Information security risk management.* This standard contains the description of the information security risk management process and its activities. It supports the general concepts specified in ISO/IEC 27001 and is designed to assist the satisfactory implementation of information security based on a risk management approach.
- ISO/IEC 27033-1:2009 *Information technology—Security techniques—Network security—Part 1: Overview and concepts.* This part of ISO/IEC 27033 provides an overview of network security and related definitions and defines and describes the concepts associated with, and provides management guidance on, network security.[3]
- (Draft) ISO/IEC 27033-2 *Information technology—Security techniques—Network security—Part 2: Guidelines for the design and implementation of network security.* This part of ISO/IEC 27033 describes the possible technical security architecture/design and implementation options as a means for the examination of different solutions and a basis for trade-off analysis. This guideline also facilitates the resolution of issues associated with technical constraints, and contentions between the requirements of the business and of security, that will often arise.
- (Draft) ISO/IEC 27035 *Information technology—Security techniques—Information security incident management.* This document provides guidance on information security incident management for information security managers and for information system, service, and network managers, primarily in large and medium-sized organizations.

2. This standard was previously known as ISO/IEC 17799:2005, but it was renumbered in 2007.
3. For this standard, network security applies to the security of devices, security of management activities related to the devices, applications/services, and end-users, in addition to security of the information being transferred across the communication links.

- (Draft) ISO/IEC 27037 *Information technology—Security techniques—Guidelines for identification, collection and/or acquisition and preservation of digital evidence.* This document provides guidance on digital evidence management, describing the processes of recognition and identification, collection and/or acquisition, and preservation of digital data that may contain information of potential evidential value.
- ISO/IEC 27799:2008 *Health informatics—Information security management in health using ISO/IEC 27002.* This standard specifies a set of detailed controls for managing health information security and provides health information security best practice guidelines to support the interpretation and implementation in health informatics of ISO/IEC 27002, to which it is a companion.
- (Draft) ISO/IEC 29100 *Information technology—Security techniques—Privacy framework.* This document provides a high-level framework for the protection of personally identifiable information within information and communication technology (ICT) systems. It is general in nature and places organizational, technical, and procedural aspects in an overall privacy framework.
- (Draft) ISO/IEC 29101 *Information technology—Security techniques—Privacy reference architecture.* This document provides a high-level reference architecture for planning and building information and communication technology (ICT) systems that facilitate the proper handling of personally identifiable information (PII). This privacy reference architecture can be used as a best practice to build necessary privacy controls into an ICT environment in a way that is compatible with information security controls.

The ISO/IEC standards and drafts can be purchased and downloaded at http://www.iso.org/iso/iso_catalogue.htm. In some cases they are available at the ANSI Standards Store at http://webstore.ansi.org.

B. NIST Publications

The National Institute of Standards and Technology (NIST), an agency of the U.S. Department of Commerce, provides standards and technology to protect U.S. government information systems against threats to the confidentiality, integrity, and availability of information and services. The following documents and drafts are worth noting:

- NIST Federal Information Processing Standard (FIPS) 199, *Standards for Security Categorization of Federal Information and Information Systems.* This document establishes security categories for both federal information and information systems that are based on the potential impact (three levels are defined) on an organization should certain events occur that jeopardize the information and information systems needed by the organization to accomplish its assigned mission, protect its assets, fulfill its legal responsibilities, maintain its day-to-day functions, and protect individuals. Security categories are to be used in conjunction with vulnerability and threat information in assessing the risk to an organization.
- NIST FIPS 200, *Minimum Security Requirements for Federal Information and Information Systems.* This document specifies minimum security requirements that cover seventeen (17) security-related areas with regard to protecting the

confidentiality, integrity, and availability of federal information systems and the information processed, stored, and transmitted by those systems. The security-related areas include: access control; awareness and training; audit and accountability; certification, accreditation, and security assessments; configuration management; contingency planning; identification and authentication; incident response; maintenance; media protection; physical and environmental protection; planning; personnel security; risk assessment; systems and services acquisition; system and communications protection; and system and information integrity.

- NIST IR 7621, *Small Business Information Security: The Fundamentals.* This Interagency Report (IR) can assist small business management to understand how to provide basic security for information, systems, and networks. It defines practices that must be done to provide basic information security for information, computers, and networks as well as important practices that are highly recommended.
- NIST Special Publication (SP) 800-12, *An Introduction to Computer Security: The NIST Handbook.* This handbook provides a broad overview of computer security to help readers understand their computer security needs and develop a sound approach to the selection of appropriate security controls. It can assist in securing computer-based resources (including hardware, software, and information) by explaining important concepts, cost considerations, and interrelationships of security controls; it does not describe detailed steps necessary to implement a computer security program, provide detailed implementation procedures for security controls, or give guidance for auditing the security of specific systems.
- NIST SP 800-30, *Risk Management Guide for Information Technology Systems.* This federal guide describes the risk management methodology, how it fits into each phase of the Systems Development Life Cycle (SDLC), and how the risk management process is tied to the process of system authorization (or accreditation). It provides a foundation for the development of an effective risk management program, containing both the definitions and the practical guidance necessary for assessing and mitigating risks identified within IT systems.
- NIST SP 800-34, *Contingency Planning Guide for Information Technology Systems.* This document provides guidelines to individuals responsible for preparing and maintaining information system contingency plans. It discusses essential contingency plan elements and processes, highlights specific considerations and concerns associated with contingency planning for various types of information system platforms, and provides examples to assist readers in developing their own plans. This document does not address facility-level information system planning (commonly referred to as a disaster recovery plan), organizational mission continuity (commonly referred to as a continuity of operations plan), or continuity of business processes.
- NIST SP 800-37 Revision 1, *Guide for Applying the Risk Management Framework to Federal Information Systems: A Security Life Cycle Approach.* This publication provides guidelines for applying the six-step risk management

framework to federal information systems to include conducting the activities of security categorization, security control selection and implementation, security control assessment, information system authorization, and security control monitoring.

- NIST SP 800-39, *Integrated Enterprise-wide Risk Management: Organization, Mission and Information Systems View.* This document provides guidelines for managing risk to organizational operations and assets, individuals, other organizations, and the nation resulting from the operation and use of information systems. It is the flagship document in the series of FISMA-related publications and provides, through the implementation of a risk management framework, a structured yet flexible approach for managing that portion of risk resulting from the incorporation of information systems into the mission and business processes of organizations.
- NIST SP 800-53 Revision 3, *Recommended Security Controls for Federal Information Systems and Organizations.* This publication provides guidelines for selecting and specifying security controls for information systems supporting the executive agencies of the federal government to meet the requirements of FIPS 200. It includes a catalog of security controls that can be effectively used to demonstrate compliance with a variety of governmental, organizational, or institutional security requirements.
- NIST SP 800-53A, *Guide for Assessing the Security Controls in Federal Information Systems.* This publication provides guidelines for building effective security assessment plans and a comprehensive set of procedures for assessing the effectiveness of security controls employed in information systems supporting the executive agencies of the federal government. It applies to the security controls defined in SP 800-53 (as amended).
- NIST SP 800-60 Volumes I and II, *Guide for Mapping Types of Information and Information Systems to Security Categories.* This publication contains the basic guidelines for mapping types of federal information and information systems to security categories. The appendices contained in Volume II include security categorization recommendations for mission-based information types and the rationale for security categorization recommendations.
- NIST SP 800-100, *Information Security Handbook: A Guide for Managers.* This publication informs members of the information security management team about various aspects of information security that they will be expected to implement and oversee in their respective organizations. In addition, it provides guidance for facilitating a more consistent approach to information security programs across the federal government.
- NIST SP 800-122, *Guide to Protecting the Confidentiality of Personally Identifiable Information (PII).* This publication provides guidance to federal agencies to assist in protecting the confidentiality of personally identifiable information (PII) in information systems. It explains the importance of protecting the confidentiality of PII in the context of information security and explains its relationship to privacy using the Fair Information Practices, which are the principles underlying most privacy laws and privacy best practices.

- (Draft) NIST SP 800-128, *Guide for Security Configuration Management of Information Systems.* This document provides guidelines for managing the configuration of information system architectures and associated components for secure processing, storing, and transmitting of information.

C. Other Publications

Several other organizations have published important security documents to assist with efforts like audit and governance as well as to provide sector-specific and general security guidance. These documents include:

- Information Security Forum, *The Standard of Good Practice for Information Security* (http://www.isfsecuritystandard.com). The Information Security Forum (ISF) is an international, independent, nonprofit organization dedicated to providing guidance on information security to its members and the public. The Standard of Good Practice provides guidance on key elements that should be addressed in an organization-wide information security program, including security management, critical business applications, computer installations, networks, systems development, and end-user environment.
- ISACA/IT Governance Institute, *Control Objectives for Information and Related Technology (COBIT)* (http://www.isaca.org). COBIT helps bridge the gaps between business requirements, control needs, and technical issues and helps communicate the level of control to stakeholders.
- Committee of Sponsoring Organizations of the Treadway Commission (COSO), *Internal Control—Integrated Framework* (http://www.coso.org). This document is an internationally accepted set of tools organized into a framework for IT governance. It provides a common language for executives and IT professionals to align IT with business objectives, deliver value, and manage associated risks.
- Federal Financial Institutions Examination Council (FFIEC), *Information Technology (IT) Examination Handbook, Information Security Booklet* (http://www.ffiec.gov). This document is used by financial regulators in executing audits of information technology and systems of financial institutions, and it provides a baseline against which a financial institution subject to the GLBA can be evaluated. It attempts to provide a high-level, comprehensive overview of the major types of information security controls one would necessarily expect to be operating effectively in a financial institution.
- PCI Security Standards Council (SSC), *PCI Data Security Standard (PCI DSS)* (https://www.pcisecuritystandards.org). This document represents the mandated and enforced contractual obligations between payment card industry members (card issuers, card holders, merchants, acquirers, and card associations) to ensure that card transactions occurring across multiple private and public networks are subject to end-to-end transaction security. Enforcement of the security requirements is done by the card associations and through a certification process of each association member.
- BITS, *BITS Framework for Managing Technology Risk for Service Provider Relationships* (http://www.bitsinfo.org). This document specifies a framework to ensure service providers implement controls in conformance with the ISO/IEC 27002 standard for information security controls.

A.2 RESOURCES FOR SYSTEMS SECURITY

Improperly configured and vulnerable applications and operating systems are often exploited by cyber attacks from criminals and nation-states. Understanding the vulnerability and attack trends as well as the security controls that can mitigate the risks with the most negative impacts is critical for most organizations. The following resources can play an important role in establishing a strong defense:

- NIST SP 800-14, *Generally Accepted Principles and Practices for Securing Information Technology Systems.* This publication provides a common baseline of requirements that can be used within and outside organizations by internal auditors, managers, users, and computer security officers. The concepts presented are generic and can be applied to organizations in private and public sectors.
- NIST SP 800-70 Revision 1, *National Checklist Program for IT Products—Guidelines for Checklist Users and Developers.* This document describes security configuration checklists and their benefits and explains how to use the NIST National Checklist Program (NCP) to find and retrieve checklists. The document also describes the policies, procedures, and general requirements for participation in the NCP.
- NIST SP 800-123, *Guide to General Server Security.* The purpose of this document is to assist organizations in understanding the fundamental activities performed as part of securing and maintaining the security of servers that provide services over network communications as a main function.
- The Center for Internet Security (CIS), *CIS Benchmarks* (http://www.cisecurity.org). CIS provides these consensus-based, best-practice security configuration guides that are both developed and accepted by government, business, industry, and academia.
- The SANS Institute, *Top Cyber Security Risks* (http://www.sans.org). This document identifies existing and emerging threats that pose significant risk to networks and the critical information that is generated, processed, transmitted, and stored on those networks. It summarizes vulnerability and attack trends, focusing on those threats that have the greatest potential to negatively impact networks and businesses. It also identifies key elements that enable these threats and associates these key elements with security controls that can mitigate risks.
- The Open Web Application Security Project (OWASP), *Top Web Application Security Risks* (http://www.owasp.org). This document identifies the top risks associated with the use of web applications in an enterprise. It includes examples and details that explain these risks to software developers, managers, and anyone interested in the future of web security.
- National Security Agency (NSA), *Security Configuration Guides* (http://www.nsa.gov/ia/guidance/index.shtml). These documents provide configuration guidance for a wide variety of software, both open source and proprietary; this software spans applications, operating systems, database servers, network devices, and so on. These guides are currently being used throughout the government and by numerous entities as a security baseline for their systems.

- American Institute of Certified Public Accountants (AICPA) and Canadian Institute of Chartered Accountants (CICA), *SYSTRUST Principles and Criteria for Systems Reliability*. This document provides a review process for systems reliability—security, availability, integrity, maintainability.
- CERT, The OCTAVE (Operationally Critical Threat, Asset, and Vulnerability Evaluation) (http://www.cert.org/octave/). OCTAVE is a suite of tools, techniques, and methods for risk-based information security strategic assessment and planning.

A.3 STANDARDS FOR SECURE SOFTWARE DEVELOPMENT

Building security into systems during their development is critical to ensuring some level of trustworthiness. It is often impossible or impractical to add security after a system has been developed. The following resources can play an important role in the integration of security during the system development lifecycle:

- ISO/IEC 21827:2008 *Information technology—Security techniques—Systems Security Engineering—Capability Maturity Model® (SSE-CMM®)*. This standard is a process reference model focused on the requirements for implementing security in a system or series of related systems that are the information technology security (ITS) domain. It is focused on the processes used to achieve ITS, most specifically on the maturity of those processes.
- (Draft) ISO/IEC TR 29193, *Information technology—Security techniques—Secure system engineering principles and techniques*. This document offers guidance on the principles, best practices, and techniques for secure system engineering for ICT systems or products and emphasizes security engineering aspects of the system/product lifecycle, from requirements to disposal.
- NIST SP 800-27 Revision A, *Engineering Principles for Information Technology Security (A Baseline for Achieving Security)*. This document has been prepared for use by federal agencies and presents generic principles that apply to all systems. It is anticipated that the application of these generic principles to specific technology areas will enable the development of more detailed guidance.
- NIST SP 800-64 Revision 2, *Security Considerations in the System Development Life Cycle*. This guideline is intended to assist federal agencies in building security into their IT development processes. This should result in more cost-effective, risk-appropriate security control identification, development, and testing. This guide focuses on the information security components of the SDLC.
- Forum for Incident Response and Security Teams (FIRST), *The Common Vulnerability Scoring System (CVSS) Version 2* (http://www.first.org/cvss). CVSS is a vendor agnostic industry open standard designed to convey vulnerability severity and help determine urgency and priority of response. It solves the problem of multiple, incompatible scoring systems and is usable and understandable by anyone.
- (Draft) NIST Interagency Report (IR) 7502, *The Common Configuration Scoring System (CCSS): Metrics for Software Security Configuration Vulnerabilities*. This document describes a set of measures of the severity of software security

configuration issues for federal agencies. It is derived from the official CVSS Version 2 from FIRST.

- (Draft) NIST IR 7517, *The Common Misuse Scoring System (CMSS): Metrics for Software Feature Misuse Vulnerabilities.* This document describes the Common Misuse Scoring System (CMSS) for federal agencies. It consists of a set of measures of the severity of software feature misuse vulnerabilities. CMSS uses the basic components of CVSS and adjusts them to account for the differences between software flaws and misuse vulnerabilities.
- NIST IR 7435, *The Common Vulnerability Scoring System (CVSS) and Its Applicability to Federal Agency Systems.* This document describes common software flaw vulnerabilities for federal agency use. It is based on the official CVSS Version 2 from FIRST.

A.4 STANDARDS FOR PRODUCT SECURITY

- NIST FIPS 140-2,[4] *Security Requirements for Cryptographic Modules.* This standard specifies the security requirements that will be satisfied by a cryptographic module utilized within a security system protecting sensitive but unclassified information. The security requirements cover areas related to the secure design and implementation of a cryptographic module, including cryptographic module specification; cryptographic module ports and interfaces; roles, services, and authentication; finite state model; physical security; operational environment; cryptographic key management; electromagnetic interference/electromagnetic compatibility (EMI/EMC); self-tests; design assurance; and mitigation of other attacks.
- ISO/IEC 19790:2006 *Information technology—Security techniques—Security requirements for cryptographic modules.* This standard specifies the security requirements for a cryptographic module utilized within a security system protecting sensitive information in computer and telecommunications systems (including voice systems). It is closely aligned with FIPS 140-2 and is intended to be used by the international community.
- ISO/IEC 15408 Parts 1–3:2008, *Information technology—Security techniques—Evaluation criteria for IT security.*[5] This multipart standard includes an introduction and general model (Part 1), specification of security functional components (Part 2), and specification of security assurance components (Part 3). It provides a common set of requirements for the security functionality of IT products and for assurance measures applied to these IT products during a

4. The NIST has published the second draft, FIPS 140-3, for public review.
5. This standard is functionally equivalent to the *Common Criteria for Information Technology Security Evaluation* version 3.1 (also known as Common Criteria, or CC) produced by the Common Criteria Organization (see http://www.commoncriteriaportal.org). CC evaluations typically use the Common Criteria Organization documents because they reflect the most current evaluation criteria.

security evaluation. These IT products may be implemented in hardware, firmware, or software.

- Institute for Security and Open Methodologies (ISECOM), *Open Source Security Testing Methodology Manual (OSSTMM)* (http://www.isecom.org/osstmm). OSSTMM is a peer-reviewed methodology for performing security tests and metrics that collectively test: information and data controls, personnel security awareness levels, fraud and social engineering control levels, computer and telecommunications networks, wireless devices, mobile devices, physical security access controls, security processes, and physical locations such as buildings, perimeters, and military bases.

A.5 STANDARDS FOR CRYPTOGRAPHY

Increasingly, cryptography plays an important role in guarding against unauthorized disclosure of sensitive information, but it is also critical in verifying data integrity as well as enabling digital signatures and nonrepudiation of actions. This section identifies important standards and publications associated with these technologies.

A. Encryption and Key Management

- ISO/IEC 10116:2006 *Information technology—Security techniques—Modes of operation for an* n-*bit block cipher.* This standard specifies modes of operation for an n-bit block cipher, which provides methods for encrypting and decrypting data where the bit length of the data may exceed the size *n* of the block cipher. It includes the Electronic Codebook (ECB), Cipher Block Chaining (CBC), Cipher Feedback (CFB), Output Feedback (OFB), and the Counter (CTR) modes of operation.
- ISO/IEC 11770-1:1996 *Information technology—Security techniques—Key management—Part 1: Framework.* This part of the standard establishes the general model on which key management mechanisms are based, defines the basic concepts of key management that are common to all the parts of this multipart standard, specifies the characteristics of key management services, establishes general principles on the management of keying material during its lifecycle, and establishes the conceptual model of key distribution.
- ISO/IEC 11770-2:2008 *Information technology—Security techniques—Key management—Part 2: Mechanisms using symmetric techniques.* This part of the standard defines key establishment mechanisms using symmetric cryptographic techniques. It addresses three environments for the establishment of keys: Point-to-Point, Key Distribution Centre (KDC), and Key Translation Centre (KTC).
- ISO/IEC 11770-3:2008 *Information technology—Security techniques—Key management—Part 3: Mechanisms using asymmetric techniques.* This part of the standard defines key management mechanisms based on asymmetric cryptographic techniques.
- ISO/IEC 18033-1:2005 *Information technology—Security techniques—Encryption algorithms—Part 1: General.* This part of the standard is general in nature

and provides definitions that apply in subsequent parts. The nature of encryption is introduced, and certain general aspects of its use and properties are described.

- ISO/IEC 18033-2:2005 *Information technology—Security techniques—Encryption algorithms—Part 2: Asymmetric ciphers.* This part of the standard specifies several asymmetric ciphers, including: ECIES-HC, PSEC-HC, ACE-HC, RSA-HC, RSAES, and HIME(R).
- ISO/IEC 18033-3:2005 *Information technology—Security techniques—Encryption algorithms—Part 3: Block ciphers.* This part of the standard specifies block ciphers that map blocks of *n* bits to blocks of *n* bits, under the control of a key of *k* bits. Six different block ciphers are defined: TDEA (128 or 192 bits), MISTY1 (128 bits), CAST-128 (128 bits), AES (128, 192, or 256 bits), Camellia (128, 192, or 256 bits), and SEED (128 bits).
- NIST Federal Information Processing Standard (FIPS) 180-3, *Secure Hash Standard (SHS).* This standard specifies five secure hash algorithms: SHA-1, SHA-224, SHA-256, SHA-384, and SHA-512. All five of the algorithms are iterative, one-way hash functions that can process a message to produce a condensed representation called a message digest.
- NIST FIPS 198-1, *Secure Hash Standard (SHS).* This standard specifies an algorithm for applications requiring message authentication. Message authentication is achieved via the construction of a message authentication code (MAC). MACs based on cryptographic hash functions are known as HMACs.
- NIST FIPS 197, *Advanced Encryption Standard (AES).* This standard specifies the Rijndael algorithm, a symmetric block cipher that can process data blocks of 128 bits, using cipher keys with lengths of 128, 192, and 256 bits. Rijndael was designed to handle additional block sizes and key lengths; however, they are not adopted in this standard.
- NIST SP 800-21, *Guideline for Implementing Cryptography in the Federal Government.* This document provides a structured yet flexible set of guidelines for selecting, specifying, employing, and evaluating cryptographic protection mechanisms in federal information systems and thus makes a significant contribution toward satisfying the security requirements of the Federal Information Security Management Act (FISMA) of 2002, Public Law 107-347.
- NIST SP 800-38A, *Recommendation for Block Cipher Modes of Operation: Methods and Techniques.* This document defines five confidentiality modes of operation for use with an underlying symmetric key block cipher algorithm: Electronic Codebook (ECB), Cipher Block Chaining (CBC), Cipher Feedback (CFB), Output Feedback (OFB), and Counter (CTR). Used with an underlying block cipher algorithm that is approved in a Federal Information Processing Standard (FIPS), these modes can provide cryptographic protection for sensitive, but unclassified, computer data.
- NIST SP 800-38B, *Recommendation for Block Cipher Modes of Operation: The CMAC Mode for Authentication.* This document specifies a message authentication code (MAC) algorithm based on a symmetric key block cipher. This block cipher–based MAC algorithm, called CMAC, may be used to provide assurance of the authenticity and, hence, the integrity of binary data.

- NIST SP 800-38C, *Recommendation for Block Cipher Modes of Operation: The CCM Mode for Authentication and Confidentiality.* This document specifies a mode of operation, called CCM, for a symmetric key block cipher algorithm. CCM may be used to provide assurance of the confidentiality and the authenticity of computer data by combining the techniques of the Counter (CTR) mode and the Cipher Block Chaining-Message Authentication Code (CBC-MAC) algorithm.
- NIST SP 800-38D, *Recommendation for Block Cipher Modes of Operation: Galois/Counter Mode (GCM) and GMAC.* This document specifies the Galois/Counter Mode (GCM), an algorithm for authenticated encryption with associated data, and its specialization, GMAC, for generating a message authentication code (MAC) on data that is not encrypted. GCM and GMAC are modes of operation for an underlying approved symmetric key block cipher.
- NIST SP 800-38E, *Recommendation for Block Cipher Modes of Operation: The XTS-AES Mode for Confidentiality on Storage Devices.* This publication approves the XTS-AES mode of the AES algorithm by reference to IEEE Std 1619-2007, subject to one additional requirement, as an option for protecting the confidentiality of data on storage devices. The mode does not provide authentication of the data or its source.
- NIST SP 800-57 Part 1, *Recommendation on Key Management—Part 1: General (Revised).* This document encompasses cryptographic algorithms, infrastructures, protocols, and applications, and the management thereof. All cryptographic algorithms currently approved by NIST for the protection of unclassified but sensitive information are in scope. This recommendation focuses on issues involving the management of cryptographic keys: their generation, use, and eventual destruction. Related topics, such as algorithm selection and appropriate key size, cryptographic policy, and cryptographic module selection, are also included in this recommendation.
- NIST SP 800-57 Part 2, *Recommendation on Key Management—Part 2: Best Practices for Key Management Organization.* This document provides a framework and general guidance to support establishing cryptographic key management policies and procedures and the infrastructure within an organization as a basis for satisfying key management aspects of statutory and policy security planning requirements for federal government organizations.
- NIST SP 800-57 Part 3, *Recommendation on Key Management—Part 3: Application-Specific Key Management Guidance.* This document is intended to address the key management issues associated with currently available cryptographic mechanisms. It is designed for system installers, system administrators, and end-users of existing key management infrastructures, protocols, and other applications, as well as the people making purchasing decisions for new systems using currently available technology.
- NIST SP 800-107, *Recommendation for Applications Using Approved Hash Algorithms.* This document provides security guidelines for achieving the required or desired security strengths of several cryptographic applications that employ the approved cryptographic hash functions specified in FIPS 180-

3, such as digital signature applications (FIPS 186-3), Keyed-hash Message Authentication Codes (HMACs; FIPS 198-1), and Hash-based Key Derivation Functions (HKDFs; SP 800-56A and SP 800-56B).

- NIST SP 800-111, *Guide to Storage Encryption Technologies for End User Devices.* This document assists organizations in understanding storage encryption technologies for end-user devices[6] and in planning, implementing, and maintaining storage encryption solutions. It provides practical, real-world guidance for three classes of storage encryption techniques: full disk encryption, volume and virtual disk encryption, and file/folder encryption. It also discusses important security elements of a storage encryption deployment, including cryptographic key management and authentication. It only discusses the encryption of data at rest (storage) and does not address the encryption of data in motion (transmission).
- (Draft) NIST SP 800-130, *A Framework for Designing Cryptographic Key Management Systems.* This document is intended for designers, implementers, security analysts, managers, system procurers, and users of cryptographic key management systems (CKMS) to manage and protect keys. While some introductory material is provided to explain the framework components and to justify the requirements, this document assumes that the reader knows the principles of key management or is able to find that information elsewhere (e.g., NIST SP 800-57 Part 1).
- (Draft) NIST SP 800-131, *Recommendation for the Transitioning of Cryptographic Algorithms and Key Sizes.* This document provides more detail than NIST SP 800-57 Part 1 about the transitions associated with the use of cryptography by federal agencies for the protection of sensitive but unclassified information. The recommendation addresses the use of algorithms and key lengths; the validation of cryptographic modules that utilize them will be provided in a separate document.

B. PKI and Digital Signatures

- NIST Federal Information Processing Standard (FIPS) 186-3, *Digital Signature Standard (DSS).* This standard specifies algorithms for applications requiring a digital signature rather than a written signature. A digital signature is represented in a computer as a string of bits. A digital signature is computed using a set of rules and a set of parameters that allow the identity of the signatory and the integrity of the data to be verified. Digital signatures may be generated on both stored and transmitted data.
- NIST SP 800-25, *Federal Agency Use of Public Key Technology for Digital Signatures and Authentication.* This document provides guidance to federal agencies

6. The types of end-user devices addressed in this document are personal computers (desktops and laptops), consumer devices (e.g., personal digital assistants, smart phones), and removable storage media (e.g., USB flash drives, memory cards, external hard drives, writeable CDs and DVDs).

that are considering the use of public key technology for digital signatures or authentication over open networks such as the Internet. This includes communications with other federal or non-federal entities, such as members of the public, private firms, citizen groups, and state and local governments.

- NIST SP 800-106, *Randomized Hashing for Digital Signatures.* This document provides a technique to randomize messages that are input to a cryptographic hash function during the generation of digital signatures using the Digital Signature Algorithm (DSA), Elliptic Curve Digital Signature Algorithm (ECDSA), and RSA.
- ABA Section of Science and Technology Law, Information Security Committee, *Digital Signature Guidelines* (1996) and *PKI Assessment Guidelines* (2003).

APPENDIX B

Glossary of Terms, References, and Industry Standards

TERM	*DEFINITION*	*REFERENCES AND INDUSTRY STANDARDS*
Access	The ability or the means necessary to read, write, modify, or communicate data/information or otherwise use any computer or network.	
Access Control	The ability to restrict *Access* to information to authorized personnel, organizations, or devices. *Access Control* may be based on a number of factors including organizational role or job function, level of assigned security clearance, or purchased access. *Access Control* is one of the nine *Principle Security Capabilities.*	
Accountability	The ability to identify the person or organization that performed, or is responsible for, the actions affecting information. *Accountability* is one of the nine *Principle Security Capabilities.*	
Addressable	Under the *HIPAA Security Rule*, for an *Implementation Specification* that is *Addressable, Covered Entities* and *Business Associates* must assess whether each implementation specification is a reasonable and appropriate safeguard in its environment. All implementation specifications are either *Required* or *Addressable*.	

TERM	*DEFINITION*	*REFERENCES AND INDUSTRY STANDARDS*
Adequacy	Article 25(6) of the *EU Data Protection Directive* provides that *Personal Data* may only be transferred to countries outside the *EU/EEA* if that country provides an adequate level of protection (by reason of its domestic law or of the international commitments it has entered into). If a country offers adequate protection, then *Personal Data* can flow from the 27 EU member states and three EEA member countries (Norway, Liechtenstein, and Iceland) to that third country without any further safeguards. The Commission has so far recognized Switzerland, Canada, Argentina, Guernsey, Isle of Man, the U.S. *Safe Harbor* Privacy Principles, and the transfer of Air Passenger Name Record to the U.S. Bureau of Customs and Border Protection as providing adequate protection.	http://ec.europa.eu/justice_home/fsj/privacy/thirdcountries/index_en.htm
Administrative Safeguards	Administrative actions policies, and procedures to manage the selection, development, implementation, and maintenance of security measures to protect restricted information and to manage the conduct of an organization's *Workforce* in relation to the protection of that information. The *HIPAA Security Rule* requires *Covered Entities* and *Business Associates* to implement appropriate administrative safeguards to ensure the *Confidentiality, Integrity*, and security of *PHI*.	NIST Special Publication 800-37 Rev. 1—*Applying the Risk Management Framework to Federal Information Systems: A Security Life Cycle Approach* (February 2010) NIST Special Publication 800-66 Rev. 1—*An Introductory Resource Guide for Implementing the Health Insurance Portability and Accountability Act (HIPAA) Security Rule* (October 2008) 45 C.F.R. § 164.304
Affirmative Consent	An individual's express agreement (opt-in) to receive certain types of communication or consent to the transfer of his or her personal information.	

TERM	*DEFINITION*	*REFERENCES AND INDUSTRY STANDARDS*
Aggregate Information	Compiled or statistical information that is not personally identifiable. Examples of aggregate information include demographics, domain names, and website traffic counts.	
APEC **(Asia-Pacific Economic Cooperation)**	*Asia-Pacific Economic Cooperation*, or APEC, is a forum for facilitating economic growth, cooperation, trade, and investment in the Asia-Pacific region. APEC has 21 members referred to as Member Economies: Australia; Brunei Darussalam; Canada; Chile; People's Republic of China; Hong Kong, China; Indonesia; Japan; Republic of Korea; Malaysia; Mexico; New Zealand; Papua New Guinea; Peru; The Republic of the Philippines; The Russian Federation; Singapore; Chinese Taipei; Thailand; United States of America; Vietnam.	http://www.apec.org/apec/apec_groups/committee_on_trade/electronic_commerce.html
The American Recovery and Reinvestment Act of 2009 (ARRA)	ARRA was enacted on February 17, 2009, and expanded the privacy and security requirements applicable to *PHI*. ARRA provisions were incorporated into existing *HIPAA* regulations where possible. Some amendments were to other legislation, such as the *Social Security Act*.	45 C.F.R. § 164.306(d)(3)
Assurance	Confidence that a system works to its specifications without defect or vulnerability. *Assurance* is one of the nine *Principle Security Capabilities*.	
Authentication	The process by which a person or a computer system determines whether a person is who he or she claims to be. Authentication identifies an individual based on some credential (e.g., password, *Biometric Identifier*). *Authentication* is one of the nine *Principle Security Capabilities*.	

TERM	*DEFINITION*	*REFERENCES AND INDUSTRY STANDARDS*
Authorization	The process by which a user is granted *Access* rights and permissions to restricted information. *Authorization* can determine if the user, once identified, is permitted to have *Access* to the information. *Authorization* is one of the nine *Principle Security Capabilities.*	
Availability	Providing *Assurances* that information and systems can be reliably and promptly *Accessed* and used when they are needed. *Availability* is one of the nine *Principle Security Capabilities.*	
Binding Corporate Rules (BCRs)	BCRs provide legally binding protection for data processing within the corporate group, meeting the *Adequacy* requirement of the *EU Data Protection Directive.* Once approved by the applicable data protection authorities, BCRs permit *Personal Data* to be transferred from that particular *EU/EEA* country to any member of the corporate group in any non-*EU/EEA* country.	
Biometric Identifier	A personal identifier that identifies a human from a measurement of a physical feature or repeatable action of the individual (e.g., hand geometry, retinal scan, iris scan, fingerprint patterns, facial characteristics, DNA sequence characters, voice prints, and handwritten signature).	

TERM	*DEFINITION*	*REFERENCES AND INDUSTRY STANDARDS*
Breach (of PHI)	Unauthorized acquisition, *Access*, use, or *Disclosure* of *Unsecured PHI* that compromises the security or privacy of the *PHI* and poses a significant risk of financial, reputational, or other harm to the affected individual. To determine if a *Breach* has occurred, a risk assessment must be performed to determine if the security or privacy of the *PHI* has been compromised. *Limited Data Sets* (except those that exclude patient zip code and date of birth) are subject to the *Breach* notification reporting requirements. The term *Breach* does not include the following three scenarios: (1) Any unintentional acquisition, *Access*, or use of *PHI* by a *Workforce* member or individual acting under the authority of a *Covered Entity* or *Business Associate* if: • the acquisition, *Access*, or use was made in good faith and within the scope of authority; and • the *PHI* is not further used or disclosed in a manner not permitted. (2) Any inadvertent *Disclosure* by a person authorized to *Access PHI* provided such information is not further used or *Disclosed* in a manner not permitted. (3) A *Disclosure* of *PHI* where a *Covered Entity* or *Business Associate* has a good faith belief that an unauthorized person to whom the *Disclosure* was made would not reasonably have been able to *Access* such information.	NIST Special Publication 800-122 (Draft)—*Guide to Protecting the Confidentiality of Personally Identifiable Information (PII)* (January 2009)

TERM	*DEFINITION*	*REFERENCES AND INDUSTRY STANDARDS*
Business Associate	A person or entity (that is not a member of a *Covered Entity*'s *Workforce*) that performs or assists a *Covered Entity* in any of the following: (1) Any function or activity involving the use, *Disclosure*, transmission, or storage of *PHI* or any *Individually Identifiable Health Information* of a patient (e.g., claims, data analysis, processing or administration, quality assurance, billing, benefit management, practice management, and repricing); (2) Any other function or activity regulated by *HIPAA*; or (3) Provision of legal, actuarial, accounting, consulting, data aggregation, management, administrative, accreditation, or financial services involving the disclosure of *Individually Identifiable Health Information* of a patient. Section 3408 of *ARRA* extended the definition of "*Business Associate*" to recently emerged entities such as health information exchanges, regional health information organizations, *PHR* vendors and operators, and e-prescribing gateways.	
Business Associate Contract	The written assurance from a *Business Associate* of a *Covered Entity* that the *Business Associate* will: (1) Comply with the requirements of *HIPAA* and the *HITECH Act*; and (2) Report any noncompliance to the *Covered Entity* that it notices and request the *Covered Entity* to correct the situation or cease doing business with it.	
Choice	See *Consent*.	
Confidential Information	Information, whether oral, written, or otherwise recorded, related to the business and operations of an organization that is not known to, and is not readily ascertainable by proper means by, the public (e.g., trade secrets, business plans, financial information, IT security information, and network passwords).	

TERM	*DEFINITION*	*REFERENCES AND INDUSTRY STANDARDS*
Confidentiality	The ability to protect information against intentional or accidental or unauthorized *Access* or *Disclosure*. *Confidentiality* is one of the nine *Principle Security Capabilities.*	
Consent	*Consent* is one of the *Fair Information Practices* requiring organizations to provide an individual choice about the use or disclosure of his or her information. *Consent* is the individual's grant of permission for such use or disclosure. *Consent* may be affirmative (e.g., opt in) or implied (e.g., the individual didn't opt out). In Europe, the equivalent principle is Choice. Individuals must be provided with clear and conspicuous, readily available, and affordable mechanisms to exercise choice over the use of their *Personal Data*. Individuals have the right to *Consent* (opt out) whether their *Personal Data* may be disclosed to a third party or used for a different purpose. For *Sensitive Data*, the *Data Subject* must provide affirmative or explicit (opt in) *Consent*.	
Cookies	Small text files that are stored on a client machine and that may be later retrieved by a web server from a client machine. Cookie files allow the web server to keep track of the end-user's web browser activities. Cookies can also be used to prevent users from having to be authorized for every password-protected page they access during a session by recording that they have successfully supplied their user name and password already.	
COPPA	The FTC's *Children's Online Privacy Protection Act* (COPPA) governing the online collection of information from children under the age of 13.	www.ftc.fov/privacy/privacyinitiatives/children.html
Covered Entity	A *Covered Entity* is a: (1) Health care provider that conducts certain transactions in electronic form (a "covered health care provider"); (2) Health care clearinghouse; or (3) Health plan.	Decision tools for determining status as a *Covered Entity* are available at http://www.cms.gov/apps/hipaa2decisionsupport/default.asp.

TERM	*DEFINITION*	*REFERENCES AND INDUSTRY STANDARDS*
CPNI	Every telecommunications carrier has a duty to protect a customer's *Customer Proprietary Network Information* (CPNI). CPNI includes information about a customer's telephone services and information contained in the customer's bill. CPNI does not include "subscriber list information" (i.e., directory information).	Section 222(a) of the Communications Act of 1934, as amended, 47 U.S.C. §§ 222 and FCC Regulations 47 C.F.R. § 64.2010
Data Controller	The *EU Data Protection Directive* defines a *Data Controller* as "the natural or legal person, public authority, agency or any other body which alone or jointly with others determines the purposes and means of the processing of personal data; where the purposes and means of processing are determined by national or community laws or regulations, the controller or the specific criteria for his nomination may be designated by national or community law."	
Data Importer	An organization located outside the *EU/EEA* that receives *Personal Data* of a resident of the *EU/EEA.*	
Data Processor	A person or organization that processes *Personal Data* on behalf of and under the authority of a *Data Controller.*	
Data Subject	An identified or identifiable natural person for purposes of the *EU Data Protection Directive*. An identifiable person is one who can be identified, directly or indirectly, in particular by reference to an identification number or to one or more factors specific to her or his physical, physiological, mental, economic, cultural, or social identity.	

TERM	*DEFINITION*	*REFERENCES AND INDUSTRY STANDARDS*
Degaussing	Means to remove or erase a residual magnetic field from a magnetized object, such as a tape or disk, usually by introducing much stronger and gradually diminishing magnetic fields of alternating polarity.	NIST Special Publication 800-99—*Guidelines for Media Sanitization, Recommendations of the National Institute of Standards and Technology* (September 2006)
Digital Certificate	A specially formatted block of data that contains a public key and the name of its owner thereby binding the identity of the owner (or some other attribute) to a public/private key pair. The certificate also carries the *Digital Signature* of a trusted third party in order to *Authenticate* it.	
Digital Signature	The process used to verify to the person receiving the information through an electronic transmission (the receiver) that the person sending the information (the transmitter) is who he or she purports to be and that the message has not changed from the time it was transmitted. In a digital signature, there is a data value generated by a public key algorithm based on the contents of a block of data and a private key, yielding an individual checksum that verifies the identity of the signer and the integrity of the data that is signed.	
Disclose **Disclosure**	Means to release, transfer, provide *Access* to, or divulge *PHI*, including e-*PHI*, outside a *Covered Entity* or *Business Associate*.	

TERM	*DEFINITION*	*REFERENCES AND INDUSTRY STANDARDS*
DMCA	The *Digital Millennium Copyright Act* (DMCA) prohibits the circumvention of technological measures implemented by copyright owners to protect their works and also prohibits tampering with copyright management information.	
DRM	Digital Rights Management.	
Electronic Media	(1) Electronic storage media, including memory devices in computers (hard drives) and any removable/transportable digital memory medium, such as magnetic tape or disk, optical disk, or digital memory card; or (2) Transmission media used to exchange information already in electronic storage media. Transmission media include the Internet, extranet (using Internet technology to link a business with information accessible only to collaborating parties), leased lines, private networks, and the physical movement of removable/transportable electronic storage media. Certain transmissions, including paper via facsimile and voice via telephone, are not considered transmissions via electronic media because the information being exchanged did not exist in electronic form before the transmission.	
Electronic Protected Health Information (e-PHI)	*Protected Health Information* that is: (1) Transmitted by *Electronic Media*; or (2) Maintained in *Electronic Media*.	

TERM	*DEFINITION*	*REFERENCES AND INDUSTRY STANDARDS*
Encryption	Used as a security measure, *Encryption* software scrambles data so that it is unreadable to interceptors without the descrambling information. The *HHS* defines acceptable *Encryption* as: • *PHI* that is encrypted as specified in the *HIPAA Security Rule* by "the use of an algorithmic process to transform data into a form in which there is a low probability of assigning meaning without use of a confidential process or key"; • Valid *Encryption* processes for data in databases, file systems, and other storage methods consistent with *National Institute of Standards and Technology (NIST) Special Publication 800-111, Guide to Storage Encryption Technologies for End User Devices*; and • Valid *Encryption* processes for data moving through a network, including wireless, which comply with requirements of *Federal Information Processing Standards (FIPS) 140-2*. Note: FIPS 140-2 will be replaced with a new version FIPS 140-3 once published.	FIPS 140-3 (Draft) will replace the current Federal Information Processing Standards Publication 140-2: *Security Requirements for Cryptographic Modules.* NIST Special Publication 800-37 Rev. 1—*Applying the Risk Management Framework to Federal Information Systems: A Security Life Cycle Approach* (February 2010) NIST Special Publication 800-111—*Guide to Storage Encryption Technologies for End-User Devices* 45 C.F.R. § 164.304 (Definition of Encryption)
ESI	*Electronically Stored Information* (ESI) is generally understood to mean information created, manipulated, communicated, stored, and best utilized in digital form, requiring the use of computer hardware and software. *ESI* is distinguished from information derived from "conventional" media, such as writing or images on paper, photographic images, analog recordings, and microfilm.	Federal Rules of Civil Procedure

TERM	*DEFINITION*	*REFERENCES AND INDUSTRY STANDARDS*
EU Data Protection Directive	Directive 95/46/EC of the European Parliament and of the Council of 24 October 1995 on the protection of individuals with regard to the processing of *Personal Data* and on the free movement of such data.	http://ec.europa.eu/justice_home/fsj/privacy/law/index_en.htm
European Economic Area (EEA)	An economic region that includes 32 member countries and six cooperating countries. The 32 member countries include the 27 European Union Member States together with Iceland, Liechtenstein, Norway, Switzerland, and Turkey. The six West Balkan countries are cooperating countries: Albania, Bosnia and Herzegovina, Croatia, the former Yugoslav Republic of Macedonia, Montenegro, and Serbia.	
European Union (EU)	The EU is an organization of European countries dedicated to increasing economic integration and strengthening cooperation among its Member States.	
FACTA	The *Fair and Accurate Credit Transactions Act of 2003* (FACTA, or the FACT Act) includes provisions to prevent identity theft and to provide redress for victims of identity theft. Also see *Red Flag Rules*.	
Fair Information Practices	The *Fair Information Practices* are the following five core principles of privacy protection: Notice/Awareness; Choice/Consent; Access/Participation; Integrity/Security; and Enforcement/Redress.	http://www.ftc.gov/reports/privacy3/fairinfo.shtm
FCRA	The *Fair Credit Reporting Act of 1970* (FCRA) requires consumer credit reporting agencies to implement "reasonable procedures" that are "fair and equitable to the consumer, with regard to confidentiality, accuracy, relevancy, and proper utilization" of consumer credit, personnel, insurance, and other covered information.	

TERM	*DEFINITION*	*REFERENCES AND INDUSTRY STANDARDS*
Federal Trade Commission (FTC)	The *Federal Trade Commission* is the nation's consumer protection agency, working to prevent fraud, deception, and unfair business practices in the marketplace.	http://www.ftc.gov/bcp/index.shtml
FERPA	The *Family Educational Rights and Privacy Act* (FERPA) applies to educational agencies and institutions that receive funds from the U.S. Department of Education. Generally, FERPA prohibits educational agencies and institutions from disclosing "students' education records" without written parental consent, unless an exception applies.	
Firewall	A *Firewall* is a hardware or software solution to enforce security policies. In the physical security analogy, a *Firewall* is equivalent to a door lock on a perimeter door or on a door to a room inside the building—it permits only authorized users such as those with a key or access card to enter. A *Firewall* has built-in filters that can disallow unauthorized or potentially dangerous material from entering the system. It also logs attempted intrusions.	NIST Special Publication 800-37 Rev. 1—*Applying the Risk Management Framework to Federal Information Systems: A Security Life Cycle Approach* (February 2010)
FISMA	The *Federal Information Security Management Act* (FISMA) requires federal agencies to identify and provide information security protections commensurate with the risk and magnitude of harm resulting from unauthorized access, use, disclosure, disruption, modification, or destruction of information collected or stored by the agency.	
Gramm-Leach-Bliley Act (GLBA)	The *Financial Services Modernization Act of 1999* regulates the privacy of personal information collected, used, or disclosed by financial institutions. The law requires that consumers be given an adequate privacy notice as well as the opportunity to opt out of any disclosure of personal information to nonaffiliated third parties for marketing purposes. Financial institutions must also have appropriate information security programs.	

TERM	*DEFINITION*	*REFERENCES AND INDUSTRY STANDARDS*
HHS	The *Department of Health and Human Services (HHS)* is the United States government's principal agency for protecting the health of all Americans and providing essential human services.	http://www.hhs.gov
HIPAA	The *Health Insurance Portability and Accountability Act of 1996* and its implementing regulations, including the *Privacy Rule* and the *Security Rule*, as amended.	http://www.hhs.gov/ocr/privacy/index.html
HITECH Act	The *Health Information Technology for Economic and Clinical Health Act* enacted February 17, 2009, and its implementing regulations and guidance, as amended. The HITECH Act (Title XIII of ARRA, pages 112–65) provisions include technology adoption incentives, education, and *Workforce* training, and new privacy provisions addressing the confidentiality of *PHI* in electronic systems.	
Health Information	Any information, whether oral or recorded, in any form or medium, that is created or received by a *Covered Entity* and relates to the past, present, or future physical or mental health or condition of an individual; the provision of health care to an individual; or the past, present or future payment for the provision of health care to an individual.	
Implementation Specifications	Specific requirements or instructions for implementing a *Standard.* The *HIPAA Security Rule* includes 42 Implementation Specifications that *Covered Entities* and *Business Associates* must address in conducting a risk assessment and analysis. Implementation Specifications are either *Addressable* or *Required*.	NIST Special Publication 800-66 Rev. 1—*An Introductory Resource Guide for Implementing the Health Insurance Portability and Accountability Act (HIPAA) Security Rule* (October 2008) 45 C.F.R. § 164.306(d)(3)
Individually Identifiable Health Information	A subset of *Health Information*, including demographic information, in any medium, that identifies a patient or for which there is a reasonable basis to believe the information can be used to identify a patient.	

TERM	DEFINITION	REFERENCES AND INDUSTRY STANDARDS
Integrity	The ability to protect information against unauthorized and either accidental or intentional corruption, tampering, or other alteration. *Integrity* includes safeguarding the accuracy and completeness of the information. *Integrity* is one of the nine *Principle Security Capabilities.*	
Internet Protocol (IP)	The *IP* specifies the format of packets and the addressing scheme. Most networks combine *IP* with a higher-level protocol called transmission control protocol (TCP), which establishes a virtual connection between a destination and a source.	
Intrusion Detection System (IDS)	Software/hardware that detects and logs inappropriate, incorrect, or anomalous activity. *Intrusion Detection Systems* are typically characterized based on the source of the data they monitor: host or network. A host-based *IDS* uses system log files and other electronic audit data to identify suspicious activity. A network-based *IDS* uses a sensor to monitor packets on the network to which it is attached.	NIST Special Publication 800-37 Rev. 1—*Applying the Risk Management Framework to Federal Information Systems: A Security Life Cycle Approach* (February 2010)
IP Address	A unique string of numbers that identifies a computer on the Internet or on a TCP/IP network. The *IP Address* is expressed in four groups of up to three numbers, separated by periods. For example: 123.123.23.2. An *IP Address* may be dynamic or static: A dynamic *IP Address* is assigned temporarily whenever a device connects to a network or an Internet service provider. A static *IP Address* does not change—it is permanently assigned to one computer or device.	

TERM	*DEFINITION*	*REFERENCES AND INDUSTRY STANDARDS*
Limited Data Set	To be a *Limited Data Set*, the *Health Information* must not include any of the following identifiers of the individual and any relatives, employees, or household members of the individual: (a) names; (b) geographic subdivisions smaller than a state, including street address or precinct, other than town or city and zip code; (c) telephone numbers; (d) fax numbers; (e) electronic mail addresses; (f) Social Security numbers; (g) medical record numbers; (h) health plan beneficiary numbers; (i) account numbers; (j) certificate/license numbers; (k) vehicle identifiers and serial numbers, including license plate numbers; (*l*) device identifiers and serial numbers; (m) URLs; (n) *IP Addresses*; (o) *Biometric Identifiers*; (p) full-face photographic images and any comparable images; and (q) any other unique identifying number, characteristic, or code, except as permitted by the regulation (45 C.F.R. § 164.514(c)) to allow the data to be reidentified by the sender.	45 C.F.R. § 164.512(e)
Malware	*Malware*, short for malicious software, is software designed specifically to disrupt a computer system. A Trojan horse, worm, or virus could be classified as *Malware*. Some advertising software can be malicious in that it can try to reinstall itself after its removal.	

TERM	*DEFINITION*	*REFERENCES AND INDUSTRY STANDARDS*
Migration	The transfer of digital materials from one hardware or software configuration to another or from one generation of computer technology to another. A *Migration* ensures the preservation and integrity of data in rapidly changing technology environments without having to undergo a major conversion.	
Model Contracts	*Model Contracts* (also referred to as *Standard Contractual Clauses*) for the transfer of *Personal Data* outside the *EU/EEA* approved by the European Commission offer *Adequate* safeguards as required by Article 26(2) of the *EU Data Protection Directive*.	
OECD	The *Organisation for Economic Co-operation and Development* (OECD) provides a setting where governments compare policy experiences, seek answers to common problems, identify good practice, and coordinate domestic and international policies.	http://www.oecd.org

TERM	*DEFINITION*	*REFERENCES AND INDUSTRY STANDARDS*
OECD Security Guidelines	The *OECD Guidelines for the Security of Information Systems and Networks: Towards a Culture of Security.* The *Security Guidelines* set forth the following nine principles: *1. Awareness.* Participants should be aware of the need for security of information systems and networks and what they can do to enhance security. *2. Responsibility.* All participants are responsible for the security of information systems and networks. *3. Response.* Participants should act in a timely and cooperative manner to prevent, detect, and respond to security incidents. *4. Ethics.* Participants should respect the legitimate interests of others. *5. Democracy.* The security of information systems and networks should be compatible with essential values of a democratic society. *6. Risk Assessment.* Participants should conduct risk assessments. *7. Security Design and Implementation.* Participants should incorporate security as an essential element of information systems and networks. *8. Security Management.* Participants should adopt a comprehensive approach to security management. *9. Reassessment.* Participants should review and reassess the security of information systems and networks and make appropriate modifications to security policies, practices, measures, and procedures. In addition to the *Security Guidelines,* the OECD has published the 1980 *OECD Guidelines Governing the Protection of Privacy and Transborder Flows of Personal Data* and the 1997 *OECD Guidelines for Cryptography Policy.*	http://www.oecd.org/document

TERM	*DEFINITION*	*REFERENCES AND INDUSTRY STANDARDS*
Nonrepudiation	*Nonrepudiation* is the assurance that someone cannot deny something. Typically, *Nonrepudiation* refers to the ability to ensure that a party to a contract or a communication cannot deny the authenticity of his or her signature on a document or the sending of a message that he or she originated. A *Digital Signature* is used not only to ensure that a message or document has been electronically signed by the person that purported to sign the document, but also, because a *Digital Signature* can only be created by one person, to ensure that a person cannot later deny that she or he furnished the signature. E-mail *Nonrepudiation* involves methods such as e-mail tracking that are designed to ensure that the sender cannot deny having sent a message and/or that the recipient cannot deny having received it.	
Peer to Peer (P2P)	A method of file sharing over a network in which individual computers are linked via the Internet or a private network to share programs/files, often illegally. Users download files directly from other users' computers, rather than from a central server.	
Personal Data	Any information relating to an identified or identifiable natural person (*Data Subject*); an identifiable person is one who can be identified, directly or indirectly, in particular by reference to an identification number or to one or more factors specific to her or his physical, physiological, mental, economic, cultural, or social identity.	*EU Data Protection Directive*—Article 2(a). See Opinion No. 4/2007 on the concept of personal data issued by the Article 29 Working Party.

TERM	*DEFINITION*	*REFERENCES AND INDUSTRY STANDARDS*
Personal Information Protection and Electronic Documents Act (PIPEDA)	The Canadian federal data protection law enacted in 2001. *PIPEDA* applies to "every organization" in respect to "personal information" that the organization collects, uses, or discloses in the "course of commercial activities" regarding customer and employee information. Personal information is defined as information about an identifiable individual, but does not include the name, title, business address, or telephone number of an employee of an organization.	
Personally Identifiable Information (PII)	Information, in any media: (1) that identifies or can be used to identify, contact, or locate the person to whom such information pertains; or (2) from which identification or contact information of an individual person can be derived. *PII* includes, but is not limited to: name, address, phone number, fax number, e-mail address, Social Security number or other government-issued identifier, *Health Information*, and credit card/financial information. Additionally, to the extent any other information (such as, but not necessarily limited to, a personal profile, unique identifier, *Biometric Identifier*, and/or *IP Address*) is associated or combined with personal information, then such information also will be considered *PII*.	NIST Special Publication 800-122 (Draft)—*Guide to Protecting the Confidentiality of Personally Identifiable Information (PII)* (January 2009)
Physical Safeguards/ Security	Physical measures, policies, and procedures to protect an organization's information systems and related buildings and equipment from natural and environmental hazards and unauthorized intrusion. The *Security Rule* requires *Covered Entities* and *Business Associates* to implement appropriate administrative, physical, and technical safeguards to ensure the *Confidentiality*, *Integrity*, and security of *e-PHI*.	NIST Special Publication 800-37 Rev. 1—*Applying the Risk Management Framework to Federal Information Systems: A Security Life Cycle Approach* (February 2010) NIST Special Publication 800-66 Rev. 1—*An Introductory Resource Guide for Implementing the Health Insurance Portability and Accountability Act (HIPAA) Security Rule* (October 2008) 45 C.F.R. § 164.304

TERM	*DEFINITION*	*REFERENCES AND INDUSTRY STANDARDS*
Portable Device	Any electronic device that has the potential to store, process, or transmit *e-PHI* and is designed for mobility or is small enough to be easily transported or concealed such as a laptop computer, tablet computer, USB drive, or personal digital assistant (PDA).	NIST Special Publication 800-111—*Guide to Storage Encryption Technologies for End-User Devices*
Principle Security Capabilities	The nine *Principle Security Capabilities* are: *Confidentiality, Integrity, Availability, Authentication, Authorization, Access Controls, Accountability, Assurance,* and *Nonrepudiation.*	
Privacy Rule	The *HIPAA Privacy Rule* requires appropriate safeguards to protect the privacy of *Health Information* and sets limits and conditions on the use and disclosure of *PHI* without patient authorization. The rule also gives patients rights over their *Health Information*, including rights to examine and obtain a copy of their health records and to request corrections.	The *Privacy Rule* is located at 45 C.F.R. Part 160 and Subparts A and E of Part 164. http://www.hhs.gov/ocr/privacy/hipaa/understanding/summary/index.html
Protected Health Information (PHI)	*Health Information* that is created or received by a *Covered Entity* or *Business Associate* and that is individually identifiable (i.e., is not de-identified). Under *HIPAA, PHI* does not include employment records held by a *Covered Entity* or *Business Associate* in its role as employer.	
Protocol	A set of formal rules that describe how to transmit data, especially across a network. Low-level protocols define the electrical and physical *Standards* to be observed, bit- and byte-ordering, and the transmission and error detection and correction of the bit stream. High-level protocols deal with data formatting, including the syntax of messages, the terminal to computer dialogue, character sets, and sequencing of messages.	

TERM	*DEFINITION*	*REFERENCES AND INDUSTRY STANDARDS*
Proxy Server	A web server that sits between a client application, such as a web browser, and a real server (such as a web server on the Internet). The proxy server intercepts all requests to the web server to determine whether it can fulfill the requests itself. If not, it forwards the requests to the web server. In many corporate or institutional networks, all requests for web pages go through a proxy server. Proxy servers can dramatically improve performance for groups of users, because they save the results of all requests for a certain amount of time. Frequently requested pages can be loaded from the proxy server, which is faster than loading them over the Internet. Proxy servers can also be used to filter requests. For example, a company might use a proxy server to prevent its employees from accessing a specific set of websites.	
Public Key Infrastructure (PKI)	A system of digital certificates, authorities, and other registration entities that verifies the authenticity of each party involved in an electronic transaction through the use of cryptography.	
Red Flag Rules	In November 2007, the FTC and the federal banking agencies published a final interagency rule, *Identity Theft Red Flags and Address Discrepancies Under the Fair and Accurate Credit Transactions Act of 2003*. The rule, referred to as the *Red Flags Rule*, requires "financial institutions" and "creditors" with "covered accounts" to implement a written Identity Theft Prevention Program to detect, prevent, and mitigate identity theft.	
Remote Access	*Remote Access* is the ability to get access to a computer or a network from a remote distance, such as when traveling or telecommuting. Common methods of *Remote Access* include wireless, cable modem, and Digital Subscriber Line (DSL).	

TERM	*DEFINITION*	*REFERENCES AND INDUSTRY STANDARDS*
Remote Access Server	*Remote Access Server* (or a *communication server*) is the computer and associated software configured to handle users seeking access to a network remotely. A *Remote Access Server* usually includes or is associated with a *Firewall* server to ensure security and a router that can forward the remote access request to another part of an organization's network. A *Remote Access Server* may be used as part of a *VPN*.	
Removable Media	Any *Electronic Media* that has the potential to store information and can easily be removed from a system such as magnetic tapes, CDs or DVDs, or external hard drives.	NIST Special Publication 800-111—*Guide to Storage Encryption Technologies for End-User Devices*
Required	Under the *HIPAA Security Rule*, an *Implementation Specification* that is *Required* must be implemented. All implementation specifications are either *Required* or *Addressable*.	45 C.F.R. § 164.306(d)(2)
Secure Destruction	*Secure Destruction* includes placing the material in a designated disposal container; shredding; erasing or *Degaussing* electronic media; or otherwise modifying the *Information* so that it is unreadable or undecipherable through any means. *HHS* defines acceptable destruction (for paper and electronic records containing *PHI*) as paper, film, or other hard copy media that have been shredded or destroyed consistent with NIST Special Publication 800-88, *Guidelines for Media Sanitization*.	NIST Special Publication 800-88—*Guidelines for Media Sanitization, Recommendations of the National Institute of Standards and Technology*, (September 2006) *Best Practices for the Secure Destruction of Personal Health Information*—Joint publication between Ontario Privacy Commissioner and the National Association for Information Destruction (NAID) (October 2009)

TERM	*DEFINITION*	*REFERENCES AND INDUSTRY STANDARDS*
Secure Sockets Layer (SSL)	*Secure Sockets Layer (SSL)* and its predecessor Transport Layer Security (TLS) are cryptographic protocols that provide security for communications over networks such as the Internet. TLS and *SSL* encrypt the segments of network connections at the Application Layer to ensure secure end-to-end transit at the Transport Layer. Several versions of the protocols are in widespread use in applications like web browsing, electronic mail, Internet faxing, instant messaging, and voice-over-IP (VoIP).	
Security Incident	A potential or actual breach of security of an organization's IT systems and/or *Confidential Information* or *PII.* For security incidents involving *PHI,* please see the definition of *Breach*. A *Security Incident* can include: (1) Attempted or successful unauthorized *Access*, use, *Disclosure*, modification, or destruction of *Confidential Information* or *PII* or interference with IT system operations by individuals or computer programs; (2) Network activity designed to result in unauthorized *Access*, use, *Disclosure*, modification, or destruction of *Confidential Information* or *PII* or interference with IT system operations; (3) Disclosure or loss of a password, pin, token (e.g., card or device used for authentication), certificate (e.g., electronic digital certificate used to provide an electronic digital identity), or any mechanism that identifies the individual to a *Covered Entity*, IT system, or building (e.g., ID badge); and (4) Damage to or loss of IT systems and/or *Confidential Information* or *PII*.	NIST Special Publication 800-122 (Draft)—*Guide to Protecting the Confidentiality of Personally Identifiable Information (PII)* (January 2009)

TERM	*DEFINITION*	*REFERENCES AND INDUSTRY STANDARDS*
Security Officer	An individual designated as responsible for the development and implementation of an organization's security policies and procedures. The *HIPAA Security Rule* requires *Covered Entities* and *Business Associates* to appoint a *Security Officer*.	45 C.F.R. § 164.308(a)(2)
(HIPAA) Security Rule	The *HIPAA Security Rule* establishes national *Standards* to protect individuals' *e-PHI* that is created, received, used, or maintained by a *Covered Entity* or *Business Associate*. The *Security Rule* requires appropriate administrative, physical, and technical safeguards to ensure the confidentiality, integrity, and security of *e-PHI*.	The *Security Rule* is located at 45 C.F.R. Part 160 and Subparts A and C of Part 164. www.hhs.gov/ocr/privacy/hipaa/understanding/srsummary.html
Sensitive Data	The *EU Data Protection Directive*, Article 8, prohibits the processing of special categories of *Personal Data* revealing racial or ethnic origin, political opinions, religious or philosophical beliefs, and trade-union membership, and the processing of data concerning health or sex life. Exceptions include where the *Data Subject* has given his or her explicit *Consent*.	
Spyware	Software that sends information about the user's web surfing habits to its website. *Spyware* is often installed without the user's *Consent* in combination with a free download.	

TERM	*DEFINITION*	*REFERENCES AND INDUSTRY STANDARDS*
Standard	A rule, condition, or requirement describing specifications or procedures. The *HIPAA Privacy Rule* establishes *Standards* for the privacy of individually identifiable *Health Information.*	45 C.F.R. §160.103
Standard Contractual Clauses	See *Model Contracts.*	
Strong Authentication	*Strong Authentication* relies on the use of a public-key cryptosystem, whereby each user possesses two keys, one public and one private, the latter of which is known only to the user. Each of these keys may be used to encipher or decipher the user's *Authentication* information, in a complementary fashion (i.e., if the information was enciphered with the private key, it must be deciphered with the public key, and vice versa). If a user's public key is held by a directory, it can be used to confirm the user's identity if the user submits authentication information encrypted using his or her private key.	
Strong Password	A password is sufficiently long, random, or otherwise producible only by the user who creates it. A strong password should be eight or more characters in length and contain at least one number, one letter, and one symbol (e.g., Smith#123).	NIST Special Publication 800-118—*Guide to Enterprise Password Management* (Draft, April 2009)

TERM	*DEFINITION*	*REFERENCES AND INDUSTRY STANDARDS*
Technical Safeguards	The technology and the policy and procedures for its use that protect *Confidential Information* and *PII* and control *Access* to such restricted information. The *HIPAA Security Rule* requires *Covered Entities* and *Business Associates* to implement appropriate technical safeguards to ensure the *Confidentiality, Integrity,* and security of *e-PHI.*	NIST Special Publication 800-37 Rev. 1—*Applying the Risk Management Framework to Federal Information Systems: A Security Life Cycle Approach* (February 2010) NIST Special Publication 800-66 Rev. 1—*An Introductory Resource Guide for Implementing the Health Insurance Portability and Accountability Act (HIPAA) Security Rule* (October 2008) NIST Special Publication 800-77—*Guide to IPSec VPNs* NIST Special Publication 800-113—*Guide to SSL VPNs* NIST Special Publication 800-111—*Guide to Storage Encryption Technologies for End-User Devices* 45 C.F.R. § 164.304
Unsecured PHI	*PHI* that is not *Encrypted* and rendered unusable, unreadable, or indecipherable to unauthorized individuals through the use of a technology or methodology specified by the Secretary of *HHS*.	
Virus	A program written to cause mischief or damage to a computer system.	

TERM	DEFINITION	REFERENCES AND INDUSTRY STANDARDS
VPN	A technology that establishes a private or secure network connection within a public network, such as the Internet, permitting secure *Remote Access* to a network.	NIST Special Publication 800-77—*Guide to IPSec VPNs* NIST Special Publication 800-113—*Guide to SSL VPNs*
Verifiable Parental Consent	The *Children's Online Privacy Protection Act (COPPA)* requires operators of websites to obtain *Verifiable Parental Consent* prior to collecting information from children under the age of 13. Acceptable methods include the use of a consent form that can be downloaded and printed so the parent can fill it out, sign it, and send it back by fax or mail; or credit card verification in which the card number is verified in the course of a transaction or by other reliable means.	
Vulnerability	In network security, vulnerability refers to any flaw or weakness in the network defense that could be exploited to gain unauthorized *Access* to, damage, or otherwise affect the network. This term most commonly refers to *Vulnerabilities* that may be exploited in software, such as operating systems and applications.	
Web Beacon	A graphic on a web page or in an e-mail message that is designed to monitor who is reading the web page or e-mail message. Among the information collected is the *IP Address* of the computer that the *Web Beacon* is sent to, the URL of the page the *Web Beacon* comes from, and the time it was viewed. *Web Beacons* are also known as Web Bugs, GIFs, and invisible GIFs.	
Workforce	Employees, volunteers, trainees, and other persons whose performance of work for a *Covered Entity* and/or *Business Associate* is under the control of the *Covered Entity/Business Associate*.	

TERM	***DEFINITION***	***REFERENCES AND INDUSTRY STANDARDS***
Worm	A self-replicating computer program, similar to a computer virus. A virus attaches itself to, and becomes part of, another executable program. A *Worm* is self-contained and does not need to be part of another program to propagate itself. *Worms* are often designed to exploit the file transmission capabilities found on many computers.	

APPENDIX C

U.S. State Information Security and Privacy Laws

Alaska Breach of Security: Definitions—Alaska Stat. § 45.48.090

Alaska Breach of Security: Allowable Delay in Notification—Alaska Stat. § 45.48.020

Alaska Breach of Security: Exception for Employees and Agents—Alaska Stat. § 45.48.050

Alaska Breach of Security: Methods of Notice—Alaska Stat. § 45.48.030

Alaska Breach of Security: Notification to Certain Other Agencies—Alaska Stat. § 45.48.040

Alaska Breach of Security: Treatment of Certain Breaches—Alaska Stat. § 45.48.070

Alaska Breach of Security: Violations—Alaska Stat. § 45.48.080

Alaska Disclosure of Breach of Security—Alaska Stat. § 45.48.010

Arizona Notification of Breach of Security System—Ariz. Rev. Stat. § 44-7501

Arkansas Disclosure of Breach of Security—Ark. Code Ann. § 4-110-105

Arkansas Protection of Personal Information: Definitions— Ark. Code Ann. § 4-110-103

Arkansas Protection of Personal Information: Exemptions— Ark. Code Ann. § 4-110-106

Arkansas Protection of Personal Information: Penalties— Ark. Code Ann. § 4-110-108

California Disclosure of Breach of Security: Cal. Civ. Code § 1798.29

California Legislation: Amended Data Breach Law—2009 Bill Text Cal. S.B. 20

California Customer Records: Definitions—Cal. Civ. Code § 1798.80

California Customer Records: Violations and Remedies—Cal. Civ. Code § 1798.84

California Disclosure of Breach Insecurity—Cal. Civ. Code § 1798.82

Colorado Legislation: Security Breach—2010 Bill Text Colo. H.B. 1422

Colorado Notification of Security Breach—Colo. Rev. Stat. § 6-1-716

Connecticut Breach of Security—Conn. Gen. Stat. § 36a-701b

Delaware Disclosure of Breach of Security—6 Del. Code § 12B-102

Delaware Disclosure of Breach of Security: Definitions—6 Del. Code § 12B-101

Delaware Disclosure of Breach of Security: Procedures Deemed in Compliance—6 Del. Code § 12B-103

Delaware Disclosure of Breach of Security: Violations—6 Del. Code § 12B-104

District of Columbia Consumer Personal Information Security Breach Notification Act of 2006—54 D.C. Reg. 393

District of Columbia Notification of Security Breach—D.C. Code § 28-3852

District of Columbia Notification of Security Breach: Definitions—D.C. Code § 28-3851

District of Columbia Notification of Security Breach: Enforcement—D.C. Code § 28-3853

Florida Data Breach Statute—Fla. Stat. § 817.5681

Georgia Notification Required Upon Breach of Security—Ga. Code Ann. § 10-1-912

Georgia Notification Required Upon Breach of Security: Definitions—Ga. Code Ann. § 10-1-911

Hawaii Notification of Security Breach—Haw. Rev. Stat. § 487N-2

Hawaii Notification of Security Breach: Definitions—Haw. Rev. Stat. § 487N-1

Hawaii Notification of Security Breach: Penalties— Haw. Rev. Stat.§ 487N-3

Idaho Amends Idaho Data Breach Law—2010 Bill Text Idaho H.B. 566

Idaho Disclosure of Breach of Security—Idaho Code § 28-51-105

Idaho Disclosure of Breach of Security: Definitions—Idaho Code § 28-51-104

Idaho Disclosure of Breach of Security: Procedures Deemed in Compliance—Idaho Code § 28-51-106

Idaho Disclosure of Breach of Security: Violations—Idaho Code § 28-51-107

Illinois Notice of Breach—815 Ill. Comp. Stat. 530/10

Illinois Notice of Breach: Definitions—815 Ill. Comp. Stat.530/5

Illinois Notice of Breach: Violation—815 Ill. Comp. Stat.530/20

Indiana "Breach of the Security of Data" defined—Burns Ind. Code Ann. § 24-4.9-2-2

Indiana "Database Owner" defined—Burns Ind. Code Ann. § 24-4.9-2-3

Indiana "Personal Information" defined—Burns Ind. Code Ann. § 24-4.9-2-10

Indiana Disclosure of Security Breach: Applicability—Burns Ind. Code Ann. § 24-4.9-1-1

Indiana Disclosure of Security Breach: Enforcement; Action by Attorney General—Burns Ind. Code Ann. § 24-4.9-4-2

Indiana Disclosure of Security Breach: Enforcement; Deceptive Act—Burns Ind. Code Ann. § 24-4.9-4-1

Indiana Methods of Disclosure—Burns Ind. Code Ann. § 24-4.9-3-4

Indiana Person Maintaining Computerized Data to Notify Database Owner—Burns Ind. Code Ann. § 24-4.9-3-2

Indiana Person to Make Disclosure Without Unreasonable Delay—Burns Ind. Code Ann. § 24-4.9-3-3

Indiana Personal Records; Keeping, Handling, Safeguarding, and Disposal—Burns Ind. Code Ann. § 28-1-2-30.5

Indiana Persons to Be Notified by Database Owner—Burns Ind. Code Ann. § 24-4.9-3-1

Iowa Security Breach—Consumer Notification—Iowa Code § 715C.2

Iowa Security Breach—Consumer Notification: Definitions—Iowa Code § 715C.1

Kansas Consumer Information; Security Breach: Definitions—Kan. Stat. Ann. § 50-7a01

Kansas Security Breach: Requirements—Kan. Stat. Ann. § 50-7a02

Kentucky (Proposed) Data Breach/Consumer Protection—2010 Bill Text Ky. H.B. 581

Louisiana Database Security Breach Notification Law—2005 La. Rev.Stat. 51:3071-3077,

Louisiana Disclosure Upon Breach in the Security of PI—La. Rev. Stat. 51:3074

Louisiana Disclosure Upon Breach in the Security of PI: Definitions—La. Rev. Stat. 51:3073

Louisiana Disclosure Upon Breach in the Security of PI: Recovery of Damages—La. Rev. Stat. 51:3075

Maine Security Breach Notice Requirements—10 Me. Rev. Stat. § 1348

Maine Security Breach Notice Requirements: Definitions—10 Me. Rev. Stat. § 1347

Maine Security Breach Notice Requirements: Enforcement; Penalties—10 Me. Rev. Stat. § 1349

Maryland Security Breach—Md. Code Ann., Com. Law § 14-3504

Maryland Security Breach: Definitions—Md. Code Ann., Com. Law § 14-3501

Maryland Security Breach: Notification to Credit Reporting Agencies—Md. Code Ann., Com. Law § 14-3506

Maryland Security Breach: Violations; Penalties—Md. Code Ann., Com. Law § 14-3508

Massachusetts Security Breaches: Definitions—Ann. Laws Mass. Gen. Law ch. 93H, § 1

Massachusetts Security Breaches: Notice Exception for Criminal Investigations—Ann. Laws Mass. Gen. Law ch. 93H, § 4

Massachusetts Security Breaches: Notice Required— Ann. Laws Mass. Gen. Law ch. 93H, § 3

Massachusetts Security Breaches: Violation Remedies— Ann. Laws Mass. Gen. Law ch. 93H, § 6

Massachusetts Standards for the Protection of Personal Information: Duty to Protect and Standards for Protecting Personal Information—201 Mass. Code Regs. 17.03

Michigan Identity Theft Protection Act: Definitions—Mich. Comp. Laws Serv. § 445.63

Michigan Identity Theft Protection Act: Misrepresentation— Mich. Comp. Laws Serv. § 445.72b

Michigan Identity Theft Protection Act: Penalties— Mich. Comp. Laws Serv. § 445.69

Michigan Identity Theft Protection Act: Notice of Security Breach— Mich. Comp. Laws Serv. § 445.72

Minnesota Notice Required for Certain Disclosures—Minn. Stat. § 325E.61

Mississippi Notice of Breach of Security—2010 Bill Text Miss. H.B. 583

Missouri Data Breach Notification—Mo. Rev. Stat. § 407.1500

Montana Computer Security Breach—Mont. Code Ann. § 30-14-1704

Montana Department to Restrain Unlawful Acts: Penalty—Mont. Code Ann. § 30-14-1705

Nebraska Breach of Security—Neb. Rev. Stat. § 87-803

Nebraska Breach of Security: Applicability—Neb. Rev. Stat. § 87-807

Nebraska Breach of Security: Attorney General: Powers—Neb. Rev. Stat. § 87-806

Nebraska Breach of Security: Compliance with Notice Requirements— Neb. Rev. Stat. § 87-804

Nebraska Breach of Security: Terms, Defined—Neb. Rev. Stat. § 87-802

Nevada Security of Personal Information; "Personal Information" defined—Nev. Rev. Stat. Ann. § 603A.040

Nevada "Breach of the Security of the System Data" defined—Nev. Rev. Stat. Ann. § 603A.020

Nevada Amends Nevada Code: PCI DSS—2009 Bill Text Nev. S.B. 227

Nevada Disclosure of Breach of Security—Nev. Rev. Stat. Ann. § 603A.220

Nevada Disclosure of Breach of Security: Civil Action—Nev. Rev. Stat. Ann. § 603A.900

Nevada Disclosure of Breach of Security: Restitution—Nev. Rev. Stat. Ann. § 603A.910

Nevada Remedies and Penalties; Injunction—Nev. Rev. Stat. Ann. § 603A.920

Nevada Security of Personal Information; "Data Collector" defined—Nev. Rev. Stat. Ann. § 603A.030

New Hampshire Notice of Security Breach: Definitions—N.H. Rev. Stat. Ann. § 359-C:19

New Hampshire Notice of Security Breach: Violation— N.H. Rev. Stat. Ann.§ 359-C:21

New Hampshire Notification of Security Breach Required— N.H. Rev. Stat. Ann.§ 359-C:20

New Jersey Definitions Relative to Security of Personal Information—N.J. Stat. § 56:8-161

New Jersey Disclosure of Breach of Security to Customers—N.J. Stat. § 56:8-163

New Jersey Unlawful Practice; Violation—N.J. Stat. § 56:8-166

New York Notification of Unauthorized Acquisition of Private Information—N.Y. Gen. Bus. Law § 899-aa

New York City Disclosure of Security Breach—NYC Admin. Code § 20-11

North Carolina Identity Theft Protection Act: Definitions—N.C. Gen. Stat. § 75-61

North Carolina Protection from Security Breaches—N.C. Gen. Stat. § 75-65

North Dakota Notice of Security Breach for Personal Information—N.D. Cent. Code § 51-30-02

North Dakota Notice of Security Breach: Alternate Compliance—N.D. Cent. Code § 51-30-06

North Dakota Notice of Security Breach: Definitions—N.D. Cent. Code § 51-30-01

North Dakota Notice of Security Breach: Delayed Notice—N.D. Cent. Code § 51-30-04

North Dakota Notice of Security Breach: Enforcement—N.D. Cent. Code § 51-30-07

North Dakota Notice of Security Breach: Method of Notice—N.D. Cent. Code § 51-30-05

Ohio Notification of Security Breach—Ohio Rev. Code Ann. § 1349.19

Ohio Notification of Security Breach: Civil Action; Penalties— Ohio Rev. Code Ann. § 1349.192

Ohio Notification of Security Breach Investigation by Attorney General— Ohio Rev. Code Ann. § 1349.191

Oklahoma Disclosure of Breach of Security—74 Okla. Stat. § 3113.1

Oregon Identity Theft Prevention: Definitions—Or. Rev. Stat. § 646A.602

Oregon Identity Theft Prevention: Powers of Directors: Penalties— Or. Rev. Stat. § 646A.624

Oregon Notice of Breach of Security— Or. Rev. Stat. § 646A.604

Pennsylvania Notification of Breach—73 Pa. Stat. § 2303

Pennsylvania Notification of Breach: Civil Relief—73 Pa. Stat. § 2308

Pennsylvania Notification of Breach: Definitions—73 Pa. Stat. § 2302

Pennsylvania Notification of Breach: Exceptions—73 Pa. Stat. § 2304

Pennsylvania Notification of Breach: Notice Exemption—73 Pa. Stat. § 2307

Puerto Rico Security Breach Statute—10 P.R. Laws Ann. § 4052

Rhode Island Notification of Breach—R.I. Gen. Laws § 11-49.2-3

Rhode Island Notification of Breach: Agencies with Security Breach Procedures—R.I. Gen. Laws § 11-49.2-7

Rhode Island Notification of Breach: Definitions—R.I. Gen. Laws § 11-49.2-5

Rhode Island Notification of Breach: Penalties for Violation—R.I. Gen. Laws § 11-49.2-6

South Carolina Breach of Security of Business Data—S.C. Code Ann. § 39-1-90

Tennessee Release of Personal Consumer Information—Tenn. Code Ann. § 47-18-2107

Texas Data Breach Legislation—2009 Bill Text Tex. H.B. 2004

Texas Legislation: Privacy of Consumer Information/Access Devices—2009 Bill Text Tex. H.B. 345

Texas Business Duty to Protect Sensitive PI: Civil Penalty; Injunction—Tex. Bus. & Com. Code § 521.151

Texas Notification Required Following Breach of Security—Tex. Bus. & Com. Code § 521.053

Utah Disclosure of System Security Breach—Utah Code Ann. § 13-44-202

Utah Protection of Personal Information: Definitions—Utah Code Ann. § 13-44-102

Utah Protection of Personal Information: Enforcement—Utah Code Ann. § 13-44-301

Vermont Notice of Security Breaches—9 Vt. Stat. Ann. § 2435

Vermont Protection of Personal Information: Definitions—9 Vt. Stat. Ann. § 2430

Virgin Islands Disclosure of Breach of Security—14 V.I. Code Ann. § 2209

Virgin Islands Identity Theft: Definitions—14 V.I. Code Ann. § 2201

Virgin Islands Notice of Security Breach: Remedies—14 V.I. Code Ann. § 2211

Virgin Islands Notices of Security Breach—14 V.I. Code Ann. § 2208

Virginia Amends data breach law to add health information—2010 Bill Text Va. H.B. 1039

Virginia Breach of Personal Information Notification—Va. Code Ann. § 18.2-186.6

Washington Legislation: Security Breach and Cardholder Data—2009 Bill Text Wash. H.B. 1149

Washington Notice of Security Breaches—Wash. Rev. Code Ann. § 19.255.010

West Virginia Notice of Breach of Security—W. Va. Code § 46A-2A-102

West Virginia Notice of Breach of Security: Definitions—W. Va. Code § 46A-2A-101

West Virginia Notice of Breach of Security: Procedures Deemed in Compliance—W. Va. Code § 46A-2A-103

West Virginia Notice of Breach of Security: Violations—W. Va. Code § 46A-2A-104

Wisconsin Notice of Unauthorized Acquisition of Personal Information—Wis. Stat. § 134.98

Wyoming Computer Security Breach; Notice to Affected Persons—Wyo. Stat. § 40-12-502

Wyoming Computer Security Breach; Notice to Affected Persons: Definitions—Wyo. Stat. § 40-12-501

Wyoming Computer Security Breach; Notice to Affected Persons: Violations; Penalties—Wyo. Stat. § 40-12-508

APPENDIX D

Best Practice Example Documents

The following are examples provided only to further the understanding of readers and should not be utilized in place of legal advice addressing the particular facts of each individual situation.

D.1. HIPAA/HITECH BUSINESS ASSOCIATE AGREEMENT

SAMPLE BUSINESS ASSOCIATE AGREEMENT

This Agreement is made effective as of [DATE], by and between ________________ ("Covered Entity"), and ___________________________ ("Business Associate") (individually, a "Party" and collectively, the "Parties").

WITNESSETH

WHEREAS, the *American Recovery and Reinvestment Act of 2009,* pursuant to Title XIII of Division A and Title IV of Division B, the *Health Information Technology for Economic and Clinical Health ("HITECH") Act,* modifies the *HIPAA Security and Privacy Rule* (hereinafter, all references to the "HIPAA Security and Privacy Rule" are deemed to include all amendments contained in the *HITECH Act* and any accompanying regulations, and any subsequently adopted amendments or regulations); and

WHEREAS, Covered Entity and Business Associate wish to enter into this Agreement in order to comply with the requirements of the HIPAA Security and Privacy Rule and to protect the interests of both Parties;

THEREFORE, in consideration of the Parties' obligations and for other good and valuable consideration, the receipt and sufficiency of which is hereby acknowledged, the Parties agree to the provisions of this Agreement.

DEFINITIONS

Except as defined herein, capitalized terms in this Agreement shall have the definitions set forth in the HIPAA Security and Privacy Rule. In the event of an inconsistency, the HIPAA Security and Privacy Rule shall control. Where provisions of this Agreement are different than those mandated in the HIPAA Security and Privacy Rule, but are nonetheless permitted by the HIPAA Security and Privacy Rule, the provisions of this Agreement shall control.

"**Electronic Protected Health Information**" ("e-PHI") means PHI which is transmitted by Electronic Media or maintained in Electronic Media.

"**Protected Health Information**" ("PHI") means individually identifiable health information including, without limitation, all information, data, documentation, and materials, including without limitation, demographic, medical, and financial information, that relates to the past, present, or future physical or mental health or condition of an individual; the provision of health care to an individual; or the past, present, or future payment for the provision of health care to an individual; and that identifies the individual or with respect to which there is a reasonable basis to believe the information can be used to identify the individual. "Protected Health Information" includes without limitation "Electronic Protected Health Information."

"**Security Incident**" means the attempted or successful unauthorized access, use, disclosure, modification, or destruction of information or interference with system operations in an information system.

"**Services**" means those services to be provided by Business Associate as set forth in Appendix A.

CONFIDENTIALITY AND SECURITY REQUIREMENTS

(a) Business Associate agrees:
   (i) to use or disclose PHI solely: (1) to provide the Services; or (2) as required by applicable law, rule, or regulation, or by accrediting or credentialing organization to whom Covered Entity is required to disclose such information or as otherwise permitted under this Agreement; and (3) as would be permitted by the HIPAA Security and Privacy Rule if such use or disclosure were made by Covered Entity. All such uses and disclosures shall be subject to the limits set forth in 45 C.F.R. § 164.514 regarding limited data sets and 45 C.F.R. § 164.502(b) regarding the minimum necessary requirements;
   (ii) at termination of this Agreement, or upon request of Covered Entity, whichever occurs first, Business Associate will return or destroy all PHI received from or created or received by Business Associate on behalf of Covered Entity;
   (iii) Business Associate agrees to take reasonable steps to ensure that its employees' actions or omissions do not cause Business Associate to breach the terms of this Agreement;
   (iv) Business Associate will not directly or indirectly receive remuneration in exchange for any PHI, subject to the exceptions contained in the HITECH Act, without a valid authorization from the applicable individual; and
   (v) Business Associate will not engage in any communication that might be deemed to be "marketing" under the HITECH Act.

(b) Notwithstanding the prohibitions set forth in this Agreement, Business Associate may use and disclose PHI if necessary for the proper management and administration of Business Associate or to carry out the legal responsibilities of Business Associate, provided that the following requirements are met:
   (i) the disclosure is required by law; or
   (ii) Business Associate obtains reasonable assurances from the person to whom the information is disclosed that it will be held confidentially and used or further disclosed only as required by law or for the purpose for which it was disclosed to the person, and the person notifies Business Associate of any instances of which it is aware in which the confidentiality of the information has been breached.

(c) Business Associate will implement appropriate safeguards to prevent use or disclosure of PHI other than as permitted in this Agreement. Business Associate will implement administrative, physical, and technical safeguards that reasonably and appropriately protect the confidentiality, integrity, and availability of any e-PHI that it creates, receives, maintains, or transmits on behalf of Covered Entity as required by the HIPAA Security and Privacy Rule.

(d) The Secretary of Health and Human Services shall have the right to audit Business Associate's records and practices related to use and disclosure of PHI to ensure Covered Entity's compliance with the terms of the HIPAA Security and Privacy Rule.

(e) Business Associate shall report to Covered Entity any use or disclosure of PHI which is not in compliance with the terms of this Agreement of which it becomes aware. Business Associate shall report to Covered Entity any Security Incident of which it becomes aware. In addition, Business Associate agrees to mitigate, to the extent practicable, any harmful effect that is known to Business Associate of a use or disclosure of PHI by Business Associate in violation of the requirements of this Agreement.

AVAILABILITY OF PHI

Business Associate agrees to comply with any requests for restrictions on certain disclosures of PHI pursuant to the HIPAA Security and Privacy Rule to which Covered Entity has agreed and of which Business Associate is notified by Covered Entity. Business Associate agrees to make available PHI to the extent and in the manner required by Section 164.524 of the HIPAA Security and Privacy Rule. If Business Associate maintains PHI electronically, it agrees to make such PHI electronically available to the applicable individual. Business Associate agrees to make PHI available for amendment and incorporate any amendments to PHI in accordance with the requirements of the HIPAA Security and Privacy Rule. In addition, Business Associate agrees to make PHI available for purposes of accounting of disclosures and provide any accounting required on a timely basis.

NOTIFICATION OF BREACH

Business Associate shall, following the discovery of a Breach of Unsecured PHI, notify Covered Entity of such breach and cooperate in Covered Entity's breach analysis procedures, if requested. A breach shall be treated as discovered by Business Associate as of the first day on which such breach is known to Business Associate or, by exercising reasonable diligence, would have been known to Business Associate. Business Associate will provide notification to Covered Entity without unreasonable delay and in no event later than _____ (__) calendar days after discovery of the breach. Such notification shall contain the elements required in 45 C.F.R. § 164.410.

TERMINATION

Covered Entity shall have the right to terminate this Agreement immediately if Covered Entity determines that Business Associate has violated any material term of this Agreement.

MISCELLANEOUS

Except as expressly stated herein or the HIPAA Security and Privacy Rule, the Parties to this Agreement do not intend to create any rights in any third parties. The obligations of Business Associate under this Section shall survive the expiration, termination, or cancellation of this Agreement and shall continue to bind Business Associate, its agents, employees, contractors, successors, and assigns as set forth herein.

This Agreement may be amended or modified only in a writing signed by the Parties. No Party may assign its respective rights and obligations under this Agreement without the prior written consent of the other Party.

This Agreement will be governed by the laws of the State of [STATE]. No change, waiver, or discharge of any liability or obligation hereunder shall be deemed a waiver of performance of any continuing or other obligation, or shall prohibit enforcement of any obligation, on any other occasion.

Business Associate acknowledges and agrees that all PHI that is created or received by Covered Entity and disclosed or made available in any form to Business Associate, or is created or received by Business Associate on Covered Entity's behalf, shall be subject to this Agreement.

The provisions of this Agreement are intended to establish the minimum requirements regarding Business Associate's use and disclosure of PHI.

In the event that any provision of this Agreement is held by a court of competent jurisdiction to be invalid or unenforceable, the remainder of the provisions of this Agreement will remain in full force and effect.

IN WITNESS WHEREOF, the Parties have executed this Agreement as of date written above.

COVERED ENTITY	BUSINESS ASSOCIATE
By:______________________	By:______________________
Title:____________________	Title:____________________

Table of Authorities

U.S. FEDERAL STATUTES AND RULES

(Note: U.S. State laws are contained in Appendix C)

INTERNATIONAL STATUTES AND RULES

New Brunswick, Personal Health Information Privacy and Access Act, S.N.B. 2009, ch. P-7.05, 75 n.260

Newfoundland, Personal Health Information Act, S.N.L. 2008, ch. P-7.01, 75 n.260

Nova Scotia, Personal Health Information Act (introduced 2009), 75 n.260

EU Data Protection Directive, Directive 95/46/EC of the European Parliament and of the Council of 24 October 1995 on the protection of individuals with regard to the processing of personal data and on the free movement of such data, 80

Safe Harbor Privacy Principles, 81 n.287

Directive 2002/58/EC concerning the processing of personal data and the protection of privacy in the electronic communications sector, 81 n.290

Directive 2009/136/EC of the European Parliament and of The Council of 25 November 2009 amending, 82 n.291

Directive 2002/22/EC on universal service and users' rights relating to electronic communications networks and services, 82 n.291

Regulation (EC) No 2006/2004 on cooperation between national authorities responsible for the enforcement of consumer protection laws, 82 n.291

APEC Privacy Framework (2004), 83 n.294

Australia, Privacy Act of 1988, 84 n.298

China, Administrative Regulations for Employment Services and Employment, 85

China, Tortious Liability Law of 2009, 85

China, Computer Information Network and Internet Security, Protection and Management Regulations, 85 n.302

China, Measures for the Administration of Internet E-mail Services, 85 n.303

China, Electronic Banking Regulations, 85 n.304

Hong Kong, Personal Data (Privacy) Ordinance of 1995, 86, n.305

India, Information Technology Act of 2000, 87 n.310

Indonesia, Electronic Information and Electronic Transactions Law (2008), 88 n.317

Japan, Act on the Protection of Personal Information (2005), 4 n.2, 88

Malaysia, Personal Data Protection Act of 2010, 89 n.320

New Zealand, Privacy Act of 1993, 90

New Zealand, Privacy (Cross-border Information) Amendment Act 2010, 90 n.321

The Philippines, Electronic Commerce Act of 2000, 91 n.324

Russia, Federal Law No. 152-FZ,On Personal Data (2006), 91, n.326

Singapore, Model Data Protection Code for the Private Sector (2002), 92 n.331

Singapore, Electronic Transactions Act (2010), 92 n.335

South Korea, Law on the Promotion of Utilization of Information and Communication Networks and the Protection of Data (2001), 92 n.336

TECHNICAL STANDARDS AND DEFINITIONS

(Note: Further standards are contained in Appendices A and B)

ISO/IEC 27000, Information Technology—Security Techniques—Information Security Management Systems—Overview and Vocabulary (2009)

ISO/IEC 27001, Information Technology—Security Techniques—Information Security Management Systems—Requirements (2005)

ISO/IEC 27002, Information Technology—Security Techniques—Code of Practice for Information Security Management (2005)

ISO/IEC 27003, Information Technology—Security Techniques—Information Security Management Systems Implementation Guidance (2010)

ISO/IEC 27004, Information Technology—Security Techniques—Information Security Management—Measurement (2009)

ISO/IEC 27005, Information Technology—Security Techniques—Information Security Risk Management (2008)

ISO/IEC 27006, Information Technology—Security Techniques—Requirements for Bodies Providing Audit and Certification of Information Security Management Systems (2007)

ISO/IEC 27011, Information Technology—Security Techniques—Information Security Management Guidelines for Telecommunications Organizations Based on ISO/IEC 27002 (2008)

NIST SP 800-18 Rev. 1, Guide for Developing Security Plans for Federal Information Systems (2006)

NIST SP 800-30 Risk Management Guide for Information Technology Systems (2002)

NIST SP 800-34 Rev. 1, Contingency Planning Guide for Federal Information Systems (2010)

NIST SP 800-37 Rev. 1, Guide for Applying the Risk Management Framework to Federal Information Systems (2010)

NIST SP 800-39, Managing Risk from Information Systems: An Organizational Perspective (2010)

NIST SP 800-52, Guidelines for the Selection and Use of Transport Layer Security (TLS) Implementations (2005)

NIST SP 800-53 Rev. 3, Recommended Security Controls for Federal Information Systems and Organizations (2009)

NIST SP 800-53A Rev. 1, Guide for Assessing the Security Controls in Federal Information Systems (2010)

NIST SP 800-60 Vol. 1, Rev. 1, Guide for Mapping Types of Information and Information Systems to Security Categories (2008)

NIST SP 800-61 Rev. 1, Computer Security Incident Handling Guide (2008)

NIST SP 800-66, Rev. 1, An Introductory Resource Guide for Implementing the Health Insurance Portability and Accountability Act (HIPAA) Security Rule (2008)

NIST SP 800-70 Rev. 1, National Checklist Program for IT Products—Guidelines for Checklist Users and Developers (2009)

NIST SP 800-77, Guide to IPSec VPNs (2005)

NIST SP 800-86, Guide to Integrating Forensic Techniques into Incident Response (2006)

NIST SP 800-88, Guidelines for Media Sanitization (2006)

NIST SP 800-111, Guide to Storage Encryption Technologies for End-User Devices (2007)

NIST SP 800-113, Guide to SSL VPNs (2008)

NIST SP 800-115, Technical Guide to Information Security Testing and Assessment (2008)

NIST SP 800-118, Guide to Enterprise Password Management (2009)

NIST SP 800-122, Guide to Protecting the Confidentiality of Personally Identifiable Information (2010)

NIST Definition of Cloud Computing, Ver. 15 (2009)

NIST IR 7628 (Draft), Smart Grid Cyber Security Strategy and Requirements (2010)

NIST IR 7628, Guidelines for Smart Grid Cyber Security: Vol. 1, Smart Grid Cyber Security Strategy, Architecture, and High-Level Requirements; Vol. 2, Privacy and the Smart Grid; Vol. 3, Supportive Analyses and References (2010)

FIPS Publication 199, Standards for Security Categorization of Federal Information and Information Systems (2004)

FIPS Publication 200, Minimum Security Requirements for Federal Information and Information Systems (2006)

ISACA Control Objectives for Information and Related Technology 4.1 (2007)

ISACA COBIT®, Mapping: Mapping of NIST SP800-53 Rev 1 with COBIT® 4.1 (2007) and COBIT® Mapping: Mapping of ISO/IEC 17799:2005 with COBIT® 4.0 (2006)

ISACA The Risk IT Framework (2009)

Payment Card Industry, Data Security Standard Requirements and Security Assessment Procedures Version 2.0 (2010)

AICPA Trust Services Principles, Criteria and Illustrations (2006)

AICPA Statement on Auditing Standards 70, Service Organizations (1992)

IAASB International Standard on Assurance Engagements (ISAE) 3402 Assurance Reports on Controls at a Third Party Service Organization

AICPA Statement on Standards for Attestation Engagements (SSAE) 16 Reporting on Controls at a Service Organization

Best Practices for the Secure Destruction of Personal Health Information—Joint Publication between Ontario Privacy Commissioner and the National Association for Information Destruction (NAID) (2009)

Reassessing Your Security Practices in a Health IT Environment, Office of the National Coordinator for Health Information and Technology (ONC)

Application Security Questionnaire, Healthcare Information and Management Systems Society (HIMSS)

ANSI/ARMA Vital Records Programs: Identifying, Managing, and Recovering Business-Critical Records (2003)

FFIEC Information Technology Examination Handbook

NACHA Operating Rules

IEEE 1619.3, Standard for Key Management Infrastructure for Cryptographic Protection of Stored Data (2007)

ISO 22399, Societal Security—Guideline for Incident Preparedness and Operational Continuity

Management (2007)

ISO/CD 22301, Societal Security—Preparedness and Continuity Management Systems—Requirements

British Standards Institution, BS25999-1: 2006, Code of Practice for Business Continuity Management and BS25999-2: 2007, Specification for Business Continuity Management

NFPA Standard 1600 on Disaster/Emergency Management and Business Continuity Programs

Table of Cases

Index

E

G